OXFORD MANAGEMENT READERS

ENTREPRENEURSHIP

The OXFORD MANAGEMENT READERS series reflects the interdisciplinary nature of much teaching of management. The aim of the series is to bring together carefully selected contributions on particular issues. The volumes will be based around either key themes or topics on the management curriculum.

Also published in the series

Firms, Organizations, and Contracts
Edited by Peter J. Buckley and Jonathan Michie

Leadership
Edited by Keith Grint

Resources, Firms, and Strategies
Edited by Nicolai J. Foss

ENTREPRENEURSHIP

The Social Science View

Edited by

Richard Swedberg

OXFORD
UNIVERSITY PRESS

OXFORD
UNIVERSITY PRESS

Great Clarendon Street, Oxford OX2 6DP

Oxford University Press is a department of the University of Oxford.
It furthers the University's objective of excellence in research, scholarship,
and education by publishing worldwide in

Oxford New York

Auckland   Cape Town Dar es Salaam   Hong Kong   Karachi
Kuala Lumpur Madrid Melbourne Mexico City   Nairobi
New Delhi Shanghai Taipei Toronto
With offices in
Argentina Austria Brazil Chile Czech Republic France Greece
Guatemala Hungary Italy Japan South Korea Poland Portugal
Singapore Switzerland Thailand Turkey Ukraine Vietnam

Published in the United States
by Oxford University Press Inc., New York

Introduction and compilation © Richard Swedberg 2000

Database right Oxford University Press (maker)

Reprinted 2009

ISBN 978-0-19-829461-0

Printed in the United Kingdom by
Lightning Source UK Ltd., Milton Keynes

Acknowledgements

Extracts from Joseph A. Schumpeter, *The Theory of Economic Development* (Harvard University Press, 1911, reprinted 1934). Reprinted by permission of Harvard University Press.

Extracts from Mark Blaug, *Economic History and the History of Economics* (New York University Press, 1986). Reprinted by permission of New York University Press.

Extracts from Ludwig von Mises, 'Profit and Loss', in *Planning for Freedom* (Libertarian Press, 1978). Reprinted by permission of Libertarian Press.

Extracts from S.M. Lipset, *Revolution and Counterrevolution* (Transaction Books, 1970, reprinted 1988). Reprinted by permission of Transaction Books.

Alexander Gerschenkron, 'The Modernization of Entrepreneurship', in Myron Weiner (ed.) *Modernization: The Dynamics of Growth* (Basic Books, 1966). Reprinted by permission of Basic Books.

Fredrik Barth, 'Economic Spheres in Darfur', in Raymond Firth (ed.) *Themes in Economic Anthropology* (Tavistock Publications, 1978). Reprinted by permission of Tavistock Books.

Rosabeth Moss Kanter, 'When a Thousand Flowers Bloom: Structural Collective, and Social Conditions for Innovation in Organization', *Research in Organizational Behaviour* 10 (1988), 169–211, by permission of JAI Press Inc.

Howard Aldrich, 'Entrepreneurial Strategies in New Organizational Populations', in Ivan Bull, Howard Thomas, and Gary Willard (eds.) *Entrepreneurship: Perspectives on Theory Building* (Pergamon, 1995). Reprinted by permission of Pergamon Press.

Kenneth Arrow, 'Innovation in Large and Small Firms', in Joshua Ronen (ed.) *Entrepreneurship* (Lexington Books, 1983). Reprinted by permission of Lexington Books.

Mark Granovetter, 'The Economic Sociology of Firms and Entrepreneurs', in Alejandro Portes (ed.) *The Economic Sociology of Immigration* (Russell Sage Foundation, 1995). Reprinted by permission of the Russell Sage Foundation.

Acknowledgements

Ronald Burt, 'The Network Entrepreneur', in Richard Swedberg (ed.) *Explorations in Economic Sociology* (Russell Sage Foundation, 1993). Reprinted by permission of the Russell Sage Foundation.

AnnaLee Saxenian, 'The Origins and Dynamics of Production Networks in Silicon Valley', *Research Policy*, 20 (1991), 423–37. Reprinted by permission of Elsevier Science Publishers B.V.

Extracts from Roger Waldinger, Howard Aldrich, and Robin Ward, *Ethnic Entrepreneurs* (Sage, 1990). Reprinted by permission of Sage Publications.

Contents

I. INTRODUCTION

II. DIFFERENT SOCIAL SCIENCE PERSPECTIVES ON ENTREPRENEURSHIP

Contents

....

III. ENTREPRENEURSHIP AND THE FIRM
(Small Firms, Large Firms, and How Can a Manager Also be an Entrepreneur?)

....

IV. ENTREPRENEURSHIP IN A CHANGING WORLD
(New Actors, New Questions, New Strategies)

Contents

List of Contributors

Howard Aldrich	Professor of Sociology at University of North Carolina at Chapel Hill
Kenneth Arrow	Professor of Economics at Stanford University
Fredrik Barth	Professor Emeritus, Oslo, Norway
Mark Blaug	Professor of Economics, University of London
Alexander Gerschenkron (1904–1978)	Russian-born economic historian, mainly active at Harvard University in Cambridge, Massachusetts
Mark Granovetter	Professor of Sociology, Stanford University
Monica Lindh de Montoya	Assistant Professor of Social Anthropology, Stockholm University, Sweden
Seymour Martin Lipset	Professor of Sociology at the Hoover Institution, Stanford
Ludwig von Mises (1881–1993)	Austrian-born economist active for many years at New York University
Rosabeth Moss Kanter	Professor at the Harvard Business School in Cambridge, Massachusetts
AnnaLee Saxenian	Professor of the Department of City and Regional Planning at the University of California at Berkeley
Joseph A. Schumpeter (1883–1950)	Austrian-born economist active at the University of Bonn and Harvard University in Cambridge, Massachusetts
Richard Swedberg	Professor of Sociology, Stockholm University, Sweden
Roger Waldinger	Professor of Sociology at City University of New York
Robin Ward	Professor at Nottingham Business School

Illustrations

Tables

I. INTRODUCTION

1

The Social Science View of Entrepreneurship: Introduction and Practical Applications

Richard Swedberg

The basic argument of this introduction—as well as the rationale for this whole reader—is that the social sciences have a very important contribution to make, not only to the theoretical understanding of entrepreneurship but also to entrepreneurship as a practical enterprise.[1] This viewpoint has tended to get lost in the surge of studies in this field, which has characterized the development during the last ten to fifteen years within the business school community. The social sciences, I argue, can provide new and fresh ideas about the theory and practice of entrepreneurship, by looking at innovative business behaviour in other times, in other societies, and in other cultures—and also by looking at entrepreneurship from novel angles and from the perspective of a much wider range of actors than is commonly done. It should be emphasized that quite a few of the insights that the social sciences have already generated can also be more or less directly translated into do's and don't's for the entrepreneur-to-be. And when this is still the case, it is not often possible to establish what the practical implications of a particular social science analysis might be. Indeed, the very process of trying to figure out how to extract practical knowledge about entrepreneurship from existing social science literature represents a useful exercise for the student of entrepreneurship. How this can be done will be illustrated in the rest of this introductory essay as well as in the introductions to the different parts of the reader.

'Entrepreneurial fervor in the 1980s', a historian of the entrepreneurial movement writes, 'became a worldwide movement, spreading across countries, regardless of their level of development or even of their basic mentality or value orientation towards business activities' (Alvarez 1996:192; cf. Alvarez 1991). Exactly why this movement came into being and is still going strong is not clear, but may well be due to a number of interacting causes. There is, for one thing, the revival of small businesses, seen for more than a decade in Europe as well as in the United States. The change in the ruling economic-political ideology that took place with the coming to power in 1979–80 of Thatcher and Reagan—from Keynesianism to a radical pro-market ideology—has probably also been important. There is, furthermore, the deep concern with unemployment and the general insight that only the creation of new businesses can provide jobs on a sufficient scale in a society with a shrinking industrial labour force. For any business to survive in a global economy, it is also increasingly realized, constant change and innovations are simply a necessity (e.g. Kanter 1995). As *The Economist* (1999) recently put it, 'Innovation has become the industrial religion of the late 20th century'.

People in and around the business-school community—not social scientists— have been leading the way in the current surge in studies of entrepreneurship. It is they who have given the topic of entrepreneurship a new legitimacy in the eyes of the public. They have also helped to institute new chairs in entre-preneurship and they have started up a number of important publications, such as *Frontiers of Entrepreneurship* (1981–), *Journal of Business Venturing* (1985–), and *Entrepreneurship and Regional Development* (1989–). Research on innovation in the business school community has been encouraged and has resulted in a number of high-quality studies which are far ahead of what has been accom-plished in the social sciences (see for example the literature referred to by Kanter in '*When a Thousand flowers Bloom: Structural, Collective, and Social Conditions for Innovation in Organization*'). Practically all business schools have by now at least one course in entrepreneurship, and it is increasingly being realized that to-day's managers and businessmen need not only *managerial skills* but *entrepre-neurial skills* as well (e.g. Drucker [1985] 1993). A number of prominent mem-bers of the business school community have also argued that the time has come to demystify entrepreneurship and transform it into a skill that can be routinely taught to the average MBA student.

The minor role that social scientists have played in renewing the study of entrepreneurship during this period has led some people in the business-school community to question the value of social science for developing entrepre-neurial skills. Social science may be good for whatever it wants to accomplish, the general sentiment seems to be, but it is not useful in courses where the aim is to teach entrepreneurship to future business leaders. A typical example of this type of attitude can be found in an important article by two influential teachers of entrepreneurship which appeared some years ago in *Strategic Management Journal*. In 'A Paradigm of Entrepreneurship: Entrepreneurial Management', Carlos Jarillo and Howard Stevenson argue that while the social sciences can help to explain the causes of entrepreneurship ('*Why?*') and its effects ('*What?*'), they have nothing to contribute to the understanding of entrepreneurial behaviour ('*How?*'). It is, however, this last question—'What do entrepreneurs do when they are entrepreneurial?'—that the business schools should focus on, according to Jarillo and Stevenson. The authors provide a definition of entrepreneurship which is tailored to the 'how' question: 'entrepreneurship is a process by which individuals—either on their own or inside organizations—pursue opportunities without regard to the resources they currently control' (Jarillo and Stevenson 1990: 23). They also advance several suggestions for how to turn an ordinary corporation, managed in a routine manner, into an entrepreneurial organization. It is, for example, possible according to the authors to train the people in an organization to detect opportunities; one can also reward them for pursuing opportunities; and one can lessen the consequences of failing.

While the Jarillo–Stevenson article contains a number of suggestive proposals, its view of the social sciences and the contribution that these can make to the study of entrepreneurship is partly mistaken. First, the social sciences look as often at what entrepreneurs do ('*How?*'), as they look at the causes of entrepreneurship ('*Why?*') and its cumulative effects ('*What?*'). And second, although practical use is not what exclusively drives the social sciences, quite a bit of what these have to say about entrepreneurship *does* have practical consequences; and these insights are well worth being taught in today's business schools. Jarillo and Stevenson are in my opinion on target when they argue that business schools should concentrate on the 'how'—but their view of the social sciences, and the contribution that these can make to the study of entrepreneurship, needs to be corrected.

While it is clear that the Jarillo–Stevenson type of sceptical attitude towards the social sciences deserves to be criticized, something should also be said about its origin since this is part of the story. The fact is that much of what the social sciences have produced insofar as the economy is concerned, has been of a very abstract nature and out of touch with economic realities. This is particularly true of economic theory, while the empirically oriented social sciences—such as sociology, psychology, and economic history—are less prone to this. The non-economic social sciences also lack the kind of unitary theory that mainstream economics has; and this makes it easier for them to relate to the practical knowledge of business people.

Richard Swedberg

A particularly useful critique of the tendency in economic theory to underestimate the importance of concrete, practical knowledge for economic activities, and thereby exclude large parts of the relevant reality from science, had already been made in the 1940s in a famous article by Friedrich von Hayek, entitled 'The Use of Knowledge in Society'; and since its main thesis fits the current situation in studies of entrepreneurship very well, it is worth repeating. The type of knowledge that has come to be known as 'scientific knowledge' in economics, Hayek argues, has distanced itself far too much from 'practical knowledge', which it views with a mixture of distrust and contempt. Practical knowledge (which Hayek defines as 'knowledge of the practical circumstances of time and place' and which is an integral part of what anthropologists call 'local knowledge') is, however, crucial to successful entrepreneurship; and knowledge that may seem trivial to the theoretical economist can be absolutely necessary for a business venture (Geertz 1983). Hayek writes:

To know of and put to use a machine not fully employed, or somebody's skill which could be better utilized, or to be aware of a surplus stock which can be drawn upon during an interruption of supplies, is socially quite as useful as the knowledge of better alternative techniques. The shipper who earns his living from using otherwise empty or half-filled journeys of tramp-steamers, or the estate agent whose whole knowledge is almost exclusively one of temporary opportunities, or the *arbitrageur* who gains from local differences of commodity prices—are all performing eminently useful functions based on special knowledge of circumstances and the fleeting moment not known to others (Hayek [1945] 1972: 80).

One conclusion that can be drawn from Hayek's argument is that economics, as well as the other social sciences, need to incorporate some of this 'practical knowledge' into their analyses. By this is not meant that the social sciences should become a depository for all empirical facts that have ever played a role in successful business ventures—this would clearly be absurd and also make it impossible to produce any science. What it does mean, however, is that *if the social sciences are to get a better handle on entrepreneurship, they will have to learn to pay more attention to the concrete ways in which entrepreneurs locate and exploit opportunities*. This type of knowledge has a certain degree of generality to it; and it is precisely this generality which makes it relevant to the social sciences.

Hayek's purpose in 'The Use of Knowledge in Society' can be described in more general terms as an attempt to improve scientific knowledge by drawing it closer to 'practical knowledge', and also to make it clear that if social scientists are ever to truly understand economic behaviour they will have to change their attitudes toward this type of knowledge. This introductory essay is inspired by a similar purpose, and in the coming pages I shall try to show how practical guidelines for opportunity spotting and creative economic behaviour, can either be directly derived from social science work on entrepreneurship or are implicit in it.

1. The Social Science Literature on Entrepreneurship (Part 1): The Contribution of the Economists

The word 'entrepreneur' comes from the French word 'entreprendre', which means 'to do something', and it was originally used in the Middle Ages in the sense of 'a person who is active, who gets things done' (Hoselitz 1951). The first economic theory of entrepreneurship is to be found in a work entitled *Essay on the Nature of Commerce in General* (*circa* 1730), written by a Paris banker of Irish extraction who had a real flair for economic analysis, Richard Cantillon (*circa* 1680–1734). The term 'entrepreneur' was given general currency among English economists by John Stuart Mill in the mid-nineteenth century (Schumpeter 1954: 556). Since the turn of the century studies of entrepreneurship have been carried out within a number of other social science disciplines than economics—such as sociology, psychology, economic history (including business history), and economic anthropology—but no competent survey which covers all of these exists. It is also difficult to find surveys of what has been accomplished in the individual social sciences, except for economics. That there, none the less, is a huge and interesting social science literature on entrepreneurship 'out there' is however not to be doubted.

Most people who are not economists would probably expect the economics literature to be full of analyses of entrepreneurship, since economics after all is the social science that deals most directly with contemporary economic reality. This, however, is not the case, and the economics literature has relatively little to say about entrepreneurship. The reason for this is primarily that mainstream economics has had great difficulty in fitting entrepreneurship into its theory, and as a result has tended to ignore the entrepreneur. Economic models, which have proved very useful for other purposes, have turned out to be resistant to the phenomenon of entrepreneurship. Economists who have done work on entrepreneurship have therefore tended to be in a minority, and they have either had to invent some way of fitting the entrepreneur into a conventional model or they have had to develop an alternative model for how the economy works.

Among those economists who have tried to develop an economic theory centred around the entrepreneur, Joseph Schumpeter is by far the most important; and the first half of this section on entrepreneurship and economic theory has been devoted to his work. In the second half, the mainstream position on entrepreneurship is presented and discussed, and a few words are also said about the texts by economists which have been included in this reader. I will argue that the various attempts that have been made to theoretically integrate entrepreneurship into mainstream economic theory are of little practical interest to the entrepreneur-to-be; and that these mainly raise theoretical questions. The situation is, however, somewhat different with the basic notions of what constitutes entrepreneurship, according to economic theorists; and here it can be quite interesting to try to figure out what the implicit (practical) consequences of some theoretical approach are.

1.1. Joseph Schumpeter's Contribution

One obvious reason for devoting quite a bit of space in this introductory essay to Joseph A. Schumpeter (1883–1950) is that he is *the* main figure in the literature on entrepreneurship. Another is that practically nowhere in the literature, either on entrepreneurship or on economic theory, can one find a well-rounded picture of Schumpeter's theory of the entrepreneur. What is rarely, if ever mentioned, is that Schumpeter's theory of entrepreneurship is part of an attempt to construct a whole new type of economic theory, which was to complement Walras' theory of a static (and stationary) economy; that Schumpeter's ideas about how to best study entrepreneurship changed considerably over time; and that his approach is interdisciplinary in nature or, more precisely, that Schumpeter looked at different aspects of entrepreneurship during different periods of his life, and that he used a variety of approaches in doing so, including economic theory, psychology, sociology, and economic history. To this can be added—and also this is rarely, if ever, mentioned—that Schumpeter produced the first competent history of entrepreneurship in economic theory. Schumpeter's approach to this topic has deeply influenced the history of economic thought, and is still the dominant one.

Despite his versatility and multi-disciplinary approach, Schumpeter never produced concrete guidelines for how the entrepreneur should behave, of the type that today's business schools are trying to develop. Whether this was due to a lack of imagination on his part or to the fact that he did not believe that such guidelines could be produced is not clear; it is most likely that this type of task never occurred to him. Schumpeter did, however, repeatedly point out that while ordinary economic behaviour is more or less automatic in nature, the entrepreneur always has to think very carefully about what action to take since he or she is involved in doing something that is fundamentally *new*—and this is perhaps an insight also worth considering today. Whenever you do something new, you do not know how to proceed—and are in extra need of practical guidelines.

To complete the picture of Schumpeter and practical entrepreneurship, it can be mentioned that he came from an entrepreneurial family (see Swedberg 1991). Schumpeter was born in 1883 in a little town on the outskirts of the Austrian Hungarian Empire called Triesch (today in Slovakia), and the first textile mill in this place had been founded by Schumpeter's great grandfather. His grandfather, as well as his father, also ran the mill; the former introduced new machinery and methods, while we have no information about the activities of Schumpeter's father. Since Schumpeter's father died when Schumpeter was four years old and his mother moved away from Triesch with her little son and remarried, the issue of whether Schumpeter should take over the textile factory was never raised.

It is true that during a few years in the early 1920s Schumpeter did try to make a living as an investor or venture capitalist. The whole thing, however, ended badly, and Schumpeter lost all his investments and quite a bit of borrowed money as well. While the main lines of Schumpeter's financial ventures are known—he had invested in a couple of local industries as well as in a bank—few concrete details are available (see Stolper 1994: 307–25; cf. Allen 1991: 184–9). The general impression one gets, however, is that Schumpeter had far too little concrete knowledge about what was going on in the companies where he had invested his money to be on top of things. The unstable political and economic situation of Austria in the 1920s no doubt added to Schumpeter's difficulties.

Schumpeter's writings on entrepreneurship fall naturally into two periods, both from a chronological viewpoint and in terms of their emphasis. Until *circa* 1940 Schumpeter was mainly interested in developing his own ideas about entrepreneurship and to integrate these into a novel system of economic theory, which was centred around economic change or development. During his last decade—Schumpeter died in 1950—he mainly looked at the sociological aspects of entrepreneurship and also tried to sketch a research programme in entrepreneurship for economic history. Both periods, as we soon shall see, are also of some interest for an understanding of entrepreneurship in more practical terms.

Schumpeter started his career as an economic theorist with a dissertation very much in the spirit of the great mathematical economist Léon Walras; and at this point in his life he thought that all problems in economic theory could be solved with the help of equilibrium theory, applied to a stationary economy. Soon, however, he began to feel that Walras had left something essential out of his analysis and also had a rather restrictive view of economics. Walras, Schumpeter now began to feel, viewed the economy as a system which only reacted to impulses from *outside* the economy, such as population increases, new inventions, discoveries of gold, and so on. These outside impulses, Walras argued, set off an adaptive response or change in the economic system, which after a while reached a new equilibrium; and it was *this* process, from one equilibrium to another, that economists should study. Schumpeter even contacted Walras to ask him if this was indeed how he viewed the task of economics, and the answer was affirmative. Schumpeter was later to describe his reaction to Walras' answer in the following manner:

I felt very strongly that this was wrong, and that there was a source of energy within the economic system which would of itself disrupt any equilibrium that might be attained. If this is so, then there must be a purely economic theory of economic change which does not merely rely on external factors propelling the economic system from one equilibrium to another. It is such a theory that I have tried to build (Schumpeter [1937] 1989: 166).

Schumpeter made a first attempt to develop such a theory in a book entitled *The Theory of Economic Development* (1911), which bears all the signs of youthful enthusiasm. It is in this work, it should be noted, that Schumpeter's famous theory of the entrepreneur is to be found. He clearly tried to develop a totally new economic theory and relied very little on what earlier economists had accomplished. His general argument was that all truly important changes in the economy are set off by the entrepreneur, and that these changes then slowly work themselves through the economic system, in the form of a business cycle. Schumpeter also suggested that his idea of internally generated change, as opposed to change induced from the outside, was not only applicable to economic phenomena, but to *all* social phenomena. Art, politics, and so on could all be conceptualized as consisting of two types of activities; on the one hand, there were creative and innovative activities and, on the other hand, repetitive and mechanical activities.

The second edition of *The Theory of Economic Development* (1926)—produced more than a dozen years later, and the edition that is read today—is considerably less ambitious. Schumpeter now tightened up his argument, systematized it, and eliminated its broader implications. In 1939 Schumpeter published a work entitled *Business Cycles*, which carried this process even further; and while entrepreneurship had been described in terms of creativity and intuition in the first edition of *The Theory of Economic Development* (1911), Schumpeter now spoke of entrepreneurship in a considerably more technical and dispassionate manner. Innovation, which the young Schumpeter in 1911 had described in a nearly dionysian manner, had now become more apollonian in nature, and is simply defined in *Business Cycles* as 'the setting up of a new production function' (Schumpeter 1939: 87).

It is consequently in the second edition of *The Theory of Economic Development* (1926)—or more precisely in the translated version (1934) of the second German edition—that we can find what most people mean when they refer to 'Schumpeter's theory of the entrepreneur'. When they speak of this theory, it should also be noted, they have exclusively in mind the famous second chapter in the English translation from 1934, partly included in this volume as *Entrepreneurship as Innovation*. And this is indeed the place where Schumpeter speaks most directly of the entrepreneur, even if it deserves to be mentioned that the main bulk of the book consists of an attempt to develop a number of new economic theories—of interest, capital, credit, profit, and the business cycle—by relating them to the theory of entrepreneurship. What we have, in other words, is a whole new economic theory, centred around the entrepreneur, rather than just a theory of the entrepreneur.

The main reason why very few people discuss anything but chapter 2 in *The Theory of Economic Development* is that what Schumpeter says in the rest of the book has failed to make any impact on economics whatsoever. Also from a practical viewpoint, it may be added, it is less interesting to look at these parts of Schumpeter's work, since they basically only raise questions that are relevant to economic theory. It is furthermore in chapter 2 that we can find most of Schumpeter's well-known statements about entrepreneurship. This is where he says that entrepreneurship can be defined as the making of a '*new combination*' of already existing materials and forces; that entrepreneurship consists of making innovations, as opposed to inventions; and that no one is an entrepreneur for ever, only when he or she is actually doing the innovative activity.

Schumpeter presents three key typologies in chapter 2 of *The Theory of Economic Development*, and all of these are of practical interest to the student of entrepreneurship (see also the introduction to Part I of this reader). The first of these typologies is very famous and has to do with the main types of entrepreneurial behaviour. These are the following five: (1) the introduction of a new good; (2) the introduction of a new method of production; (3) the opening of a new market; (4) the conquest of a new source of supply of raw material; and (5) the creation of a new organization of an industry.

One practical implication of Schumpeter's typology of entrepreneurial behaviour has to do with the very concept of *combination*; and a useful exercise for a student of practical entrepreneurship might be to train himself/herself in thinking up new combinations, using case studies. Another exercise could be to try to add to (or subtract from) Schumpeter's typology. Would it, for example, be possible also to speak of financial innovations (so why does Schumpeter not do so?); and how should this type of innovation be defined? Are venture capitalists entrepreneurs or do they just help entrepreneurs? Schumpeter does not speak of innovations in the organizational structure of firms, but only of innovations in the organizational structure of industries. What would some examples of the former be, and do this type of innovations translate into higher profits?

Also Schumpeter's second typology, which has to do with the motivation of the entrepreneur, is famous. What drives the entrepreneur, Schumpeter says, are primarily three things: (1) 'the dream and the will to found a private kingdom'; (2) 'the will to conquer'; and (3) 'the joy of creating' (Schumpeter [1934] 1961: 93). We can translate Schumpeter's formulations into modern language as: (1) the desire for power and independence; (2) the will to succeed; and (3) the satisfaction of getting things done. It should be pointed out that money *per se* is not what ultimately motivates the entrepreneur, according to Schumpeter. 'Entrepreneurs', as he says elsewhere, 'are certainly not economic men in the theoretical sense' (Schumpeter [1946] 1991:408). He adds, in *The Theory of Economic Development*, that his idea about the motivation of the entrepreneur falls within the field of psychology and has therefore no place in economic theory. Again, it can be noticed, we are in the presence of a case where the practical implications of Schumpeter's ideas are much easier to spot, when he distances himself from the higher regions of economic theory. To ferret out the practical implications of Schumpeter's typology one might ask questions like, how do you design incentives to promote entrepreneurship? and, how do you spot people who are likely to become good entrepreneurs?

During the last decade of his life the emphasis in Schumpeter's writings on entrepreneurship shifted from economic theory to sociology and economic history. *Capitalism, Socialism and Democracy* (1942) is mainly a sociological work, in the sense that it focuses on the institutional structure of society; and what Schumpeter has to say about the entrepreneur in this book is primarily of a sociological character. The thrust of his ideas is clear from the title of its most important section on entrepreneurship—'The Obsolescence of the

Entrepreneurial Function' (some interesting observations on this topic can also be found in 'The Process of Creative Destruction'; see Schumpeter [1950] 1976: 81–6, 131–4). A number of institutional factors, Schumpeter here argues, are weakening entrepreneurship and contributing to the stagnation of capitalism as a social system. People, for example, are getting increasingly used to change, and there is consequently less opposition to entrepreneurship—something which makes for less strong headed and original entrepreneurs. The big corporations are also beginning to develop innovative technologies in a routine fashion by putting together teams of specialists. Finally, capitalism has a general tendency to rationalize and demystify everything in society, including entrepreneurship.

During the 1940s Schumpeter also got involved with the Research Center in Entrepreneurial History at Harvard University and wrote a few articles under its influence. These articles constitute some of the best that Schumpeter ever wrote on entrepreneurship and contain many new ideas as well as some interesting reformulations of old ideas (see especially Schumpeter [1947] 1989, [1949] 1989). For one thing, Schumpeter now made clear that the entrepreneur does not have to be a single person but can equally well be an organization, either a political or an economic one. What matters is the behaviour, not the actor. He also encouraged the writing of 'a comprehensive history of entrepreneurship', which he envisioned as including a history of the various ways that entrepreneurship has been financed throughout the ages as well as a discussion of the different types of entrepreneurs that have existed (industrial entrepreneurs, financial entrepreneurs, aristocratic entrepreneurs, and so on; cf. Schumpeter [1949] 1989: 264ff). Schumpeter furthermore argued that the theory of entrepreneurship should be based on 'the actual activity of the entrepreneur', as opposed to preconceived notions by economic theorists (including those that could be found in his own work; ibid.). The key to a future understanding of entrepreneurship, he repeatedly emphasized, was to draw economic history and economic theory much closer to one another. Doing this, we may add today, will probably also make it easier to develop practical guidelines for the entrepreneur-to-be.

It is often said that Schumpeter glorifies the entrepreneur and portrays him as a kind of aristocratic hero who has little in common with the businessman in the real world. To some extent this is true; Schumpeter had a taste for what is dashing and bold, and this rubbed off on his theory of the entrepreneur. Still, it is also clear that Schumpeter's work on entrepreneurship is much richer than is commonly thought; and it is furthermore my distinct impression that a thorough study of Schumpeter's work, from the viewpoint of practical entrepreneurship, would pay off. Schumpeter once noted that what made him especially proud of his work was that behind it all was 'a living piece of reality' (Schumpeter 1943). He also pointed out that it was exactly this that made his work so refractory to mathematical formulation. One wonders, however, if it is not precisely this quality that still makes Schumpeter's work on the entrepreneur seem so relevant and alive.

It should finally also be mentioned that quite a bit of contemporary research on innovation has been inspired by Schumpeter's ideas. People from a variety of fields—organizational economics, evolutionary economics and so on—have picked up one or another idea from Schumpeter's work and incorporated it into their own analyses. Much of the emphasis in this type of literature has been on technological innovations, rather than on organizational innovations, but this may well be changing (for an overview of research on innovations in the Schumpeterian tradition, see Kamien and Schwartz 1982; see also the annual volumes based on the conferences of the International Joseph A. Schumpeter Society, e.g. Scherer and Perlman 1992).

1.2. The Contribution of Mainstream Economics

For a long time it has been realized that mainstream economics has very little to say about entrepreneurship. In 1968 well-known economist William Baumol published what was soon to become a famous article on this theme, stating that the entrepreneur had 'virtually disappeared' from mainstream economics, and that the whole thing was a little like a performance of *Hamlet* with the Danish prince missing (Baumol 1968: 64). Summing up the situation many years later, a well-known historian of economic thought noted that the situation was more or less the same, adding that it constituted a 'scandal' that students of economics were taught so little about entrepreneurship (Blaug 1986: 229: 'Entrepreneurship Before and After Schumpeter').

But even if mainstream economics on the whole has ignored entrepreneurship, it does contain some material on the topic. The way economists have discussed (or avoided) entrepreneurship before *circa* 1930 has been discussed by Schumpeter and, as already mentioned, his account is still the dominant one in the history of economic thought (see Schumpeter 1928, [1949] 1989, 1954). Modern accounts of entrepreneurship usually add a section on Schumpeter's theory (Schumpeter never discussed his own theories); they typically also contain a discussion of the works of a few other individuals, such as

Israel Kirzner and Mark Casson. More complete versions add something about the works of the two founders of neo-Austrian economics, Friedrich von Hayek and Ludwig von Mises, and also mention the work of William Baumol (see Baumol 1993).

How are the theories of entrepreneurship, which have been developed by mainstream economists, to be read and interpreted by those who are mainly interested in entrepreneurship from a practical viewpoint? Before suggesting an answer to this question, I would like to quickly summarize the most important landmarks in the mainstream history of entrepreneurship. The first two economists to write in an original manner on the entrepreneur were both active in France: Richard Cantillon (*circa* 1680–1734) and Jean-Baptiste Say (1776–1832). The former defined entrepreneurs as those who are willing 'to buy at a certain price and sell at an uncertain price' (cited in Blaug 1986: 220). Say, who had read Cantillon, suggested another definition: entrepreneurship consists of combining the factors of production into an organism.

The British economists, from Adam Smith and onwards, confused the capitalist with the entrepreneur and had a tendency to view economic progress as something automatic. The latter attitude was particularly pronounced in the works of Ricardo and Marx, according to Blaug. German economist Johann Heinrich von Thünen (1783–1850) distinguished, however, in a clear manner between the interest on capital, wages to the manager, and the insurance rate for all that could be insured in the business venture; and suggested that entrepreneurial profit consisted of what was left over, once these three items had been paid. Another German economist from about the same time period, Hans von Mangoldt (1824–68), proposed that entrepreneurial profit could be conceptualized as rent of ability.

What is today known as neo-classical economics emerged around the turn of the century and was ushered in by such people as Alfred Marshall and Léon Walras. Marshall (1842–1924) viewed entrepreneurship as synonymous with business management and suggested, similar to Mangoldt, that payment for this function could be seen as rent on ability. In the system of the great theoretician of general equilibrium, Léon Walras (1834–1910), the entrepreneur plays virtually no role. In a well-known formulation, Walras states that in an equilibrium situation the entrepreneur 'neither makes [money] nor loses' (cited by Schumpeter 1954: 893). An attempt to square neo-classical thought with a theory of entrepreneurship, which is much admired by other economists, can finally be found in *Risk, Uncertainty, and Profit* (1921) by Frank Knight. The objective probability of 'risk', it is here argued, can be calculated, while 'uncertainty' can never be known. Knight's view of entrepreneurial profit as gain resulting handling uncertainty, it is often noted, is fully compatible with the theories of perfect competition and of equilibrium in the long run.

Since Schumpeter's theory of the entrepreneur has already been discussed in the preceeding section, I shall pass it over here. A few words need, however, to be said about the works of Israel Kirzner and Mark Casson. The latter has a somewhat eclectic view of entrepreneurship, and defines the entrepreneur as a person who specializes in making decisions about how to coordinate scarce resources (Casson 1983: 23). Kirzner's position, which has evolved over a period of several decades, can be summarized in the following manner: entrepreneurship means alertness towards profit opportunities (Kirzner 1997; cf. 1973). The entrepreneur essentially tries to discover profit opportunities and helps to restore equilibrium in the market by acting on these. Kirzner's view of the entrepreneur as someone who restores equilibrium is often contrasted to that of Schumpeter, who sees the entrepreneur as someone who breaks an equilibrium through an innovation.

While Kirzner himself has always stated that his theory draws heavily on the works of Ludwig von Mises and Friedrich von Hayek, this is more seldom realized in conventional histories of entrepreneurship and should therefore be stressed. Friedrich von Hayek (1899–1992) is primarily important in this context for his analysis of knowledge and entrepreneurship or, more precisely, for his suggestion that lack of knowledge is constitutive for the very existence of entrepreneurship. The role that detailed and concrete knowledge about local events plays in entrepreneurship ('practical knowledge') has already been mentioned. To this should now be added that entrepreneurship, according to Hayek, does not so much mean that already existing information is diagnosed as lacking, and then acquired, but that new and unknown knowledge is being *created* through the process of entrepreneurship. To be an entrepreneur implies a 'discovery process', to use one of Hayek's well-known formulations.

As opposed to Hayek, Ludwig von Mises (1881–1973) developed a full theory of entrepreneurship. Mises starts out from the idea that when the economy is in a stable and repetitive equilibrium cycle, there is no place for entrepreneurship. His argument on this point (but not his terminology) is very similar to that of Schumpeter in the latter's discussion of 'the circular flow'. Mises, however, differs from Schumpeter by defining entrepreneurship as anticipations of uncertain events, and not as innovations. Entrepreneurship is in his view always geared to the 'uncertainty of future constellations of demand and supply' (Mises 1963: 293; cf. [1951] 1978). The entrepreneur is exclusively driven by a desire to make money; and he or she makes profits by figuring out what the consumer wants. The better the entrepreneur is at this, the more profit he or she will make. But just as the entrepreneur can make money, he or she can also lose money; and Mises is one of the few theoreticians of entrepreneurship who stresses the role of 'entrepreneurial errors'.

In my opinion, also those who are mainly interested in the practical dimensions of entrepreneurship can learn quite a bit from the theories that have been developed by economists. One of the items on the agenda of practical entrepreneurship today should, in my mind, be to carefully go through this literature and try to establish what is useful in it and what can be discarded. That the result of doing so will differ quite a bit from what mainstream economists have gotten out of this literature is to be expected.

One of the items, it seems to me, that is of minimal interest to those who are concerned with developing practical entrepreneurship is whether an individual economist's argument can easily be fitted into the theoretical system of mainstream economics or not. While Frank Knight's argument about risk versus uncertainty, for example, may be suggestive in itself, much of the praise that has been heaped on Knight is for his success in squaring this idea with neo-classical thought. Besides, Knight's distinction may well have to be seen in a different light today, especially after the introduction of successful trade in options in the 1970s. Similarly, it is totally uninteresting, from the perspective of practical entrepreneurship, whether the activities of the entrepreneur should be understood as restoring an equilibrium (Kirzner) or as disturbing an equilibrium (Schumpeter). To conceptualize entrepreneurial profit as rent on ability, as Mangoldt and Marshall do, is also of minimal interest from a practical perspective. What is much more relevant is to figure out what this 'ability' consists of, how to develop it, and how to spot it.

What about the recent discussion in economics which attempts to determine exactly how the entrepreneur is made to disappear from mainstream economics—is it only of academic interest or is it of some value to those who primarily view entrepreneurship from a practical perspective? There are, for example, some economists who accomplish this vanishing act by assuming that economic progress is automatic or that economies will advance without the help of an entrepreneur. Others claim that there is simply no place for the entrepreneur in an equilibrium system; and finally there are those who state that input and output in the firm have to be determined as well as be identical for the theory to work—even though this unfortunately means that the entrepreneur is eliminated. My own answer is that this type of discussion may often seem irrelevant, but none the less has some positive qualities to it since its main goal, after all, is to restore a place to the entrepreneur in economic theory; and that it is therefore also of some interest to the practitioner.

But there do exist some very fine insights into the nature of entrepreneurship in the economics literature, and the problem here is more of how to locate these and to dig them out, than to determine whether they are of interest or not from a practical perspective. Some comments on how to do this are in place. First of all, to find these insights one definitely has to look at a much broader range of works than those which are today discussed in mainstream economics. Second, this whole literature needs to be sifted through for practical statements about entrepreneurship, including statements about the experience that economists themselves have had of engaging in business ventures. And third, there are different ways in which the economists have conceptualized the very idea of entrepreneurship, and these have some practical implications. I shall say something about each of these three topics.

First, that the literature on entrepreneurship which has been produced by economists is much larger than the one that is usually being discussed, is clear to anyone who has done research on the history of economic thought. There is, for example, the work on entrepreneurship which was carried out within the German Historical School and which is practically unexplored. The modern institutionalist tradition, including evolutionary economics, is also relevant in this context (e.g. Nelson 1993). Those who want some references to start with may, for example, consult Hébert and Link's *The Entrepreneur: Mainstream Views and Radical Critiques* (1982). But it should also be pointed out that the mainstream tradition itself is much richer than it is usually given credit for. That this is the case is well illustrated by the text of Kenneth Arrow, which has been included in this reader ('Innovation in Large and Small Firms'), and also by the work of William Baumol (1990). In the latter it is, for example, argued that entrepreneurship can be found in many societies throughout history, but while it is productive in some, it is unproductive and even destructive in others. Arrow's article contains an interesting attempt to explain what kind of innovations large firms are good at, as opposed to small firms. (For other important research on small firms and entrepreneurship, see e.g. Acs 1996; Acs *et al.* 1998; the practical implications of Arrow's "Innovation in Large and Small Firms" are discussed in the introduction to Part II.)

When going through the literature by economists on entrepreneurship it can, to reiterate, be profitable to look for explicitly practical statements. A related research task would be to investigate the relationship between *writing* about entrepreneurship and *being* an entrepreneur; and as we know, several of the most important theoreticians of entrepreneurship also had some business experience, such as Cantillon, Say, and Schumpeter. In discussing the work of Say, Schumpeter (1954: 492–3) notes that Say drew on his own experience as a businessman, and adds that 'intellectuals who know business only from newspapers are in the habit of congratulating themselves on their detachment; but obviously there is another side to the matter'. Another case of an economic theorist, who was also a skilful investor, is that of Keynes, and what he has to say about 'animal spirits' is of course applicable in this context. Due to human nature we all have some 'animal spirits', Keynes says, and display an 'innate urge to act' as well as 'spontaneous optimism'; and this has important consequences for the way the market operates (Keynes [1936] 1960: 161–3). An entrepreneur, from this perspective, can perhaps be characterized as someone who combines some vigorous animal spirits with skill and resources in building up and leading an enterprise. Spontaneous optimism may also act as a kind of shield for the entrepreneur, according to another economist. Many businessmen, Albert O. Hirschman says, would never have started up their businesses in the first place, if they had known in advance how difficult it was going to be (Hirschman 1967: 9–34; see also Sawyer 1951–2).

And, finally, one should also try to ferret out the practical implications of the economic theories of entrepreneurship. A few examples of how this can be done have already been given in the section on Schumpeter. The neo-Austrian school of entrepreneurship also seems promising in this respect. It deserves to be pointed out that one of the most suggestive theories of entrepreneurship that has emerged within the business school community—Howard Stevenson's notion that entrepreneurship consists of a relentless pursuit of opportunities, regardless of resources—has its roots in Ludwig von Mises's work and what Israel Kirzner has added to this. Both Mises and Kirzner also talk about 'entrepreneurial errors', a notion which clearly deserves to be more developed in the current discussion of practical entrepreneurship (Gratzer, forthcoming). To Mises as well as Kirzner, one entrepreneur's error basically creates another entrepreneur's opportunity. To this can be added that an entrepreneur can also learn quite a bit from his or her own mistakes; and that the entrepreneur benefits from being imbued with a spirit of not giving up after the first attempt. Many entrepreneurial feats have furthermore become possible in the first place just because they have been preceded by a number of what one may call 'innovative errors' (see e.g. Bailyn 1955). Hayek's ideas about entrepreneurship and knowledge similarly have some interesting practical implications. How, for example, do you learn to sort out relevant practical knowledge from irrelevant practical knowledge? And when, in the attempt to develop a new innovation, can you expect to discover the new entrepreneurial information that Hayek talks about?

In concluding this section it should be emphasized that it is utopian to believe that practical entrepreneurship and the economic theory of entrepreneurship one day will merge. As I note towards the end of this introduction, this is not even desirable. What can be accomplished—and also wished for—is, however, that the two get considerably closer than they currently are. For economic theorists this would mean that they would have to rethink the relationship of economic theory to economic practice. And for those interested in practical entrepreneurship, it would mean being more sensitive to—and curious about—the practical implications of economic theory.

2. The Social Science Literature on Entrepreneurship (Part 2): The Contribution of Social Scientists Other than Economists

Many fascinating analyses of entrepreneurship can be found in the enormous body of work that has been produced over the years by social scientists other than economists. The sciences I am talking about are, first and foremost, the following ones: sociology, psychology, anthropology, and economic history. But there also exist other sciences which are important in this context, as 'The Origins and Dynamics of Production Networks in Silicon Valley' by regional planner AnnaLee Saxenian illustrates. Work by sociologists, psychologists, and so on, it also deserves to be emphasized, differs from that of the economists in several respects. It is, for one thing, much more descriptive in nature, and the theoretical part is more directly shaped by empirical research. In none of the non-economic social sciences, it should furthermore be noted, does there exist such a cohesive theoretical doctrine as in mainstream economics.

All of this makes for a very lively and multifaceted literature on entrepreneurship, which is much closer to practical reality than the writing which can be found in mainstream economics. It, unfortunately, also makes for a very sprawling literature and one that is hard to survey. Only a few, rather incomplete inventories of what has been produced about entrepreneurship in the individual social sciences exist (for economic history, see Soltow 1968 and Mathias 1983; for anthropology, see Owens 1978; for psychology, see Chell, Haworth, and Brearley, 1991; and for sociology, see Martinelli 1994). This naturally makes the task of presenting the main accomplishments of the non-economic social science literature more difficult, and I will therefore do this in a somewhat impressionistic way.

2.1. The Contribution of Max Weber

Some of the most brilliant ideas on entrepreneurship within the social sciences can be traced back to the work of Max Weber (1864–1920). This alone is a good reason for devoting a separate section to his contribution; another is that what Weber says on entrepreneurship nearly always gets garbled, due to the complexity of his thought. Adding to the difficulty of getting a handle on Weber's ideas on entrepreneurship, it should also be added, is that these were never summarized in one single text but are scattered throughout his work (and hence no reading of Weber has been included in this volume).

Weber is usually thought of as a sociologist, and during the last period of his life he indeed spent about a decade trying to develop a sociological type of analysis, including an economic sociology (see Swedberg 1998). He was, however, primarily trained as a legal historian, and the field in which he may well have been the most proficient was the history of law. For a couple of years he also taught economics at the universities of Freiburg and Heidelberg, mainly a mixture of historical economics and marginal utility economics. Most of his life, however, was spent as a private scholar, and during this time Weber did work in the philosophy of the social sciences, economic history, political science and a few other fields as well.

Weber's view of entrepreneurship is often identified with his theory of charisma; and, according to this interpretation, his main contribution is to be found in his analysis of that special type of human being—the charismatic person—who makes other people want to follow him or her, simply by virtue of his or her extraordinary personality. This view, however, is largely mistaken. According to Weber, charisma has only functioned as an important motor of change during the early stages of mankind; and it is much less important in capitalist society, where economic change is mainly due to enterprises being geared to profit opportunities in the market. Also, the general trend towards rationalization in human society—especially the replacement of myth and religion by science and methodical, calculable thought—has limited the place for charisma in the modern world.

According to Weber, the entrepreneur can (1) only be found in an exchange economy, and (2) entrepreneurship has much more to do with the direction of economic action in the form of enterprises than with the economic operations of a single individual. An early definition of entrepreneurship that can be found in his work reads as follows: 'Entrepreneurship means the taking over and organization of some part of an economy, in which people's needs are satisfied through exchange, for the sake of making a profit and at one's own economic risk' (Weber [1898] 1990: 57).

There also are those who identify Weber's theory of the entrepreneur exclusively with his famous study *The Protestant Ethic and the Spirit of Capitalism* (1904–5; see Weber 1988); and it is indeed true that this work is central to what Weber has to say on the entrepreneur. More precisely, Weber makes two important contributions to the understanding of entrepreneurship in this study. First, he looks at the decisive change in attitude towards entrepreneurship that took place some time after the Reformation in the Western world, from being one of hostility and alienation to being one of acceptance and active promotion. And second, Weber analyses the way that a certain form of religion—what he called ascetic Protestantism (basically Calvinism, Pietism, Methodism, and Baptism)—helped to develop a positive attitude towards moneymaking and work, something which facilitated the more general change in attitude towards the entrepreneur.

Until some time after the Reformation, Weber argues in *The Protestant Ethic* (1988), moneylending, commerce, and entrepreneurship had always been looked down upon by the dominant ideology (religion) all over the world; and these activities were at best tolerated, never embraced. A certain form of Calvinism and some ascetic Christian sects in the sixteenth and seventeenth centuries, however, set off a reaction within Christianity which, inadvertently, changed the attitude to business and industry, first among the believers and later in society at large. Once society's attitude to entrepreneurship had become positive, the grip of religion began to loosen, and soon religious ideas had lost most of their power to regulate the economy. Entrepreneurship or 'the vocation to make money' had been set free.

But the ascetic Protestants, according to Weber, did not only—inadvertently!—help to change society's attitude to business from negative to positive, they also infused the economy itself with a new spirit. While greed had always existed among businessmen and other people, Weber notes, a methodical and quasi-ascetic attitude to work had not. This methodical character, however, was typical of the attitude to religion that existed among the ascetic Protestants; and from them it spread to the whole economy. The first to develop this new economic ethic were merchants who belonged to the ascetic Protestantism sects. These now became considerably more methodical—and effective—than their traditional counterparts. Soon, however, the new economic ethic would lose its original religious content and become thoroughly secular.

Weber also made a contribution to entrepreneurship in his later work, more precisely in his sociological and political writings from the 1910s (see e.g. Weber 1978: 90–100, 956–1005, 1292–6; 1994: 159–61, 272-303). As in his earlier work, the emphasis is much more on entrepreneurship as the skilful direction of enterprises, which respond to opportunities in the market economy, than on the personality of the individual entrepreneur. What is particularly interesting in the work from this period is the way that Weber counterposes the entrepreneur to the bureaucrat. As society becomes more rationalized, Weber argues, bureaucracy becomes ever more important, both within the enterprises and within the state. If the political bureaucracy succeeds in taking over all of the economy, say through a socialist revolution, economic progress will grind to a halt and political democracy will be replaced by dictatorship. In a capitalist society, in other words, the economic sector operates as a counterbalance to the political sector.

But the economy can also be stifled from within, Weber argues, and this is what happens if the bureaucratic tendencies within the individual enterprises are allowed to take over. If this happens—and it was Weber's personal fear that it indeed would happen—rent would replace profit, the economy would slow down, and a repressive, political climate would soon emerge. The entrepreneur, in Weber's opinion, is the only person in the economy who can keep the bureaucracy in its place. The entrepreneur is used to taking his or her own decisions and to assuming responsibility for a whole organization—not to obeying orders and yielding, as is the bureaucrat. Only the entrepreneur, Weber adds, has better knowledge of a firm than the bureaucrats.

What then are the practical implications of Weber's theories about entrepreneurship? I have to admit that in trying to give an answer to this question I feel a bit like Freud, who when someone drew his attention to the psychoanalytical significance of smoking cigars (Freud loved cigars), meekly answered: 'There are times when a cigar is only a cigar'. In other words, Weber's ideas are surely innovative and brilliant—but they do not seem to have any obvious practical implications. They are just good social science. Still, with a bit of good will it can be shown that it is possible also to use Weber's work as a point of departure for an interesting discussion about practical entrepreneurship. Weber's early definition of entrepreneurship may, for example, help us to put Schumpeter's individualistic entrepreneur into perspective. For entrepreneurship to exist, according to Weber, you first and foremost need a modern enterprise or organization that is capable of successfully and methodically exploiting profit opportunities; a creative personality with lots of good ideas is not enough. Such notions in *The Protestant Ethic* as methodical work and 'moneymaking as a vocation' also raise a number of questions. First of all, what precisely is meant by methodical work and moneymaking as a vocation and how exactly do they relate to entrepreneurship? Do these two types of behaviour thrive in post-industrial society or do they belong to an earlier epoch? Can they be taught and, if so, how? To compare, contrast, and otherwise explore the differences between the entrepreneur and the bureaucrat on a number of practical issues may also be a useful exercise for the entrepreneur-to-be. Indeed, Howard Stevenson and David Gumpert have tried to do exactly this in their well-known article called 'The Heart of Entrepreneurship' (1992). A final question that it may be interesting to discuss is whether the current attempt in the business school community to turn entrepreneurship into a teachable skill is not itself an example of rationalization and disenchantment. Is it perhaps true that the mythical entrepreneur is on his way out, about to be replaced by a score of methodical and innovative MBA students? Can entrepreneurship really be taught?

2.2. *The Contributions of Sociologists, Anthropologists, Psychologists, and Economic Historians*

The topic of entrepreneurship has never been particularly popular in *sociology* but a number of studies, some of which are of high quality, have none the less been produced over the years (for a survey, see Martinelli 1994; for a general introduction to economic sociology, see Smelser and Swedberg 1994). It should also be noted that there exist a number of general theories of change and innovation in sociology, which are of interest in this context. While Weber's theory of charisma may not be identical to his theory of entrepreneurship, the concept of charisma can none the less be used to elucidate certain aspects of entrepreneurship, as a well-known study by Nicole Woolsey Biggart— *Charismatic Capitalism: Direct Selling Organizations in America* (1989)—illustrates.

Emile Durkheim's notion that new institutions and new values appear in situations of 'collective effervescence'—when the intensity of social interaction reaches such a pitch that it practically boils over—is another interesting theory of innovation (Durkheim [1912] 1965: 240–55). Examples of such moments in history, according to Durkheim, include the Renaissance and the French

Revolution. Examples from the economy would perhaps be the early stages of the Industrial Revolution in England, the time around the turn of the century in the United States—or the more recent history of Silicon Valley (for the last example, see "The Origins and Dynamics of Production Networks in Silicon Valley" by AnnaLee Saxenian).

Robert K. Merton's idea that many discoveries are made by accident ('serendipity') is also evocative in this context (Merton 1968: 157ff). In one of his most famous articles Merton has furthermore suggested that there may exit an inadvertent link between entrepreneurship and crime. In cultures where there is a very strong emphasis on what people should strive for (such as economic success in the United States), but where there also exist few means through which the average person can reach this goal, the result is often an attempt to find a new way to succeed—innovative behaviour for businessmen, but sometimes also deviance and crime for those without access to legitimate means (Merton 1968: 181–214). Some sociologists have also suggested that entrepreneurship can be conceptualized as a social movement; and that there exist entrepreneurs in other spheres of society than the economy. Concepts such as moral entrepreneurs, political entrepreneurs, and so on have as a result become quite common (see e.g. Becker 1963: 147–83, Jenkins 1983, Weber 1994: 338–47).

Sociologists, as opposed to economists, often apply a comparative perspective on entrepreneurship, and S. M. Lipset's article "Values and Entrepreneurship in the Americas" is a fine example of this. Lipset argues that cultural values deeply affect entrepreneurship and the level of economic development, and to show this he contrasts Latin America to North America. While the former was deeply influenced by early Iberian culture, with its tendency to downgrade manual labour as well as commerce and industry, Puritan values with their emphasis on work and moneymaking, as a vocation in God's honour, predominated in many parts of the United States. While landed property became the mark of success in Latin America, it was fortunes made in business in the United States. The educational ideals have also differed, with humanist education being popular in Latin America, as opposed to engineering and science in the United States (cf. Cardoso 1967).

One topic that has nearly become a growth industry in contemporary sociology is that of entrepreneurship and ethnicity (e.g. Aldrich and Waldinger 1990; Waldinger, Aldrich, and Ward 1990; "Ethnic Entrepreneurs"). It has been well established, for example, that ethnic groups have a natural market for certain commodities among their own members, but also that this market cannot grow beyond a certain size. Ethnic minorities tend to favour family businesses, and these are often kept alive through self-exploitation. It can be added that some interesting insights about entrepreneurship in developing countries have also emerged within the framework of ethnic entrepreneurship. In discussing some particular ethnic group, this type of study usually also says something about the economic (and entrepreneurial) conditions in the country from where the members of the ethnic group originate. It is furthermore common that the ethnic group which is being studied operates in a developing country—with its own attitudes to entrepreneurship and business.

What Mark Granovetter has to say about the emergence of the firm is also of relevance for an understanding of entrepreneurship in developing countries ("The Economic Sociology of Firms and Entrepreneurs"). He points out, for example, that extended kin ties and family solidarity can constitute an obstacle for a businessman if the latter is obliged to care for distant kin members; but that the same strong family feelings can turn into an advantage once the businessman has emigrated—as long as the distant kin members stay behind. Granovetter also discusses another important element in many entrepreneurial ventures, namely *trust*. In social groups and societies where people are isolated from each other, he argues, it may be difficult to develop the kind of confidence that is absolutely necessary to start a firm or otherwise cooperate in economic matters.

Sociologists have also looked at aspects of modern entrepreneurship other than ethnicity. One method that has been used in some of their studies is that of networks, as illustrated in this volume by Ronald Burt's article on 'structural holes', ("The Network Entrepreneur"). According to Burt, entrepreneurial opportunities exist in a person's network if this is structured in a special way. More precisely, person A's network contains entrepreneurial opportunities (or structural holes) to the extent that it contains groups of people who want to do business with each other and who have no other way of communicating than via person A. Sociologists have also shown that it is possible to relate entrepreneurship to the rise and decline of organizational populations. This means that an entrepreneur's chance of succeeding is to some extent dependent on when he or she starts the business—at the same time, before or later than other people (see in this context "Entrepreneurial Strategies in New Organizational Populations" by Howard Aldrich). The reader should also be aware that there is a rather complex process, which has been little studied, which takes place *before* a firm is founded (Aldrich 1999).

As illustrated by another text in this reader, the study of entrepreneurship within large firms has also attracted some attention among sociologists. According to Rosabeth Moss Kanter, a well-known sociologist at the Harvard

Business School, innovations within firms (intrapreneurship) can be consciously cultivated with excellent results ("When a Thousand Flowers Bloom: Structural, Collective, and Social Conditions for Innovation in Organization"; cf. Kanter 1983, 1997). 'Innovations', she argues, 'can grow wild, springing up weed-like despite unfavorable circumstances, but they can also be cultivated, blossoming in greater abundance under favorable conditions' (Kanter 1988: 170). You have, first of all, to create a corporate environment that is positive to the generation of ideas; then put resources at the disposal of the idea generators; and, finally, have an organizational structure that facilitates the completion of the new project and helps diffuse the innovation.

A few words need finally to be said about the way that sociologists have dealt with the issue of gender and entrepreneurship. Some solid sociological insights on intrapreneurship and gender have been developed by Rosabeth Moss Kanter (1977, 1983); and there also exists the previously mentioned study by Nicole Woolsey Biggart of female direct selling organizations. A few other studies—of women and self-employment more generally, for example—can also be found (e.g. Carter and Cannon 1992, Kovalainen 1993, Moore and Buttner 1997). On the whole, however, much more work needs to be done on this topic—a statement which is not only true for sociologists, but also for scholars from other disciplines who do research in this important field.

Compared to sociology, relatively few studies of entrepreneurship are to be found in *anthropology*. The only overview that exists is quite old, even though it should be added that comparatively little work has been produced on this topic during the last ten to fifteen years (see Owens 1978; see also Greenfield 1979, Greenfield and Strickon 1986, and "Entrepreneurship and Anthropology: The Case of Freddy, the Strawberry Man" by Monica Lindh de Montoya). Still, some of the work that has been produced by anthropologists on this topic—especially by Fredrik Barth and Clifford Geertz—belongs to the absolute finest in the social sciences. A student at a business school in, say, Europe or the United States may, of course, wonder what studies of non-Western and pre-industrial societies, of the type that anthropologists specialize in, have to do with entrepreneurship in the modern world. There are two answers to this question, as I see it. First, anthropologists, like other social scientists, aim at generality in their research, which means that the concepts they use and the insights they develop may also be applied to behaviour in contemporary western society. And second, modern-day anthropologists do not only deal with pre-industrial societies but also with developing countries and fully industrialized countries. Geertz' best known study of entrepreneurship, for example, is an analysis of two Indonesian villages in the 1950s (Geertz 1963).

Richard Swedberg

Fredrik Barth made his first attempt to develop an anthropological theory of entrepreneurship in his native Norway in the 1960s, but it is in a study of a Central African village from a few years later that his ideas have come to their clearest and most mature expression (for Norway, see Barth 1963; for Africa, "Economic Spheres in Darfur"). According to Barth, entrepreneurship has essentially to do with connecting two spheres in society, between which there exists a difference in value (see also Granovetter forthcoming). Something which is cheap in one sphere, in other words, may be expensive in another sphere. In the Norwegian study, for example, Barth argues that economics and politics constitute two different spheres, and that it can be very difficult (but also lucrative) to transfer value from one sphere to the other. It is, for example, illegal to use money to buy support in the political sphere. It is, on the other hand, possible to make financial contributions to political parties; and in this way some licence may be procured, a road may be built or something else be accomplished, which is worth much more than the amount that was given to the political party.

In his case study from Central Africa, Barth uses an example of an economy which has two distinct spheres. In one of these cash is used, in the other not. In the former people trade on the market in a few products, such as onions and tomatoes; while the second economic sphere is characterized by millet production and work to build houses, which only can be exchanged for beer, not for cash. That these two spheres should be kept separate from one another was seen as self-evident by the local population; and this was also the way it had 'always' been. One day, however, an Arab merchant appeared and connected the two spheres by offering beer in exchange for help in cultivating tomatoes—which he then sold for cash on the market at a good profit for himself. Barth's analysis of economic spheres illustrates not only that entrepreneurship is about spotting new opportunities, but also, as Robert K. Merton has suggested, that entrepreneurship may involve a challenge to some of the basic values that exist in a community.

More studies on entrepreneurship may well have been carried out within the field of *psychology* than in either mainstream economics or in sociology (for a survey of the field, see Chell *et al.* 1991). Psychological studies of the entrepreneur have none the less a fairly low status among social scientists who study entrepreneurship, and the main reason for this is that the attempt to single out one or several psychological traits as typical for the entrepreneurial personality is generally considered to have failed. That such a personality exists in the first place is also seriously doubted. To this can be added that psychologists often try to explain far too much, according to the other social sciences, including those aspects of entrepreneurship that, for example, sociology or economic history are better equipped to handle.

It is possible to roughly divide the psychological studies of entrepreneurship into two groups: one where the main goal is to isolate the entrepreneurial personality; and another which is more social-psychological in nature and where the personality of the entrepreneur is seen as decisively shaped by something from the outside, such as the minority status of the parents or the way that children are socialized. The former types of study are typically conducted on a population of a few dozen to one or two hundred subjects, who are either interviewed or given a questionnaire to complete. Control groups are rarely, if ever, used. The list of traits that supposedly characterize entrepreneurs is long—independence, problem solving style, flexibility, creativity, high self-esteem, endurance and so on—but none of these (or no combination of them) has won general acceptance. The results, to cite some knowledgeable psychologists, are 'contradictory', and there is 'little agreement' among the researchers as to the nature of the psychological makeup of the entrepreneur (Chell *et al.* 1991: 29, 37; cf. Brockhaus and Horwitz 1986).

Some of the best known attempts to unlock the secrets of entrepreneurship with the help of psychology can more appropriately be labelled social-psychological, since they are centred around the interaction of the entrepreneur with his or her social surroundings. There are in particular two studies of this type that have become famous: David McClelland's *The Achieving Society* (1961) and Everett E. Hagen's *On The Theory of Social Change* (1962). McClelland's basic thesis is that entrepreneurship has to do with an individual's so-called need for achievement (referred to as *n* Achievement); while Hagen (trained as an economist) argues that people who have grown up in certain minorities develop a much stronger psychological propensity for entrepreneurship than those who have not.

The approaches of McClelland and Hagen are generally seen as discredited today (see for example *'The Modernization of Entrepreneurship'* by Alexander Gerschenkron; see also Schatz 1965). Both theories may well contain a grain of truth, but McClelland as well as Hagen try to bite off far too much in their analyses and especially disregard the complicated institutional environment that surrounds the entrepreneur. As an example of this one can mention McClelland's argument that the achievement motive of the ascetic Protestants created modern capitalism (while Weber had argued something different, namely that the ascetic Protestants had helped to create the spirit of modern capitalism but none of its many institutions, from commercial law to the modern enterprise). Hagen's argument is similarly tenuous: status withdrawal from a minority supposedly leads to the development among future male children of a certain 'retreatism'; after having lived with such retreatist males for a few generations, their wives get annoyed and try to install an achievement motive in their sons—and thereby social change and economic growth begin.

Despite all the critique that can be directed at the works of McClelland and Hagen, it is also clear that much can be learned from their studies—something which is also true for many works in the psychological literature on entrepreneurs. McClelland in particular is a very creative thinker and has introduced fascinating new types of material into the discussion of entrepreneurship, such as children's tales and different forms of popular culture (McClelland 1962 is a good and easy-to-read example of this). It would also seem obvious that there *does* exist a psychological dimension to entrepreneurship, and that psychologists have an important contribution to make to this field. Exactly how this can be done is not clear today, even if it is often suggested that in order to be successful, psychological research has to be better coordinated with the insights of the other social sciences. It is unlikely, in other words that the 'entrepreneurial personality' will ever be discovered. It also seems likely that psychologists would do better if they focused on some unit other than the entrepreneur's personality—for example on different types of entrepreneurs, on the gender dimension of entrepreneurship or on entrepreneurship in different kinds of organizations.

The number of studies which have been carried out within the field of *economic history* is enormous and probably exceeds what all the other social sciences have produced together. This literature not only includes traditional economic history (in all its national variations), but also business history and the kind of monographs which corporations like to publish in connection with their jubilees. Adding to the difficulty in summarizing the main trends in this giant literature is also the fact that the only available surveys of studies of entrepreneurship within economic history are incomplete, somewhat old and heavily biased to Anglo-Saxon contributions (Soltow 1968, Mathias 1983; see also Hannah 1983 and Livesay 1989). Judging from what my colleagues in economic history tell me, the current profile of entrepreneurial study may look something like this: there is an increasing number of sophisticated studies of entrepreneurship within single corporations and also attempts to use concepts and theories from microeconomics on economic development; studies of entrepreneurship within small enterprises, of female entrepreneurs and of commercial failures are, on the other hand, still very much underrepresented.

A great landmark in entrepreneurial studies is represented by what was accomplished during the decade that the Research Center for Entrepreneurial

History was in operation at Harvard University (1948–58). The main spirit behind the Center, economic historian A. H. Cole, felt that entrepreneurial history must be interdisciplinary in nature and did his best to get people from a number of different social science disciplines interested in its activities. A list of those who in one way or another participated in the Center includes the following: Bernard Bailyn (history), Thomas Cochran (economic history), Alexander Gerschenkron (economic history), David Landes (economic history), Talcott Parsons (sociology), Fritz Redlich (economic history), and Joseph Schumpeter (economics). Also a small number of anthropologists were involved, such as Richard Wohl and Cyril Belshaw.

That scholars of this calibre would leave behind many interesting studies is obvious, and this is also what happened (see e.g. Aitkin 1965). Some of these exist in the form of monographs, while others were published in the journal of the Center, *Explorations in Entrepreneurial History*. A central theme in much of this work was that entrepreneurship should not be studied by focusing on the individual entrepreneur but rather by looking at the enterprise. Special attention was often paid to the social relations within the enterprise and to the relations between the enterprise and its surroundings. A special effort was made by several members at the Center to apply the concepts of social role and social attitude to the study of entrepreneurship—but there also existed some significant opposition to this. Marshalling a number of historical examples in his support, Alexander Gerschenkron, in particular, countered that entrepreneurship has flourished in many places where the general attitude of the population to economic innovations had been negative. In countries where the prerequisites for an industrial takeoff did not exist, he also noted, substitutes had usually been found, with the state or the banks filling in for local entrepreneurs ("The Modernization of Entrepreneurship").

One of the most solid contributions to the study of entrepreneurship during the post-World War II period has been made by business historian Alfred Chandler. In several huge volumes, which began to appear in the 1960s, Chandler more or less singlehandedly wrote the history of an extremely important innovation in US economic history: the huge industrial corporation, which appeared at the end of the nineteenth century. Chandler, however, was not so much interested in writing the history of the entrepreneurs who had started these corporations, as in understanding the new type of administration that characterized them. These huge corporations, he argued, could produce products which were considerably cheaper than their competitors, for mainly two reasons: decreasing costs, due to large production (*size*), and a big repertoire in products (*scale*; cf. Chandler 1990). To Chandler, it is these giant industrial corporations which have driven economic growth and entrepreneurship during the twentieth century in the OECD countries; and he is convinced that they will also do so in the future. (For a counterargument which highlights the importance of small and flexible firms in contemporary society, see "The Origins and Dynamics of Production Networks in Silicon Valley" by AnnaLee Saxenian on Silicon Valley in the 1970s; see also Saxenian's well-known study *Regional Advantage* [1994]).

It was perhaps not to be expected that those scholars who wanted to apply microeconomic concepts to economic history would be particularly interested in entrepreneurship; and this has also turned out to be the case. In the work of economic historian and Nobel Laureate Douglass North, for example, the entrepreneur plays a very small role, when mentioned at all. In *The Rise of the Western World* (1973) North and Thomas argue that differences in relative prices create incentives for the emergence of efficient organizations, and it is these latter which produce economic growth. In a later study North backtracks and says that political rulers devise property rights in their own interest, something which can lead to the creation of inefficient economic organizations and a blocking of economic development. In *Institutions, Institutional Change and Economic Performance* (1990)—North's latest, major statement—it is explicitly stated that the individual entrepreneur is 'the agent of change' and that he or she responds to incentives embodied in the institutional framework (North 1990: 83). As in North's earlier work, however, the entrepreneur is only mentioned in passing, and there is no real attempt to flesh out what a new institutional theory of the entrepreneur might look like.

Finally, the reader may have noted that in discussing the non-economic sciences I have not mentioned their possible contributions to practical entrepreneurship. The main reason for this has been my desire not to unduly tax the patience of the reader; another reason is that it is fairly easy to spot the practical implications of the type of analysis that one can find in the non-economic social sciences. That it is easy to do so is probably due to their close link to empirical material; and in many cases the theories of sociologists, economic historians and so on are little but generalizations, based on a number of individual cases. This can be exemplified by the sociological literature on ethnic entrepreneurship, where quite a few of the insights can be directly translated into practical advice for how to start up a business, what traps to avoid, and so on. Some social scientists, it should be noted, also write because they want to change reality, and in this case the step from text to practical advice is naturally minimal.

It would, however, be a pity to close the section on the practical implications of the non-economic social sciences without mentioning one type of insight which can be found in this literature, but which is absent in most of the economics literature. This is the fact that successful entrepreneurship usually involves more actors than the entrepreneur himself or herself, and that the behaviour of these other actors must be taken into account in the analysis. One of these actors is clearly the state, and I have also mentioned Gerschenkron's observation that the state can substitute for a native group of entrepreneurs under certain conditions ('The Modernization of Entrepreneurship'). Another type of state intervention—which is more in tune with the ideological climate of today—would be for the state to sponsor entrepreneurial education, supplied in schools, to the unemployed or to youths in the ghetto. This, for example, is what sociologists Ivan Light and Carolyn Rosenstein suggest for the United States (Light and Rosenstein 1995: 205–28). That parents can also play a role in entrepreneurial education is implied in several studies in psychology; but exactly how this is to happen is not clear. Intermediate organizations of the type that civil society is made up of, may also be very helpful in furthering entrepreneurship. Tocqueville, for example, pointed out in Democracy in America (1835–1840) that active political participation in the townships had helped the American population in the early 1800s to acquire skills which they later used for setting up and operating their own businesses.

3. Summing Up the Argument: Bringing Practical Knowledge and Scientific Knowledge Closer Together

Even if one goes through the social science literature in as quick and summary a fashion as I have done here, it should be clear that the social sciences not only have a contribution to make to the analysis of entrepreneurship but also to *practical entrepreneurship*. Some social science ideas, as I have tried to show, can be directly translated into advice for how to run a business, while in other cases a bit of ingenuity may be needed to ferret out the practical implications of some arguments. In a number of cases, finally, it is hard to find any practical implications whatsoever.

It deserves to be emphasized that the absence of practical implications is not necessarily a disadvantage since the social sciences also have other tasks than being of practical use. Certain questions—including ethical ones—need to be discussed, regardless of practical results or implications. Successful entrepreneurship may, for example, benefit some groups in a society, but not all; and it is the duty of the social scientist to figure out if this is the case. It is similarly the duty of the social scientist to point out, as Baumol (1993) has done, that throughout history entrepreneurship has many times been destructive to all but a small minority in society. Finally, according to a common view in the social sciences, all values are scientifically undemonstrable (Weber 1994). If one should be for—or against—entrepreneurship is consequently something that social science cannot pronounce on.

It is clear that a social science which sees as its only task to produce practical recipes for entrepreneurs-to-be would soon become sterile. There exists a playful and impractical element to social science which is absolutely necessary for its development, but which has no place in the world of practical business. Businessmen, as David McClelland (1962) has pointed out, want quick results and plenty of money in exchange for their efforts, while scientists like to get involved in projects which stretch over a long period of time and where the 'payoff' is often neither very clear nor supplied in money.

The general thrust of this essay can be summarized and given some generality with the help of Hayek's argument about 'practical knowledge' versus 'scientific knowledge', which was mentioned at the outset. Hayek, to recall, contrasts scientific knowledge to practical knowledge, defining the latter as concrete knowledge about an individual case, and the former as a much more general and analytical kind of knowledge. In Hayek's view, practical knowledge has often been looked upon with a certain disdain by scientists, something which he felt was wrong.

With a bit of oversimplification it is possible to conceptualize practical knowledge and scientific knowledge as being situated along one and the same continuum, with a minimum of abstraction and analytical complexity at one of the ends and a maximum of the two at the other. What has earlier been said about social science and practical entrepreneurship can then be placed along this continuum, and a typology suggested. First of all, there exists the kind of detailed, practical knowledge which the entrepreneur has of his or her own business deals (*Type 1: practical knowledge of the entrepreneur*). Next comes the kind of knowledge that is often taught in courses on entrepreneurship at business schools today. This type of knowledge about how to spot and develop business opportunities is very concrete in nature but differs from Type 1 in that it is more general, especially since it has to be taught to a plurality of students (*Type 2: practical knowledge about entrepreneurship, as taught in the business schools*). Social scientists can sometimes contribute to this type of knowledge by directly translating some of their insights into practical advice, but most of the research that the social scientists produce can be found at the next stage of abstraction. This type of knowledge is often rich in practical implications for entrepreneurship (*Type 3: social science knowledge with practical implications for entrepreneurship*). And finally, the most abstract type of social science knowledge is of such generality that it is often totally impractical or otherwise irrelevant for practical entrepreneurship (*Type 4: pure social science or social science with no implications for practical entrepreneurship*).

Hayek's critique of scientific knowledge in the 1940s, and the critique of the social sciences that today is coming from some of those who teach entrepreneurship in the business schools, can be interpreted as a plea for shifting the emphasis in current social science research from Type 4 (or pure science) to something like Type 3 (or social science research with direct implications for practical entrepreneurship). In my opinion this is a reasonable request; it would also be good if it was possible to develop more of a direct overlap between practical entrepreneurship, as taught in the business schools, and social science research at the universities. Both parties would no doubt benefit from this.

Notes

1. For information, criticism and/or assistance, I would like to thank José Luis Alvarez, Patrik Aspers, Frédéric Delmar, Erik Ljungar, Stephen Gudeman, Mark Granovetter, Ulf Hannerz, Karl Gratzer, Shahram Khosravi, and Cecilia Swedberg. David Musson, editor at Oxford University Press, should be especially thanked for encouragement in general as well as many good suggestions. For financial assistance, I am grateful to Magnus Bergvalls Stiftelse at S-E-Banken in Sweden.

References

Acs, Zoltan (ed.) 1996. *Small Firms and Growth*. Cheltenham: Elgar.
Acs, Zoltan, Bo Carlsson, and Charlie Karlsson (eds.) 1998. *Entrepreneurship, Small and Medium Sized Enterprises and the Macroeconomy.* Cambridge: Cambridge University Press.
Aitken, Hugh 1965. 'Entrepreneurial Research: The History of an Intellectual Innovation'. pp. 3–19 in *Explorations in Enterprise*. Cambridge, MA: Harvard University Press.
Aldrich, Howard 1999. *Organizations Evolving*. London: Sage.

Richard Swedberg

Aldrich, Howard and Roger Waldinger 1990. 'Ethnicity and Entrepreneurship', *Annual Review of Sociology* 16: 111–35.

Allen, Robert Loring 1991. *Opening Doors: The Life and Work of Joseph Schumpeter*. New Brunswick: Transaction Press.

Alvarez, José Luis 1991. *The International Diffusion and Institutionalization of the New Entrepreneurship Movement: A Study in the Sociology of Organizational Knowledge.* Unpublished Ph.D. thesis. Harvard University, Department of Sociology, and Harvard Business School.

Alvarez, José Luis 1996. 'The Role of Business Ideas in the Promotion of Unemployment: The Case of Entrepreneurship in the 1980s', in Jordi Gual (ed.) *The Social Challenge of the Creation of Employment in Europe.* Cheltenham, England: Edward Elgar, pp. 190–214.

Bailyn, Bernard 1955. *The New England Merchants in the Seventeenth Century.* Cambridge, MA: Harvard University Press.

Barth, Fredrik (ed.) 1963. *The Role of the Entrepreneur in Social Change in Northern Norway.* Oslo: Universitetsforlaget.

Baumol, William 1968. 'Entrepreneurship in Economic Theory', *American Economic Review (Papers and Proceedings)* 58: 64–71.

Baumol, William 1990. 'Entrepreneurship: Productive, Unproductive, and Destructive', *Journal of Political Economy* 98: 893–921.

Baumol, William 1993. *Entrepreneurship, Management, and The Structure of Payoffs.* Cambridge, MA: The MIT Press.

Becker, Howard 1963. *The Outsiders: Studies in the Sociology of Deviance.* New York: The Free Press.

Berger, Brigitte (ed.) *The Culture of Entrepreneurship.* San Francisco: ICS.

Biggart, Nicole Woolsey 1989. *Charismatic Capitalism: Direct Selling Organizations in America.* Chicago: University of Chicago Press.

Blaug, Mark 1986. 'Entrepreneurship Before and After Schumpeter', in *Economic History and the History of Economics.* New York: New York University Press, pp. 219–30.

Brockhaus, Robert and Pamela Horwitz 1986. 'The Psychology of the Entrepreneur', in Donald Sexton and Raymond Smilor (eds.) *The Art and Science of Entrepreneurship.* Cambridge, MA: Ballinger Publishing Company, pp. 25–48.

Cardoso, Fernando 1967. 'The Industrial Elite', in Seymour Martin Lipset and Aaldo Solari (eds.) *Elites in Latin America.* New York: Oxford University Press, pp. 94–114.

Carter, Sara and Tom Cannon 1992. *Women as Entrepreneurs.* London: Academic Press.

Casson, Mark 1983. *The Entrepreneur: An Economic Theory.* Oxford: Martin Robertson.

Chandler, Alfred 1990. *Scale and Scope: The Dynamics of Industrial Capitalism.* Cambridge, MA: Harvard University Press.

Chell, Elizabeth, Jean Haworth, and Sally Brearley 1991. 'The Search for Entrepreneurial Traits', in *The Entrepreneurial Personality.* London: Routledge, pp. 29–53.

Delmar, Frédéric 1996. *Entrepreneurial Behavior and Business Performance.* Stockholm: Handelshögskolan (EFI).

Drucker, Peter [1985] 1993. *Innovation and Entrepreneurship.* New York: Harper-Business.

Durkheim, Emile [1912] 1965. *Elementary Forms of Religious Life*. New York: The Free Press.

The Economist 1999. 'A Survey of Innovation in Industry'. February 20 (28 pp).

Geertz, Clifford 1963. *Peddlers and Princes: Social Change and Economic Modernization in Two Indonesian Towns*. Chicago: University of Chicago Press.

Geertz, Clifford 1983. *Local Knowledge: Further Essays in Interpretive Anthropology*. New York: Basic Books.

Granovetter, Mark (forthcoming). Draft Chapter 4 in *Society and Economy*. Cambridge, MA: Harvard University Press.

Gratzer, Karl (forthcoming). 'Entrepreneurial Errors'. Södertörn Highschool, Huddinge, Sweden.

Greenfield, Sidney (ed.) 1979. *Entrepreneurs in Cultural Context*. Albuquerque: University of New Mexico Press.

Greenfield, Sidney and Arnold Strickon (eds.) 1986. *Entrepreneurship and Social Change*. Monographs in Economic Anthropology, No. 2. New York: University Press of America.

Hagen, Everett 1962. *On The Theory of Social Change: How Economic Growth Begins*. Homewood, IL: Dorsey Press.

Hannah, Leslie 1983. *Entrepreneurs and the Social Sciences (An Inaugural Lecture)*. London: London School of Economics and Political Science.

Hayek, Friedrich von [1945] 1972. 'The Use of Knowledge in Society', in *Individualism and Economic Order*. Chicago: Henry Regnery Company, pp. 77–91.

Hébert, Robert and Albert Link. 1982. *The Entrepreneur: Mainstream Views and Radical Critiques*. New York: Praeger.

Hirschman, Albert O. 1967. *Development Projects Observed*. Washington, DC: The Brookings Institution.

Hoselitz, Bert 1951. 'The Early History of Entrepreneurial Theory', *Explorations in Entrepreneurial History* 3: 193–220.

Jarillo, Carlos and Howard Stevenson 1990. 'A Paradigm of Entrepreneurship: Entrepreneurial Management', *Strategic Management Journal* 11: 17–27.

Jenkins, J. Craig 1983. 'Resource Mobilization Theory of the Study of Social Movements', *Annual Review of Sociology* 9: 527–53.

Kamien, Morton I. and Nancy L. Scwartz 1982. *Market Structure and Innovation*. Cambridge: Cambridge University Press.

Kanter, Rosabeth Moss 1977. *Men and Women of the Corporation*. New York: Basic Books.

Kanter, Rosabeth Moss 1983. *The Change-Masters: Innovation and Entrepreneurship in the American Corporation*. New York: Simon and Schuster.

Kanter, Rosabeth Moss 1988. 'When A Thousand Flowers Bloom: Structural, Collective, and Social Conditions for Innovation in Organization', *Research in Organizational Behavior* 10: 169–211. (Also reproduced in this reader.)

Kanter, Rosabeth Moss 1995. *World Class: Thriving Locally in the Global Economy*. New York: Simon and Schuster

Kanter, Rosabeth Moss 1997. *On the Frontiers of Management*. Boston: Harvard Business Review Book.

Keynes, John Maynard [1936] 1960. *The General Theory of Employment, Interest and Money*. London: Macmillan & Co.

Kidder, Tracy 1981. *The Soul of a New Machine*. Boston: Little, Brown and Company.

Kirzner, Israel 1973. *Competition and Entrepreneurship*. Chicago: University of Chicago Press.

Kirzner, Israel 1997. 'Entrepreneurial Discovery and the Competitive Market Process: An Austrian Approach', *Journal of Economic Literature* 35: 60–85.

Knight, Frank 1921. *Risk, Uncertainty and Profit*. New York: Houghton Mifflin Company.

Kovalainen, Anne 1993. *At the Margins of the Economy: Women's Self-Employment in Finland 1960–1990*. Turku: Turku School of Economics and Business Administration.

Light, Ivan and Carolyn Rosenstein 1995. *Race, Ethnicity and Entrepreneurship in Urban America*. New York: Aldine de Gruyter.

Livesay, Harold 1989. 'Entrepreneurial Dominance in Business Large and Small, Past and Present', *Business History Review* 63: 1–21.

McClelland, David 1961. *The Achieving Society*. Princeton: D. Van Nostrand Co.

McClelland, David 1962. 'Business Drive and National Achievement', *Harvard Business Review* 40 (July–August): 99-112.

McClelland, David 1965. 'Achievement Motivation Can Be Developed', *Harvard Business Review* 41(November-December): 6-24, 178.

Martinelli, Alberto 1994. 'Entrepreneurship and Management', in Neil Smelser and Richard Swedberg (eds.) *Handbook of Economic Sociology*. Princeton and New York: Princeton University Press and the Russell Sage Foundation, pp. 476–503.

Mathias, Peter 1983. 'Entrepreneurship and Economic History: The State of the Debate', in Michael Earl (ed.) *Perspectives on Management*. Oxford: Oxford University Press, pp. 40–54.

Merton, Robert K. 1968. *Social Theory and Social Structure*. 3rd enlarged edn. New York: The Free Press.

Mises, Ludwig von [1951] 1978. 'Profit and Loss', in *Planning for Freedom*. South Holland, IL: Libertarian Press, pp. 108–50.

Mises, Ludwig von 1963. *Human Action: A Treatise on Economics*, rev. edn. New Haven: Yale University Press.

Mises, Ludwig von 1966. *Human Action: A Treatise on Economics*. 3rd rev. edn. Chicago: Contemporary Books.

Moore, Dorothy P. and E. Holly Buttner 1997. *Women Entrepreneurs: Moving Beyond the Glass Ceiling*. London: Sage.

Nelson, Richard (ed.) 1993. *National Innovation Systems*. New York: Oxford University Press.

North, Douglass 1990. *Institutions, Institutional Change and Economic Performance*. Cambridge: Cambridge University Press.

North, Douglass and Robert Paul Thomas 1973. *The Rise of the Western World: A New Economic History*. Cambridge: Cambridge University Press.

Owens, Raymond 1978. 'The Anthropological Study of Entrepreneurship', *Eastern Anthropologist* 31: 65–80.

Sawyer, John E. 1951–52. 'Entrepreneurial Error and Economic Growth', *Explorations in Entrepreneurial History* 4: 199–204.

Saxenian, AnnaLee 1994. *Regional Advantage*. Cambridge, MA: Harvard University Press.

Schatz, Sayre P. 1965. ''n Achievement and Economic Growth: A Critique', *Quarterly Journal of Economics* 79: 235–41. See also the debate between Schatz and McClelland on pp. 242-7.

Scherer, Frederic M. and Mark Perlman (eds.) 1992. *Entrepreneurship, Technological Innovation, and Economic Growth: Studies in the Schumpeterian Tradition*. Ann Arbor: University of Michigan Press.

Schumpeter, Joseph A. 1928. 'Unternehmer', in Vol. 8 of Ludwig Elster *et al* (eds.) *Handwörterbuch der Staatswissenschaften*. Jena: Gustav Fischer Verlag, pp. 476–87.

Schumpeter, Joseph A. [1934] 1961. *The Theory of Economic Development*. New York: Oxford University Press. This represents a translation of the second edition from 1926 of a work that originally appeared in 1911.

Schumpeter, Joseph A. [1937] 1989. 'Preface to Japanese translation of *Theorie der Wirtschaftlichen Entwicklung*', in *Essays*. New Brunswick: Transaction Publishers. pp. 165–8.

Schumpeter, Joseph A. 1939. *Business Cycles: A Theoretical, Historical and Statistical Analysis of the Capitalist Process*. New York: McGraw-Hill.

Schumpeter, Joseph A. 1943. Letter to David McCord Wright dated December 6, in Richard Swedberg, *Schumpeter—A Biography*. Princeton: Princeton University Press, 1991, pp. 230–1.

Schumpeter, Joseph A. [1946] 1991. 'Comments on a Plan for the Study of Entrepreneurship', in *The Economics and Sociology of Capitalism*. Princeton: Princeton University Press. pp. 406–28.

Schumpeter, Joseph A. [1947] 1989. 'The Creative Response in Economic History', in *Essays*. New Brunswick: Transaction Publishers, pp. 216–26. For the original, fuller version, see Schumpeter [1946] 1991.

Schumpeter, Joseph A. [1949] 1989. 'Economic Theory and Entrepreneurial History', in *Essays*. New Brunswick: Transaction Publishers, pp. 253–71.

Schumpeter, Joseph A. [1950] 1976. *Capitalism, Socialism and Democracy*. New York: Harper.

Schumpeter, Joseph A. 1954. *History of Economic Analysis*. London: George Allen & Unwin.

Smelser, Neil and Richard Swedberg (eds.) 1994. *Handbook of Economic Sociology*. Princeton and New York: Princeton University Press and the Russell Sage Foundation.

Soltow, James 1968. 'The Entrepreneur in Economic History', *American Economic Review (Papers and Proceedings)* 58: 84–92.

Stevenson, Howard and David Gumpert, 1992. 'The Heart of Entrepreneurship', in William Sahlman and Howard Stevenson (eds.), *The Entrepreneurial Venture*. Boston: Harvard Business School, pp. 9–25.

Stevenson, Howard and Carlos Jarillo. 1990. 'A Paradigm of Entrepreneurship: Entrepreneurial Management', *Strategic Management Journal* 11: 17–27.

Stolper, Wolfgang 1994. *Joseph Alois Schumpeter: The Public Life of A Private Man*. Princeton: Princeton University Press.

Swedberg, Richard 1991. *Schumpeter—A Biography*. Princeton: Princeton University Press.

Swedberg, Richard 1998. *Max Weber and the Idea of Economic Sociology*. Princeton: Princeton University Press.

Tocqueville, Alexis de. [1835-1840] 1990. *Democracy in America*. 2 vols. New York: Vintage Books.

Waldinger, Roger, Howard Aldrich, and Robin Ward 1980. *Ethnic Entrepreneurs*. London: Sage.

Weber, Max [1898] 1990. *Grundriss zu den Vorlesungen über Allgemeine ('theoretische') Nationalökonomie*. Tübingen: J.C.B. Mohr.

Weber, Max 1978. *Economy and Society: An Outline of Interpretive Sociology*. Ed. Guenther Roth and Claus Wittich. 2 vols. Berkeley: University of California Press.

Weber, Max 1988. *The Protestant Ethic and the Spirit of Capitalism*. Trans. Talcott Parsons. Gloucester, MA: Peter Smith.

Weber, Max 1994. *Political Writings*. Cambridge: Cambridge University Press.

Wong, Bernard 1998. *Ethnicity and Entrepreneurship: The New Chinese Immigrants in the San Francisco Bay Area*. Boston: Allyn and Bacon.

II. DIFFERENT SOCIAL SCIENCE PERSPECTIVES ON ENTREPRENEURSHIP

This section contains major statements on the nature of entrepreneurship from different social science perspectives. Several articles have been written by economists, reflecting the fact that economists still have something of an ideological monopoly on this topic ('*Entrepreneurship as Innovation*', '*Entrepreneurship Before and After Schumpeter*', and '*The Entrepreneur and Profit*'). Even if economists have not produced a generally accepted theory of entrepreneurship, they are none the less the ones who are expected to do so. One article by a sociologist ('*Values and Entrepreneurship in the Americas*'), one by an economic historian ('*The Modernization of Entrepreneurship*'), and one by an anthropologist ('*Economic Spheres in Darfur*') have also been included. All the authors are major figures within their respective disciplines. That no contribution by a psychologist has been included is not by design, but by accident. A few possible articles were located, but none worked out in the end. (The reader may, however, wish to read Chapter 2 in David McClelland's *The Achieving Society* or Chapter 3 in *The Entrepreneurial Personality* by Elizabeth Chell, Jean Haworth, and Sally Brearley).

In what follows, a few words will be said about each article and author. In general, it seems to me that a good way for students in business schools and similar institutions to approach the individual articles in this reader would be to submit them to a number of questions on the following key theme: how does this argument help to better understand entrepreneurship as a practical enterprise? To facilitate this process, I shall indicate what kind of questions might be asked for each individual article, in order to ferret out possible practical implications. There is, of course, also the fact that certain aspects of the social science literature cannot be translated into practical considerations, and that this is not necessarily something negative (see the 'Introduction' on this point).

The first reading, 'Entrepreneurship as Innovation', is an excerpt from Chapter 2 in The Theory of Economic Development by economist Joseph Schumpeter (1883–1950). This text is regarded as the classic statement on entrepreneurship, not only by economists but also by other social scientists. The general context of Schumpeter's work is discussed in section 1.1 'Joseph Schumpeter's Contribution' in the Introduction. In the excerpt which has been included in this volume Schumpeter outlines a theory which is centred around the idea of entrepreneurship as putting together a *new combination*: the entrepreneur combines already existing materials and thereby produces something novel and innovative. It is only at the very moment when someone actually puts together such a combination that he or she is engaged in entrepreneurship. Schumpeter also suggests several useful typologies in his text: one on the constitutive parts of entrepreneurship; another on the different motives that drive the entrepreneur; and a third which covers the main types of innovative behaviour that entrepreneurship may result in.

A few practical implications of Schumpeter's view of entrepreneurship have already been cited in the introductory essay, so here I shall only mention a few additional ones. Schumpeter argues, for example, that overcoming *resistance* to change represents one of the integral parts of entrepreneurship; and it might be interesting to explore the practical consequences of this observation. Is it possible, for example, to train people to face general disapproval or even ostracism? Schumpeter's statement that the entrepreneur needs to rely on intuition rather than on rational reasoning is another thought-provoking idea—as is his suggestion that knowing something in a very thorough manner can sometimes block the right decision. The answers one can make up in response to the question when intuition is preferable to rationality may also be relevant for understanding another theme in Schumpeter, namely that someone is only an entrepreneur when he or she engages in entrepreneurship. Is it, for example, possible to be intuitive over a long period of time—or does intuitive thinking and rationality tend to alternate over periods of time?

The second reading, 'Entrepreneurship Before and After Schumpeter', consists of a brief history of the way that entrepreneurship has been viewed in mainstream economics. Its author, Mark Blaug, is a well-known economist and the author of a number of works on the history of economics. Blaug mentions the way that the entrepreneur has been viewed from the eighteenth century until today, paying particular attention to the failure of his fellow economists to integrate the entrepreneur into mainstream theory. Economists, he also says, have only 'scratched the surface' of the topic of entrepreneurship.

My own opinion (also expressed in the introductory essay) is that the attempt by economists to fit the entrepreneur into the existing models of mainstream economics may be exciting to those who are concerned with improving economic theory, but not of much interest to those who wish to learn about practical entrepreneurship. From a practical perspective, it is of no consequence whatsoever if the entrepreneur is seen as creating an equilibrium (Kirzner) or as breaking one (Schumpeter). There does exist a practical dimension to the way that economists have conceptualized the very essence of entrepreneurship. Cantillon's idea that entrepreneurship consists of buying at a fixed price and selling at an uncertain price surely deserves a discussion from a practical perspective; and so does Frank Knight's famous distinction between risk and uncertainty. When should the entrepreneur follow Cantillon's prescription? And is the line between risk and uncertainty fixed or can it be moved—and what would be the advantage of moving it?

The author of 'The Entrepreneur and Profit'—Ludwig von Mises (1881–1993 —is one of the founders of Austrian economics, which was once regarded as a radical critique of mainstream economics, but which today is increasingly becoming part of it. According to Mises' text, entrepreneurship consists of correctly anticipating the market or, what amounts to the same thing, correctly figuring out what the customers want well ahead of the competition. If the entrepreneur is successful in doing this, he or she will be able to produce more cheaply than the competitors and hence make a profit. Mises argues that the entrepreneur earns his or her profit by being useful to the customer; indeed, the more useful the entrepreneur is in this respect, the larger the profit will be. It would therefore be utterly destructive, he says, to tax or otherwise confiscate the profit of the entrepreneur. People in general, Mises notes with dismay, are often envious of the entrepreneur and hostile to the idea of profit. To Mises, this is outrageous and wrong.

Mises' essay is sharp and provocative, and its practical implications are many. If so much hinges on correctly anticipating what the consumer wants, for example, how does the entrepreneur go about doing this?—through intuition, market research or what? Can the entrepreneur directly influence the consumer and thereby facilitate the whole thing? In his discussion of the entrepreneur's attempt to figure out what the customer wants, Mises also points out that the entrepreneur may fail. To Mises, this failure ('entrepreneurial error') is totally negative and results in a loss of money—but the notion that failures can also be positive deserves to be discussed. Is it not through errors that individuals (and groups in society?) learn; and is it not so that some of the most successful entrepreneurs have failed a few times in their careers? Does society need 'serial entrepreneurs', to use a term that one can find in The Economist? Mises' attacks on the general public's tendency to envy the entrepreneur and on politicians tendency to tax entrepreneurial profit similarly raise a number of questions.

Should the entrepreneur, for example, try to educate the public and fight politicians? If so, how is this to be done?

Seymour Martin Lipset—author of 'Values and Entrepreneurship in the Americas'—is one of the best-known sociologists in the world and the author of a long series of works, from Political Man (1950) to American Exceptionalism (1997). In his contribution to this volume, Lipset compares entrepreneurship in North America to entrepreneurship in Latin America. The main emphasis in the analysis is on the role of culture in promoting or blocking entrepreneurial behaviour. The social structure, Lipset argues, imposes constraints as well as creates possibilities in society; while culture very much decides which of the possible alternatives will be chosen. According to Lipset, a culture is influenced by a host of social factors, including religion, education, the role of the military, and so on.

Similar to Mises, but in a more subtle manner, Lipset points out that entrepreneurship involves more actors than the entrepreneur; and this raises the practical question of how the entrepreneur should relate to these. First of all, there is obviously the state—or rather, all the different institutions that make up the state (the legislature, the courts, the military, the educational system, and so on). And then there are the religious groups, from the state church to the local sect. Should the entrepreneur have any relationship to religious groups and if so, why and with what type of church? Sects may at one point in history have produced excellent entrepreneurs (Weber)—but could that really happen again? Are today's Mormons, Calvinists, and so on better entrepreneurs than Lutherans, Catholics and secular persons? Furthermore, should the entrepreneur try to have an impact on culture (for example, via a church or via politics) or is it impossible to influence something as nebulous as 'culture'? Should entrepreneurs in principle ignore all those factors which affect entrepreneurship in important ways, but which cannot be changed? Or do entrepreneurs need to cooperate and form organizations to fight for their long-range goals?

The next essay in this part, 'The Modernization of Entrepreneurship', is written by Alexander Gerschenkron (1904-1978), who is one of the foremost economic historians of the twentieth century. Gerschenkron was born in Russia, raised in Austria and produced most of his academic work while at Harvard University in the United States. His text contains, among other things, a critique of the theory that people's capacity for entrepreneurship is decisively influenced by the way that they were socialized as children. The main thrust of his argument, however, has to do with entrepreneurship in the process of industrialization; and his thesis is that some scholars have exaggerated the role that prerequisites play in this process, including the prerequisite that there has to exist a number of native entrepreneurs. What history teaches us, Gerschenkron notes, is something else, namely that industrialization has been successfully carried out in countries where some prerequisite has been missing, including that of native entrepreneurs; and the reason for this is that some substitute for the missing prerequisite usually has been found. Maybe the state or the banking community supplied the capital, when the entrepreneurs were unable to do so, or maybe foreign entrepreneurs were imported when native entrepreneurs could not be found.

Gerschenkron raises the question of the practicality of psychological theories about entrepreneurship by stating that if innovative economic behaviour is as dependent on childhood socialization as some psychologists suggest, there is little one can do about it. This may be correct—but does it also mean that everything psychology has to say about entrepreneurship is impractical? Would it, for example, be possible to develop personality tests which measure the individual's capacity for entrepreneurship? Can therapy be used to release entrepreneurial creativity (or would it rather block it, as Schumpeter might have argued)? The most important question that Gerschenkron's essay raises, however, has to do with substitutes for entrepreneurship. Does his theory of substitutes constitute a general theory of entrepreneurship—with entrepreneurship being defined as behaviour in a situation in which you create something new by making up for a missing element or a prerequisite? Should the entrepreneur train himself/herself to be on the outlook for substitutes? Is it possible to use more than one substitute in a specific situation or is one missing element the maximum you can make up for?

Fredrik Barth—the author of 'Economic Spheres in Darfur'—is one of the world's leading anthropologists. His text takes the reader to a small community in Central Africa which mainly lives off agriculture and which Barth studied in the 1960s. The author suggests that the economy of this community can be conceptualized in terms of spheres, and he adds that this perspective can be generalized to all societies. This also goes for Barth's theory of entrepreneurship, according to which entrepreneurial behaviour means to connect two different spheres in society, between which there is a huge discrepancy in value.

The idea that entrepreneurship in a small, pre-industrial community would be essentially the same as entrepreneurship in a modern society, like ours, is intriguing and worth reflecting on. The notion of economic spheres is also interesting and displays some similarities to Schumpeter's idea of resistance to entrepreneurship. The very heart of Barth's proposal—that entrepreneurship means connecting or bridging two separate spheres—is, however, the one that needs to be discussed the most. Is it, for example, meaningful to see the modern economy as consisting of different spheres, and can profit always be made by connecting these? Is it, for example, of value for someone in the economic sphere to get something from the sphere of the family (or from the sphere of politics or the sphere of culture)? Barth's perspective also raises some questions about values and ethics in the economy. Should certain spheres always be kept distinct and should attempts to join them be repelled? Does entrepreneurship usually entail a crossing, or getting close to a crossing, of some ethical barrier?

Richard Swedberg

I shall not try to summarize my own answers to all of the questions I have raised in these comments. I do think, however, that the readings in Part II of this volume clearly show that there exists a wealth of good ideas about entrepreneurship in the social science literature, and that these also have some important implications for the practice of entrepreneurship. While it is clear that this type of reading about entrepreneurship cannot replace texts of a more practical nature, they may none the less complement these in a creative fashion.

2 Entrepreneurship as Innovation

Joseph A. Schumpeter

To produce means to combine materials and forces within our reach. To produce other things, or the same things by a different method, means to combine these materials and forces differently. In so far as the "new combination" may in time grow out of the old by continuous adjustment in small steps, there is certainly change, possibly growth, but neither a new phenomenon nor development in our sense. In so far as this is not the case, and the new combinations appear discontinuously, then the phenomenon characterising development emerges. For reasons of expository convenience, henceforth, we shall only mean the latter case when we speak of new combinations of productive means. Development in our sense is then defined by the carrying out of new combinations.

This concept covers the following five cases: (I) The introduction of a new good—that is one with which consumers are not yet familiar—or of a new quality of a good. (2) The introduction of a new method of production, that is one not yet tested by experience in the branch of manufacture concerned, which need by no means be founded upon a discovery scientifically new, and can also exist in a new way of handling a commodity commercially. (3) The opening of a new market, that is a market into which the particular branch of manufacture of the country in question has not previously entered, whether or not this market has existed before. (4) The conquest of a new source of supply of raw materials or half-manufactured goods, again irrespective of whether this source already exists or whether it has first to be created. (5) The carrying out of the new organisation of any industry, like the creation of a monopoly position (for example through trustification) or the breaking up of a monopoly position.

Now two things are essential for the phenomena incident to the carrying out of such new combinations, and for understanding of the problems involved. In the first place it is not essential to the matter—though it may happen—that the new combinations should be carried out by the same people who control the productive or commercial process which is to be displaced by the new. On the contrary, new combinations are, as a rule, embodied, as it were, in new firms which generally do not arise out of the old ones but start producing beside them; to keep to the example already chosen, in general it is not the owner of stage-coaches who builds railways. This fact not only puts the discontinuity which characterises the process we want to describe in a special light, and creates so to speak still another kind of discontinuity in addition to the one mentioned above, but it also explains important features of the course of events. Especially in a competitive economy, in which new combinations mean the competitive elimination of the old, it explains on the one hand the process by which individuals and families rise and fall economically and socially and which is peculiar to this form of organisation, as well as a whole series of other phenomena of the business cycle, of the mechanism of the formation of private fortunes, and so on. In a non-exchange economy, for example a socialist one, the new combinations would also frequently appear side by side with the old. But the economic consequences of this fact would be absent to some extent, and the social consequences would be wholly absent. And if the competitive economy is broken up by the growth of great combines, as is increasingly the case to-day in all countries, then this must become more and more true of real life, and the carrying out of new combinations must become in ever greater measure the internal concern of one and the same economic body. The difference so made is great enough to serve as the water-shed between two epochs in the social history of capitalism.

We must notice secondly, only partly in connection with this element, that whenever we are concerned with fundamental principles, we must never assume that the carrying out of new combinations takes place by employing means of production which happen to be unused. In practical life, this is very often the case. There are always unemployed workmen, unsold raw materials, unused productive capacity, and so forth. This certainly is a contributory circumstance, a favorable condition and even an incentive to the emergence of new combinations; but great unemployment is only the consequence of non-economic events—as for example the World War—or precisely of the development which we are investigating. In neither of the two cases can its existence play a fundamental role in the explanation, and it cannot occur in a well balanced circular flow from which we start. Nor would the normal yearly increment meet the case, as it would be small in the first place, and also because it would normally be absorbed by a corresponding expansion of production within the circular flow, which, if we admit such increments, we must think of as adjusted to this rate of growth.[1] As a rule the new combinations must draw the necessary means of production from some old combinations—and for reasons already mentioned we shall assume that they *always* do so, in order to put in bold relief what we hold to be the essential contour line. The carrying out of new combinations means, therefore, simply the different employment of the economic system's existing supplies of productive means—which might provide a second definition of development in our sense. That rudiment of a pure economic theory of development which is implied in the traditional doctrine of the formation of capital always refers merely to saving and to the investment of the small yearly increase attributable to it. In this it asserts nothing false. but it entirely overlooks much more essential things. The slow and continuous increase in time of the national supply of productive means and of savings is obviously an important factor in explaining the course of economic history through the centuries, but it is completely overshadowed by the fact that development consists primarily in employing existing resources in a different way, in doing new things with them, irrespective of whether those resources increase or not. In the treatment of shorter epochs, moreover, this is even true in a more tangible sense. Different methods of employment, and not saving and increases in the available quantity of labor, have changed the face of the economic world in the last fifty years. The increase of population especially, but also of the sources from which savings can be made, was first made possible in large measure through the different employment of the then existing means.

The next step in our argument is also self-evident: command over means of production is necessary to the carrying out of new combinations. Procuring the means of production is one distinct problem for the established firms which work within the circular flow. For they *have* them already procured or else can procure them currently with the proceeds of previous production (as was explained in the first chapter). There is no fundamental gap here between receipts and disbursements, which, on the contrary, necessarily correspond to one another just as both correspond to the means of production offered and to the products demanded. Once set in motion, this mechanism works automatically. Furthermore, the problem does not exist in a non-exchange economy even if new combinations are carried out in it; for the directing organ, for example a socialist economic ministry, is in a position to direct the productive resources of the society to new uses exactly as it can direct them to their previous employments. The new employment may, under certain circumstances, impose temporary sacrifices, privations, or increased efforts upon the members of the community; it may presuppose the solution of difficult problems, for example the question from which of the old combinations the necessary productive means should be withdrawn; but there is no question of procuring means of production not already at the disposal of the economic ministry. Finally, the problem also does not exist in a competitive economy in the case of the carrying out of new combinations, if those who carry them out have the necessary productive means or can get them in exchange for others which they have or for any other property which they may possess. This is not the privilege of the possession of property *per se*, but only the privilege of the possession of disposable property, that is such as is employable either immediately for carrying out the new combination or in exchange for the necessary goods and services.[2] In the contrary case—and this is the rule as it is the fundamentally interesting case—the possessor of wealth, even it if is the greatest combine, must resort to credit if he wishes to carry out a new combination, which cannot like an established business be financed by returns from previous production. To provide this credit is clearly the function of that category of individuals which we call "capitalists." It is obvious that this is the characteristic method of the capitalist type of society—and important enough to serve as its *differentia specifica*—for forcing the economic system into new channels, for putting its means at the service of new ends, in contrast to the method of a non-exchange economy of the kind which simply consists in exercising the directing organ's power to command.

It does not appear to me possible to dispute in any way the foregoing statement. Emphasis upon the significance of credit is to be found in every textbook. That the structure of modern industry could not have been erected without it, that it makes the individual to a certain extent independent of inherited possessions, that talent in economic life "ride to success on its debts," even the most conservative orthodoxy of the theorists cannot well deny. Nor is the connection established here between credit and the carrying out of innovations, a connection which will be worked out later, anything to take offence at. For it is as clear *a priori* as it is established historically that credit is primarily necessary to new combinations and that it is from these that it forces its way into the circular flow, on the one hand because it was originally necessary to the founding of what are now the old firms, on the other hand because its mechanism, once in existence, also seizes old combinations for obvious reasons. First, *a priori*: borrowing is not a necessary element of production in the normal circular flow within accustomed channels, is not an element without which we could not understand the essential phenomena of the latter. On the other hand, in carrying out new combinations, "financing" as a special act is fundamentally necessary, in practice as in theory. Second, historically: those who lend and borrow for industrial purposes do not appear early in history. The pre-capitalistic lender provided money for other than business purposes. And we all remember the type of industrialist who felt he was losing caste by borrowing and who therefore shunned banks and bills of exchange. The capitalistic credit system has grown out of and thrived on the financing of new combinations in all countries, even though in a different way in each (the origin of German joint stock banking is especially characteristic). Finally there can be no stumbling block in our speaking of receiving credit in "money or money substitutes." We certainly do not assert that one can produce with coins, notes, or bank balances, and do not deny that services of labor, raw materials, and tools are the things wanted. We are only speaking of a method of procuring them.

Nevertheless there is a point here in which, as has already been hinted, our theory diverges from the traditional view. The accepted theory sees a problem in the existence of the productive means, which are needed for new, or indeed any, productive processes, and this accumulation therefore becomes a distinct function or service. We do not recognise this problem at all; it appears to us to be created by faulty analysis. It does not exist in the circular flow, because the running of the latter presupposes given quantities of means of production. But neither does it exist for the carrying out of new combinations,[3] because the productive means required in the latter are drawn from the circular flow whether they already exist there in the shape wanted or have first to be produced by other means of production existing there. Instead of this problem another exists for us: the problem of detaching productive means (already employed somewhere) from the circular flow and allotting them to new combinations. This is done by credit, by means of which one who wishes to carry out new combinations outbids the producers in the circular flow in the market for the required means of production. And although the meaning and object of this process lies in a movement of goods from their old towards new employments, it cannot be described entirely in terms of goods without overlooking something essential, which happens in the sphere of money and credit and upon which depends the explanation of important phenomena in the capitalist form of economic organisation, in contrast to other types.

Finally one more step in this direction: whence come the sums needed to purchase the means of production necessary for the new combinations if the individual concerned does not happen to have them? The conventional answer is simple: out of the annual growth of social savings plus that part of resources which may annually become free. Now the first quantity was indeed important enough before World War I—may perhaps be estimated as one-fifth of total private incomes in Europe and North America—so that together with the latter sum, which it is difficult to obtain statistically, it does not immediately give the lie quantitatively to this answer. At the same time a figure representing the range of all the business operations involved in carrying out new combinations is also not available at present. But we may not even start from total "savings." For its magnitude is explicable only by the results of previous development. By far the greater part of it does not come from thrift in the strict sense, that is from abstaining from the consumption of part of one's regular income, but it consists of funds which are themselves the result of successful innovation and in which we shall later recognise entrepreneurial profit. In the circular flow there would be on the one hand no such rich source, out of which to save, and on the other hand essentially less incentive to save. The only big incomes known to it would be monopoly revenues and the rents of large landowners; while provision for misfortunes and old age, perhaps also irrational motives, would be the only incentives. The most important incentive, the chance of participating in the gains of development, would be absent. Hence, in such an economic system there could be no great reservoirs of free purchasing power, to which one who wished to form new combinations could turn—and his own savings would only suffice in exceptional cases. All money would circulate, would be fixed in definite established channels.

Even though the conventional answer to our question is not obviously absurd, yet there is another method of obtaining money for this purpose, which claims our attention, because it, unlike the one referred to, does not presuppose the existence of accumulated results of previous development, and hence may be considered as the only one which is available in strict logic. This method of obtaining money is the creation of purchasing power by banks. The form it takes is immaterial. The issue of bank-notes not fully covered by specie withdrawn from circulation is an obvious instance, but methods of deposit banking render the same service, where they increase the sum total of possible expenditure. Or we may think of bank acceptances in so far as they serve as money to make payments in wholesale trade. It is always a question, not of transforming purchasing power which already exists in someone's possession, but of the creation of new purchasing power out of nothing—out of nothing even if the credit contract by which the new purchasing power is created is supported by securities which are not themselves circulating media—which is added to the existing circulation. And this is the source from which new combinations *are* often financed, and from which they would have to be financed *always*, if results of previous developmental did not actually exist at any moment.

These credit means of payment, that is means of payment which are created for the purpose and by the act of giving credit, serve just as ready money in trade, partly directly, partly because they can be converted immediately into ready money for small payments or payments to the non-banking classes—in particular to wage-earners. With their help, those who carry out new combinations can gain access to the existing stocks of productive means, or, as the case may be, enable those from whom they buy productive services to gain immediate access to the market for consumption goods. There is never, in this nexus, granting of credit in the sense that someone must wait for the equivalent of his service in goods, and content himself with a claim, thereby fulfilling a special function; not even in the sense that someone has to accumulate means of maintenance for laborers or landowners, or produced means of production, all of which would only be paid for out of the final results of production. Economically, it is true, there is an essential difference between these means of payment if they are created for new ends, and money or other means of payment of the circular flow. The latter may be conceived on the one hand as a kind of certificate for completed production and the increase in the social product effected through it, and on the other hand as a kind of order upon, or claim to, part of this social product. The former have not the first of these two characteristics. They too are orders, for which one can immediately procure consumption goods, but not certificates for previous production. Access to the national dividend is usually to be had only on condition of some productive service previously rendered or of some product previously sold. This condition is, in this case, not yet fulfilled. It will be fulfilled only after the successful completion of the new combinations. Hence this credit will in the meantime affect the price level.

The banker, therefore, is not so much primarily a middleman in the commodity "purchasing power" as a *producer* of this commodity. However, since all reserve funds and savings to-day usually flow to him, and the total demand for free purchasing power, whether existing or to be created, concentrates on him, he has either replaced private capitalists or become their agent; he has himself become the capitalist par excellence. He stands between those who wish to form new combinations and the possessors of productive means. He is essentially a phenomenon of development, though only when no central authority directs the social process. He makes possible the carrying out of new combinations, authorises people, in the name of society as it were, to form them. He is the ephor of the exchange economy.

We now come to the third of the elements with which our analysis works, namely the "new combination of means of production," and credit. Although all three elements form a whole, the third may be described as the fundamental phenomenon of economic development. The carrying out of new combinations we call "enterprise"; the individuals whose function it is to carry them out we call "entrepreneurs." These concepts are at once broader and narrower than the usual. Broader, because in the first place we call entrepreneurs not only those "independent" businessmen in an exchange economy who are usually so designated, but all who actually fulfil the function by which we define the concept, even if they are, as is becoming the rule, "dependent" employees of a company, like managers, members of boards of directors, and so forth, or even if their actual power to perform the entrepreneurial function has any other foundations, such as the control of a majority of shares. As it is the carrying out of new combinations that constitutes the entrepreneur, it is not necessary that he should be permanently connected with an individual firm; many "financiers," "promoters," and so forth are not, and still they may be entrepreneurs in our sense. On the other hand, our concept is narrower than the traditional one in that it does not include all heads of firms or managers or industrialists who merely may operate an established business, but only those who actually perform that function. Nevertheless I maintain that the above definition does no more than formulate with greater precision what the traditional doctrine really means to convey. In the first place our definition agrees with the usual one on the fundamental point of distinguishing between "entrepreneurs" and "capitalists"—irrespective of whether the latter are regarded as owners of money, claims to money, or material goods. This distinction is common property to-day and has been so for a considerable time. It also settles the question whether the ordinary shareholder as such is an entrepreneur, and disposes of the conception of the entrepreneur as risk bearer.[4] Furthermore, the ordinary characterisation of the entrepreneur type by such expressions as "initiative," "authority," or "foresight" points entirely in our direction. For there is little scope for such qualities within the routine of the circular flow, and if this had been sharply separated from the occurrence of changes in this routine itself, the emphasis in the definition of the function of entrepreneurs would have been shifted automatically to the latter. Finally there are definitions which we could simply accept. There is in particular the well known one that goes back to J. B. Say: the entrepreneur's function is to combine the productive factors, to bring them together. Since this is a performance of a special kind only when the factors are combined for the first time—while it is merely routine work if done in the course of running a business—this definition coincides with ours. When Mataja (in *Unternehmergewinn*) defines the entrepreneur as one who receives profit, we have only to add (see conclusion of the first chapter) that there is no profit in the circular flow, in order to trace this formulation too back to ours.[5] And this view is not foreign to traditional theory, as is shown by the construction of the *entrepreneur faisant ni bénéfice ni perte*, which has been worked out rigorously by Walras, but is the property of many other authors. The tendency is for the entrepreneur to make neither profit nor loss in the circular flow—that is he has no function of a special kind there, he simply does not exist; but in his stead, there are heads of firms or business managers of a different type which we had better not designate by the same term.

It is a prejudice to believe that the knowledge of the historical origin of an institution or of a type immediately shows us its sociological or economic nature. Such knowledge often leads us to understand it, but it does not directly yield a theory of it. Still more false is the belief that "primitive" forms of a type are also *ipso facto* the "simpler" or the "more original" in the sense that they show their nature more purely and with fewer complications than later ones. Very frequently the opposite is the case, amongst other reasons because increasing specialisation may allow functions and qualities to stand out sharply, which are more difficult to recognise in more primitive conditions when mixed with others. So it is in our case. In the general position of the chief of a primitive horde it is difficult to separate the entrepreneurial element from the others. For the same reason most economists up to the time of the younger Mill failed to keep capitalist and entrepreneur distinct because the manufacturer of a hundred years ago was both; and certainly the course of events since then has facilitated the making of this distinction, as the system of land tenure in England has facilitated the distinction between farmer and landowner, while on the Continent this distinction is still occasionally neglected, especially in the case of peasant who tills his own soil.[6] But in our case there are still more of such difficulties. The entrepreneur of earlier times was not only as a rule the capitalist too, he was also often—as he still is to-day in the case of small concerns—his own technical expert, in so far as a professional specialist was not called in for special cases. Likewise he was (and is) often his own buying and selling agent, the head of his office, his own personnel manager, and sometimes, even though as a rule he of course employed solicitors, his own legal adviser in current affairs. And it was performing some or all of these functions that regularly filled his days. The carrying out of new combinations can no more be a *vocation* than the making and execution of strategical decisions, although it is this function and not his routine work that characterises the military leader. Therefore the entrepreneur's essential function must always appear mixed up with other kinds of activity, which as a rule must be much more conspicuous than the essential one. Hence the Marshallian definition of the entrepreneur, which simply treats the entrepreneurial function as "management" in the widest meaning, will naturally appeal to most of us. We do not accept it, simply because it does not bring out what we consider to be the salient point and the only one which specifically distinguishes entrepreneurial from other activities.

Nevertheless there are types—the course of events has evolved them by degrees—which exhibit the entrepreneurial function with particular purity. The "promoter," to be sure, belongs to them only with qualifications. For, neglecting the associations relative to social and moral status which are attached to this type, the promoter is frequently only an agent intervening on commission, who does the work of financial technique in floating the new enterprise. In this case he is not its creator nor the driving power in the process. However, he *may* be the latter also, and then he is something like an "entrepreneur by profession." But the modern type of "captain of industry"[7] corresponding more closely to what is meant here, especially if one recognises his identity on the one hand with, say, the commercial entrepreneur of twelfth-century Venice—or, among later types, with John Law—and on the other hand with the village potentate who combines with his agriculture and his cattle trade, say, a rural brewery, an hotel, and a store. But whatever the type, everyone is an entrepreneur only when he actually "carries out new combinations," and loses that character as soon as he has built up his business, when he settles down to running it as other people run their businesses. This is the rule, of course, and hence it is just as rare for anyone always to remain an entrepreneur throughout the decades of his active life as it is for a businessman never to have a moment in which he is an entrepreneur, to however modest a degree.

Because being an entrepreneur is not a profession and as a rule not a lasting condition, entrepreneurs do not form a social class in the technical sense, as, for example, landowners or capitalists or workmen do. Of course the entrepreneurial function will *lead* to certain class positions for the successful entrepreneur and his family. It can also put its stamp on an epoch of social history, can form a style of life, or systems of moral and aesthetic values; but in itself it signifies a class position no more than it presupposes one. And the class position which may be attained is not as such an entrepreneurial position, but is characterised as landowning or capitalist, according to how the proceeds of the enterprise are used. Inheritance of the pecuniary result and of personal qualities may then both keep up this position for more than one generation and make further enterprise easier for descendants, but the function of the entrepreneur itself cannot be inherited, as is shown well enough by the history of manufacturing families.[8]

But now the decisive question arises: why then is the carrying out of new combinations a special process and the object of a special kind of "function"? Every individual carries on his economic affairs as well as he can. To be sure, his own intentions are never realised with ideal perfection, but ultimately his behavior is moulded by the influence on him of the results of his conduct, so as to fit circumstances which do not as a rule change suddenly. If a business can never be absolutely perfect in any sense, yet it in time approaches a relative perfection having regard to the surrounding world, the social conditions, the knowledge of the time, and the horizon of each individual or each group. New possibilities are continuously being offered by the surrounding world, in particular new discoveries are continuously being added to the existing store of knowledge. Why should not the individual make just as much use of the new possibilities as of the old, and, according to the market position as he understands it, keep pigs instead of cows, or even choose a new crop rotation, if this can be seen to be more advantageous? And what kind of special new phenomena or problems, not to be found in the established circular flow, can arise there?

While in the accustomed circular flow every individual can act promptly and rationally because he is sure of his ground and is supported by the conduct, as adjusted to this circular flow, of all other individuals, who in turn expect the accustomed activity from him, he cannot simply do this when he is confronted by a new task. While in the accustomed channels his own ability and experience suffice for the normal individual, when confronted with innovations he needs guidance. While he swims with the stream in the circular flow which is familiar to him, he swims against the stream if he wishes to change its channel. What was formerly a help becomes a hindrance. What was a familiar datum becomes an unknown. Where the boundaries of routine stop, many people can go no further, and the rest can only do so in a highly variable manner. The assumption that conduct is prompt and rational is in all cases a fiction. But it proves to be sufficiently near to reality, if things have time to hammer logic into men. Where this has happened, and within the limits in which it has happened, one may rest content with this fiction and build theories upon it. It is then not true that habit or custom or non-economic ways of thinking cause a hopeless difference between the individuals of different classes, times, or cultures, and that, for example, the "economics of the stock exchange" would be inapplicable say to the peasants of to-day or to the craftsmen of the Middle Ages. On the contrary the same theoretical picture[9] in its broadest contour lines fits the individuals of quite different cultures, whatever their degree of intelligence and of economic rationality, and we can depend upon it that the peasant sells his calf just as cunningly and egotistically as the stock exchange member his portfolio of shares. But this holds good only where precedents without number have formed conduct through decades and, in fundamentals, through hundreds and thousands of years, and have eliminated unadapted behavior. Outside of these limits our fiction loses its closeness to reality.[10] To cling to it there also, as the traditional theory does, is to hide an essential thing and to ignore a fact which, in contrast with other deviations of our assumptions from reality, is theoretically important and the source of the explanation of phenomena which would not exist without it.

Therefore, in describing the circular flow one must treat combinations of means of production (the production-functions) as data, like natural possibilities, and admit only small[11] variations at the margins, such as every individual can accomplish by adapting himself to changes in his economic environment, without materially deviating from familiar lines. Therefore, too, carrying out of new combinations is a special function, and the privilege of a type of people who are much less numerous than all those who have the "objective" possibility of doing it. Therefore, finally, entrepreneurs are a special type,[12] and their behavior a special problem, the motive power of a greater number of significant phenomena. Hence, our position may be characterised by three corresponding pairs of opposites. First, by the opposition of two real processes: the circular flow or the tendency towards equilibrium on the one hand, a change in the channels of economic routine or a spontaneous change in the economic data arising from within the system on the other. Secondly, by the opposition of two theoretical *apparatuses:* statics and dynamics.[13] Thirdly, by the opposition of two types of conduct, which, following reality, we can picture as two types of individuals: mere managers and entrepreneurs. And therefore the "best method" of producing in the theoretical sense is to be conceived as "the most advantageous among the methods which have been empirically tested and become familiar." But it is not the "best" of the methods "possible" at the time. If one does not make this distinction, the concept becomes meaningless and precisely those problems remain unsolved which our interpretation is meant to provide for.

Let us now formulate precisely the characteristic feature of the conduct and type under discussion. The smallest daily action embodies a huge mental effort. Every schoolboy would have to be a mental giant, if he himself had to create all he knows and uses by his own individual activity. And every man would have to be a giant of wisdom and will, if he had in every case to create anew all the rules by which he guides his everyday conduct. This is true not only of those decisions and actions of individual and social life the principles of which are the product of tens of thousands of years, but also of those products of shorter periods and of a more special nature which constitute the particular instrument for performing vocational tasks. But precisely the things the performance of which according to this should involve a supreme effort, in general demand no special individual effort at all; those which should be especially difficult are in reality especially easy; what should demand superhuman capacity is accessible to the least gifted, given mental health. In particular within the ordinary routine there is no need for leadership. Of course it is still necessary to set people their tasks, to keep up discipline, and so forth; but this is easy and a function any normal person can learn to fulfil. Within the lines familiar to all, even the function of directing other people, though still necessary, is mere "work" like any other, comparable to the service of tending a machine. All people get to know, and are able to do, their daily tasks in the customary way and ordinarily perform them by themselves; the "director" has his routine as they have theirs; and his directive function serves merely to correct individual aberrations.

This is so because all knowledge and habit once acquired becomes as firmly rooted in ourselves as a railway embankment in the earth. It does not require to be continually renewed and consciously reproduced, but sinks into the strata of subconsciousness. It is normally transmitted almost without friction by inheritance, teaching, upbringing, pressure of environment. Everything we think, feel, or do often enough becomes automatic and our conscious life is unburdened of it. The enormous economy of force, in the race and the individual, here involved is not great enough, however, to make daily life a light burden and to prevent its demands from exhausting the average energy all the same. But it is great enough to make it possible to meet the ordinary claims. This holds good likewise for economic daily life. And from this it follows also for economic life that every step outside the boundary of routine has difficulties and involves a new element. It is this element that constitutes the phenomenon of leadership.

The nature of these difficulties may be focused in the following three points. First, outside these accustomed channels the individual is without those data for his decisions and those rules of conduct which are usually very accurately known to him within them. Of course he must still foresee and estimate on the basis of his experience. But many things must remain uncertain, still others are only ascertainable within wide limits, some can perhaps only be "guessed." In particular this is true of those data which the individual strives to alter and of those which he wants to create. Now he must really to some extent do what tradition does for him in everyday life, viz. consciously plan his conduct in every particular. There will be much more conscious rationality in this than in customary action, which as such does not need to be reflected upon at all; but this plan must necessarily be open not only to errors greater in degree, but also to other kinds of errors than those occurring in customary action. What has been done already has the sharp-edged reality of all the things which we have seen and experienced; the new is only the figment of our imagination. Carrying out a new plan and acting according to a customary one are things as different as making a road and walking along it.

How different a thing this is becomes clearer if one bears in mind the impossibility of surveying exhaustively all the effects and counter-effects of the projected enterprise. Even as many of them as could in theory be ascertained if one had unlimited time and means must practically remain in the dark. As military action must be taken in a given strategic position even if all the data potentially procurable are not available, so also in economic life action must be taken without working out all the details of what is to be done. Here the success of everything depends upon intuition, the capacity of seeing things in a way which afterwards proves to be true, even though it cannot be established at the moment, and of grasping the essential fact, discarding the unessential, even though one can give no account of the principles by which this is done. Thorough preparatory work, and special knowledge, breadth of intellectual understanding, talent for logical analysis, may under certain circumstances be sources of failure. The more accurately, however, we learn to know the natural and social world, the more perfect our control of facts becomes; and the greater the extent, with time and progressive rationalisation, within which things can be simply calculated, and indeed quickly and reliably calculated, the more the significance of this function decreases. Therefore the importance of the entrepreneur type must diminish just as the importance of the military commander has already diminished. Nevertheless a part of the very essence of each type is bound up with this function.

As this first point lies in the task, so the second lies in the psyche of the businessman himself. It is not only objectively more difficult to do something new than what is familiar and tested by experience, but the individual feels reluctance to it and would do so even if the objective difficulties did not exist. This is so in all fields. The history of science is one great confirmation of the fact that we find it exceedingly difficult to adopt a new scientific point of view or method. Thought turns again and again into the accustomed track even if it has become unsuitable and the more suitable innovation in itself presents no particular difficulties. The very nature of fixed habits of thinking, their energy-saving function, is founded upon the fact that they have become subconscious, that they yield their results automatically and are proof against criticism and even against contradiction by individual facts. But precisely because of this they become drag chains when they have outlived their usefulness. So it is also in the economic world. In the breast of one who wishes to do something new, the forces of habit rise up and bear witness against the embryonic project. A new and another kind of effort of will is therefore necessary in order to wrest, amidst the work and care of the daily round, scope and time for conceiving and working out the new combination and to bring oneself to look upon it as a real possibility and not merely as a day-dream. This mental freedom presupposes a great surplus force over the everyday demand and is something peculiar and by nature rare.

The third point consists in the reaction of the social environment against one who wishes to do something new. This reaction may manifest itself first of all in the existence of legal or political impediments. But neglecting this, any deviating conduct by a member of a social group is condemned, though in greatly varying degrees according as the social group is used to such conduct or not. Even a deviation from social custom in such things as dress or manners arouses opposition, and of course all the more so in the graver cases. This opposition is stronger in primitive stages of culture than in others, but it is never absent. Even mere astonishment at the deviation, even merely noticing it, exercises a pressure on the individual. The manifestation of condemnation may at once bring noticeable consequences in its train. It may even come to social ostracism and finally to physical prevention or to direct attack. Neither the fact that progressive differentiation weakens this opposition—especially as the most important cause of the weakening is the very development which we wish to explain—nor the further fact that the social opposition operates under certain circumstances and upon many individuals as a stimulus, changes anything in principle in the significance of it. Surmounting this opposition is always a special kind of task which does not exist in the customary course of life, a task which also requires a special kind of conduct. In matters economic this resistance manifests itself first of all in the groups threatened by the innovation, then in the difficulty in finding the necessary cooperation, finally in the difficulty in winning over consumers. Even though these elements are still effective to-day, despite the fact that a period of turbulent development has accustomed us to the appearance and the carrying out of innovations, they can be best studied in the beginnings of capitalism. But they are so obvious there that it would be time lost for our purposes to dwell upon them.

There is leadership *only* for these reasons—leadership, that is, as a special kind of function and in contrast to a mere difference in rank, which would exist in every social body, in the smallest as in the largest, and in combination with which it generally appears. The facts alluded to create a boundary beyond which the majority of people do not function promptly by themselves and require help from a minority. If social life had in all respects the relative immutability of, for example, the astronomical world, or if mutable this mutability were yet incapable of being influenced by human action, or finally if capable of being so influenced this type of action were yet equally open to everyone, then there would be no special function of leadership as distinguished from routine work.

The specific problem of leadership arises and the leader type appears only where new possibilities present themselves. That is why it is so strongly marked among the Normans at the time of their conquests and so feebly among the Slavs in the centuries of their unchanging and relatively protected life in the marshes of the Pripet. Our three points characterise the nature of the *function* as well as the *conduct* or behavior which constitutes the leader type. It is no part of his function to "find" or to "create" new possibilities. They are always present, abundantly accumulated by all sorts of people. Often they are also generally known and being discussed by scientific or literary writers. In other cases, there is nothing to discover about them, because they are quite obvious. To take an example from political life, it was not at all difficult to see how the social and political conditions of France at the time of Louis XVI could have been improved so as to avoid a breakdown of the *ancien régime*. Plenty of people as a matter of fact did see it. But nobody was in a position to *do* it. Now, it is this "doing the thing," without which possibilities are dead, of which the leader's function consists. This holds good of all kinds of leadership, ephemeral as well as more enduring ones. The former may serve as an instance. What is to be done in a casual emergency is as a rule quite simple. Most or all people may see it, yet they want someone to speak out, to lead, and to organise. Even leadership which influences merely by example, as artistic or scientific leadership, does not consist simply in finding or creating the new thing but in so impressing the social group with it as to draw it on in its wake. It is, therefore, more by will than by intellect that the leaders fulfil their function, more by "authority," "personal weight," and so forth than by original ideas.

Economic leadership in particular must hence be distinguished from "invention." As long as they are not carried into practice, inventions are economically irrelevant. And to carry any improvement into effect is a task entirely different from the inventing of it, and a task, moreover, requiring entirely different kinds of aptitudes. Although entrepreneurs of course *may* be inventors just as they may be capitalists, they are inventors not by nature of their function but by coincidence and vice versa. Besides, the innovations which it is the function of entrepreneurs to carry out need not necessarily be any inventions at all. It, is therefore, not advisable, and it may be downright misleading, to stress the element of invention as much as many writers do.

The entrepreneurial kind of leadership, as distinguished from other kinds of economic leadership such as we should expect to find in a primitive tribe or a communist society, is of course colored by the conditions peculiar to it. It has none of that glamour which characterises other kinds of leadership. It consists in fulfilling a very special task which only in rare cases appeals to the imagination of the public. For its success, keenness and vigor are not more essential than a certain narrowness which seizes the immediate chance and *nothing else.* "Personal weight" is, to be sure, not without importance. Yet the personality of the capitalistic entrepreneur need not, and generally does not, answer to the idea most of us have of what a "leader" looks like, so much so that there is some difficulty in realizing that he comes within the sociological category of leader at all. He "leads" the means of production into new channels. But this he does, not by convincing people of the desirability of carrying out his plan or by creating confidence in his leading in the manner of a political leader—the only man he has to convince or to impress is the banker who is to finance him—but by buying them or their services, and then using them as he sees fit. He also leads in the sense that he draws other producers in his branch after him. But as they are his competitors, who first reduce and then annihilate his profit, this is, as it were, leadership against one's own will. Finally, he renders a service, the full appreciation of which takes a specialist's knowledge of the case. It is not so easily understood by the public at large as a politician's successful speech or a general's victory in the field, not to insist on the fact that he seems to act—and often harshly—in his individual interest alone. We shall understand, therefore, that we do not observe, in this case, the emergence of all those affective values which are the glory of all other kinds of social leadership. Add to this the precariousness of the economic position both of the individual entrepreneur and of entrepreneurs as a group, and the fact that when his economic success raises him socially he has no cultural tradition or attitude to fall back upon, but moves about in society as an upstart, whose ways are readily laughed at, and we shall understand why this type has never been popular, and why even scientific critique often makes short work of it.[14]

We shall finally try to round off our picture of the entrepreneur in the same manner in which we always, in science as well as in practical life, try to understand human behavior, viz. by analysing the characteristic motives of his conduct. Any attempt to do this must of course meet with all those objections against the economist's intrusion into "psychology" which have been made familiar by a long series of writers. We cannot here enter into the fundamental question of the relation between psychology and economics. It is enough to state that those who on principle object to *any* psychological considerations in an economic argument may leave out what we are about to say without thereby losing contact with the argument of the following chapters. For none of the results to which our analysis is intended to lead stands or falls with our "psychology of the entrepreneur," or could be vitiated by any errors in it. Nowhere is there, as the reader will easily satisfy himself, any necessity for us to overstep the frontiers of observable behavior. Those who do not object to *all* psychology but only to the *kind* of psychology which we know from the traditional textbook, will see that we do not adopt any part of the time-honored picture of the motivation of the "economic man."

In the theory of the circular flow, the importance of examining motives is very much reduced by the fact that the equations of the system of equilibrium may be so interpreted as not to imply any psychic magnitudes at all, as shown by the analysis of Pareto and of Barone. This is the reason why even very defective psychology interferes much less with results than one would expect. There may be rational *conduct* even in the absence of rational *motive*. But as soon as we really wish to penetrate into motivation, the problem proves by no means simple. Within given social circumstances and habits, most of what people do every day will appear to them primarily from the point of view of duty carrying a social or a superhuman sanction. There is very little of conscious rationality, still less of hedonism and of *individual* egoism about it, and so much of it as may safely be said to exist is of comparatively recent growth. Nevertheless, as long as we confine ourselves to the great outlines of constantly repeated economic action, we may link it up with wants and the desire to satisfy them, on condition that we are careful to recognise that economic motive so defined varies in intensity very much in time; that it is society that shapes the particular desires we observe; that wants must be taken with reference to the group which the individual thinks of when deciding his course of action—the family or any other group, smaller or larger than the family; that action does not promptly follow upon desire but only more or less imperfectly corresponds to it; that the field of individual choice is always, though in very different ways and to very different degrees, fenced in by social habits or conventions and the like: it still remains broadly true that, within the circular flow, everyone adapts himself to his environment so as to satisfy certain *given* wants—of himself or others—as best he can. In *all* cases, the *meaning* of economic action is the satisfaction of wants in the sense that there would be no economic action if there were no wants. In the case of the circular flow, we may also think of satisfaction of wants as the normal *motive*.

The latter is not true for our type. In one sense, he may indeed be called the most rational and the most egotistical of all. For, as we have seen, conscious rationality enters much more into the carrying out of new plans, which themselves have to be worked out before they can be acted upon, than into the mere running of an established business, which is largely a matter of routine. And the typical entrepreneur is more self-centred than other types, because he relies less than they do on tradition and connection and because his characteristic task—theoretically as well as historically—consists precisely in breaking up old, and creating new, tradition. Although this applies primarily to his economic action, it also extends to the moral, cultural, and social consequences of it. It is, of course, no mere coincidence that the period of the rise of the entrepreneur type also gave birth to Utilitarianism.

But his conduct and his motive are "rational" in no other sense. And in *no* sense is his characteristic motivation of the hedonist kind. If we define hedonist motive of action as the wish to satisfy one's wants, we may indeed make "wants" include any impulse whatsoever, just as we may define egoism so as to include all altruistic values too, on the strength of the fact that they also mean something in the way of self-gratification. But this would reduce our definition to tautology. If we wish to give it meaning, we must restrict it to such wants as are capable of being satisfied by the consumption of goods, and to that kind of satisfaction which is expected from it. Then it is no longer true that our type is acting on a wish to satisfy his wants.

For unless we assume that individuals of our type are driven along by an insatiable craving for hedonist satisfaction, the operations of Gossen's law would in the case of business leaders soon put a stop to further effort. Experience teaches, however, that typical entrepreneurs retire from the arena only when and because their strength is spent and they feel no longer equal to their task. This does not seem to verify the picture of the economic man, balancing probable results against disutility of effort and reaching in due course a point of equilibrium beyond which he is not willing to go. Effort, in our case, does not seem to weigh at all in the sense of being felt as a reason to stop. And activity of the entrepreneurial type is obviously an obstacle to hedonist enjoyment of those kinds of commodity which are usually acquired by incomes beyond a certain size, because their "consumption" presupposes leisure.

Hedonistically, therefore, the conduct which we usually observe in individuals of our type would be irrational.

This would not, of course, prove the absence of hedonistic motive. Yet it points to another psychology of non-hedonist character, especially if we take into account the indifference to hedonist enjoyment which is often conspicuous in outstanding specimens of the type and which is not difficult to understand.

First of all, there is the dream and the will to found a private kingdom, usually, though not necessarily, also a dynasty. The modern world really does not know any such positions, but what may be attained by industrial or commercial success is still the nearest approach to medieval lordship possible to modern man. Its fascination is specially strong for people who have no other chance of achieving social distinction. The sensation of power and independence loses nothing by the fact that both are largely illusions. Closer analysis would lead to discovering an endless variety within this group of motives, from spiritual ambition down to mere snobbery. But this need not detain us. Let it suffice to point out that motives of this kind, although they stand nearest to consumers' satisfaction, do not coincide with it.

Then there is the will to conquer: the impulse to fight, to prove oneself superior to others, to succeed for the sake, not of the fruits of success, but of success itself. From this aspect, economic action becomes akin to sport—there are financial races, or rather boxing-matches. The financial result is a secondary consideration, or, at all events, mainly valued as an index of success and as a symptom of victory, the displaying of which very often is more important as a motive of large expenditure than the wish for the consumers' goods themselves. Again we should find countless nuances, some of which, like social ambition, shade into the first group of motives. And again we are faced with a motivation characteristically different from that of "satisfaction of wants" in the sense defined above, or from, to put the same thing into other words, "hedonistic adaptation."

Finally, there is the joy of creating, of getting things done, or simply of exercising one's energy and ingenuity. This is akin to a ubiquitous motive, but nowhere else does it stand out as an independent factor of behavior with anything like the clearness with which it obtrudes itself in our case. Our type seeks out difficulties, changes in order to change, delights in ventures. This group of motives is the most distinctly anti-hedonist of the three.

Only with the first groups of motives is private property as the result of entrepreneurial activity an essential factor in making it operative. With the other two it is not. Pecuniary gain is indeed a very accurate expression of success, especially of *relative* success, and from the standpoint of the man who strives for it, it has the additional advantage of being an objective fact and largely independent of the opinion of others. These and other peculiarities incident to the mechanism of "acquisitive" society make it very difficult to replace it as a motor of industrial development, even if we would discard the importance it has for creating a fund ready for investment. Nevertheless it is true that the second and third groups of entrepreneurial motives may in principle be taken care of by other social arrangements not involving private gain from economic innovation. What other stimuli could be provided, and how they could be made to work as well as the "capitalistic" ones do, are questions which are beyond our theme. They are taken too lightly by social reformers, and are altogether ignored by fiscal radicalism. But they are not insoluble, and may be answered by detailed observation of the psychology of entrepreneurial activity, at least for given times and places.

Notes

1. On the whole it is much more correct to say that population grows slowly up to the possibilities of any economic environment than, that it has any tendency to outgrow it and to become thereby an independent cause of change. [Editor's note : By the term 'circular flow', used here and elsewhere in the text, Schumpeter means a changeless economic system.]

2. A privilege which the individual can achieve through saving. In an economy of the handicraft type this element would have to be emphasised more. Manufactures' "reserve funds" assume an existing development.

3. Of course the productive means do not fall from heaven. In so far as they are not given by nature or non-economically, they were and are created at some time by the individual waves of development in our sense, and henceforth incorporated in the circular flow. But every individual wave of development and every individual new combination itself proceeds again from the supply of productive means of the existing circular flow—a case of the hen and the egg.

4. Risk obviously always falls on the owner of the means of production or of the money-capital which was paid for them, hence never on the entrepreneur *as such*. A shareholder *may* be an entrepreneur. He may even owe to his holding a controlling interest the power to act as an entrepreneur. Shareholders *per se*, however, are never entrepreneurs, but merely capitalists, who in consideration of their submitting to certain risks participate in profits. That this is no reason to look upon them as anything but capitalists is shown by the facts, first, that the average shareholder has normally no power to influence the management of his

company, and secondly, that participation in profits is frequent in cases in which everyone recognises the presence of a loan contract. Compare, for example, the Graeco-Roman *foenus nauticum*. Surely this interpretation is more true to life than the other one, which, following the lead of a faulty legal construction—which can only be explained historically—attributes functions to the average shareholder which he hardly ever thinks of discharging.

5. The definition of the entrepreneur in terms of entrepreneurial profit instead of in terms of the function the performance of which creates the entrepreneurial profit is obviously not brilliant. But we have still another objection to it: we shall see that entrepreneurial profit does not fall to the entrepreneur by "necessity" in the same sense as the marginal product of labor does to the worker.

6. Only this neglect explains the attitude of many socialistic theorists towards peasant property. For smallness of the individual possession makes a difference only for the petit-bourgeois, not for the socialist. The criterion of the employment of labor other than that of the owner and his family is economically relevant only from the standpoint of a kind of exploitation theory which is hardly tenable any longer.

7. Cf. for example the good description in Wiedenfeld, "Das Persönliche im modernen Unternehmertum." Although it appeared in Schmoller's *Jahrbuch* in 1910 (from which this text has been taken) this work was not known to me when the first edition of this book was published in 1911.

8. On the nature of the entrepreneurial function also compare my statement in the article "Unternehmer" [1928] in the Handwörterbuch der Staatswissenschaften.

9. The same *theoretical* picture, obviously not the same sociological, cultural, and so forth.

10. How much this is the case is best seen to-day in the economic life of those nations, and within our civilization in the economics of those individuals, whom the development of the last century has not yet completely drawn into its stream, for example, in the economy of the Central European peasant. This peasant "calculates"; there is not deficiency of the "economic way of thinking" (*Wirtschaftsgesinnung*) in him. Yet he cannot take a step out of the beaten path; his economy has not changed at all for centuries, except perhaps through the exercise of external force and influence. Why? Because the choice of new methods is not simply an element in the concept of rational economic action, nor a matter of course, but a distinct process which stands in need of special explanation.

11. Small disturbances which may indeed, as mentioned earlier, in time add up to great amounts. The decisive points is that the businessman, if he makes them, never alters his routine. The usual case is one of small, the exception one of great (*uno actu* great), disturbances. Only in this sense is emphasis put upon "smallness" here. The objection that there can be no difference in principle between small and large disturbances is not effective. For it is false in itself, in so far as it is based upon the disregard of the principle of the infinitesimal method, the essence of which lies in the fact that one can assert of "small quantities" under certain

circumstances what one cannot assert of "large quantities." But the reader who takes umbrage at the large-small contrast may, if he wishes, substitute for it the contrast adapting-spontaneous. Personally I am not willing to do this because the latter method of expression is much easier to misunderstand than the former and really would demand still longer explanations.

12. In the first place it is a question of a type of *conduct* and of a type of *person* in so far as this conduct is accessible in very unequal measure and to relatively few people, so that it constitutes their outstanding characteristic. Because the exposition of the first edition of the book from which this text has been taken was reproached with exaggerating and mistaking the peculiarity of this conduct, and with overlooking the fact that it is more or less open to every businessman, and because the exposition in a later paper ("Wellenbewegung des Wirtschaftslebens," [1928] *Archiv für Sozialwissenschaft*) was charged with introducing an intermediate type ("half-static" businessmen), the following may be submitted. The conduct in question is peculiar in two ways. First, because it is directed towards something different and signifies doing something different from other conduct. One may indeed in this connection include it with the latter in a higher unity, but this does not alter the fact that a theoretically relevant difference exists between the two, and that only one of them is adequately described by traditional theory. Secondly, the type of conduct in question not only differs from the other in its object, "innovation" being peculiar to it, but also in that it presupposes aptitudes differing *in kind* and not only in degree from those of mere rational economic behavior.

Now these aptitudes are presumably distributed in an ethically homogeneous population just like others, that is the curve of their distribution has a maximum ordinate, deviations on either side of which become rarer the greater they are. Similarly we can assume that every healthy man can sing if he will. Perhaps half the individuals in an ethically homogeneous group have the capacity for it to an average degree, a quarter in progressively diminishing measure, and, let us say, a quarter in a measure above the average; and within the quarter, through a series of continually increasing singing ability and continually diminishing number of people who possess it, we come finally to the Carusos. Only in this quarter are we struck in general by the singing ability, and only in the supreme instance can it become the characterising mark of the person. Although practically all men can sing, singing ability does not cease to be a distinguishable characteristic and attribute of a minority, indeed not exactly of a type, because this characteristic—unlike ours—affects the total personality relatively little.

Let us apply this: Again, a quarter of the population may be so poor in those qualities, let us say here provisionally, of economic initiative that the deficiency makes itself felt by poverty of their moral personality, and they play a wretched part in the smallest affairs of private and professional life in which this element is called for. We recognise this type and know that many of the best clerks, distinguished by devotion to duty, expert knowledge, and exactitude, belong to it. Then comes the "half," and "normal." These prove themselves to be better in the things which even within the established channels cannot simply be dispatched but must also be decided and carried out. Practically all business people belong here, otherwise they would never have attained their positions; most represent a selection—individually or hereditarily tested. A textile manufacturer travels no "new" road when he goes to a wool auction. But the situations there are never the same, and the success of the business depends so much upon skill and initiative in buying wool that the fact that textile industry has so far exhibited no trustification comparable with that in heavy manufacturing is undoubtedly partly explicable by the reluctance of the cleverer manufacturers to renounce the advantage of their own skill in buying wool. From there, rising in the scale we come finally into the highest quarter, to people who are a type characterised by super-normal qualities of intellect and will. Within this type there are not only many varieties (merchants, manufacturers, financiers, etc.) but also a continuous variety of degrees of intensity in "initiative." In our argument types of every intensity occur. Many a one can steer a safe course, where no one has yet been; others follow where first another went before; still others only in the crowd, but in this among the first. So also the great political leader of every kind and time is a type, yet not a thing unique, but only the apex of a pyramid from which there is a continuous variation down to the average and from it to the sub-normal values. And yet not only is "leading" a special function, but the leader also something special, distinguishable—wherefore there is no sense in our case in asking: "Where does that type begin then?" and then to exclaim: "This is no type at all!"

13. It has been objected against the first edition of the book from which this text has been taken that it sometimes defines "statics" as a theoretical construction, sometimes as the picture of an actual state of economic life. I believe that the present exposition gives no ground for this opinion. "Static" theory does not assume a stationary economy; it also treats of the effects of changes in data. In itself, therefore, there is no necessary connection between static theory and stationary reality. Only in so far as one can exhibit the fundamental form of the economic course of events with the maximum simplicity in an unchanging economy does this assumption recommend itself to theory. The stationary economy is for uncounted thousands of years, and also in historical times in many places for centuries, an incontrovertible fact, apart from the fact, moreover, which Sombart emphasised, that there is a tendency towards a stationary state in every period of depression. Hence it is readily understood how this historical fact and that theoretical construction have allied themselves in a way which led to some confusion. The words "statics" and "dynamics" the author would not now use in the meaning they carry above, where they are simply short expressions for "theory of the circular flow" and "theory of development." One more thing: theory employs two methods of interpretation, which may perhaps make difficulties. If it is to be shown how all the elements of the economic system are determined in equilibrium by one another, this equilibrium system is considered as not yet existing and is built up before our eyes *ab ovo*. This

does not mean that its coming into being is genetically explained thereby. Only its existence and functioning are made logically clear by mental dissection. And the experiences and habits of individuals are assumed as existing. How just these productive combinations have come about is not thereby explained. Further, if two contiguous equilibrium positions are to be investigated, then sometimes (not always), as in Pigou's *Economics of Welfare*, the "best" productive combination in the first is compared with the "best" in the second. And this again need not, but may, mean that the two combinations in the sense meant here differ not only by small variations in quantity but in their whole technical and commercial structure. Here too the coming into being of the second combination and the problems connected with it are not investigated, but only the functioning and the outcome of the already existing combination. Even though justified as far as it goes, this method of treatment passes over our problem. If the assertion were implied that this is also settled by it, it would be false.

14. It may, therefore, not be superfluous to point out that our analysis of the role of the entrepreneur does not involve any "glorification" of the type, as some readers of the first edition of the book from which this text has been taken seemed to think. We do hold that entrepreneurs *have* an economic function as distinguished from, say, robbers. But we neither style every entrepreneur a genius or a benefactor to humanity, nor do we wish to express any opinion about the comparative merits of the social organisation in which he plays his role, or about the question whether what he does could not be effected more cheaply or efficiently in other ways.

3 Entrepreneurship Before and After Schumpeter

Mark Blaug

Capitalism is usually defined as an economic system in which the means of production are privately held. But private ownership of the means of production may involve a number of separate functions: the provision of financial capital, the employment and co-ordination of the factors of production, the management and administration of the entire enterprise, and the ultimate power of making strategic decisions about investment. The existence of capital markets and the invention of the principle of limited liability makes it possible completely to separate the supply of financial capital from all the other functions. Likewise, the hiring of inputs and the functions of routine management and administration can be almost completely delegated to salaried employees. That leaves the power of making the fundamental decisions to invest or not to invest, to enter a new market or to leave an old one, etcetera, as the only function that cannot be hived off: a businessman need not be a "capitalist" or "manager" but he must be a decision-maker, whether he liked it or not. It is his function and this function alone that deserves the title of "entrepreneurship".

Given the vital role of entrepreneurship in an economic system characterised by private ownership of capital, the analysis of entrepreneurship must, surely, occupy a central role in the investigations of economists? Or so one might have thought before studying the subject! However, when we open any current textbook of elementary economics, we discover that entrepreneurship is hardly mentioned, or mentioned only in passing. Is this some sinister conspiracy of silence, or are economists so confused about the nature of economics as to ignore what is staring them in the face ?

It was not always thus: the strange disappearance of the entrepreneur from the centre of the stage of economic debate has a long history. Adam Smith in *The Wealth of Nations* (1776) clearly separated the functions of the capitalist from those of the manager, and he emphasised the fact that "profits" of the capitalist exclude the "wages" of management as a payment for "the labour of inspection and direction". However, Adam Smith did not distinguish in any way between the capitalist as the provider of the "stock" of the enterprise and the entrepreneur as the ultimate decision-maker. He did use the terms "projector" and "undertaker" as the English equivalents of the French word "entrepreneur" but only as synonyms for the business proprietor. This failure to isolate the entrepreneurial function from that of pure ownership of capital became the standard practice of all the English classical economists. Thus, the term "entrepreneur" or any of its English equivalents is totally absent in the writings of David Ricardo and so is the concept of the businessman as the principal agent of economic change.

Some would argue that the English classical economists may be forgiven for having amalgamated the functions of the capitalist and the entrepreneur. Of course, the corporate form of business organisation, in which the capitalist role of the stockholders is sharply distinguished from the decision-making role of managers and entrepreneurs, had been invented centuries before. Nevertheless, until the "railway mania" of the 1840s, trading on the British stock exchange was largely confined to government bonds and public utility stocks and the prevalent form of business ownership in the heyday of the Industrial Revolution was the small to medium-sized family firm, the capital funds being provided by the owner, his relatives, or his friends. No wonder then that the classical economists failed to highlight the distinctive character of the entrepreneurial function.

On further reflection, however, this historical explanation of the neglect of entrepreneurship in English classical political economy appears somewhat unconvincing. The fact of the matter is that the concept of the entrepreneur as having a function quite distinct from that of both the capitalist and the manager had already been formalised by a remarkable French economist of the eighteenth century, Richard Cantillon, writing some twenty years before Adam Smith.

Richard Cantillon had the remarkable insight that discrepancies between demand and supply in a market create opportunities for someone to buy cheap and to sell dear and that it is precisely this sort of arbitrage which brings competitive markets into equilibrium. He named people who take advantage of these unrealised profit opportunities "entrepreneurs", that is, those who are willing "to buy at a certain price and sell at an uncertain price". Moreover, he noted that action of this kind need not involve manufacture and need not absorb the personal funds of the entrepreneur, although it frequently did. In short, for Cantillon entrepreneurship is a matter of foresight and willingness to assume risk, which is not necessarily connected with the employment of labour in some productive process. Cantillon therefore left no doubt of the difference between the functions of the entrepreneur and the capitalist.[1]

Adam Smith read Cantillon but took no notice of his analysis of entrepreneurship. Similarly, David Ricardo had the benefit of Jean Baptiste Say's writings, which leaned heavily on Cantillon in distinguishing between the provision of capital to a business enterprise, on the one hand, and the function of superintendence, direction, control, and judgment, on the other (Hébert and Link, 1982, pp. 29–35). Nevertheless, there is not so much as a hint of the special role of entrepreneurship in Ricardo. It is evident that Ricardo, and for that matter virtually all the other leading English classical economists, regarded production and the investment of capital as a more or less automatic process, involving no critical decision-making and certainly no risky judgment or imagination of any kind. Ricardo recognised that the first capitalist to introduce a novel improvement such as a new machine is liable to reap extra returns but this did not lead him to single out the capacity to innovate as the feature which distinguished one capitalist from another.

And exactly the same thing is true of Marx. Despite his emphasis on the constant accumulation of capital, on the remorseless pressure under competition to introduce labour-saving machinery to keep ahead of rivals, on the need under capitalism to innovate or to perish, Marx too treated the business process as virtually automatic once the required capital was forthcoming.[2] The only aspect of production that was problematic for Marx was what he called "the labour process", the control and direction of the work force so as to secure the intensity of human effort that could never be properly specified in the written employment contract. According to Marx, squeezing the work force to make greater efforts is one of the two principal sources of extra profits for capitalists, the other being the introduction of new machinery. But there is never any problem in Marx about which new machines the capitalist is to introduce; likewise in Marx, there appear to be no choices to make about the size of the business, or the number of products to manufacture, or the type of market to penetrate. The businessman in Marx is simply capital personified as the "despot' of the work place. In other words, Marx, like all economists before him and since him, realised that the action of competition requires differences in behaviour among economic agents (after all, if they all acted exactly the same in the face of the same circumstances, economic change and progress would be impossible to explain). Nevertheless, Marx took no interest in these individual differences among capitalists that alone account for the dynamic evolution of the capitalist system.

Marx knew perfectly well that capitalists can borrow all their capital from banks, which is why he regarded "interest" on capital as a deduction from the "profits" of the enterprise. He also knew that the special skills of managers, including the skills of monitoring and supervising the labour force, can be hired on the labour market. But he never considered whether the residual income left over after paying the interest on borrowed capital and the wages of management corresponds to any particular economic function, for example, the function of buying inputs at certain prices and selling the output at uncertain prices, as a result of which there may be losses rather than profits. He must have thought either that decision-making under uncertainty, which is what is involved in operating a business enterprise, entails no risks, or that if it does, there is an unlimited supply of people in a capitalist economy willing to take such risks. At any rate, Marx simply conflated the functions of the capitalist and the entrepreneur and in that sense simply carried on where Adam Smith and David Ricardo left off. In short, Marx, who claimed to be alone in truly analysing the "laws of motion" of capitalism, had simply no explanation to give of the actual source of the acknowledged technical dynamism of capitalism.

For the first entirely adequate statement of the entrepreneurial role, we must go not to Marx, or even to Cantillon or Say, but to the nineteenth-century German economist, Johann von Thünen. His remarkable but hopelessly obscure book, *The Isolated State*, Volume II (1850), defines the gains of the entrepreneur as being that which is left over from the gross profits of a business operation after paying (1) the actual or imputed interest on invested capital, (2) the wages of management, and (3) the insurance premium against the calculable risk of losses. The rewards of the entrepreneur, Thünen went on the say, are therefore the returns for incurring those risks which no insurance company will cover because they are unpredictable. Since novel action is precisely the condition under which it is impossible to predict the probability of gain or loss, the entrepreneur is "inventor and explorer in his field" *par excellence* (Hébert and Link, 1982, pp. 45–7). Notice: this masterful grasp of the entrepreneur as the residual income claimant of a risky, unpredictable income, typified by but not confined to the innovative entrepreneur, predates the publication of Marx's *Capital* by seventeen years! Moreover, Marx had read Thünen's *Isolated State*. In short, let us not say that Marx identified the entrepreneur and the capitalist because he could not have known better.

John Stuart Mill's *Principles of Economics* (1848) popularised the term "entrepreneur" among English economists but failed to break the hold of the Smith–Ricardo tradition of the entrepreneur as simply a multifaceted capitalist. Soon thereafter, the new economic analysis that increasingly came to characterise professional economics after 1870 shifted attention away from the internal organisation of the business enterprise, thus eliminating the role of both the capitalist and the entrepreneur. The general equilibrium theory of Léon Walras, a central figure in the marginal revolution which ushered in the era of the neoclassical economics, provides a perfect example of how the new microeconomics caused the entrepreneur, as it were, to disappear. Every productive agent in a competitive economy, Walras tells us, is rewarded according to his marginal product, that is, the increment of output which is contributed by the marginal unit of that agent. Now suppose some economic agent hires others to produce a certain product; the hiring agent will be forced by competition to pay all the agents whom he employs their marginal product; this may leave him with something over and above the marginal product of his own services; if so, this merely induces the hired agents themselves to become the hiring agent, thus eliminating the positive residual; if, on the other hand, the residual proves to be negative, the hiring agent ceases to be a residual income recipient and rents the use of his services to others at the value of its marginal product; in either case, the residual always tends to become zero. The hiring agent is, of course, our friend the entrepreneur but Walras assumed that entrepreneurship is not itself a factor of production but rather a function that can be carried on by any agent, say, the capitalist or the salaried manager. In any case, with a zero residual income, the total product is, as neoclassical economists were fond of saying, exactly "exhausted" when all productive agents are paid their marginal products. When perfect competition has done its work, when we have reached short-run and long-run equilibrium, labour receives "wages" in accordance with the marginal product of labour, capital receives "interest" in accordance with the marginal product of capital goods, but "profits" have been eliminated and the entrepreneur, as Walras said, "neither benefits, nor loses" (Hébert and Link, 1982, pp. 63–4).

We are now at the heart of the question with which we began: why do modern economists neglect entrepreneurship? So long as economic analysis is preoccupied with the nature of static equilibrium under conditions of perfect competition, there is simply no room either for a theory of entrepreneurship or a theory of profits as the residual income-claim of persons who assume the risks associated with uncertainty. What the older classical economists had called "profits", or what Marx called "surplus value", is now said to be "interest" and of course perfect competition produces a positive rate of interest even in stationary equilibrium. But a permanent, positive residual over and above wages and interest can only be the result of constant technical progress disrupting the stationary state and the new neoclassical economics has little to say about the circumstances governing technical progress.

The growing popularity of general equilibrium theory set the seal on the possibility of theorising about entrepreneurship. As a matter of fact, static equilibrium analysis increasingly came to typify the study of economics as the nineteenth century gave way to the twentieth. And even in the 1930s when Keynesian macroeconomics arrived on the scene, Walrasian static equilibrium analysis was refurbished, a process which reached even greater stages of refinement in the 1950s. Despite valiant attempts to dynamise microeconomics, large parts of modern economics remain trapped in a static framework. Worse than that is the fact that modern economics lacks any true theory of the competitive *process*; what it actually possesses is the theory of the outcome of that process in an equilibrium *state*. In short, it emphasises equilibrium at the expense of disequilibrium. By assuming that all economic agents have free access to all the information they require for taking decisions, decision-making in modern economics is largely trivialised into the mechanical application of mathematical rules for optimisation. No wonder then that the elementary textbook of today is rich in the treatment of consumer behaviour, the profit-maximising decisions of business firms (in short-run equilibrium), the theory of wages, the theory of interest, the theory of international trade, etcetera, but poor in the analysis of technical change, the growth of big business, the causes of the wealth and poverty of nations—and the theory of entrepreneurship.[3]

This is the more remarkable in that this virtual consensus about the unimportance of entrepreneurship has been seriously questioned on at least two notable occasions in the twentieth century. The first occasion came with the publication of Frank Knight's *Risk, Uncertainty and Profit* (1921), an acknowledged classic of modern economics.

Knight began by elaborating on Thünen's distinction between "risk" and "uncertainty". Many uncertainties of economic life are like the chances of dying at a certain age: their objective probability can be calculated and to that extent they can be shifted via insurance to the shoulders of others. Such risks thus become an element in the costs of production, a deduction from and not a cause of profits or losses. There are other uncertainties, however, which can never be reduced to objective measurement because they involve unprecedented situations. "The only 'risk' which leads to profit", Knight remarked, "is a unique uncertainty resulting from an exercise of ultimate responsibility which in its very nature cannot be insured nor capitalized nor salaried" (quoted by Hébert and Link, 1982, p. 71).

The beauty of Knight's argument was to show that the presence of true "uncertainty" about the future may allow entrepreneurs to earn positive profits despite perfect competition, long-run equilibrium and "product exhaustation". Production takes place in anticipation of consumption, and since the demand for factors of production is derived from the expected demand of consumers for output, the entrepreneur is forced to speculate on the price of his final product. But it is impossible to determine the price of the final product without knowing what payments are being made to the factors of production. The entrepreneur resolves this dilemma by guessing the price at which output will sell, thereby translating the *known* marginal physical products of the factors of production into their *anticipated* marginal value products. Although the factors are hired on a contractual basis and therefore must be paid their anticipated marginal value product, the entrepreneur as a residual, non-contractual income claimant may make a windfall gain if actual receipts prove greater than forecasted receipts.

Knight denied that this uncertainty theory of profits provides some sort of social justification for profits as a type of personal income. The argument is a subtle one: we cannot describe this non-contractual, windfall gain as a necessary price that must be paid for the performance of a specific service, the "painful" cost of bearing uncertainty, for that would imply a definite connection between the level of profit and the burden of bearing uncertainty. But no such definite connection exists. If it did exist, uncertainty-bearing would have all the characteristics of a productive factor and marginal productivity theory would apply to it: profits would equal the marginal product of entrepreneurship and would therefore constitute a standard charge on production. But profits are the windfall difference between the expected and realised returns of an enterprise and as such would cease to exist in a stationary economy in which all future events could be perfectly foreseen. So, it is not that profits are justified under capitalism but that capitalism is one way of ensuring that someone is willing to assume the "gamble" of undertaking production under uncertainty. This "gamble" can be socialised by collective ownership of the means of production and we can then ask: which system is better at generating successful "gambles"?: what we cannot do is to deny that production under any social system necessarily involves a "gamble".

Knight's book, although published over sixty years ago, has withstood criticism remarkably well. There was little problem about assimilating his contributions to orthodox economic ideas because Knight did not question static economic analysis so far as it went. Unfortunately, he failed to persuade orthodox economics that the uncertainty theory of profits was anything more than a footnote to mainstream analysis, tying together some loose ends that had been left lying around ever since Adam Smith. Economics was now provided with a satisfactory explanation of profits and entrepreneurship but, of course, the main focus of analysis continued to be the pricing of factors of production in accordance with marginal productivity principles under stationary conditions.

Ten years before the appearance of Knight's book, the young Schumpeter had contributed a wholly different view of *the* economic problem in *The Theory of Economic Development* (1911). In this book, entrepreneurship and its connection with dynamic uncertainty is placed at the centre of economic inquiry.[4] Schumpeter developed his argument by constructing a model of an economy in which technical change of any kind is absent. Such an economy, he contended, would settle down to a repetitive and perfectly routine economic process in which there is no uncertainty about the future. Hence, there would be no profits in such an economy and, moreover, even the rate of interest would fall to zero. In short, competitive long-run stationary equilibrium as visualised in traditional theory rules out both profit and interest. Schumpeter's claim that only technical innovations and dynamic change can produce a positive rate of interest has been hotly disputed (see Haberler, 1951; Samuelson, 1981) but at the expense of considering his associated views on innovation and enterprise. Distinguishing between "invention" and "innovation"—the discovery of new technical knowledge and its practical application to industry—and defining "innovations" broadly as the introduction of new technical methods, new products, new sources of supply, and new forms of industrial organisation, Schumpeter traced all disrupting economic change to innovations and identified the innovator with the entrepreneur. The entrepreneur is the source of all dynamic change in an economy and for Schumpeter (1942, Chs. 7, 12) the capitalist system cannot be understood except in terms of the conditions giving rise to entrepreneurship.

As in all the previous theories of entrepreneurship, the entrepreneur in Schumpeter is a functional role which is not necessarily embodied in a single physical person and certainly not in a well-defined group of people. The entrepreneur may be a capitalist or even a corporate manager but whether all these different functions are combined in one or more persons depends on the nature of capital markets and on the forms of industrial organisation. But Schumpeter went even further than his predecessors in recognising that the same person may be an entrepreneur when he is an innovating businessman, only to lose that character as soon as he has built up his business and settled down to running it along routine lines. Thus, the actual population of entrepreneurs in a capitalist economy is constantly changing because the function of entrepreneurship is typically mixed up with other kinds of activity.

Schumpeter's influence on entrepreneurial theory has been overwhelming and subsequent writers on entrepreneurship have usually defined their own position by contrasting it with his. In the meanwhile, however, mainstream economic theory has continued to neglect Schumpeter's writings on entrepreneurship as it continues to neglect Knight's theory of profits because neither fits in with static equilibrium analysis. The theory of entrepreneurship has, however, been given a new lease of life by the modern Austrian school, descending from Ludwig von Mises and Friedrich Hayek. In two closely reasoned books, *Competition and Entrepreneurship* (1973) and *Perception, Opportunity and Profit* (1979), a student of von Mises, Israel Kirzner, has sought once again to persuade his fellow economists that the properties of disequilibrium states deserve as much attention as those of equilibrium states. Disequilibria are due to intertemporal and interspatial differences in demand and supply and hence give rise to unrealised profit opportunities. The essence of entrepreneurship, for Cantillon as much as for Kirzner, consists in the personal alertness to such potential sources of gain. There is a subtle change of emphasis in Kirzner's discussion of entrepreneurship from that of Schumpeter's: Schumpeter always portrayed the entrepreneur-innovator as a disequilibrating force disturbing a previous equilibrium, whereas Kirzner (1973, pp. 72–4, 79–81, 126–31; 1979, Ch. 7) depicts him as seizing upon a disequilibrium situation and working to restore equilibrium. But not too much should be made of this change of emphasis, which is no doubt a reflection of the state of contemporary economic theory in 1911 and 1973: in the days before World War I, economists needed convincing that an achieved state of general equilibrium is the exception and not the rule, whereas nowadays economists need convincing that the process of arriving at general equilibrium has never been satisfactorily explained.

Unfortunately, the new Austrian theory of entrepreneurship reduces entrepreneurship to any kind of arbitrage and in so doing wipes out most of the crucial questions that have been posed about entrepreneurship. The popular stereotype of the entrepreneur as a swashbuckling business tycoon may take too narrow a view of entrepreneurship but, on the other hand, the Austrian conception of the entrepreneur as anyone who buys cheap and sells dear is so general as to dissolve practically all the questions one cares to ask about entrepreneurship. As Demsetz has said (in Ronen, 1983, p. 277) entrepreneurship in new Austrian theory is "little more than profit maximization in a context in which knowledge is costly and imitation is not instantaneous". A more promising approach to the theory of entrepreneurship is offered in a recent study by Mark Casson who synthesises and extends previous work by Knight, Schumpeter, Kirzner and many others. Casson defines an entrepreneur as "someone who specializes in taking judgmental decisions about the coordination of scarce resources" (Casson, 1982, p. 23), every term in this definition being carefully chosen to highlight the specific content of the entrepreneurial role. The entrepreneur is a person, not a team, committee or organisation, and he is someone who has a comparative advantage in making decisions; moreover, he reaches a different decision from other people in the face of identical circumstances either because of access to better information or because of a different interpretation of the same information. The entrepreneurial function is, in principle, performed in all societies by individuals whose judgment differs from the norm, and military and political life may provide as much scope for entrepreneurship as the economic one. Capitalism then is simply an economic system that harnesses entrepreneurship to industrial decisions. Even economic entrepreneurship under capitalism, however, may range from pure arbitrage or financial speculation to the non-routine decisions of salaried managers and the daring innovations of self-employed businessmen. It is true, as Schumpeter argued, that ownership and entrepreneurship are conceptually separate functions and that one can be an entrepreneur without being a capitalist. Nevertheless, entrepreneurship in practice is likely to be packaged together with asset ownership because financial intermediaries are reluctant to lend to an entrepreneur precisely because the entrepreneur's assessment of a situation necessarily differs from everybody else's assessment, including that of the lender. In other words, personal wealth, or at least the wealth of friends and relatives, is in fact a major constraint on the scale of entrepreneurial activity and bank credit has only a limited role to play.

Casson's theory throws new light on the long-lived reluctance in economic thought to divorce proprietorship from entrepreneurship, thus identifying the capitalist with the entrepreneur. The industrial entrepreneur frequently was and still is a capitalist, and this association between the two roles is not accidental but stems from the very nature of entrepreneurship as consisting of an eccentric evaluation of economic events which other people are unwilling to support. Casson's theory also clears up another longstanding bone of contention in the history of entrepreneurship (see Kanbur, 1980; Ronen, 1983, pp. 147–9). Schumpeter (1951, pp. 251–2; 1954, p. 556) always insisted paradoxically that risk-bearing is not an entrepreneurial function and that all the risks of an enterprise are borne by the capitalist. Even accepting the Knightian distinction between risk and uncertainty, Schumpeter agreed with Knight that profits cannot be construed simply as an earned reward for the psychic pain of bearing uncertainty in the sense that smaller profits would discourage people from becoming entrepreneurs; it might or it might not, depending entirely on the number of risk-averters in a society. If we taxed away the profits of entrepreneurship or cut off industrial entrepreneurship by collectivising the means of production, all we might do, according to Schumpeter, is to drive entrepreneurship into non-economic activity. Casson (1982, Ch. 17) argues, however, that the profits of entrepreneurship are "earned income" in the true sense of the term. In the short run, the entrepreneur's reward is a "rent of ability", a temporary monopoly rent to superior judgment, and in the long run, it is in fact a necessary compensation for the time and effort involved in identifying and making judgmental decisions and obtaining financial backing to undertake the search for information. Since it is frequently the entrepreneur's own wealth that supports his activity, the entrepreneur risks his own capital but, in addition, he always risks the opportunity cost of his time and effort and the value of his "good will" for future operations.

Be that as it may, private ownership of the means of production and private entitlement to the profits of entrepreneurship do not lack economic justification. Entrepreneurship may be a universal feature of all society but capitalism provides a unique institutional setting to release the entrepreneurial spirit. The technical dynamism of capitalism, which Marx attributed to the organisational invention of the factory, the despotic control of the workers by capitalists, and the restless urge of the bourgeoisie to save and invest, must instead be credited in large part to the institution of private property rights, which channels the entrepreneurial spirit into productive outlets where previously it remained locked into speculative and purely merchandising activity. If we fully understood the nature of industrial entrepreneurship and the conditions under which is flourishes, and I do not claim that we have done more than scratch the surface of that subject, we would at long last be near to answering the great question with which economics began: what *are* the causes of the wealth of nations?

I do believe that Schumpeter in some respects takes us further towards an answer to this great question than does Marx. The entrepreneurial function is central to the workings of a capitalist society and yet there is no entrepreneurial function in Marx. Ah, Marxists will say, where is the entrepreneur without capitalist backing and without capitalist control of "the labour process"? Why label the entrepreneurial function the principal agent of economic change when the entrepreneur is in practice frequently capitalist and manager as well? I can only imagine how Schumpeter might have answered that question. Yes, he might have said, without control of the work force, without the constant monitoring of job performance, there are no profits and there is no growth. But is this a specifically capitalist phenomenon? Would a socialist society be able to dispense with the "labour process"? Yes, if labour-managed enterprises are feasible (as Marx thought they were) and No otherwise.[5] In short, Schumpeter would have said, any industrialised society must somehow get workers to work effectively. But industrial entrepreneurship—an individual taking a chance to introduce a new method or a new product—is specifically capitalist: it cannot be collectivised without being destroyed. That is why the growth of the large corporation is worrying because it may erode the institutional basis of dynamic entrepreneurship.

Let us call a halt to his imaginary dialogue and return to the main subject at hand: the neglect of entrepreneurship in modern, mainstream economics. Surely, this neglect must give us pause? It is a scandal that nowadays students of economics can spend years in the study of the subject before hearing the term "entrepreneur", that courses in economic development provide exhaustive lists of all the factors impeding or accelerating economic growth without mentioning the conditions under which entrepreneurship languishes or flourishes, and that learned comparisons between "socialism" and "capitalism" are virtually silent about the role of entrepreneurship under regimes of collective rather than private ownership.

....

Notes

1. See the detailed treatment of Cantillon in Hébert and Link (1982, Ch. 3).
2. I am not the first to have noticed this. As Schumpeter (1954, p. 556) said: "Ricardo, the Ricardians and also Senior . . . almost accomplished what I have described as an impossible feat, namely, the exclusion of the figure of the entrepreneur completely. For them—as well as for Marx—the business process runs substantially by itself, the one thing needful to make it run being an adequate supply of capital". See also Schumpeter (1951, p. 250) and Kirzner (1979, Ch. 3).
3. Again, this has been said before by others (e.g. Baumol, 1968; Leff, 1979; Kirzner, 1979, Ch. 7).
4. Even twenty-three years later, when Schumpeter (1934, p. xi) wrote a preface to the English translation of his book, he found himself moved to exclaim that the arguments of his book "might usefully be contrasted with the theory of [static]

equilibrium, which explicitly or implicitly always has been and still is the centre of traditional theory".

5. In this respect, see the interesting discussion by A. Bergson of the innovatory process in Yugoslavian labour-managed enterprises (Ronen, 1983, Ch. 8).

References

Baumol, W. (1968), "Entrepreneurship in Economic Theory", *American Economic Review*, 58, No. 2 (May 1968).

Casson, M. (1982), *The Entrepreneur. An Economic Theory* (Oxford).

Haberler, G. (1951), "Schumpeter's Theory of Interest", in *Schumpeter; Social Scientist*, ed. S. Harris (Cambridge, Mass.).

Hébert, R.F., Link, A.N. (1982), *The Entrepreneur. Mainstream Views and Radical Critiques* (New York).

Kanbur, S.M. (1980), "A Note on Risk Taking, Entrepreneurship, and Schumpeter". *History of Political Economy*, 12, No. 4, (Winter).

Kirzner, I (1973). *Competition and Entrepreneurship* (Chicago).

——(1979), *Perception, Opportunity, and Profit. Studies in the Theory of Entrepreneurship* (Chicago).

Leff, N.H. (1979), "Entrepreneurship and Development: The Problem Revisited", *Journal of Economic Literature* 17, No. 1 (March 1979).

Ronen, J. ed. (1983), *Entrepreneurship* (Lexington, Mass.).

Samuelson, P.A. (1981), "Schumpeter as an Economic Theorist", in *Schumpeterian Economics*, ed. H. Frisch (New York).

Schumpeter, J.A. (1934), *The Theory of Economic Development* (Boston, Mass.).

——(1942), *Capitalism, Socialism, and Democracy* (New York).

——(1951), *Essays of Joseph A. Schumpeter*, ed. R. V. Clemence (Cambridge, Mass.)

——(1954), *History of Economic Analysis* (New York).

4 The Entrepreneur and Profit

Ludwig von Mises

A. The Economic Nature of Profit and Loss

1. The Emergence of Profit and Loss

In the capitalist system of society's economic organization the entrepreneurs determine the course of production. In the performance of this function they are unconditionally and totally subject to the sovereignty of the buying public, the consumers. If they fail to produce in the cheapest and best possible way those commodities which the consumers are asking for most urgently, they suffer losses and are finally eliminated from their entrepreneurial position. Other men who know better how to serve the consumers replace them.

If all people were to anticipate correctly the future state of the market, the entrepreneurs would neither earn any profits nor suffer any losses. They would have to buy the complementary factors of production at prices which would, already at the instant of the purchase, fully reflect the future prices of the products. No room would be left either for profit or for loss. What makes profit emerge is the fact that the entrepreneur who judges the future prices of the products more correctly than other people do buys some or all of the factors of production at prices which, seen from the point of view of the future state of the market, are too low. Thus the total costs of production—including interest on the capital invested—lag behind the prices which the entrepreneur receives for the product. This difference is entrepreneurial profit.

On the other hand, the entrepreneur who misjudges the future prices of the products allows for the factors of production prices which, seen from the point of view of the future state of the market, are too high. His total costs of production exceed the prices at which he can sell the product. This difference is entrepreneurial loss.

Thus profit and loss are generated by success or failure in adjusting the course of production activities to the most urgent demand of the consumers. Once this adjustment is achieved, they disappear. The prices of the complementary factors of production reach a height at which total costs of production coincide with the price of the product. Profit and loss are ever-present features only on account of the fact that ceaseless change in the economic data makes again and again new discrepancies, and consequently the need for new adjustments originate.

2. The Distinction Between Profits and Other Proceeds

Many errors concerning the nature of profit and loss were caused by the practice of applying the term profit to the totality of the residual proceeds of an entrepreneur.

Interest on the capital employed is not a component part of profit. The dividends of a corporation are not profit. They are interest on the capital invested plus profit or minus loss.

The market equivalent of work performed by the entrepreneur in the conduct of the enterprise's affairs is entrepreneurial quasi-wages but not profit.

If the enterprise owns a factor on which it can earn monopoly prices, it makes a monopoly gain. If this enterprise is a corporation, such gains increase the dividend. Yet they are not profit proper.

Still more serious are the errors due to the confusion of entrepreneurial activity and technological innovation and improvement.

The maladjustment the removal of which is the essential function of entrepreneurship may often consist in the fact that new technological methods have not yet been utilized to the full extent to which they should be in order to bring about the best possible satisfaction of consumers' demand. But this is not necessarily always the case. Changes in the data, especially in consumers' demand, may require adjustments which have no reference at all to technological innovations and improvements. The entrepreneur who simply increases the production of an article by adding to the existing production facilities a new outfit without any change in the technological method of production is no less an entrepreneur than the man who inaugurates a new way of producing. The business of the entrepreneur is not merely to experiment with new technological methods, but to select from the multitude of technologically feasible methods those which are best fit to supply the public in the cheapest way with the things they are asking for most urgently. Whether a new technological procedure is or is not fit for this purpose is to be provisionally decided by the entrepreneur and will be finally decided by the conduct of the buying public. The question is not whether a new method is to be considered as a more "elegant" solution of a technological problem. It is whether, under the given state of economic data, it is the best possible method of supplying the consumers in the cheapest way.

The activities of the entrepreneur consist in making decisions. He determines for what purpose the factors of production should be employed. Any other acts which an entrepreneur may perform are merely accidental to his entrepreneurial function. It is this that laymen often fail to realize. They confuse the entrepreneurial activities with the conduct of the technological and administrative affairs of a plant. In their eyes not the stockholders, the promoters and speculators, but hired employees are the real entrepreneurs. The former are merely idle parasites who pocket the dividends.

Nobody ever contended that one could produce without working. But neither is it possible to produce without capital goods, the previously produced factors of further production. These capital goods are scarce, i.e., they do not suffice for the production of all things which one would like to have produced. Hence the economic problem arises: to employ them in such a way that only those goods should be produced which are fit to satisfy the most urgent demands of the consumers. No good should remain unproduced on account of the fact that the factors required for its production were used—wasted—for the production of another good for which the demand of the public is less intense. To achieve this is under capitalism the function of entrepreneurship that determines the allocation of capital to the various branches of production. Under socialism it would be a function of the state, the social apparatus of coercion and oppression. The problem whether a socialist directorate, lacking any method of economic calculation, could fulfill this function is not to be dealt with in this essay.

There is a simple rule of thumb to tell entrepreneurs from non-entrepreneurs. The entrepreneurs are those on whom the incidence of losses on the capital employed falls. Amateur-economists may confuse profits with other kinds of intakes. But it is impossible to fail to recognize losses on the capital employed.

3. Non-Profit Conduct of Affairs

What has been called the democracy of the market manifests itself in the fact that profit-seeking business is unconditionally subject to the supremacy of the buying public.

Non-profit organizations are sovereign unto themselves. They are, within the limits drawn by the amount of capital at their disposal, in a position to defy the wishes of the public.

A special case is that of the conduct of government affairs, the administration of the social apparatus of coercion and oppression, viz. the police power. The objectives of government, the protection of the inviolability of the individuals' lives and health and of their efforts to improve the material conditions of their existence, are indispensable. They benefit all and are the necessary prerequisite of social cooperation and civilization. But they cannot be sold and bought in the way merchandise is sold and bought; they have therefore no price on the market. With regard to them there cannot be any economic calculation. The costs expended for their conduct cannot be confronted with a price received for the product. This state of affairs would make the officers entrusted with the administration of governmental activities irresponsible despots if they were not curbed by the budget system. Under this system the administrators are forced to comply with detailed instructions enjoined upon them by the sovereign, be it a self-appointed autocrat or the whole people acting through elected representatives. To the officers limited funds are assigned which they are bound to spend only for those purposes which the sovereign has ordered. Thus the management of public administration becomes bureaucratic, i.e., dependent on definite detailed rules and regulations.

Bureaucratic management is the only alternative available where there is no profit and loss mangement.[1]

4. The Ballot of the Market

The consumers by their buying and abstention from buying elect the entrepreneurs in a daily repeated plebiscite as it were. They determine who should own and who not and how much each owner should own.

As is the case with all acts of choosing a person—choosing holders of public office, employees, friends or a consort—the decision of the consumers is made on the ground of experience and thus necessarily always refers to the past.

There is no experience of the future. The ballot of the market elevates those who in the immediate past have best served the consumers. However, the choice is not unalterable and can daily be corrected. The elected who disappoints the electorate is speedily reduced to the ranks.

Each ballot of the consumers adds only a little to the elected man's sphere of action. To reach the upper levels of entrepreneurship he needs a great number of votes, repeated again and again over a long period of time, a protracted series of successful strokes. He must stand every day a new trial, must submit anew to reelection as it were.

It is the same with his heirs. They can retain their eminent position only by receiving again and again confirmation on the part of the public. Their office is revocable. If they retain it, it is not on account of the deserts of their predecessor, but on account of their own ability to employ the capital for the best possible satisfaction of the consumers.

The entrepreneurs are neither perfect nor good in any metaphysical sense. They owe their position exclusively to the fact that they are better fit for the performance of the functions incumbent upon them than other people are. They earn profit not because they are clever in performing their tasks, but because they are more clever or less clumsy than other people are. They are not infallible and often blunder, but they are less liable to err, and blunder less than other people do. Nobody has the right to take offense at the errors made by the entrepreneurs in the conduct of affairs and to stress the point that people would have been better supplied if the entrepreneurs had been more skillful and prescient. If the grumbler knew better, why did he not himself fill the gap and seize the opportunity to earn profits? It is easy indeed to display foresight after the event. In retrospect all fools become wise.

A popular chain of reasoning runs this way: The entrepreneur earns profit not only on account of the fact that other people were less successful than him in anticipating correctly the future state of the market. He himself contributed to the emergence of profit by not producing more of the article concerned; but for intentional restriction of output on his part, the supply of this article would have been so ample that the price would have dropped to a point at which no surplus of proceeds over costs of production expended would have emerged. This reasoning is at the bottom of the spurious doctrines of imperfect and monopolistic competition. It was resorted to a short time ago by the American Administration when it blamed the enterprises of the steel industry for the fact that the steel production capacity of the United States was not greater than it really was.

Certainly those engaged in the production of steel are not responsible for the fact that other people did not likewise enter this field of production. The reproach on the part of the authorities would have been sensible if they had conferred on the existing steel corporations the monopoly of steel production. But in the absence of such a privilege, the reprimand given to the operating mills is not more justified than it would be to censure the nation's poets and musicians for the fact that there are not more and better poets and musicians. If somebody is to blame for the fact that the number of people who joined the voluntary civilian defense organization is not larger, then it is not those who have already joined but only those who have not.

That the production of a commodity p is not larger than it really is, is due to the fact that the complementary factors of production required for an expansion were employed for the production of other commodities. To speak of an insufficiency of the supply of p is empty rhetoric if it does not indicate the various products m which were produced in too large quantities with the effect that their production appears now, i.e., after the event, as a waste of scarce factors of production. We may assume that the entrepreneurs who instead of producing additional quantities of p turned to the production of excessive amounts of m and consequently suffered losses, did not intentionally make their mistake.

Neither did the producers of p intentionally restrict the production of p. Every entrepreneur's capital is limited; he employs it for those projects which, he expects, will, by filling the most urgent demand of the public, yield the highest profit.

An entrepreneur at whose disposal are 100 units of capital employs, for instance, 50 units for the production of p and 50 units for the production of q. If both lines are profitable, it is odd to blame him for not having employed more, e.g., 75 units, for the production of p. He could increase the production of p only by curtailing correspondingly the production of q. But with regard to q the same fault could be found by the grumblers. If one blames the entrepreneur for not having produced more p, one must blame him also for not having produced more q. This means: one blames the entrepreneur for the facts that there is a scarcity of the factors of production and that the earth is not a land of Cockaigne.

Perhaps the grumbler will object on the ground that he considers p a vital commodity, much more important than q, and that therefore the production of p should be expanded and that of q restricted. If this is really the meaning of his criticism, he is at variance with the valuations of the consumers. He throws off his mask and shows his dictatorial aspirations. Production should not be directed by the wishes of the public but by his own despotic discretion.

But if our entrepreneur's production of q involves a loss, it is obvious that his fault was poor foresight and not intentional.

Entrance into the ranks of the entrepreneurs in a market society, not sabotaged by the interference of government or other agencies resorting to violence, is open to everybody. Those who know how to take advantage of any business opportunity cropping up will always find the capital required. For the market is always full of capitalists anxious to find the most promising employment for their funds and in search of the ingenious newcomers, in partnership with whom they could execute the most remunerative projects.

People often failed to realize this inherent feature of capitalism because they did not grasp the meaning and the effects of capital scarcity. The task of the entrepreneur is to select from the multitude of technologically feasible projects those which will satisfy the most urgent of the not yet satisfied needs of the public. Those projects for the execution of which the capital supply does not suffice must not be carried out. The market is always crammed with visionaries who want to float such impracticable and unworkable schemes. It is these dreamers who always complain about the blindness of the capitalists who are too stupid to look after their own interests. Of course, the investors often err in the choice of their investments. But these faults consist precisely in the fact that they preferred an unsuitable project to another that would have satisfied more urgent needs of the buying public.

People often err very lamentably in estimating the work of the creative genius. Only a minority of men are appreciative enough to attach the right value to the achievement of poets, artists and thinkers. It may happen that the indifference of his contemporaries makes it impossible for a genius to accomplish what he would have accomplished if his fellow men had displayed better judgment. The way in which the poet laureate and the philosopher *à la mode* are selected is certainly questionable.

But it is impermissible to question the free market's choice of the entrepreneurs. The consumers' preference for definite articles may be open to condemnation from the point of view of a philosopher's judgment. But judgments of value are necessarily always personal and subjective. The consumer chooses what, as he thinks, satisfies him best. Nobody is called upon to determine what could make another man happier or less unhappy. The popularity of motor cars, television sets and nylon stockings may be criticized from a "higher" point of view. But these are the things that people are asking for. They cast their ballots for those entrepreneurs who offer them this merchandise of the best quality at the cheapest price.

In choosing between various political parties and programs for the commonwealth's social and economic organization most people are uninformed and groping in the dark. The average voter lacks the insight to distinguish between policies suitable to attain the ends he is aiming at and those unsuitable. He is at a loss to examine the long chains of aprioristic reasoning which constitute the philosophy of a comprehensive social program. He may at best form some opinion about the short-run effects of the policies concerned. He is helpless in dealing with the long-run effects. The socialists and communists in principle often assert the infallibility of majority decisions. However, they belie their own words in criticizing parliamentary majorities rejecting their creed, and in denying to the people, under the one-party system, the opportunity to choose between different parties.

But in buying a commodity or abstaining from its purchase there is nothing else involved than the consumer's longing for the best possible satisfaction of his instantaneous wishes. The consumer does not—like the voter in political voting—choose between different means whose effects appear only later. He chooses between things which immediately provide satisfaction. His decision is final.

An entrepreneur earns profit by serving the consumers, the people, as they are and not as they should be according to the fancies of some grumbler or potential dictator.

5. The Social Function of Profit and Loss

Profits are never normal. They appear only where there is a maladjustment, a divergence between actual production and production as it should be in order to utilize the available material and mental resources for the best possible satisfaction of the wishes of the public. They are the prize of those who remove this maladjustment; they disappear as soon as the maladjustment is entirely removed. In the imaginary construction of an evenly rotating economy there are no profits. There the sum of the prices of the complementary factors of production, due allowance being made for time preference, coincides with the price of the product.

The greater the preceding maladjustments, the greater the profit earned by their removal. Maladjustments may sometimes be called excessive. But it is inappropriate to apply the epithet "excessive" to profits.

People arrive at the idea of excessive profits by confronting the profit earned with the capital employed in the enterprise and measuring the profit as a percentage of the capital. This method is suggested by the customary procedure applied in partnerships and corporations for the assignment of quotas of the total profit to the individual partners and shareholders. These men have contributed to a different extent to the realization of the project and share in the profits and losses according to the extent of their contribution.

But it is not the capital employed that creates profits and losses. Capital does not "beget profit" as Marx thought. The capital goods as such are dead things that in themselves do not accomplish anything. If they are utilized according to a good idea, profit results. If they are utilized according to a mistaken idea, no profit or losses result. It is the entrepreneurial decision that creates either profit or loss. It is mental acts, the mind of the entrepreneur, from which profits ultimately originate. Profit is a product of the mind, of success in anticipating the future state of the market. It is a spiritual and intellectual phenomenon.

The absurdity of condemning any profits as excessive can easily be shown. An enterprise with a capital of the amount c produced a definite quantity of p which it sold at prices that brought a surplus of proceeds over costs of s and consequently a profit of n per cent. If the entrepreneur had been less capable, he would have needed a capital of $2c$ for the production of the same quantity of p. For the sake of argument we may even neglect the fact that this would have necessarily increased costs of production as it would have doubled the interest on the capital employed, and we may assume that s would have remained unchanged. But at any rate s would have been confronted with $2c$ instead of c and thus the profit would have been only $n/2$ per cent of the capital employed. The "excessive" profit would have been reduced to a "fair" level. Why? Because the entrepreneur was less efficient and because his lack of efficiency deprived his fellow men of all the advantages they could have got if an amount c of capital goods had been left available for the production of other merchandise.

In branding profits as excessive and penalizing the efficient entrepreneurs by discriminatory taxation, people are injuring themselves. Taxing profits is tantamount to taxing success in best serving the public. The only goal of all production activities is to employ the factors of production in such a way that they render the highest possible output. The smaller the input required for the production of an article becomes, the more of the scarce factors of production is left for the production of other articles. But the better an entrepreneur succeeds in this regard, the more is he vilified and the more is he soaked by taxation. Increasing costs per unit of output, that is, waste, is praised as a virtue.

The most amazing manifestation of this complete failure to grasp the task of production and the nature and functions of profit and loss is shown in the popular superstition that profit is an addendum to the costs of production, the height of which depends uniquely on the discretion of the seller. It is this belief that guides governments in controlling prices. It is the same belief that has prompted many governments to make arrangements with their contractors according to which the price to be paid for an article delivered is to equal costs of production expended by the seller increased by a definite percentage. The effect was that the purveyor got a higher surplus, the less he succeeded in avoiding superfluous costs. Contracts of this type enhanced considerably the sums the United States had to expend in the two World Wars. But the bureaucrats, first of all the professors of economics who served in the various war agencies, boasted of their clever handling of the matter.

All people, entrepreneurs as well as non-entrepreneurs, look askance upon any profits earned by other people. Envy is a common weakness of men. People are loath to acknowledge the fact that they themselves could have earned profits if they displayed the same foresight and judgment the successful businessman did. Their resentment is the more violent, the more they are subconsciously aware of this fact.

There would not be any profits but for the eagerness of the public to acquire the merchandise offered for sale by the successful entrepreneur. But the same people who scramble for these articles vilify the businessman and call his profit ill-gotten.

The semantic expression of this enviousness is the distinction between earned and unearned income. It permeates the textbooks, the language of the laws and administrative procedure. Thus, for instance, the official Form 201 for the New York State Income Tax Return calls "Earnings" only the compensation received by employees and, by implication, all other income, also that resulting from the exercise of a profession, unearned income. Such is the terminology of a state whose governor is Republican and whose state assembly has a Republican majority.

Public opinion condones profits only as far as they do not exceed the salary paid to an employee. All surplus is rejected as unfair. The objective of taxation is, under the ability-to-pay principle, to confiscate this surplus.

Now one of the main functions of profits is to shift the control of capital to those who know how to employ it in the best possible way for the satisfaction of the public. The more profits a man earns, the greater his wealth consequently becomes, the more influential does he become in the conduct of business affairs. Profit and loss are the instruments by means of which the consumers pass the direction of production activities into the hands of those who are best fit to serve them. Whatever is undertaken to curtail or to confiscate profits, impairs this function. The result of such measures is to loosen the grip the consumers hold over the course of production. The economic machine becomes, from the point of view of the people, less efficient and less responsive.

The jealousy of the common man looks upon the profits of the entrepreneurs as if they were totally used for consumption. A part of them is, of course, consumed. But only those entrepreneurs attain wealth and influence in the realm of business who consume merely a fraction of their proceeds and plough back the much greater part into their enterprises. What makes small business develop into big business is not spending, but saving and capital accumulation.

6. Profit and Loss in the Progressing and in the Retrogressing Economy

We call a stationary economy an economy in which the per head quota of the income and wealth of the individuals remains unchanged. In such an economy what the consumers spend more for the purchase of some articles must be equal to what they spend less for other articles. The total amount of the profits earned by one part of the entrepreneurs equals the total amount of losses suffered by other entrepreneurs.

A surplus of the sum of all profits earned in the whole economy above the sum of all losses suffered emerges only in a progressing economy, that is in an economy in which the per head quota of capital increases. This increment is an effect of saving that adds new capital goods to the quantity already previously available. The increase of capital available creates maladjustments insofar as it brings about a discrepancy between the actual state of production and that state which the additional capital makes possible. Thanks to the emergence of additional capital, certain projects which hitherto could not be executed become feasible. In directing the new capital into those channels in which it satisfies the most urgent among the previously unsatisfied wants of the consumers, the entrepreneurs earn profits which are not counterbalanced by the losses of other entrepreneurs.

The enrichment which additional capital generates goes only in part to those who have created it by saving. The rest goes, by raising the marginal productivity of labor and thereby wage rates, to the earners of wages and salaries and, by raising the prices of definite raw materials and food stuffs, to the owners of land, and, finally, to the entrepreneurs who integrate this new capital into the most economical production processes. But while the gain of the wage earners and of the landowners is permanent, the profits of the entrepreneurs disappear once this integration is accomplished. Profits of the entrepreneurs are, as has been mentioned already, a permanent phenomenon only on account of the fact that maladjustments appear daily anew by the elimination of which profits are earned.

Let us for the sake of argument resort to the concept of national income as employed in popular economics. Then it is obvious that in a stationary economy no part of the national income goes into profits. Only in a progressing economy is there a surplus of total profits over total losses. The popular belief that profits are a deduction from the income of workers and consumers is entirely fallacious. If we want to apply the term deduction to the issue, we have to say that this surplus of profits over losses as well as the increments of the wage earners and the landowners is deducted from the gains of those whose saving brought about the additional capital. It is their saving that is the vehicle of economic improvement, that makes the employment of technological innovations possible and raises productivity and the standard of living. It is the entrepreneurs whose activity takes care of the most economical employment of the additional capital. As far as they themselves do not save, neither the workers nor the landowners contribute anything to the emergence of the circumstances which generate what is called economic progress and improvement. They are benefited by other people's saving that creates additional capital on the one hand and by the entrepreneurial action that directs this additional capital toward the satisfaction of the most urgent wants on the other hand.

A retrogressing economy is an economy in which the per head quota of capital invested is decreasing. In such an economy the total amount of losses incurred by entrepreneurs exceeds the total amount of profits earned by other entrepreneurs.

....

B. The Condemnation of Profit

1. Economics and the Abolition of Profit

Those who spurn entrepreneurial profit as "unearned" mean that it is lucre unfairly withheld either from the workers of from the consumers or from both. Such is the idea underlying the alleged "right to the whole produce of labor" and the Marxian doctrine of exploitation. It can be said that most governments—

if not all—and the immense majority of our contemporaries by and large endorse this opinion although some of them are generous enough to acquiesce in the suggestion that a fraction of profits should be left to the "exploiters."

There is no use in arguing about the adequacy of ethical precepts. They are derived from intuition; they are arbitrary and subjective. There is no objective standard available with regard to which they could be judged. Ultimate ends are chosen by the individual's judgments of value. They cannot be determined by scientific inquiry and logical reasoning. If a man says, "This is what I am aiming at whatever the consequences of my conduct and the price I shall have to pay for it may be," nobody is in a position to oppose any arguments against him. But the question is whether it is really true that this man is ready to pay any price for the attainment of the end concerned. If this latter question is answered in the negative, it becomes possible to enter into an examination of the issue involved.

If there were really people who are prepared to put up with all the consequences of the abolition of profit, however detrimental they may be, it would not be possible for economics to deal with the problem. But this is not the case. Those who want to abolish profit are guided by the idea that this confiscation would improve the material well-being of all non-entrepreneurs. In their eyes the abolition of profit is not an ultimate end but a means for the attainment of a definite end, viz., the enrichment of the non-entrepreneurs. Whether this end can really be attained by the employment of this means and whether the employment of this means does not perhaps bring about some other effects which may to some or to all people appear more undesirable than conditions before the employment of this means, these are questions which economics is called upon to examine.

2. The Consequences of the Abolition of Profit

The idea to abolish profit for the advantage of the consumers involves that the entrepreneur should be forced to sell the products at prices not exceeding the costs of production expended. As such prices are, for all articles the sale of which would have brought profit, below the potential market price, the available supply is not sufficient to make it possible for all those who want to buy at these prices to acquire the articles. The market is paralyzed by the maximum price decree. It can no longer allocate the products to the consumers. A system of rationing must be adopted.

The suggestion to abolish the entrepreneur's profit for the benefit of the employees aims not at the abolition of profit. It aims at wresting it from the hands of the entrepreneur and handing it over to his employees.

Under such a scheme the incidence of losses incurred falls upon the entrepreneur, while profits go to the employees. It is probable that the effect of this arrangement would consist in making losses increase and profits dwindle. At any rate, a greater part of the profits would be consumed and less would be saved and ploughed back into the enterprise. No capital would be available for the establishment of new branches of production and for the transfer of capital from branches which—in compliance with the demand of the customers—should shrink into branches which should expand. For it would harm the interests of those employed in a definite enterprise or branch to restrict the capital employed in it and to transfer it into another enterprise or branch. If such a scheme had been adopted half a century ago, all the innovations accomplished in this period would have been rendered impossible. If, for the sake of argument, we were prepared to neglect any reference to the problem of capital accumulation, we would still have to realize that giving profit to the employees must result in rigidity of the once attained state of production and preclude any adjustment, improvement and progress.

In fact, the scheme would transfer ownership of the capital invested into the hands of the employees. It would be tantamount to the establishment of syndicalism and would generate all the effects of syndicalism, a system which no author or reformer ever had the courage to advocate openly.

A third solution of the problem would be to confiscate all the profits earned by the entrepreneurs for the benefit of the state. A one hundred per cent tax on profits would accomplish this task. It would transform the entrepreneurs into irresponsible administrators of all plants and workshops. They would no longer be subject to the supremacy of the buying public. They would just be people who have the power to deal with production as it pleases them.

The policies of all contemporary governments which have not adopted outright socialism apply all these three schemes jointly. They confiscate by various measures of price control a part of the potential profits for the alleged benefit of the consumers. They support the labor unions in their endeavours to wrest, under the ability-to-pay principle of wage determination, a part of the profits from the entrepreneurs. And, last but not least, they are intent upon confiscating, by progressive income taxes, special taxes on corporation income and "excess profits" taxes, an ever increasing part of profits for public revenue. It can easily be seen that these policies if continued will very soon succeed in abolishing entrepreneurial profit altogether.

The joint effect of the application of these policies is already today rising chaos. The final effect will be the full realization of socialism by smoking out the entrepreneurs. Capitalism cannot survive the abolition of profit. It is profit and loss that force the capitalists to employ their capital for the best possible service to the consumers. It is profit and loss that make those people supreme in the conduct of business who are best fit to satisfy the public. If profit is abolished, chaos results.

3. The Anti-Profit Arguments

All the reasons advanced in favor of an anti-profit policy are the outcome of an erroneous interpretation of the operation of the market economy.

The tycoons are too powerful, too rich and too big. They abuse their power for their own enrichment. They are irresponsible tyrants. Bigness of an enterprise is in itself an evil. There is no reason why some men should own millions while others are poor. The wealth of the few is the cause of the poverty of the masses.

Each word of these passionate denunciations is false. The businessmen are not irresponsible tyrants. It is precisely the necessity of making profits and avoiding losses that gives to the consumers a firm hold over the entrepreneurs and forces them to comply with the wishes of the people. What makes a firm big is its success in best filling the demands of the buyers. If the bigger enterprise did not better serve the people than a smaller one, it would long since have been reduced to smallness. There is no harm in a businessman's endeavours to enrich himself by increasing his profits. The businessman has in his capacity as a businessman only one task: to strive after the highest possible profit. Huge profits are the proof of good service rendered in supplying the consumers. Losses are the proof of blunders committed, of failure to perform satisfactorily the tasks incumbent upon an entrepreneur. The riches of successful entrepreneurs is not the cause of anybody's poverty; it is the consequence of the fact that the consumers are better supplied than they would have been in the absence of the entrepreneur's effort. The penury of millions in the backward countries is not caused by anybody's opulence; it is the correlative of the fact that their country lacks entrepreneurs who have acquired riches. The standard of living of the common man is highest in those countries which have the greatest number of wealthy entrepreneurs. It is to the foremost material interest of everybody that control of the factors of production should be concentrated in the hands of those who know how to utilize them in the most efficient way.

It is the avowed objective of the policies of all present-day governments and political parties to prevent the emergence of new millionaires. If this policy had been adopted in the United States fifty years ago, the growth of the industries producing new articles would have been stunted. Motorcars, refrigerators, radio sets and a hundred other less spectacular but even more useful innovations would not have become standard equipment of most of the American family households.

The average wage earner thinks that nothing else is needed to keep the social apparatus of production running and to improve and to increase output than the comparatively simple routine work assigned to him. He does not realize that the mere toil and trouble of the routinist is not sufficient. Sedulousness and skill are spent in vain if they are not directed toward the most important goal by the entrepreneur's foresight and are not aided by the capital accumulated by capitalists. The American worker is badly mistaken when he believes that his high standard of living is due to his own excellence. He is neither more industrious nor more skillful than the workers of Western Europe. He owes his superior income to the fact that his country clung to "rugged individualism" much longer than Europe. It was his luck that the United States turned to an anticapitalistic policy as much as forty or fifty years later than Germany. His wages are higher than those of the workers of the rest of the world because the capital equipment per head of the employee is highest in America and because the American entrepreneur was not so much restricted by crippling regimentation as his colleagues in other areas. The comparatively greater prosperity of the United States is an outcome of the fact that the New Deal did not come in 1900 or 1910, but only in 1933.

If one wants to study the reasons for Europe's backwardness, it would be necessary to examine the manifold laws and regulations that prevented in Europe the establishment of an equivalent of the American drug store and crippled the evolution of chain stores, department stores, super markets and kindred outfits. It would be important to investigate the German Reich's effort to protect the inefficient methods of traditional *Handwerk* (handicraft) against the competition of capitalist business. Still more revealing would be an examination of the Austrian *Gewerbepolitik* (industrial policy), a policy that from the early eighties on aimed at preserving the economic structure of the ages preceding the Industrial Revolution.

The worst menace to prosperity and civilization to the material well-being of the wage earners is the inability of union bosses, of "union economists" and of the less intelligent strata of the workers themselves to appreciate the role entrepreneurs play in production. This lack of insight has found a classical expression in the writings of Lenin. As Lenin saw it all that production requires besides the manual work of the laborer and the designing of the engineers is "control of production and distribution," a task that can easily be accomplished "by the armed workers." For this accounting and control "have been *simplified* by capitalism to the utmost, till they have become the extraordinarily simple operations of watching, recording and issuing receipts, within the reach of everybody who can read and write and knows the first four rules of arithmetic." No further comment is needed.

4. The Moral Condemnation of the Profit Motive

As soon as the problem of profits is raised, people shift it from the praxeological sphere into the sphere of ethical judgments of value. Then everybody glories in the aureole of a saint and an ascetic. He himself does not care for money and material well-being. He serves his fellow men to the best of his abilities unselfishly. He strives after higher and nobler things than wealth. Thank God, he is not one of those egoistic profiteers.

The businessmen are blamed because the only thing they have in mind is to succeed. Yet everybody—without any exception—in acting aims at the attainment of a definite end. The only alternative to success is failure; nobody ever wants to fail. It is the very essence of human nature that man consciously aims at substituting a more satisfactory state of affairs for a less satisfactory. What distinguishes the decent man from the crook is the different goals they are aiming at and the different means they are resorting to in order to attain the ends chosen. But they both want to succeed in their sense. It is logically impermissible to distinguish between people who aim at success and those who do not.

Practically everybody aims at improving the material conditions of his existence. Public opinion takes no offense at the endeavours of farmers, workers, clerks, teachers, doctors, ministers, and people from many other callings to earn as much as they can. But it censures the capitalists and entrepreneurs for their greed. While enjoying without any scruples all the goods business delivers, the consumer sharply condemns the selfishness of the purveyors of this merchandise. He does not realize that he himself creates their profits by scrambling for the things they have to sell.

Neither does the average man comprehend that profits are indispensable in order to direct the activities of business into those channels in which they serve him best. He looks upon profits as if their only function were to enable the recipients to consume more than he himself does. He fails to realize that their main function is to convey control of the factors of production into the hands of those who best utilize them for his own purposes. He did not, as he thinks, renounce becoming an entrepreneur out of moral scruples. He chose a position with a more modest yield because he lacked the abilities required for entrepreneurship or, in rare cases indeed, because his inclinations prompted him to enter upon another career.

Mankind ought to be grateful to those exceptional men who out of scientific zeal, humanitarian enthusiasm or religious faith sacrificed their lives, health and wealth, in the service of their fellow men. But the philistines practice self-deception in comparing themselves with the pioneers of medical X-ray application or with nuns who attend people afflicted with the plague. It is not self-denial that makes the average physician choose a medical career, but the expectation of attaining a respected social position and suitable income.

Everybody is eager to charge for his services and accomplishments as much as the traffic can bear. In this regard there is no difference between the workers, whether unionized or not, the ministers and teachers on the one hand and the entrepreneurs on the other hand. Neither of them has the right to talk as if he were Francis d'Assisi.

There is no other standard of what is morally good and morally bad than the effects produced by conduct upon social cooperation. A—hypothetical—isolated and self-sufficient individual would not in acting have to take into account anything else than his own well-being. Social man must in all his actions avoid indulging in any conduct that would jeopardize the smooth working of the system of social cooperation. In complying with the moral law man does not sacrifice his own concerns to those of a mythical higher entity, whether it is called class, state, nation, race or humanity. He curbs some of his own instinctive urges, appetites and greed, that is his short-run concerns, in order to serve best his own—rightly understood or long-run—interests. He foregoes a small gain that he could reap instantly lest he miss a greater but later satisfaction. For the attainment of all human ends, whatever they may be, is conditioned by the preservation and further development of social bonds and interhuman cooperation. What is an indispensable means to intensify social cooperation and to make it possible for more people to survive and to enjoy a higher standard of living is morally good and socially desirable. Those who reject this principle as un-Christian ought to ponder over the text: "That thy days may be long upon the land which the Lord thy God giveth thee." They can certainly not deny that capitalism has made man's days longer than they were in the precapitalistic ages.

There is no reason why capitalists and entrepreneurs should be ashamed of earning profits. It is silly that some people try to defend American capitalism by declaring: "the record of American business is good; profits are not too high." The function of entrepreneurs is to make profits; high profits are the proof that they have well performed their task of removing maladjustments of production.

Of course, as a rule capitalists and entrepreneurs are not saints excelling in the virtue of self-denial. But neither are their critics saintly. And with all the regard due to the sublime self-effacement of saints, we cannot help stating the fact that the world would be in a rather desolate condition if it were peopled exclusively by men not interested in the pursuit of material well-being.

5. The Static Mentality

The average man lacks the imagination to realize that the conditions of life and action are in a continual flux. As he sees it, there is no change in the external objects that constitute his well-being. His world view is static and stationary. It mirrors a stagnating environment. He knows neither that the past differed from the present nor that there prevails uncertainty about future things. He is at a complete loss to conceive the function of entrepreneurship because he is unaware of this uncertainty. Like children who take all the things the parents give them without asking any questions, he takes all the goods business offers him. He is unaware of the efforts that supply him with all he needs. He ignores the role of capital accumulation and of entrepreneurial decisions. He simply takes it for granted that a magic table appears at a moment's notice laden with all he wants to enjoy.

This mentality is reflected in the popular idea of socialization. Once the parasitic capitalists and entrepreneurs are thrown out, he himself will get all that they used to consume. It is but the minor error of this expectation that it grotesquely overrates the increment in income, if any, each individual could receive from such a distribution. Much more serious is the fact that it assumes that the only thing required is to continue in the various plants production of those goods they are producing at the moment of the socialization in the ways they were hitherto produced. No account is taken of the necessity to adjust production daily anew to perpetually changing conditions. The dilettante-socialist does not comprehend that a socialization effected fifty years ago would not have socialized the structure of business as it exists today but a very different structure. He does not give a thought to the enormous effort that is needed in order to transform business again and again to render the best possible service.

This dilettantish inability to comprehend the essential issues of the conduct of production affairs is not only manifested in the writings of Marx and Engels, it permeates no less the contributions of contemporary pseudo-economics.

The imaginary construction of an evenly rotating economy is an indispensable mental tool of economic thinking. In order to conceive the function of profit and loss, the economist constructs the image of a hypothetical, although unrealizable, state of affairs in which nothing changes, in which tomorrow does not differ at all from today and in which consequently no maladjustments can arise and no need for any alteration in the conduct of business emerges. In the frame of this imaginary construction there are no entrepreneurs and no entrepreneurial profits and losses. The wheels turn spontaneously as it were. But the real world in which men live and have to work can never duplicate the hypothetical world of this mental makeshift.

One of the main shortcomings of the mathematical economists is that they deal with this evenly rotating economy—they call it the static state—as if it were something really existing. Prepossessed by the fallacy that economics is to be treated with mathematical methods, they concentrate their efforts upon the analysis of static states which, of course, allow a description in sets of simultaneous differential equations. But this mathematical treatment virtually avoids any reference to the real problems of economics. It indulges in quite useless mathematical play without adding anything to the comprehension of the problems of human acting and producing. It creates the misunderstanding as if the analysis of static states were the main concern of economics. It confuses a merely ancillary tool of thinking with reality.

The mathematical economics is so blinded by his epistemological prejudice that he simply fails to see what the tasks of economics are. He is anxious to show us that socialism is realizable under static conditions. As static conditions, as he himself admits, are unrealizable, this amounts merely to the assertion that in an unrealizable state of the world socialism would be realizable. A very valuable result, indeed, of a hundred years of the joint work of hundreds of authors, taught at all universities, publicized in innumerable textbooks and monographs and in scores of allegedly scientific magazines!

There is no such thing as a static economy. All the conclusions derived from preoccupation with the image of static states and static equilibrium are of no avail for the description of the world as it is and will always be.

Notes

1. Cf. Mises, *Human Action*, Yale University Press, 1949, pages 305–307; *Bureaucracy*, Yale University Press, 1994, Pages 40–73.

Values and Entrepreneurship in the Americas

Seymour Martin Lipset

Discussions of the requisites of economic development have been concerned with the relative importance of the appropriate economic conditions, rather than the presumed effects on varying rates of economic growth of diverse value systems. Much of the analysis which stems from economic thought has tended to see value orientations as derivative from economic factors. Most sociological analysts, on the other hand, following in the tradition of Max Weber, have placed a major independent role on the effect of values in fostering economic development.[1]

Although the evaluation of the casual significance of economic factors and value orientations has often taken the form of a debate pitting one against the other, increasingly more people have come to accept the premise that both sets of variables are relevant. Many economists now discuss the role of "noneconomic" factors in economic growth, and some have attempted to include concepts developed in sociology and psychology into their over-all frame of analysis. Sociologists, from Weber on, have rarely argued that value analysis could account for economic growth. Rather the thesis suggested by Weber is that, given the economic conditions for the emergence of a system of rational capital accumulation, whether or not such growth occurred in a systematic fashion would be determined by the values present. Structural conditions make development possible; cultural factors determine whether the possibility becomes an actuality. And Weber sought to prove that capitalism and industrialization emerged in Western Europe and North America because value elements inherent in or derivative from the "Protestant Ethic" fostered the necessary kinds of behavior by those who had access to capital; while conversely during other periods in other cultures, the social and religious "ethics" inhibited a systematic rational emphasis on growth.[2]

The general Weberian approach has been applied to many of the contemporary underdeveloped countries. It has been argued that these countries not only lack the economic prerequisites for growth, but that many of them preserve values which foster behavior antithetical to the systematic accumulation of capital. The relative failure of Latin American countries to develop on a scale comparable to those of North America or Australasia has been seen, in some part, as a consequence of variations in value systems dominating these two areas. The overseas offspring of Great Britain seemingly had the advantage of values derivative in part from the Protestant Ethic and from the formation of "New Societies" in which feudal ascriptive elements were missing.[3] Latin America, on the other hand, is Catholic, and has been dominated for long centuries by ruling elites who created a social structure more congruent with ascriptive social values.

Perhaps the most impressive comparative evidence bearing on the significance of value orientations for economic development may be found in the work of David McClelland and his colleagues, who have undertaken detailed content analyses of folk tales in primitive cultures and of children's storybooks in literate ones, seeking to correlate degrees of emphasis on achievement values in these books with rates of economic development.[4]

Among the primitive tribes, those which were classified as high in achievement orientation on the basis of the content of their folk tales were much more likely to contain full-time "business entrepreneurs" (persons engaged in a market economy) than those which were low. To measure the relationships in literature societies, McClelland and his coworkers analyzed the content of children's stories read by early primary school children during two time periods, 1925 and 1950, in many nations. Statistically significant correlations were found between this measure of achievement level for 1925 and the extent to which the increase in use of electrical energy (a measure of development) was higher or lower than the expected rate of growth for the period from 1925 to 1950, for a group of twenty-three countries. Similar findings are reported for forty countries for the period 1952 to 1958. As McClelland comments, the latter

finding is more striking than the earlier one, because many Communist and underdeveloped countries are included in the sample. Apparently N Achievement [his term for the achievement orientation] is a precursor of economic growth—and not only in the Western style type of capitalism . . . but also in economies controlled and fostered largely by the state.[5]

These findings are reinforced by two historical studies of the thematic content of various types of literature in England between 1400 and 1800, and in Spain between 1200 and 1700. In both countries, the "quantitative evidence is clear cut and a rise and fall of the n Ach level *preceded in time* the rise and fall of economic development."[6]

Striking differences have been found by McClelland and his collaborators in the value orientations of comparable samples of populations in less developed as compared with more developed countries. Thus, research in Brazil and the United States analyzing the achievement motivations of students aged nine to twelve, with the Brazilian sample drawn from São Paulo and Rio Claro, and the North American one from four northeastern states, reports that

Brazilian boys on the average have lower achievement motivation than their American peers . . . [that] upper, middle, and lower class Brazilians tend to have lower achievement motivation scores than Americans of a comparable class. *What is more startling is the finding that the mean score of Brazilian boys in any social class is lower than the motivation score of the Americans . . . whatever their class may be.*[7]

On a theoretical level, the systematic analysis of the relations of value systems to the conditions for economic development requires concepts which permit one to contrast the relative strength of different values. Thus far, the most useful concepts for this purpose are Talcott Parsons', which were elaborated on more fully in Chapter 2 of the work from which this chapter has been taken. These refer to basic orientations toward human action and are sufficiently comprehensive to encompass the norms affecting behavior within all social systems, both total societies and their subsystems, such as the family or the university.[8]

In his original presentation of the pattern variables, Parsons linked combinations of two of them: achievement ascription and universalism-particularism to different forms of existing societies. Thus the combination of universalism-achievement may be exemplified by the United States. It is the combination most favorable to the emergence of an industrial society since it encourages respect or deference toward others on the basis of merit and places an emphasis on achievement. It is typically linked with a stress on specificity, the judging of individuals and institutions in terms of their individual roles, rather than generally.[9]

If we turn now to studies focusing directly on the relationship between values and entrepreneurial behavior, the available materials from many Latin American countries seem to agree that the predominant values which continue to inform the behavior of the elite stem from the continued and combined strength of ascription, particularism, and diffuseness. Thomas Cochran has examined the literature from various American cultures, as well as from his own empirical research, and has conjectured that Latin American businessmen differ from North American ones in being:

1) more interested in inner worth and justification by standards of personal feeling than they are in the opinion of peer groups; 2) disinclined to sacrifice personal authority to group decisions; 3) disliking impersonal as opposed to personal arrangements, and generally preferring family relations to those with outsiders; 4) inclined to prefer social prestige to money; and 5) somewhat aloof from and disinterested in science and technology.[10]

Somewhat similar conclusions are reported in various surveys of managerial attitudes in various Latin American countries. These indicate that role specificity, i.e., separation of managerial from other activities, is relatively less common there than in more developed areas. A Latin American manager "is quite likely to devote part of his office hours to politics or family affairs."[11] Bureaucratic and competitive norms are comparatively weak. Personal characteristics are valued more than technical or organizational ability.[12]

Family particularism is much more common among Latin American business executives than among their counterparts in more developed nations. "Managers are frequently selected on the basis of family links, rather than specialized training." The entire managerial group often came from one family, and the "great majority of managers interviewed either considered this to be an appropriate arrangement under the conditions of their country, or had not thought of alternatives."[13] In Brazil, even the growth of large industries and corporate forms of ownership have not drastically changed the pattern. In many companies the modal pattern seems to involve an adjustment between family control and the rational demands of running a big business. Either the children or the in-laws of the old patriarch are technically trained, or the company involves a mixed system of family members working closely with technically educated nonfamily executives. However, the type of managers employed by family groups is known as *hombres de confianza* (men who can be trusted), and have been selected more for this quality than for their expertise.[14]

Most analysts of Latin American business behavior agree that a principal concern of the typical entrepreneur is to maintain family prestige; thus he is reluctant to give up the family-owned and managed type of corporation. Outsiders are distrusted, for the entrepreneur "is actually aware that any advantage that may be given to somebody outside his family is necessarily at the expense of himself and his own family."[15] From this evolves an unwillingness to cooperate with others outside of one's firm, and a defensiveness toward subordinates, as well as toward creditors, distributors, and others. Such assumptions about the behavior of others are, of course, self-maintaining, since people tend to behave as significant others define them, thus reinforcing a mutual state of distrust. In the family-dominated firms which constitute such a large proportion of Latin American business, non-family, middle-management personnel will often be untrustworthy and inefficient, since they will lack identification with firms in which "the 'road upward' is blocked by family barriers," and they are given limited responsibility.[16] This fear of dealing with outsiders even extends to reluctance to permit investment in the firm. For many Brazilian "industrialists, the sale of stocks to the public seems to involve . . . a loss of property." A Brazilian market research survey reported that 93 per cent of entrepreneurs interviewed stated "that they had never thought of selling stock in their enterprise."[17] As Emilio Willems points out, "such a typically modern institution as the stock-market in large metropolitan centres failed to develop because the most important joint-stock companies are owned by kin-groups which handle transfer of stock as a purely domestic matter."[18]

Although not statistically typical of Brazilian entrepreneurial behavior, some of the practices of the largest Brazilian firm, the United Industries, which in 1952 employed 30,000 workers in 367 plants, indicate the way in which family particularism and other traditional practices can continue within a massive industrial complex. In spite of its size, it is owned largely by the son of the founder, Francisco Matarazzo, Jr., and various family members. "The bleak and impeccably dressed Francisco, Jr., controls his empire from a pigskinpaneled office that is fitted with a buzzer system to summon top executives, who, on leaving, *must bow their way backward from his presence.*"[19]

The managers of foreign-owned companies, whether Brazilian or foreign are different in their behavior. They tend to emphasize a high degree of rationalization and bureaucratic practice in running their firms. Although they are interested in securing personal loyalty from subordinates, it is not the basic requirement for employment. The executive personnel are ambitious and competent employees, concerned with their personal success, and valuing ambition in themselves and others.[20]

The lack of a concern with national interests of institutional development among Latin American entrepreneurs has been related by Albert Hirschman to what he calls an "ego-focused image of change," characteristic of badly integrated, underdeveloped societies. Individuals in nations dominated by such an image, "not identifying with society," will view new developments or experiences simply as opportunities for self-aggrandizement. Although seemingly reflecting a desire to get ahead, this orientation, which inhibits efforts to advance by cooperation with others "is inimical to economic development, [since] . . . success is conceived not as a result of systematic application of effort and creative energy, combined perhaps with a 'little bit of luck,' but as due either to sheer luck or to the outwitting of others through careful scheming." And Hirschman, like other analysts of Latin America, sees the inability to trust and work with others as antithetical to effective entrepreneurship.[21]

A 1960-1961 analysis of the "technological decisions" of Mexican and Puerto Rican entrepreneurs, compared with foreign-born managers of subsidiaries of international companies, supports these interpretations.

Differences among foreign and national enterprises in ways of attracting capital, handling labor relations, arranging technical flexibility, channeling information internally and externally (and even willingness to respond to impertinent interview questions) are all consistent with an interpretation that the native entrepreneurs view society as probably malevolent and that the foreigners would have stayed home if they agreed [with this view of society].[22]

Attitudes to money similar to those frequently reported as characteristic of a nonindustrial, traditional population have been reported in studies of Latin American business leaders. A short-range rather than a long-range orientation is common: make money now "and then live happily—that is, idly—ever after."[23] This means that entrepreneurs frequently prefer to make a high profit quickly, often by charging a high price to a small market, rather than to maximize long-range profits by seeking to cut costs and prices, which would take more effort.[24] Although the concept of immediate profit "in industrial enterprise usually meant within one year or else after paying back initial loans," this does not reflect a Schumpeterian assumption about the reward or encouragement necessary to entrepreneurial risk-taking. Rather, the overwhelming majority of the Latin American businessmen interviewed argued that risk is to be avoided, and that "when there is risk there will not be new investment," that investment risk is a luxury which only those in wealthy countries can afford.[25] Reluctance to take risks may be related to the strong concern with family integrity, with viewing business property much like a family estate. "Where bankruptcy might disgrace one's family, managers will be more cautious than where it is regarded impersonally as expedient corporate strategy."[26]

It is important to note that these generalizations about the attitudes and behavior of Latin American entrepreneurs are all made in a comparative context. Those who stress their commitment to particularistic and diffuse values are generally comparing them to North Americans, or to a model of rational, bureaucratic, competitive enterprise. However, as contrasted with other groups within their societies, Latin American entrepreneurs, particularly those involved in large-scale enterprise, tend to be the carriers of "modern" values. Thus one analysis of Colombian businessmen points out: "They are urban people in a rural country. In a relatively traditionally oriented society, their values are rational and modern."[27]

The impact of Latin American orientations to entrepreneurial behavior has been summed up in the following terms:

Comparatively the Latin American complex: 1) sacrifices rigorous economically directed effort, or profit maximization, to family interests; 2) places social and personal emotional interests ahead of business obligations; 3) impedes mergers and other changes in ownership desirable for higher levels of technological efficiency and better adjustments to markets; 4) fosters nepotism to a degree harmful to continuously able top-management; 5) hinders the building up of a supply of competent and cooperative middle managers; 6) makes managers and workers less amenable to constructive criticism; 7) creates barriers of disinterest in the flow of technological communication; and 8) lessens the urge for expansion and risk-taking.[28]

···

Economic Growth and the Role of the "Deviant" in Anti-Entrepreneurial Cultures

The argument that Latin American values are antithetical to economic development can, of course, be pitted against the fact that a considerable amount of economic growth has occurred in many of these countries. Clearly, in the presence of opportunity, an entrepreneurial elite has emerged. The logic of value analysis would imply that the creation or expansion of roles which are not socially approved in terms of the traditional values should be introduced by social "deviants." This hypothesis is basic to much of the literature dealing with the rise of the businessman in different traditional societies.

In his classic analysis of economic development, Joseph Schumpeter pointed out that the key aspect of entrepreneurship, as distinct from being a manager, is the capacity for leadership in innovation, for breaking through the routine and the traditional.[29] From this perspective the analysis of the factors which resulted in the rise of an entrepreneurial group leading to economic growth under capitalism is comparable to the study of the conditions which brought about anticapitalist revolutionary modernizing elites of various countries in recent decades. The approach which emphasizes the theory of deviance assumes that those who introduce change must be deviants, since they reject the traditional elite's ways of doing things.[30] As Hoselitz puts it, "a deviant always engages in behavior which constitutes in a certain sense a breach of the existing order and is contrary to, or at least not positively weighted in the hierarchy of existing social values."[31] In societies in which the values of the dominant culture are

not supportive of entrepreneurial activity, someone who is relatively outside of the social system may have a particular advantage in entering an entrepreneurial activity. The restraints upon entrepreneurial activity imposed by the network [of social relations] would be less effective against such a person. Thus, an immigrant may be outside of many of the networks of the nation and freer to engage in entrepreneurial activity.[32]

in other words, freer socially to deviate.

If we assume, in following up such generalizations, that within the Americas the value system of Latin America has discouraged entrepreneurial activity, while that of the English-speaking Protestant world of the United States and Canada has fostered it, then a comparative study of the backgrounds of entrepreneurs in these countries should reveal that those of Latin America are recruited disproportionately from sociological "deviants," while those of North America should come largely from groups which possess traits placing them inside the central structures of the society. An examination of the research data bearing on this hypothesis indicates that it is valid.

In many countries of Latin America, members of minority groups, often recent immigrants, have formed a considerable section of the emerging business elite. "In general it appears that immigrants took the lead in establishing modern manufacturing before World War I [in Latin America]."[33] Recent studies in various countries reveal comparable patterns. Frequently, these new entrepreneurs come from groups not known for their entrepreneurial prowess at home, such as the Arabs and the Italians, although Germans and Jews are also among those who are to be found in disproportionate numbers in business leadership. A study of Mexican business leaders found that of 109 major executives, 26 had foreign paternal grandfathers; among the "32 outstanding business leaders in Mexico, 14 reported a foreign paternal grandfather."[34] Analysis of the backgrounds of 286 "prestigious" entrepreneurs, taken from the Argentine *Who's Who*, indicates that 45.5 per cent were foreign born.[35] However, many of those born in Argentina are "among the first generation born in the country."[36] Classifying the sample by origins, Imaz reports that only 10 per cent came from the traditional upper class, and they, as in many other Latin American countries, are concentrated in industries which processed agricultural products, so that their role in industry is an extension of their position as a landed class. Among the rest, almost all are of relatively recent foreign origin.[37] Data from a survey of the heads of 46 out of the 113 industrial establishments in Santiago, Chile, which employ more than 100 workers indicate that 76 per cent of them are immigrants or the children of immigrants.[38] An earlier study of the Chilean middle class reports that as of 1940 the overwhelming majority of the 107,273 foreign born in the country were in middle-class, largely self-employed occupations.[39] In Brazil also "the majority of industrial entrepreneurs are immigrants or descendants of relatively recent immigrants."[40] Thus in São Paulo, 521 enterprises out of 714 were owned by men in these categories.[41] In the other economically developed states, Rio Grande do Sul and Santa Catarina, "almost 80 per cent of the industrial activities . . . were developed by people of European immigrant extraction."[42]

Similar patterns may be found in the less developed and more traditional countries. Thus, in a recent study of Peru, François Bourricaud traces in detail the continued control of members of the ancient oligarchy over much of the economic life of the country, their maintenance in much of agriculture and traditional business and banking of the *patron* system, and family and clan control. However, in the new and risky enterprises, those which have produced the new rich of the country, one finds many recent immigrants.[43] In Colombia, like Peru, a country with relatively little immigration, a study of the members of the National Association of Industrialists reports "that in 1962, 41 per cent of a sample of business leaders in Bogotá were immigrants from other countries."[44] In Panama, in 1940 before the decree "nationalizing" commerce, "nearly 45% of the men actively engaged in commerce or manufacturing were foreigners."[45]

The various studies of the backgrounds of the Latin American entrepreneurial elite indicate that on the whole they are a well-educated group, the majority of them in most countries are university graduates. And a study of the origins of students at the University of São Paulo suggests that much of the separation in career orientations between those of native background and others takes place while in school. Thus, the proportion of students of non-Brazilian background is higher among the students than in the population of the city; only 22 per cent are of purely Brazilian descent. Even more significant is the fact that students with a higher proportion of foreign-born ancestors tend to enroll in the "modern" faculties, such as economics, engineering, pharmacy, and the like. Those with preponderantly Brazilian family backgrounds are more likely to be found in the more traditional high-prestige schools such as law and medicine. And the author of this study comments:

The children of foreign-born parents . . . are more inclined to take advantage of the new opportunities in occupations which have emerged from the economic development of the city of São Paulo. One should consider the fact that in Brazil, the schools of Law and Medicine convey special social prestige to their students. It is easier for a not completely assimilated adolescent of foreign descent to ignore that prestige than for a "pure" Brazilian.[46]

Similarly, at the University of Chile, the School of Physics suffers from low prestige, "which diminishes the attractiveness of the field. . . ." A recent study of Chilean university students reports:

Who, then, are the students in this school? Why have they rejected the natural and well-formed paths of career choice? The most obvious are those who are immigrants or sons of immigrants—primarily German refugees and Italian emigrés . . . A second and frequently overlapping group is composed of students who are critical of the traditional alternatives.[47]

Immigrant and minority groups have shown comparable abilities to take advantage of, or to create, opportunities in other parts of the underdeveloped world. Thus in sub-Saharan Africa, Arabs, Indians, and to a lesser extent Chinese, form a large part of the commercial world. In Southeast Asian countries, Chinese constitute almost the entire business community; Indians were important in Burmese economic life before they were expelled. It should be noted that it is not only "immigrants" who have been disproportionately successful. Minority religious groups such as Christians have entered the universities in relatively large numbers in various Asian states, even where they are a tiny minority in the entire population. In Indonesia, for example, more than 15 per cent of the new students entering Gadjah Mada University in 1959–1960 were Christians, although few people adhere to Christianity. In general in Southeast Asia, there is

a relatively high proportion of youth from minorities enrolled in universities and [they have a] . . . reputation as better academic achievers than youth from majority elites. Such minorities . . . include the Karens and the Indians in Burma, the Chinese in Thailand, the "burghers" in Ceylon, the Bataks and Chinese in Indonesia, and other Christians in all these countries.[48]

The creative role of the deviant, or the outsider, has in part been conceptualized by the term "marginal man," who for various reasons is partially outside the culture in which he is living, is less socially integrated in the structures which maintain conformity, and is therefore not so committed to the established values of the larger order. Hence men of this sort are more likely to be receptive to possibilities for change.[49] An analysis of those who successfully took advantage of the opportunity to shift the use of land in the vicinity of São Paulo from subsistence agriculture to lucrative commercial crops (mainly the growth of eucalyptus for firewood) illustrates this process. More than 90 per cent of those who became small-scale, relatively well-to-do entrepreneurs were recent settlers in the area, "immigrants or children of immigrants . . . or members of a small but flourishing Protestant sect (the *Evangelistas*) . . ."

Almost all of the recent settlers were as poor as the *caboclos* [the native, lowest status rural dwellers] when they arrived. They managed to see new alternatives when they arose, to buy up small plots of land and gradually increase their holdings, mostly at the expense of the *caboclos* . . . It is worth testing . . . the proposition that *participation in newly valued activities among members of low economic and prestige classes varies inversely with length of residence in a locality.* Old settlers at depressed levels have inherited habits of belief, a morality and expectation of role rights and obligations associated with their statuses . . . that they are only slowly adaptable in the presences of altered opportunities. One of the most striking occurrences in the changing situation within the *municipio* under consideration is the fact that several *caboclos* sold or were seeking to sell their properties to prospective entrepreneurs, and then turned around and hired their labor out for wages.[50]

The traits which are often associated with economic innovation lead their bearers to be frowned upon or even hated by those who adhere to conventional traditions of the society, or who resent the success of others. Thus in Brazil, Gilberto Freyre reports that many of non-Portugese descent have

shown a lack of finer moral scruples which has given many of them the reputation of being morally or ethically inferior . . . [Their actions which lead to success in politics and business] are given as an example of the fact that the sons of "immigrants" are morally inferior to the sons of old Brazilian families as political leaders, businessmen. and industrial pioneers. Of course, sons of immigrants who follow such careers are freer than the members of old and well-known families from certain moral controls that act upon men deeply rooted in their towns or countries or regions.[51]

It is indicative of the extent to which Latin Americans identify entrepreneurial or commercial abilities as "alien" to their tradition and values that ethnic myths are invented to explain the success of those of native background who do succeed. Thus both in Colombia, where the citizens of Antioquia have evidenced entrepreneurial abilities far exceeding those of other sections of the country, and in Mexico, where residents of Monterrey have shown comparable skills, the story is widely believed that both groups are descended from *maranos*, secretly practicing Jews who publically changed their religion after 1492.[52] These stories have been disproven by historical research, but the fact that many accept them as gospel tells much about attitudes toward entrepreneurship. The same factors may be involved in Gilberto Freyre's report, citing various writers, that the major center of business enterprise in Brazil, São Paulo, is "probably the nucleus of the Brazilian population with the largest strain of Semitic blood."[53]

The logic of the analysis suggested here, however, does not agree with the thesis that innovating entrepreneurs in developing societies must be recruited disproportionately from the ranks of social "deviants," as some have interpreted data such as these. Rather, it points with Weber to the fact that many minority groups have not shown such propensities. Clearly the Catholic minorities in England, or other Protestant countries, were much less likely than the general population to engage in entrepreneurial activity. In his analysis of the divergent consequences for economic behavior of Protestantism and Catholicism, Max Weber pointed to the greater business accomplishments of the Protestant *majority* as compared to the Catholic minority in Germany.[54] The key issue, as Weber has indicated, is the value system of the various groups involved. Latin America and some other less developed traditional societies are so vulnerable to economic cultural "deviants" because the predominant values of the host culture are in large measure antithetical to rational entrepreneurial orientations. Where national values support economic development, the Weberian emphasis on value would suggest that the innovating business elite would be drawn not from deviants but rather from the "in-group," from persons with socially privileged backgrounds.

An examination of the social characteristics of North American business leaders in both Canada and the United States bears out these assumptions. Compared with most other nations in the world, the United States and English-speaking Canada have been among the most hospitable cultures to economic development. The Protestant ethic as fostered by denominations spawned of Calvinist and Arminian origins strongly influenced all classes in these societies, the United States somewhat more than Canada. And a study of the business leaders of the United States in 1870, the period of its take off into industrial development, indicates that 86 per cent of them came from "colonial families" settled in the country before 1777. Only 10 per cent were foreign-born or the children of foreign-born.[55] More than 98 per cent of the post-Civil War business elite were Protestant. Although the proportions of those of non-Anglo-Saxon, non-Protestant, and foreign-born parentage have increased over the years, they have always remained considerably lower than their proportion in the population as a whole.[56] Canadian data are available only for the post-World War II period, but it should be noted that Canada's emergence as a major industrial society largely dates from the war. Previously its economy somewhat resembled that of Argentina, being largely dependent on agricultural exports. The Canadian case is extremely interesting since the country is composed of two separate cultures—English Protestant and Latin Catholic. And a comprehensive report on the Canadian elite shows a clear-cut picture: where cultural values congruent with entrepreneurship are ascendant, the business elite will be recruited largely from the dominant culture group, not from minorities. Thus those of Anglo-Saxon Protestant background are overrepresented, while those of Latin, Catholic, and minority origins are underrepresented.

An examination of the social origins of the economic elite shows that economic power belongs almost exclusively to those of British origin, even though this ethnic group made up less than half of the population in 1951. The fact that economic development in Canada has been in the hands of British Canadians has long been recognized by historians. Of the 760 people in the economic elite, only 51 (6.7 per cent) could be classified as French Canadians although the French made up about one-third of the population in 1951. . . . There were no more than a handful who . . . could be classified as top-ranking industrialists in their own province.

Ethnic groups of neither British nor French origin, which made up about one-fifth of the general population, were hardly represented at all. There were six Jews (.78 per cent of the sample as opposed to 1.4 per cent of the general population) . . . [O]nly 78 (about 10 per cent) were Catholic . . . 43 per cent of the population in 1951 was Catholic.[57]

In seeking to account for the low representation of French Canadians in the economic elite, even within Quebec, John Porter points out that the evidence does not fit the assumption that it is largely a result of the greater power of the British Canadians. For French Canadians do quite well in other power structures, e.g., politics, the intellectual world, and religion. French weakness in industry seems related to elements in their culture comparable with those in much of Latin America.

The varying origins of the business elites of the American nations clearly indicate that "out" groups, such as ethnic-religious minorities, are given the opportunity to innovate economically when the values of the dominant culture are antithetical to such activities. Thus, the comparative evidence from the various nations of the Americas sustains the generalization that cultural values are among the major forces which affect the potentiality for economic development.

Although I have focused on the direct effects of value orientations on the entrepreneurial behavior of certain groups, it should be clear that any given individual or group supports the values of his or its effective social environment. Although national values may discourage entrepreneurial activities, ethnic or religious subgroups, or links to foreign cultures may encourage them for those involved. One explanation of the comparative success of members of some minority groups in Latin America, such as the Anglo-Argentines, is that they continue to respect their ancestral national culture more than that of their host society. The fact that many ethnic minorities in some Latin American nations continue to send their children to schools conducted in their ancestral language and to speak it at home attests to their lack of acceptance of national culture and values.

The key question basically is whether one is involved in a network of social relations which sustain or negate a particular activity. Viscount Mauá, Brazil's great nineteenth-century economic innovator, although a native Brazilian, was adopted while in his early teens by an English merchant in Rio de Janeiro; his biography clearly indicates that he became an "alien" within his native culture, that English became his "native" language, the one in which he thought and wrote his private thoughts."[58] Conversely, as we have seen, many successful entrepreneurs are drawn away from total commitment to their business life by an involvement in social networks and reference groups which supply more prestige than their vocation. One of Argentina's most successful entrepreneurs, who was an immigrant, built up a complex network of industrial companies, took the time to study at the university, accepted an appointment as an associate professor of Economics and Industrial Organization at the University of Buenos Aires, when he was fifty years of age, sought to secure a regular chair three years later, and bought a 6,600-acre *estancia*, on which he spent much time.[59] To facilitate the emergence of a given new role in a society, it is necessary to help create social recognition for it within meaningful subgroups. The leaders of Meiji Japan have provided an example of the way in which one nation did this. To raise the prestige of the business class,

. . . social distinctions [were] granted to the presidents and main shareholders of the new companies. The presidents were given the privilege of the sword and family name. They were appointed by the government, as officials were. A president could walk directly into the room of a government official while common people had to wait and squat outside the building. Many other minor privileges were granted.[60]

It is important to recognize that the introduction of new activities by those linked to "foreign" cultures or minority religions is not simply one of the various ways to modernize a society. Innovations which are associated with socially marginal groups are extremely vulnerable to political attack from those who would maintain traditional values. Consequently efforts at economic modernization, changes in the educational system, or social customs which are introduced by "outsiders," may have much less effect in modifying the central value system than when they are fostered by individuals who are members of the core group, as occurred in Meiji Japan.

···

Notes

1. For an excellent general discussion of the relationships between values and economic behavior written in a Latin-American context see Thomas C. Cochran, "Cultural Factors in Economic Growth," *Journal of Economic History*, 20 (1960), 515–530; see also John Gillin, "Ethos Components in Modern Latin American Culture," *American Anthropologist*, 57 (1955), 488–500.
2. Max Weber, *The Protestant Ethic and the Spirit of Capitalism* (New York: Scribner, 1935).
3. See Louis Hartz, *The Founding of New Societies. Studies in the History of the United States, Latin America, South Africa, Canada, and Australia* (New York: Harcourt, Brace, & World, 1964).
4. David C. McClelland, *The Achieving Society* (Princeton: Van Nostrand, 1961), pp. 70–79; McClelland, "The Achievement Motive in Economic Growth," in Bert F. Hoselitz and Wilbert E. Moore (eds.), *Industrialization and Society* (Paris: UNESCO-Mouton, 1963), pp. 79–81.
5. McClelland, "The Achievement Motive in Economic Growth," p. 79.
6. Juan B. Cortés, "The Achievement Motive in the Spanish Economy between the 13th and 18th Centuries," *Economic Development and Cultural Change*, 9 (1961), 159, 144–163; Norman N. Bradburn and David E. Berlew, "Need for Achievement and English Industrial Growth," *Economic Development and Cultural Change*, 10 (1961), 8–20.
7. Bernard Rosen, "The Achievement Syndrome and Economic Growth in Brazil," *Social Forces*, 42 (1964), 345–346 (emphasis in original).
8. See Talcott Parsons, *The Social System* (Glencoe: The Free Press, 1951), pp. 58–67 and *passim*; "Pattern Variables Revisited," *American Sociological Review*, 25 (1960), 58–67; and "The Point of View of the Author," in Max Black (ed.), *The Social Theories of Talcott Parsons* (Englewood Cliffs, N.J.: Prentice-Hall, 1961), pp. 319–320, 329–336. I have discussed the pattern variables and attempted to use them in an analysis of differences among the four major English-speaking

nations. See S.M. Lipset, *The First New Nation* (New York: Basic Books, 1963), pp. 207–273.

9. See Parsons, *The Social System*, pp. 182–191.

10. Thomas C. Cochran, *The Puerto Rican Businessman* (Philadelphia: University of Pennsylvania Press, 1959), p. 131; see also pp. 151–154 and Cochran, "Cultural Factors in Economic Growth," *op. cit.*

11. Albert Lauterbach, "Managerial Attitudes and Economic Growth," *Kyklos*, 15 (1962), 384. This study is based on interviews with managers in eight countries.

12. Eduardo A. Zalduendo, *El empresário industrial en América Latina: Argentina* (Mar del Plata, Argentina: Naciones Unidas Comisión Económica para América Latina, 1963. E/CN12/642/Add 1), p. 46

13. Albert Lauterbach, "Government and Development: Managerial Attitudes in Latin America," *Journal of Inter-American Studies*, 7 (1965), 202–203; see also L. C. Bresser Pereira, "The Rise of Middle Class and Middle Management in Brazil," *Journal of Inter-American Studies*, 4 (1962), 322–323.

14. Fernando H. Cardoso, *El empresário industrial en América Latina: Brasil* (Mar del Plata, Argentina: Naciones Unidas Comisión Económica para América Latina, 1963, E/CN/12/642/Add. 2), pp. 25–26; for a description of the way in which *hombres de confianza* were incorporated into a major Argentinian industrial complex see Thomas C. Cochran and Ruben E. Reina, *Entrepreneurship in Argentine Culture. Torcuato Di Tella and S.I.A.M.* (Philadelphia: University of Pennsylvania Press, 1962), pp. 266–268; see also Emanuel de Kadt, "The Brazilian Impasse," *Encounter*, 25 (September 1965), p. 57, for a summary of Brazilian evidence on this point.

15. Thomas Roberto Fillol, *Social Factors in Economic Development. The Argentine Case* (Cambridge: M.I.T. Press, 1961), pp. 13–14.

16. *Ibid.*, p. 61.

17. Cardoso, *El empresário industrial en América Latina*, p. 31; Siegel, *op. cit.*, pp. 405–408. Robert J. Alexander, *Labor Relations in Argentina, Brazil, Chile* (New York: McGraw-Hill, 1962), pp. 48–49.

18. Emilio Willems, "The Structure of the Brazilian Family," *Social Forces*, 31 (1953), 343.

19. Richard M. Morse, *From Community to Metropolis, A Biography of São Paulo, Brasil* (Gainesville: University of Florida Press, 1958), p. 229 (my italics).

20. Cardoso, *El empresário industrial en América Latina*, pp. 35–39.

21. Albert O. Hirschman, *The Strategy of Economic Development* (New Haven: Yale University Press, 1958), pp. 14–19.

22. W. Paul Strassmann, "The Industrialist," in John Johnson, (ed.), *Continuity and Change in Latin America* (Stanford: Stanford University Press, 1964).

23. Lauterbach, "Managerial Attitudes and Economic Growth," p. 379; Fillol, *op. cit.*, pp. 13–14.

24. One report on Panama comments that "their business philosophy . . . is that of the gambler or plunger. . . . They prefer low volume and high markup; they want

quick, large profits on small investment. They cannot think in pennies," John Biesanz, "The Economy of Panama," *Inter-American Economic Affairs*, 6 (Summer, 1962), 10.

25. Lauterbach, "Government and Developments," pp. 209–210. Powell, *op. cit.*, pp. 82–83.

26. Strassmann, *op. cit.*, p. 173.

27. Aaron Lipman, *El empresário industrial en América Latina: Colombia* (Mar del Plata, Argentina: Naciones Unidas Comisión para América Latina, 1963. E/CN/12/642/ Add. 4), p. 30; Guillermo Briones, *El empresário industrial en América Latina: Chile* (Mar del Plata, Argentina: Naciones Unidas Comisión para América Latina, 1963. E/CN/12/642/Add. 3), p. 35. It should be noted that most of the above generalizations about Latin American entrepreneurs are based on interview data. And as Fernando Cardoso points out, such data may tend to be at variance with actual behavior. Many of those interviewed are well educated and aware of the nature of a modern entrepreneurial outlook. Cardoso suggests that the actual behavior of those interviewed is much less modern and rational than would be suggested by the interviews, Cardoso, *op. cit.*, pp. 47–48, 59.

28. Cochran, "Cultural Factors in Economic Growth," pp. 529–530.

29. Joseph Schumpeter, *The Theory of Economic Development* (New York: Oxford University Press, 1961), pp. 74–94.

30. Bert Hoselitz, "Main Concepts in the Analysis of the Social Implications of Technical Change," in Hoselitz and Moore, *op. cit.*, pp. 22–28.

31. Hoselitz, *Sociological Aspects*, p. 62; Peter T. Bauer and Basil S. Yamey, *The Economics of Underdeveloped Countries* (Chicago: University of Chicago Press, 1957), pp. 106–112.

32. Louis Kriesberg, "Entrepreneurs in Latin America and the Role of Cultural and Situational Processes," *International Social Science Journal*, 15 (1963), 591.

33. Strassmann, *op. cit.*, p. 164.

34. Raymond Vernon, *The Dilemma of Mexico's Development* (Cambridge: Harvard University Press, 1963), p. 156.

35. Imaz, p. 136.

36. *Ibid.*, see also Gino Germani, "The Strategy of Fostering Social Mobility," in Egbert De Vries and José Medina Echeverría (eds.), *Social Aspects of Economic Development in Latin America* (Paris: UNESCO, 1963), pp. 223–226; and Eduardo A. Zalduendo. *El empresário industrial en América Latina: Argentina* (Mar del Plata, Argentina: Naciones Unidas Comisión Económica para América Latina, 1963), p. 10. The census of 1895 reported that 84 per cent of the 18,000 business establishments were owned by foreign-born individuals. Cochran and Reina, *op. cit.*, p. 8.

37. Imaz, *op. cit.*, pp. 138–139.

38. Guillermo Briones, *El empresário industrial en América Latina: Chile* (Mar del Plata. Argentina: Naciones Unidas Comisión Económica para América Latina, (1963). p. 10.

39. Julio Vega, "La clase media en Chile," in *Materiales para el estudio de la clase media en la América latina* (Washington, D. C.: Pan American Union, 1950), pp. 81–82, as cited in Frederick P. Pike, *Chile and the United States, 1880–1962* (Notre Dame: University of Notre Dame Press, 1962), p. 279.

40. Benjamin Higgins, "Requirements for Rapid Economic Development in Latin America: The View of an Economist," in Egbert de Vries and José Medina Echeverría (eds.), *Social Aspects of Economic Development in Latin America* (Paris: UNESCO, 1963), p. 169.

41. Emilio Willems, "Immigrants and Their Assimilation in Brazil," in T. Lynn Smith and Alexander Marchant (eds.), *Brazil. Portrait of Half a Continent* (New York: Dryden Press, 1951), p. 217. These apparently are largely from Italian, German, Jewish, and Lebanese backgrounds. See also Pereira, *op. cit.*, p. 316; Richard Morse, "São Paulo in the Twentieth Century: Social and Economic Aspects," *Inter-American Economic Affairs*, 8 (Summer, 1954), 21–23, 44; George White, "Brazil: Trends in Industrial Development," in Simon Kuznets, Wilbert E. Moore and Joseph J. Spengler (eds.), *Economic Growth: Brazil, India, Japan* (Durham: Duke University Press, 1955), pp. 57, 60–62.

42. Wagener, *An Introduction to Brazil* (New York: Columbia University Press, 1971), p. 87.

43. François Bourricaud, *Pouvoir et societé dans le Pérou Contemporain* (Paris: Armand Colin, 1967), Chapter I.

44. Aaron Lipman, "Social Backgrounds of the Bogotá Entrepreneur," *Journal of Inter-American Studies*, 7 (1965), 231.

45. John Biesanz, "The Economy of Panama," *Inter-American Economic Affairs*, 6 (Summer 1962), p. 9.

46. Bertram Hutchinson, "A origem sócio-econômica dos estudantes universitários," in Hutchinson (ed.), *Mobilidada e Trabalho* (Rio de Janeiro: Centro Brasileiro de Pesquisas Educacionais Ministério de Educaçáo e Cultura, 1960), p. 145.

47. Myron Glazer, *The Professional and Political Attitudes of Chilean University Students* (Ph.D. thesis: Department of Sociology, Princeton University, 1965), 78–79.

48. Joseph Fischer, "The Student Population of a Southeast Asian University: an Indonesian Example," *International Journal of Comparative Sociology*, 2 (1961), 225, 230.

49. See Robert Park, *Race and Culture* (Glencoe: The Free Press, 1950), pp. 345–392; Everett Stonequist, *The Marginal Man* (New York: Russell & Russell, 1961).

50. Bernard J. Siegel, "Social Structure and Economic Change in Brazil," in Kuznets, Moore and Spengler (eds.), *op. cit.*, pp. 399–400 (emphases in the original).

51. Gilberto Freyre, *New World in the Tropics* (New York: Vintage Books, 1963), p. 161.

52. Strassmann, *op. cit.*, p. 166.

53. Gilberto Freyre, *The Masters and the Slaves: A Study in the Development of Brazilian Civilization* (New York: Alfred A. Knopf, 1963), p. 36. Freyre does not evaluate this thesis; rather, as with many other tales concerning Jewish traits and abilities,

he seems to be gullibly accepting. "The farmers with a deep love for the land and a thorough knowledge of agriculture were sometimes abused or exploited in Brazil by those of their fellow countrymen whose passion was for commercial adventure and urban life—most of them probably Jews" (Freyre, *New World in the Tropics*, p. 50).

54. Weber, *op. cit.*, pp. 38–46.
55. Suzanne Keller, *The Social Origins and Career Lines of Three Generations of American Business Leaders* (Ph.D. dissertation: Department of Sociology, Columbia University, 1953), pp. 37–41.
56. See S. M. Lipset and Reinhard Bendix, *Social Mobility in Industrial Society* (Berkeley: University of California Press, 1959), pp. 137–138.
57. Porter, *op. cit.*, pp. 286–289.
58. Anyda Marchant, *Viscount Mauá and the Empire of Brazil* (Berkeley: University of California Press, 1965), pp. 81, 83, 208–209, 241.
59. Cochran and Reina, *op. cit.*, pp. 147–51. It is worth noting that his two sons studied for their Ph.D.s abroad, and that both are professors, one in economics and the other in sociology.
60. Johannes Hirschmeier, *The Origins of Entrepreneurship in Meiji Japan* (Cambridge: Harvard University Press, 1964), p. 35.

6 The Modernization of Entrepreneurship

Alexander Gerschenkron

Most people will agree that the emergence of modern entrepreneurs has been an integral part of the great economic transformation known as the historical process of industrialization. The question I wish to consider is twofold: (1) What were some of the distinguishing "modern" features of industrial entrepreneurs, particularly in the early stages of that transformation? (2) How did those characteristics come about? In dealing with these questions, I shall be thinking mostly of the area of European industrializations, which should give us sufficient scope both for generalization and differentiation.

There are many ways to define an entrepreneur, and scholars have been arguing for a long time, often heatedly and confusingly, about the relative merits of this or that definition. For our purposes, it is sufficient to say that entrepreneurs are people whose task it is to make economic decisions. Naturally, there is hardly any economic activity that does not involve decisions. The man who spends his working day sorting out big and small oranges is involved in a continual process of decision making. But there are big and small decisions. The big decisions refer, for instance, to what shall be produced and how it shall be produced; what goods should be bought and sold, where and when, and at what price; whether output shall be kept constant, or whether it should be increased or reduced; and so on. All such decisions are entrepreneurial decisions.

There have been entrepreneurs in this sense at all levels in all periods of economic history. A peasant in a backward agrarian country who decides when to start plowing, what to sow, and when to reap makes entrepreneurial decisions. So did a Venetian merchant in the sixteenth century who decided what kinds of spice he should buy in the East and then carry across the Alps and whether Augsburg in Germany or Lyons in France was the most promising market for his wares. Very broadly speaking, such decisions are not different from those of an executive or group of executives in a modern American plant—say, in Wilmington, Delaware—who has decided to concentrate on the production of a new vibration-absorbing material or from those of an automobile factory in Detroit that has decided to add a small car to its list for the next fall.

But, despite a certain similarity of all entrepreneurial decisions performed in all times and climes, we all know intuitively that the differences among the cases just mentioned are enormous. Entrepreneurship on a medieval farm or in a craft-guild dominated artisan shop in Perth or Strassburg of the fifteenth century, or even in a large wool-processing mill in Flanders of the same period, was, in many important respects, not comparable to the entrepreneurial activities in the modern age, from the eighteenth century onward, when rapid industrial progress, spreading from one country to another, became the characteristic feature of economic life, primarily in Europe and North America. Let us try to make some of those differences explicit.

For one, modern industry requires large amounts of fixed capital. In other words, it demands construction of buildings and acquisition of machinery whose contribution to output must be utilized over a considerable period of time. This means that an industrial entrepreneur must look far ahead into the future. His time horizon must be high. To be sure, even in preindustrial times, there were merchants who loaded and dispatched ships on long sea voyages, waiting for many months, perhaps a year, for the reappearance of the vessel and the sale of the return cargo. But neither was even such a relatively long stretch of time, during which the merchant's capital was tied up in his risky venture, comparable with the average life span of modern machinery nor did transactions of this sort ever begin to assume, within the total volume of goods and services produced, a significance even remotely comparable to the share of industrial output in the national income of a modern industrial country.

With the heightening of the time horizon, also, something else happened that was at least indirectly related to it. Industrial entrepreneurship became a lifetime occupation. A merchant in preindustrial days who had accumulated a sizable fortune would be strongly tempted to say farewell to his mercantile pursuits, acquire a landed estate, and attempt to elevate himself into the ranks of the gentry. A modern industrial entrepreneur in Germany or England often liked to see his children marry into a noble family; he was sensitive to the social prestige and the amenities of a country house, but in valuing those things he did not cease to be what he was, that is to say, a modern industrialist.

Connected with what has been just said and partly following from it, there were other differences. The connections between a merchant and his customers were often fleeting affairs, once-over transactions. Hence the urge was strong, indeed, to deceive the buyer as to the quantity and quality of what he purchased. *Caveat emptor*—it is the buyer's lookout—warned the Roman law, and the idea of dishonesty became fully associated in the popular mind with trade and traders. Various etymologies reflect the connection. In German, for instance, the verb for exchange is "tauschen," but if two little dots are put over the "a," the word becomes "täuschen" and means to deceive. In French, the similarity between "truc" and "troque"—trick and barter—reflects the same connection; and the etymological origins of the very term "barter" in English, as in several Romance languages (whence the word came), point to cheating and deception. In Russian, an often quoted popular proverb used to advise: "If you do not cheat, you will not sell," which only repeated in a pithy form something that had been said time and again since the days of Ecclesiasticus.

It is not claimed, of course, that the modern industrial entrepreneur was at all times a paragon of impeccable probity. He was not. But it is fair to say that the permanence of his activities, the closeness of relations with the customer established by installation of equipment and delivery of spare parts, the very fact that so much of modern industrial output was sold, not to an amorphous mass of anonymous buyers, but to other industrial entrepreneurs—all these factors necessitated a much more scrupulous attitude toward the buyer. Furthermore, and no less importantly, modern industry was largely based on a well-developed credit system. The price at which a modern entrepreneur got his capital disposition—that is, the interest rate—had to be relatively low, which it could not be if the service of the debt included high risk premiums. If there was to be an industrial entrepreneurship, its standards of commercial honesty perforce had to be high.

And, finally, modern industry was inseparable from technological and organizational progress. New ways of doing things were continually emerging. Very few modern industrial entrepreneurs were truly great innovators, in the sense of being the first to apply a revolutionary, unprecedented technique. Most of them were imitators, a part of what Professor Schumpeter called the "secondary wave," which spread a new signal innovation over broad segments of the industrial economy. But, as everyone who ever worked inside a modern enterprise knows, the distinction between the innovator and the imitator is a very uncertain one. Every imitation requires a great deal of energy to overcome the inertia, to abandon the accustomed way of doing things. It raises a million technical and economic problems that must be solved. And they will not be solved unless there are alert minds to welcome the new and to see the solutions and strong wills to carry the tasks to successful termination. No comparable problems, no comparable pressures to tackle them had existed before the advent of modern industry.

Thus, modern industrial entrepreneurship has specific features that could not have been easily discovered to any similar extent and in any similar intensity in the preindustrial periods. We can now turn to an attempt to deal with the second question we asked earlier. How did these features come about? What is the historical process in the course of which entrepreneurship became modernized so that the proper functioning of modern industrial enterprises could be assured? This is a question that used to exercise—and still does exercise—very many scholars, and a considerable literature of the subject has been created. As I see it, the most interesting problem in this discussion is related to the broader problem of prerequisites of modern industrialization. This calls for a brief digression.

According to a widespread view, which has been particularly popularized and dramatized by Professor Rostow, the times of rapid industrial progress— the great spurts of industrialization—were preceded, country by country, by a more or less protracted period during which the "preconditions" of modern industrialization were created. Such "preconditions" or "prerequisites" are taken then so seriously that some scholars are willing to speak of "necessary and sufficient" preconditions, just as in a logical definition one speaks of conditions that are necessary and sufficient in order to define a given object. Thus, it would be argued, certain agrarian reforms involving a change in the system of land tenure, abolition of restrictions on the personal freedom of the peasantry, and increase in the productivity of agriculture were a necessary prerequisite for the subsequent industrialization.

Or, it would be asserted, particularly by Marxian writers, that a previous accumulation of wealth over considerable historical periods was a necessary precondition for financing the capital investment of entrepreneurs during great industrial spurts. In either case, the inference is that where such preconditions were not established, no industrialization could take place. But such arguments and assertions, presented as propositions of ubiquitous validity, do not stand up under the test of confrontation with the empirical material, even within the relatively restricted area of Europe of the nineteenth century. In important cases, considerable industrial development took place despite the absence of the allegedly necessary prerequisites, however logical the sequence of events scheduled in an abstract scheme may appear to the ear of an uncritical listener. For, analytically speaking, the attempt to convert logical conditions into historical preconditions is hardly more than a sleight of hand, a coarse analogy that insinuates into the argument the concept of historical necessity, which is something that lies on the other side of the line separating scientific pursuits from metaphysical speculation and political propaganda. And, historically speaking, the concept of necessary prerequisites fails because economic life is pregnant with many alternative solutions, so that in countries where the so-called necessary prerequisites were not present, various substitutions for them have been developed in the very course of industrial development. This was true of the lack of proper agrarian reforms, as it was true of the lack of preindustrial accumulations of wealth, even though Soviet scholars are still busy trying to find the "original accumulation of capital" in every country that ever went through the process of industrialization.

This brief discussion of prerequisites of modern industrialization has a direct bearing on the problem of creation of modern entrepreneurship with which we are concerned. Is creation of modern entrepreneurship a prerequisite of modern industrial development? And is this creation itself a protracted historical process, in the course of which the prerequisites for modern entrepreneurship are created? The first of these questions is very often based on a misunderstanding. When people say, "Of course entrepreneurs are a prerequisite of industrialization. How else could you industrialize without them?" they are again confusing preconditions with conditions. Entrepreneurs use capital and hire labor in order to produce industrial goods, but this is the very stuff industrialization is made of; these are the very conditions of any reasonable definition of industrialization. But what we are talking about is not a definition or a description of industrialization, but a historical process, more or less lengthy, in the course of which the prerequisites of modern entrepreneurship are created. And this, indeed, is a real problem that calls for some more extended discussion.

It is not difficult to argue that in *some* countries, things may be discovered that make us think that certain features of modern entrepreneurship have roots in a fairly remote historical past of those countries. Take, for instance, the experience of master artisans in towns dominated by the craft guilds in the late Middle Ages. There is no doubt that in many cases the institutional framework of the craft guilds—their rules and regulations and their ideology—served to inform the guild's membership with the instinct of workmanship, with the pride of the quality of their work, and, by the same token, with the idea of honesty in dealing with their customers; that is to say, with a characteristic that we found before to be very germane to modern industrial entrepreneurship. All this began centuries before the year 1517, in which Martin Luther started the Reformation by nailing his theses on the door of a church at Wittenberg.

But there is no reason for us to deny that Protestantism, particularly in its Calvinist branch, tended to promote the attitudes of honesty and thrift, lifetime dedication to one's work, and interest in innovation, even though it remains entirely a moot question to what extent it was the doctrines of Protestant churches rather that the adherence to a penalized minority, be it the Huguenots in France or the Nonconformists in England, that determined the attitudes. Nor is it clear that people did not tend to espouse Protestant persuasions *because* they had certain attitudes. Still, it is quite reasonable to say that in *some* countries, in the course of their preindustrial history, certain habits of thinking originated from several sources that provided a propitious climate for the exercise of modern entrepreneurial attitudes. There is nothing wrong in considering, therefore, those habits of thinking *where they actually occurred* as prerequisites for the emergence of modern entrepreneurship in the countries concerned. Yet we must be very wary of generalizing such findings and regarding them in any way as *necessary* prerequisites.

It is precisely this, however, that is done by several sociologists and psychologists who are trying to develop general theories of modern industrialization with particular stress on the entrepreneurial element therein. One body of such theories tends to emphasize the dominant value system of the society within which modern industrial development takes place. It is argued that unless the social value system that prevails is such as to bestow social approval upon the role played by the entrepreneurs, they cannot succeed, and a modern industrial development will not occur or at the very best will be hopelessly retarded. Thus, a change in the values of the society as a whole is regarded as a necessary prerequisite for the deployment of modern entrepreneurial activities and, by the same token, for industrialization. Generalizations of this sort are in obvious conflict with the facts.

Economic history, within the European framework, provides sufficient cases where magnificent entrepreneurial activities were conducted in the face of a dominant value system that was violently opposed to such activities and continued regarding the working of the land that brought forth the blessing of its fruit as the only economic activity that was pleasing in the eyes of the Lord. Theories of this sort are wrong, but they are not entirely useless because they do help to raise the interesting question of how the lack of social approval was overcome or, to put it differently, what substitutions, if any, were found for the absence of social approval as a prerequisite of modern entrepreneurship.

There is an even more comprehensive theory for the emergence of modern entrepreneurship, which combines social and psychological factors and tries to establish the necessary prerequisites in a grandiose historical scheme comprising many centuries. It is argued that modern entrepreneurship requires replacement of the "authoritarian personality" of the "traditional society" by the "innovational personality" of the modern society. In either case, the personality is said to be the product of the methods of child raising in the four or five years after birth. It is further claimed that the change is brought about by the withdrawal at some point of status respect from the "common folk" by an upper group. Thereby the traditional society is disrupted, and the common folk spend many hundreds of years in a state of "retreatism." During that period, the parent-child relationship experiences profound changes and the methods of child rearing are fundamentally altered so that in the end—in the very long end—the innovational entrepreneurial personalities emerge from the lap of the society, and modern economic growth can begin.

It is easy to see the difference between the two theories just sketched. While the former considers that what the entrepreneurs need is just approval of their activities by the dominant value system of the society, the latter envisages a thoroughgoing transformation of personality formation in the society at large as a prerequisite for the emergence of entrepreneurs. But this is not the only difference. Theories that center on "social approval" can be criticized, because, in many societies, stratified and complex as they are, approval by some groups is paralleled by disapproval by others; and a single system of dominant social values is hardly more than a fiction. Still, the historical record shows societies where the traditional agrarian beliefs have survived fairly unchanged into the modern period and are accepted, at least superficially, by groups that are rather far removed from the tillage of the land. Russia in the late nineteenth century may serve as an important example of such a society.

But the point is that with respect to this theory, it is still possible to get some empirical data in order to see how well or how badly it squares with the facts. On the other hand, the theory claiming basic changes in the methods of infant rearing and in parent-child relations over long centuries defies any empirical testing, which would require, within the meaning of the theory, psychoanalyzing huge samples of dead men who are unable to tell their tales on an analyst's couch. All we can say is that by looking at the treatment of infants and very young children in a number of countries that had gone through very successful periods of industrialization and have produced considerable entrepreneurial figures (such as Germany or Sweden before World War I), it is very difficult to discover any striking progress in this respect. Thus, the theory is little more than a figment of speculative imagination, and this particular attempt to view the emergence of modern entrepreneurship as a very prolonged process requiring creation of certain definite necessary prerequisites may be shelved as altogether unconvincing.

When general theories fail us, we must return to a more modest, but also more effective and more enlightening way of looking at the creation of modern entrepreneurship. What has been said before about substitutions in other areas of industrial development for missing prerequisites should give us some guidance also with respect to the problem of entrepreneurship. As we take a closer look at those substitutions, we are able to say that the need for them and also their complexity were not randomly distributed about the map of nineteenth-century Europe. On the contrary, there was a rather clear relationship: The more backward a country was on the eve of its big industrial spurt, the fewer in it were those elements that might be reasonably regarded as prerequisites of industrialization and the more widespread and intensive was the use of substitutes for such prerequisites. Another way of putting it is to say that in the more advanced countries, their preindustrial history presented a rich and colorful picture, while their industrial history was relatively simple. By contrast, the preindustrial landscape of backward countries was rather barren, but the history of their industrializations much more complex and variegated, precisely because it was shot through and dominated by substitutions of many kinds.

Let us apply this generalization to the field of modern industrial entrepreneurship. A backward country such as, say, Russia in the last decades of the nineteenth century no doubt suffered from many disabilities in this respect, as it did in others. The number of able entrepreneurs was relatively small, their time horizon limited, their standards of commercial honesty deplorably low; and entrepreneurial activities were viewed with suspicion by both the mass of the populace and the intelligentsia. In a less backward country, such as, for instance, Germany in the middle of the last century, most of those negative features were present (even though in an attenuated form, and, in particular, the tradition for honesty in commercial dealings was fairly high, probably as a result of the craft-guile experience in the past centuries).

One cannot go amiss, therefore, in saying that in either country the prerequisites for modern entrepreneurship were either nonexistent or present to a quite insufficient extent. And yet Germany in the second half of the century went through a magnificent industrial upsurge that brought her abreast of England, the "workshop of the world." Russia before 1914 did less well than Germany in absolute terms, but its great spurt of industrial development in the eighteen-eighties and particularly the eighteen-nineties is a matter of historical record, and the rate of industrial growth it achieved in those years was far above anything ever attained by Germany. How could that happen in the face of the disabilities just mentioned? The answer is that in either country men succeeded in developing specific substitutions.

The inadequacy in the numbers of available entrepreneurs could be remedied or substituted for by increasing the size of plant and enterprise above what otherwise would have been its optimal size. In Germany, the various incompetencies of the individual entrepreneurs were offset by the device of splitting the entrepreneurial function: the German investment banks—a powerful invention, comparable in its economic effects to that of the steam engine—were in their capital-supplying functions a substitute for the insufficiency of the previously created wealth willingly placed at the disposal of entrepreneurs. But they were also a substitute for entrepreneurial deficiencies. From their central vantage points of control, the banks participated actively in shaping the major—and sometimes even not so major—decisions of the individual enterprises. It was they who very often mapped out a firm's paths of growth, conceived farsighted plans, decided on major technological and locational innovations, and arranged for mergers and capital increases. To some extent, although less effectively, similar pressures were brought to bear upon Russian entrepreneurs by the Imperial bureaucracy—that is to say, first and foremost, the ministry of finance, which also in other respects provided substitutions similar to those incarnated in the German banks and altogether pursued very similar policies of industrial expansion. In Russia, of course, the quantitative and qualitative deficiencies of entrepreneurs were also alleviated by importation from abroad of foreign entrepreneurial talent, although the over-all extent thereof should not be exaggerated.

And, finally, also the lack of social approval of entrepreneurs, the existence of sentiments and values unfavorable to them, was overcome to a considerable extent by the fact that the power of the state—the judicial machinery as well as the police and the army—were used to protect the entrepreneurs and their interests from social forces that were hostile to them, to say nothing of many statutory provisions that pursued the same purpose.

The conclusion, therefore, must be that the processes of modern industrialization are much too variegated to allow of simple generalizations. Those processes in general vary with the degree of backwardness of the countries concerned. And this is as true of modern entrepreneurship as of other factors of industrial progress. It is simply factually incorrect to hold that in countries in which the historical roots of modern entrepreneurship were weak or even nonexistent, no industrial development could take place. It could, and did, in fact, occur because human ingenuity discovered a number of ways to substitute for the missing and allegedly necessary prerequisites.

But something else is of great importance. With the spurt of industrialization also begins a rapid process of transformation of entrepreneurs while their ranks are speedily increasing. For, more important than all historical prerequisites of modern entrepreneurship is the effect on entrepreneurs of being passed through the great training school of industrialization. Few things are more surprising than the great change in values, attitudes, and standards experienced by the Russian entrepreneurs over just one generation between the eighteen-eighties and the years preceding World War I. An astonishing process of modernization took place, not before, but in the very course—and as a consequence—of a spurt of modern industrialization.

These two conclusions, taken together, do help us understand the historical record of European industrializations in its graduated diversity. But, in addition, they also contain a message of some encouragement for the currently underdeveloped countries. In their case, too, the lack of entrepreneurial talents and the absence of historical roots of modern entrepreneurship need not be an obstacle that cannot be overcome by ingenuity, dedication, and, above all, a reasonably short passage of time after a serious industrialization effort has been launched. There is, of course, no such thing as "industrialization gratis." Industrialization always was and will remain a costly business. Still, one may perhaps express the hope that in the currently underdeveloped countries, "substitutions" will be discovered that may prove less unpleasant and more equitable than were some of the devices applied in the formerly backward countries of Europe in the nineteenth century.

7 Economic Spheres in Darfur[1]

Fredrik Barth

This paper contains a concrete account of the main structure of the Mountain Fur economy. It also pursues an argument of greater generality concerning the use of the concept of spheres in the analysis of an economic system. Concretely, I try to show in what sense the flow of goods and services is patterned in discrete spheres, and to demonstrate the nature of the unity within, and barriers between, the spheres. I point to the discrepancies of evaluation that are made possible by the existence of barriers between spheres, and to the activities of entrepreneurs in relation to these barriers. To give the material, I also have to give a sketch of some important institutional complexes that constitute especially significant factors in determining the structure of the economy. Basic to the whole analysis is the view that the demarcation of spheres must be made with respect to the total pattern of circulation of value in an economic system, and not merely with reference to the criterion of direct exchangeability.

Physical Background

Jebel Marra is a mountain massif located about 13° N. and 24° E., close to the centre of the African continent. The area is relatively self-contained, and is isolated by deserts to the North and East, arid and sparsely populated plains to the West, and the Bahr el Arab to the South. From a plain of about

2,000 to 3,000 ft in altitude the mountain rises to nearly 10,000 ft and creates an environment rather different from the surrounding savannah belt of the Sudan: despite a dry season from October till May there are perennial streams and stands of large forest. The mountain, particularly on its lower slopes, supports a dense population of Fur-speaking hoe agriculturalists, living in hamlets or villages of up to about 500 habitants (for general background, see Lampen, 1950; Lebon & Robertson, 1961).

Subsistence

The crops cultivated on the Jebel Marra form two agricultural complexes: summer rainland crops, and winter crops on irrigated land. The predominant staple is bullrush millet (*dukhn*) grown on dry terraces and completely dependent on summer rains. Millet fields are prepared and hoed during May–June, the seed is sown as the rains start, and repeated weeding is required until harvest-time in September. The fertility of the soil is prolonged by periodic fallow periods, but extended use leads to impoverishment and final indefinite abandonment to bush.

In rocky fields, and inside the compounds, tomatoes are also grown in the summer, following their introduction by Egyptian troops some hundred years ago. Occasionally, wheat is also cultivated on the dry terraces in the summer, as a final crop before the fields are laid fallow. Low terraces by streams, on the other hand, are artificially irrigated and used for the cultivation of onion, garlic, and wheat in the dry winter season. Whatever manure is available is used on these fields; and they are not normally ever left fallow. In the summer, special crops of chillies, herbs, and potatoes are grown in these fields without irrigation. Scattered among the compounds are also a fair number of cotton bushes. To an increasing extent, irrigated lands are also being developed as orchards, containing limes, lemons, oranges, mangoes, papayas, guava, and bananas.

Of domestic animals, the most important is the donkey, on which the population depends for practically all heavier transport. Pigeons are kept by most families; goats are kept in small numbers for meat, with a negligible yield of milk. Cattle are kept by some, mainly for re-sale; they are not locally bred or milked. Swarming termites, locusts, wild figs, edible grasses, honey, etc. are collected and contribute significantly to subsistence.

Institutional Forms

Besides this geographical and ecological basis for the Fur economy, there are also some basic institutions in Fur culture which may be regarded as primary, and from which forms in the economy may be derived. These relate to the size and composition of households, the forms of ownership of land, values concerning labour and reciprocal obligations, and the organization of weekly markets.

(a) First, the units of management need to be identified—the unit which organizes production and consumption and holds a separate 'purse'. In this respect, Fur society is extreme and simple, in that every individual has his own farm plots, his own grain stores, and his separate budget. Domestic units are not primary economic units; though marriage implies certain reciprocal obligations and services, it does not imply a joint household.

Husband and wife each cultivate separate fields and store their produce in separate, adjoining grain bins in their joint hut. Neither spouse is allowed to take grain from the other's store, nor are they obliged to give any foodstuffs to each other. The economic obligations in a marriage mainly concern services: the wife must provide the husband with female labour, especially for cooking and brewing beer (from the millet he supplies from his stores); the husband in return provides the wife and her issue with clothing—predominantly, and formerly almost exclusively, spun and woven by the man himself. Some spouses elect to work one or several fields jointly, and most do assist each other somewhat in cultivation; but this does not alter their basic independence as units of economic management.

Children are fed by their mother from her stores. Boys remain with their mother till the age of 8–10 years; then they leave their home village to live as wandering scholars, attending the schools of Koranic teachers (*Fakki*) and supporting themselves by begging. After three, four, or five years they pass a religious examination with the last teacher they have been attending, and return to their village, where they start cultivating fields of their own. Until marriage, they depend on a mother or a sister for the female labour of cooking and brewing. The father, and other close relatives, are obliged to assist the boy in providing a bride-price; but he alone is responsible for his own needs. Daughters, on the other hand, remain at home until marriage and, until that time, may either work together with their mother or cultivate separate fields but pool their produce.

In other words, economic activities are characteristically pursued by single individuals, though in a matrix of obligations, mainly of providing labour, to persons in specified kinship positions.

(b) This means that every person must obtain individual access to the basic means of production: land. The rights over land are institutionalized as follows:

Territorial rights are associated with descent groups of a non-unilineal kind—large blocks of kinsmen, with an endogamous tendency, often spoken of as patrilineal in form but in fact of a much looser structure allowing membership 'through our grandmothers'. This looseness in structure is possible only because the groups are non-corporate—their joint rights are vested in a title-holder, who represents the kin group in question and is responsible for its joint estate.

His responsibility consists in essence in allocating usufruct rights to fields. Such rights are given to individuals and are usually retained by them until use of the land is discontinued—i.e. the usufruct rights do not lapse when fields are left fallow in a systematic rotational pattern, only when they are abandoned. However, inside a community, it is regarded as every individual's right to obtain the land necessary for subsistence. When need arises, and when there is no unused land available, usufruct rights may be revoked and some land taken from those who have plenty and given to those who are in need. The title-holder is the person with the power to revoke such rights and redistribute the land of his descent group. Because the argument from relative need is accepted, he will be obliged to allocate fields alike to members and non-members of the 'owning' group; and the distribution of plots shows little correlation with the distribution of the users' descent-group rights.

The rights of the cultivator as *user* as distinct from *owner* are expressed in the symbolic prestation of one pot of beer to the title-holder after each harvest—a custom that is not consistently practised but is universally regarded as correct and proper. No rent in kind or services, or other obligations, are required from the cultivator.

The more shifting nature of cultivation on the unirrigated lands assures a fair circulation of usufruct rights in the population. There is some tendency for children to take over the dry farms cultivated by their parents, especially for daughters to succeed on the death of their mother; but there does not seem to be any question of the lineal transfer of usufruct rights over several generations. In the case of the irrigated lands, however, no periods of disuse intervene, and usufruct rights come up for redistribution only on the death of the cultivator. The argument of need is used to justify a reallocation of rights to small onion plots, but most of the irrigated land tends to remain in the same hands, and there is an increasing tendency, with the growth of irrigation agriculture, for title-holders to monopolize this resource (see below, p. 157).

None the less, the main picture remains that land, as the main productive resource, is made available to all without any significant rent or other counter-presentation.

(c) With every individual so characteristically constituting a separate unit of management for economic purposes, the predominant pattern of labour tends to be one where every person uses his or her own time to work for the direct satisfaction of his own needs. By Mountain Fur conventions, it is furthermore shameful to work for wages in the local community, though a few men have experience as migrant labour elsewhere. None the less, there are institutionalized opportunities for both symmetrical and asymmetrical transactions involving labour, and there are some kinship and neighbourhood obligations which commit fractions of a person's time and effort.

The Fur institution that facilitates labour exchanges is the beer party. This takes several forms, exemplified by informal reciprocal help, work parties with many participants, and house-building parties. In the simplest form, two or more friends may decide to work together for company, in which case they jointly cultivate each other's field in turn, he whose field is being cultivated providing a pot of beer for their joint consumption. Larger work parties may be arranged in a similar way, but without the obligation of reciprocity: a man will announce his intention a few days in advance, have a large amount of beer prepared, and ask his friends and neighbours to come to the work party. Besides those who are invited, any person who wishes may join the party and drink beer in return for working. In these cases, the beer must be plentiful and is supposed to compensate for the work being expended; when the beer is finished, the work party disperses. Finally, house-building has a communal and reciprocal character; a day is announced for the work—first one for the women, who plaster the hut walls, then for the men, who build the roof and thatch it. On the appointed day, kinsmen and neighbours who have been invited are obliged to come, bringing with them the materials that are needed in the building. Large amounts of beer must again be provided by the host, and other persons may join in the work, in which case they pay a 'fine' of 2 piastres (about five pence) for not having brought building materials.

Close kin of the house-builders, especially brothers and sisters, also assist by supplying one or several pots of beer at such occasions, as well as by working themselves and egging on the other guests to work well. A person's freedom to allocate his own labour is thus restricted by some commitments; and his opportunities for disposing of it on the Fur labour-for-beer labour market are restricted by the number of occasions offered by work parties in the local or adjoining villages. These are, however, very frequent in the larger communities; and with the above reservations one may say that essentially, a person's time is his own, to use for labour in his own fields or to exchange for beer on a local, relatively open, labour market. The reciprocities that limit a person's freedom on this market derive from obligations of mutual sociability, i.e. they are associated with the 'party' and not the 'work' aspect of the work party. Labour is seen as adequately compensated for in beer, and there is no restriction that each person's input of work and of beer into the system should be equivalent. This fact, together with the considerable degree of freedom allowed persons in choosing partners and occasions for transactions, means that we are dealing with a *market* for the exchange of labour and beer. The fact that persons also enjoy the 'party' aspect of the work party does not affect this argument.

(d) Fourthly, the Fur have a well-organized system of market-places, which facilitates a great number of economic exchanges. The medium of exchange used at these markets is, and has for a long time been, money issued in the Nile valley. Previously, cloth may have served as a medium of exchange.

Each market-place is active one day, or in a few cases two days, a week. They are spaced at a distance of 15 to 20 km from each other on the perimeter of the mountain, so that every community is within walking distance of at least one market-place, enabling people to attend the market and return home the same day. Particularly in the slack agricultural seasons, markets are visited by large numbers of people, amounting to several hundred through much of the day.

Villagers bring all varieties of agricultural produce to the market-place, though millet, being very bulky and heavy in proportion to its value, is rarely marketed. Most producers bring only small quantities, since they sell only to obtain cash for specific purchases, though some, anticipating a good price or because of acute need, may also bring larger quantities to sell in bulk. Occasionally, cattle or goats are also brought for sale by their owners. Craftsmen, who form a small, discrete population of male smiths and female potters, also bring their products for sale, and the smith sets up a small anvil for incidental repairs. Finally, travelling pedlars, most of them Arabs but some Fur, set up shops in booths or on mats from which they sell imported industrial consumer goods, particularly cloth, utensils, sugar, etc.

Numerous middlemen appear and mediate the flow of trade while seeking profit, either by speculating in rising prices through the day, or by accumulating products in bulk for transport and re-sale at communication entrepots 50 to

100 km away. Each will specialize in one or two products—garlic, onions, dried tomatoes, or wheat—buying from the individual producers and accumulating for re-sale on the spot, or for transport. Middlemen also buy the livestock, slaughter and partition it, and sell it in small portions to local consumers. Some sales of fresh vegetables, fruits, and other garden produce also take place directly from producer to individual consumer.

Some women also brew beer and bring it for sale in the market-place. Though there is no dearth of buyers, especially as the afternoon wears on, the sale of beer is regarded as immoral and the women who do so are looked upon as immodest. This may be both because the making of beer is an intimate female service appropriate only in a close, domestic context, and because beer, as in a work party, is a festive idiom of cooperation and companionship and not appropriate as an object of commercial bargaining.

In the market-place, then, individual villagers are able to exchange their agricultural products for tools and utensils, cloth, and a variety of other consumer goods which they do not themselves produce. They do so by freely switching between the statuses of buyer and seller, and must deal with factors of supply and demand and with fluctuating prices measured in a monetary currency.

Economic Spheres

The facts presented so far invite the use of a concept of economic spheres. They suggest the existence of two discrete spheres of exchange in the Mountain Fur economy: one that embraces a large variety of material items, including also a monetary medium, and is associated with the market-place facilities; and another that exists for the exchange of labour and beer. The two spheres are separated by the sanction of moral reprobation on conversions from labour to cash and from beer to cash. They thus would seem to fit well the definition of spheres given in Bohannan and Dalton (1965, p. 8), i.e. they each constitute a set of freely exchangeable material items and services. They also would seem to exhibit the feature of hierarchical ranking: conversions in the one direction are frowned upon; i.e. the sphere containing labour and beer would be regarded as the higher, that associated with the monetary medium the lower.

However, such a model is inconsistent with some of the empirical material. Thus some highly prestigious items of wealth, such as swords, are obtained in the cash sphere. Furthermore, the bridewealth for a wife is composed predominantly of cash and items from the cash sphere, and this would indicate a high rather than a low rating for the cash sphere.

Nor can one argue that these are the effects of breakdown associated with the introduction of money. Cash had been used in the Fur area long before colonial times, and the system described here is in this sense a traditional and relatively stable one in which cash is an integral part. If a concept of spheres is to be useful for the analysis of this system, the hierarchical assumption is best dismissed.

What is more, it is difficult to relate the labour–beer sphere significantly to the cash sphere by any patterned channels of conversion. On a more fundamental level, I would argue that a separation of spheres based on the criterion of exchangeability alone gives an unnecessarily inadequate representation of the structure of the economy. The concept of spheres has much greater analytic utility if it relates to all forms of circulation and transformation of value, whether by exchange, production, inheritance, or other means.

I shall therefore try to depict all the standard choices of alternative allocations of resources open to the units of management in the Fur economy, and to delimit the significant spheres with respect to the total pattern of circulation or flow of value. The units of management are single individuals, whose basic problem is to transform their own efforts into a range of items that satisfies their own consumption profile. The institutional forms I have described above may be regarded as the main facilities or means at their disposal to achieve this transformation; and the description of the economy is simplified by the fact that persons have approximately equal access to these facilities.[2] It is further simplified by the fact that, as members of a relatively homogeneous society, their habits and appetites are similar, except for the male-female differences which mainly reflect reciprocal obligations in marriage.

An attempt to aggregate the allocations of the whole population of management units, giving a picture of the *village* economy, is therefore unusually simple in this case. In the cash sphere, as long as there is no shortage of land, the village economy can be represented as the *sum* of decisions of management units, since these units do not seriously compete for resources and their activities do not have any great impact on market prices. Aggregating the decisions in the millet–beer–labour sphere is more difficult, since any transformation by a management unit of its beer into labour presupposes the presence of persons willing to exchange their labour for beer. The simplest procedure is to assume a certain supply of labour and beer and to see how the allocation decision of one member unit might affect the availability of these forms of value on the market, and possibly also affect the relative 'price' of each as measured in terms of the other. Some of these problems are taken up below in the section on management and

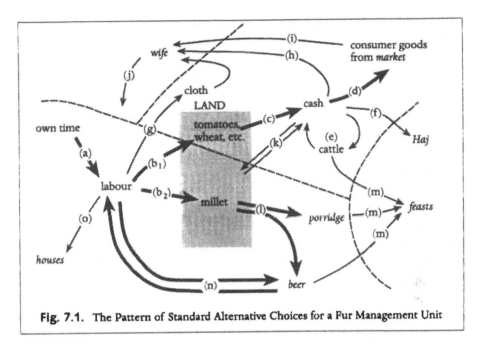

Fig. 7.1. The Pattern of Standard Alternative Choices for a Fur Management Unit

stratification (pp. 153–154) and in connection with new uses of labour and possible responses to this (pp. 154–155).

The pattern of standard alternative choices for a Fur management unit can thus be represented as in Figure 7.1. With the reservations noted above, this may simultaneously be regarded as a model of the village economy as a whole. The remainder of this paper is essentially an exposition of Figure 7.1 followed by a discussion of its implications.

Patterns and Alternatives of Allocation

(a) The input into the economic system is the person's own time, used as labour. All self-supporting persons in the society must and do have the basic skills necessary to cultivate the main varieties of crops, and to trade.

(b) To start production, a person next needs access to land. This is obtained either from a parent or close relative with plenty, or from one of the title-holders in the village. Every individual needs to obtain plots of several kinds, suitable for different crops and uses. A configuration of sizes and types of farm implies an allocation of labour to alternative products: millet, and some onions, for basic subsistence, and readily marketable crops such as tomatoes, wheat, garlic, onions for cash needs. The balance struck between these two categories of products depends on the person's obligations: women, especially those with small children, concentrate more of their effort on millet, while men, especially those with plural wives, have greater need for cash to meet the obligations of clothing their families, and to save towards bridewealth for themselves or their sons.

In the course of the year, every person will need to cultivate at least one farm in each category. One may choose to distribute the labour so that most work falls in the rainy season on millet and tomato farms, leaving much time in the winter for threshing, house-building, and trading, or to allocate the labour more equally between summer and winter crops. Individual skills and preferences, and established usufruct rights to irrigated land, will influence these allocations.

(c) Tomatoes and wheat are produced exclusively for the market, since they are used hardly at all as food by the Fur; garlic, onions, etc. are partly for own consumption and partly for sale. The weekly market-places are available to transform these products into cash. Cash again is used to obtain a variety of consumer goods from the market.

(d) In 1964 the annual cash needs of men in the prime of their lives was estimated by informants, and reported for themselves, to be about £8; that of women only £1, £2, or £3. The rate of consumption in the cash sector has, however, been increasing rapidly over the last years.

Also purchased for cash are tools—a relatively minor expense; donkeys, of which every man wishes to own one, and young cattle. These last are bought from Baggara Arabs when they are about two years old, for about £6.

(e) They are then kept for some years, tended by the children of the owner, till they are ready for sale as meat on the market at the age of 5 or 6 years, when they bring about £11 or £12. No breeding or milking takes place, but the manure that accumulates where the animals are stabled at night is valued and used in the irrigated fields.

Livestock thus constitute a possible field of investment, if one has the children to tend them. Otherwise, the possibilities for investment of cash in productive enterprises are extremely restricted. Cash savings are useful as a store of wealth to secure against crop failure or sickness in the future; and amounts up to several hundred pounds are accumulated by some. But for most people who dare not use such savings for speculation and trade on the market, they remain inactive wealth, buried in a pot under the floor of the hut, and are not used as capital.

(f) A few villagers chose, usually fairly late in life, to use such savings to perform the *Haj* pilgrimage to Mecca. The returned Haji tends to take little part in village affairs, and so this conversion of wealth to rank has limited consequences in the Fur system.

(g) Men may somewhat reduce their cash expenditure by weaving cloth for their families rather than buying it. Cotton for such thread may be bought, or produced by the man himself. He spins it by hand while walking or sitting idle, and weaves it on a horizontal loom which, though nominally it may be owned by someone, is in fact used communally by all.

(h) A major cash expense is that of bridewealth, involving various traditional prestations to the wife and to her bilateral kinsmen totalling about £35 in value. This expense is borne by the groom and his father. Most of it is given in purchasable objects (donkeys, cattle, swords, cloth) or their cash equivalents. Two lengths of cloth must, however, be produced by the groom himself and given to the bride's parents. For the rest of their married life, the husband is further obliged to provide his wife, and small children, with

(i) basic necessities from the market.

(j) In return, the wife must provide female services of sex, cooking, and brewing of beer.

(k) The other main kind of crop is millet. Some people find that they, in their initial allocation of labour (b), have struck an inadequate balance between production of cash crops and of millet. This can be corrected in the market-place: not infrequently, people run short of millet and have to buy some before the next harvest; while a few find that they have an excess which it is more convenient to store as cash than as grain. Much of the Marra mountain seems to be rather too high to offer optimal conditions for millet, and there is doubtless an overall import from lower-lying, surplus-producing areas.

(l) Millet is used for porridge and beer. Independent estimates in connection with sample budgets indicate that on an average about one-fifth of the total grain production goes into beer—more in the case of men, somewhat less in the case of women.

(m)Most of the porridge is consumed directly. On special occasions, however, connected with funerals and memorials for senior deceased relatives, or the life-crises of junior relatives, feasts are given at which porridge is also served to invited and uninvited visitors. At most feasts, beer is also given, and occasionally cattle are slaughtered. Such feasts bring honour to the person who gives them; but as they are given in the name of another person and are not formalized in grades or titles, it would be inappropriate to regard them as 'feasts of merit' in any real sense; and their effects on the political influence of the feast-giver seem to be minimal.

Beer-making is a rather complicated procedure which stretches over several days, and the product does not keep for long; so most households are unable regularly to have beer available for home consumption. Most of the beer produced thus enters the circuit of feasts and work parties,

(n) especially as a reciprocal in exchange for labour, as discussed above. Besides being used to mobilize labour in millet cultivation, where the large, uniform fields invite the use of communal labour, such beer-for-labour exchanges

(o) are used in house-building. Indeed, a final marriage obligation, after a period of successful marriage, is the building of a hut by each spouse for his or her parallel-sex parent-in-law, using only labour mobilized by beer in a kinship/friendship network, and associated with special festive customs, dances, and songs.

Possibilities for Growth

Figure 7.1 thus depicts all the main forms of goods and services in the Mountain Fur economy, how they are produced and how they can be exchanged for each other—i.e. it depicts the flow of value through the system. The whole system is seen from the point of view of an ordinary villager, not a craftsman or a market-place speculator; and it presupposes the ecological and institutional facts outlined in the first part of the paper.

From the point of view of each individual unit of management, the central purpose of economic activities must be to direct the flow of his own assets in these various channels in such a way as (i) to achieve maximal increase in them while (ii) obtaining a balanced distribution of value on the various consumption items of market goods, porridge, beer, housing, *Haj*, and feasts. The balance in question is determined by each person's consumption profile.

Some general characteristics of the economy stand out very clearly in this diagram; most clearly, the limited possibilities for cumulative growth. Such growth possibilities depend on a recognized channel for reinvestment and will show up in the diagram as possible *circles* of flow, permitting what might most vividly be described as *spirals* of growth (Barth, 1963, p. 11). Only three such circles are present: (1) labour–cash–crops–cash–wife–labour, (2) cash–cattle–cash, and (3) labour–millet–beer–labour. The first of these circles is apparent rather than real; and all have built-in brakes which prevent them from serving as true spirals of growth.

As for the labour–cash–wife–labour circle, this is controlled by a number of factors such as the availability of marriageable women, the acceptance of the marriage offer by the woman and her kinspeople, and the ultimate limit of four legal wives. Of more immediate relevance, however, is the fact that the labour obtained from a wife is not of the same kind as that invested in work on the cash crops. A woman's labour obligations to her husband concern the special female services only; as a cultivator she is independent, and the cash crops which she cultivates are her own, not her husband's. Though spouses often work together in the field, this is on a reciprocal basis. Thus, plural marriages will not only deplete a man's savings, but also increase his cash expenses without providing him with any sources of labour, from wives or from children, which he can use in the production of cash crops. There is thus no opportunity for cumulative increase of assets in this circle.

The cash–cattle–cash circle, on the other hand, offers a genuine circle for investment and increase provided that (otherwise essentially unusable) juvenile labour is available in the domestic unit. However, the erratic supply of young cattle constitutes a brake on systematic investment: there are no markets to facilitate trade in such animals, and the supply depends entirely on the whim of the Arab nomads, who offer the beasts for sale individually through random contacts and only in response to unforeseen and urgent cash needs. In a complete census of one mountain Fur community of 212 adult householders, one person owned 5 cattle, the rest fewer, and most of them none. Though restricted in this way, profits in this particular spiral are none the less frequently cited by villagers as the source of accumulated savings.

The labour–millet–beer–labour circle is the most clearly marked one in the economy. But it also has characteristic built-in brakes. General notions of reciprocity are not effective, as noted previously; but there is a tendency for labour efficiency to correlate negatively with the size of the task: the larger the field, the more beer and the more people are present, and the more quickly does the whole occasion degenerate into a pure drinking party. The host tries to control this tendency by bringing out his beer a little at a time; but if he is too careful people will leave the site in protest.

Furthermore, the circle is essentially a closed one: millet is not treated by the Mountain Fur as a cash crop, and so wealth once in this circle remains within it, and a person's incentive to try systematically to accumulate in a spiral is limited by his view of his possible consumption needs or appetites for porridge, beer, and thatched huts.

Spheres and Barriers

The items labour, millet, porridge, beer, and houses are thus closely interconnected, and most nearly constitute a sphere in terms of exchangeability. By also considering other regular modes of circulation, especially that of a production in which the factor of land is freely available, the interconnectedness of these items is more adequately depicted. It should be noted that all items are *not* freely exchangeable for each other, e.g. labour cannot be obtained in exchange for millet. But through the brewing of beer, labour is mobilized in direct proportion to the millet invested and there are no significant restrictions on the volume or timing of this transformation—i.e. it is present in the system as a constantly available possible allocation of the resources in question. It thus seems most meaningful to classify these items together as constituting a single economic sphere, and to demarcate such spheres by criteria of freedom of allocation and the facility with which each item or form can be transformed into any other.

The concept of spheres, then, serves to summarize the major structural features of a flow pattern. In this case, most items fall by such criteria clearly in either of two main spheres, that of labour, beer, etc. and that associated with cash. In addition, the diagram depicts conversions to *Haj* and feasts, in a sphere related to rank and influence that has no clear feedback into the economic system, and also some conversions into a sphere of kinship and affinal ties, represented here by wives as the only item with a significant, though limited, feedback on the labour side of the economic system.

The barriers between spheres, in this view, are barriers to ready transformation, i.e. all the factors that impede the flow of value and restrict people's freedom to allocate their resources, and reverse these allocations. Thus the allocation of cash to the purchase of a ticket to Mecca is a conversion to another sphere, since this amount of value can never be transformed back into cash. An allocation of labour to millet cultivation is likewise an allocation of resources to a non-cash sphere; because of the items in this sphere millet is for reasons of price and competition not a marketable cash crop, porridge has no buyers, the sale of beer is regarded as immoral, and the labour obtained for beer cannot be sold and has traditionally been used only in millet cultivation and house-building. Houses, finally, are not sold, because of the difficulty of finding buyers.[3] The barriers that prevent or restrict flow between spheres are thus compounded of a variety of factors, only some of them of a moral or socially sanctioned nature.

Management and Stratification

Successful management consists in allocating labour wisely to the two main spheres, and steering one's assets through the channels of each sphere in such a way as to maximize increase. In the cash sphere, this involves agricultural skills and an adequate programming of labour input in terms of the changing requirements of hoeing, watering, guarding, and harvesting—and, in the case of tomatoes, also of drying the crop. Besides, relative gains or losses result from the choice of different alternative crops in different years, as a result of fluctuations in weather conditions and market prices. In general, cultivators seemed to feel that weather fluctuations were unpredictable; and many also seemed to choose their crops on a conventional or habitual basis, without reference to prognoses of changing prices. A steady rise in the price obtained for tomatoes over the last years none the less has resulted in a very considerable increase in the quantity of tomatoes cultivated.

Finally, the time of marketing affects the price obtained. Thus the price of onions sinks, when the new crop comes in, to less than half of the peak price that obtains in early winter. Persons with cash resources to cover current expenditure are thus able to postpone their crop sales and reap the greater profits.

The linear character of the flow channel in the cash sphere does not give much scope for management finesse, and only in the small cash–cattle–cash circle can careful saving and investment produce bonuses of any importance. Not so in the millet–beer–labour sphere, however: systematic management of millet cultivation and beer–labour mobilization is the corner-stone on which the prosperity of most villagers is based.

Let us first look at the direct relation between labour input and production. The millet-growing season extends over approximately 70 days; including the preparatory period of terrace-mending and hoeing, and the considerable concluding labour of threshing and winnowing, nearly six months are probably needed to produce a final harvest of reasonable size.

Villagers estimated that a woman with no cash-cropping commitment in the summer season should be able to produce at least 10 *mid* (1,000 lb), by her own labour. As a daily rate this would correspond to more than 1/2 *mid* (5 lb), per working day.

Alternatively, much of the labour may be done with the aid of work parties. At such parties, the hosts generally estimate that a large—about 30 litre—pot of beer provides enough beer for six men for one day. By the brewing techniques generally used in the Marra mountain, millet produces about six times its own volume in finished beer. One *mid* (corresponding to about 5 litres) of grain thus makes about 30 litres of beer. The daily consumption of beer per man in a work party is thus approximately 5 litres, corresponding to 1.7 lb millet.

Given an adequate store of millet, a person can thus mobilize labour at a cost of some 1.7 lb millet/day/man and apply it to a task that produces an average of some 5 lb millet, or three times the cost, per work-day. A reasonably skilful management in this flow circle thus secures a person an adequate supply of millet from a relatively small labour input. The person who cannot husband his resources, and whose thirst or hunger tempts him to join work parties so as quickly and directly to transform his labour into beer, will constantly be on the losing end of the deal. In Mountain Fur villages, the population thus has a tendency to fall into two strata: a majority of moderately prosperous persons, and a fraction who, because of disease, age, or bad management, have inadequate grain stores, and who supplement their food resources by frequent participation in work parties, thus serving as a labour reserve for the more prosperous villagers.

Discrepancies of Evaluation

I have argued elsewhere (Barth, 1966) that the barriers which separate spheres and limit the amount and occasions of flow between them will allow considerable discrepancies of evaluation to persist as between items located in different spheres. Such discrepancies may be discovered when barriers break down and new patterns of circulation are made possible, in which cases an increased flow may force people radically to revise their evaluations (see pp. 157–158 below, on the value of land). Alternatively, these discrepancies may be demonstrated where it is possible to construct some common denominator, or coefficient, for comparing evaluations in one sphere with those of another. In the present case, such a common denominator may be constructed on the basis of the market price of millet—an 'imperfection' in the separation of the two major spheres, brought about mainly by the activities of travelling merchants who bring millet in from the adjoining ecological zone, but also occasionally by the sale of millet raised by the Mountain Fur themselves.

The price of millet in 1964 ranged from 4 to 6 piastres, i.e. around an average of 1 shilling per *mid* (10 lb) of grain. We thus get the equations:

10 lb millet = 1 shilling = 30 litres of beer = 6 man days,
or 1 man day = 5 litres of beer = 2d. worth of millet.

This evaluation of what a man-day of labour is worth in beer may be compared to that obtaining in the cash sphere. The Sudan Forestry Department, and some other public bodies, make relatively unsuccessful attempts to recruit local labour in Jebel Marra. Their basic wage offer has been about 10 piastres=2 shillings a day, or 12 times the value of the millet which a man demands for participation in a work party. Yet it has proved very difficult, especially in the initial years of recruiting in any one village or locality, to entice people to take work. Privately, I found that an arrangement for having fresh water brought to my hut, at the rate of about 1d. per 12 litre pot, was impossible to maintain because the women in the neighbourhood were dissatisfied with the rate of pay—the equivalent of half a day's 'millet pay' for 20 minutes' work. Admittedly, in these equations I have ignored the value of the labour of brewing—as indeed I suspect that the Fur themselves, particularly the men, would do if they were to attempt the comparison. But this additional factor is far from sufficient to make good the discrepancies. Likewise, one might argue that the Fur idea that it is shameful to work for a wage should be represented as an additional cost for a man entering a wage contract, and that this constitutes the balancing factor. The empirical facts would, however, rather suggest that these costs are not so very great, since once the Fur are given enough opportunities to work for wages so that they discover the advantages of these wage rates, they eagerly accept the contracts, as in some of the Jebel Marra foothills areas. No matter how one chooses to represent it, there does seem to be a very great discrepancy between the values placed on beer and labour, and those placed on money.

....

Innovating Activity

So far I have discussed the economic activity of persons within the traditional framework of alternative allocations. But to the extent that the individual units of management really attempt to maximize their assets, they will assert a constant pressure on this framework, and will seek ways of utilizing new opportunities where they are apparent and not blocked by unreasonable risk factors or supervening social sanctions.

Fredrik Barth

The most general change that is taking place along these lines in the Jebel Marra is a progressive increase in the range of crops cultivated, and a certain change in the whole agricultural regime because of the increasing importance of tree crops. This development has been initiated by some modest agricultural experimental stations, but is sustained without any supporting agricultural extension work. The development of orchards is leading to derivative changes in the views on land-ownership and tenure rights. Finally, in a few localities one can also find some truly entrepreneurial undertakings where new strategies of management and channels of conversion are being exploited. The forms which these changes take are to a marked degree determined by the economic system outlined above, and give further perspective on its structure.

Orchard Development

The development of orchards requires irrigated land—i.e. the tree crop is an alternative to the irrigated winter cash crops. Such a tree crop takes four years before it gives a significant product; however, in the intervening period the fields may also be used to raise an irrigated onion crop, so no significant loss of current production is suffered during the transition. The fruits are marketable for cash—limes, lemons, oranges, and mangoes particularly for export; papaya, guava, and bananas mainly for local consumption. The ease of production, and the relatively low value of the fruit in the case of limes and lemons, make them less attractive under present circumstances, whereas some varieties of oranges have been spectacularly profitable.

The labour to establish an orchard comes in addition to that normally required, since other cash crops must be cultivated to cover current expenses until the trees start producing. The development of an orchard thus requires an extra input of labour; and this has generally been done by the innovators with the aid of work parties, utilizing surplus millet for beer. A precedent is thus established for the use of beer-mobilized labour in the cash-crop sphere. So long as a person's millet resources are large enough to provide simultaneously for the other current uses, there are no sanctions against such an allocation; but it requires careful management, i.e. a successful large production of millet by beer work parties in the year preceding the orchard development. Perhaps for this reason, only the quite successful and prosperous have embarked on this production beyond the occasional planting of single trees. In the localities of fieldwork, the first orchards were planted in a village adjoining the foothills zone in 1956, in a high mountain village not till 1962. The mature orchards give large incomes with little input of labour, individual properties producing £20 to £30 worth of fruit annually.

Land Rights

This change in agricultural regime has created some uneasiness with regard to land-ownership and usufruct rights. The principle of individual ownership to (wild) trees is established and recognized. The trees which a person plants will according to this principle be his, no matter who owns the land on which they grow. However, an orchard on irrigated land becomes so dense that it shades other crops and monopolizes that land. A person who obtains usufruct rights to irrigated land to which he has no title can thus, by planting an orchard, render it useless to all others for an indefinite period. Some men who held titles to land on behalf of their descent group were, in 1964, quite concerned over this, and pressed for the general acceptance of a rule forbidding the planting of orchards on borrowed land. Some few of them, on the other hand, had been quick enough to evict other users in time to secure ample areas for their private orchard developments.

Others, who had no such titular rights, wished to obtain the exclusive access to irrigated land that would make the long-term investment of orchard development a safe proposition. In the most sophisticated areas, a few sales and purchases of land had taken place by 1964, tentatively establishing truly private ownership to land. Both parties to such transactions were quite uneasy about the deal, the sellers because they were alienating rights which they held in trust for larger kin groups (and only those who belonged to nearly extinct, or emigrated, kin groups were willing to consider sale at all), the buyers because they felt that the price was excessive.

Indeed, the prices demanded are an extreme illustration of the discrepancies of evaluation that can obtain where the items, in this case land and cash, have not been in circulation in the same economic sphere. I recorded those few transactions of this kind that had taken place in one community. The first sale took place in 1961, when a field was sold for £17. The buyer planted orange trees, and proceeded to cultivate onions in the three transitional years. For these onion crops he obtained £27, £22, and £25, respectively. He expected his first proper yield of oranges to bring a larger income. He was personally no longer in doubt that the transaction had been to his advantage; but he failed by this argument to convince his friend to purchase a field for £30 which had regularly been giving an onion crop worth more than £15 annually. The man in question was willing to offer £25, but would not go higher—not because he did not have the money, but because he felt that, surely, no piece of land could be worth that much. One must assume that an increasing number of such transactions will progressively lead to a general revision of relative evaluations.

Entrepreneurial Activity

On purely logical grounds I have argued elsewhere (Barth, 1966) that entrepreneurs will direct their activity pre-eminently towards those points in an economic system where the discrepancies of evaluation are greatest, and will attempt to construct bridging transactions which can exploit these discrepancies. The social factors which produce a reluctance to sell land serve as a general impediment on entrepreneurial activity in this field; besides, the profits connected with such transactions are long-term. But the disparities of evaluation between the cash and the millet–labour–beer spheres offer opportunities which have recently been discovered and exploited by a few entrepreneurs. The problem, when an entrepreneurial adventure consists in breaking through the barrier between spheres, is that of re-conversion of assets without loss— i.e. that of locating channels that allow a circle of reinvestment and growth (see above, pp. 153–4, and Barth, 1963, p. 11).

Returning to Figure 7.1 the possibility of such a circle is apparent in the combination of channels $(k)–(l)–(n)–(b_1)–(c)$. Concretely, what happened, apparently for the first time in 1961, was that an Arab merchant who regularly visited the market-places on the northern fringe of the Marra mountain, asked for permission to spend the rainy season in a village, and asked for an area of land on which to cultivate a tomato crop. He brought in his wife and settled her in a hut, and he bought a large amount of millet in the lowlands to the northeast, where the price is very low, which he transported in on his donkeys and camels. From the millet, his wife made beer; this beer he used to call work parties, applying the labour to the tomato cultivation. Without any significant labour input of his own, he thus produced a large tomato crop, which he dried and transported to el Fasher for sale after the end of the rainy season. On an investment of £5 worth of millet, he obtained a return of more than £100 for his tomatoes.

In 1962 and 1963, more merchants, and some local people, adopted the same strategy with results nearly as spectacular. The precedent of orchard labour showed the way in which assets in the beer–labour circle could be converted to the cash sphere by being used in the production of cash crops—a conversion that takes advantage of the disparity in the beer versus cash evaluations of labour. The re-conversion of assets from the cash to the non-cash sphere through the purchase of millet again takes advantage of a favourable disparity of evaluations, and is particularly simple for a trader with access to lowland markets.

The profits on trade and transport of the products also enters into the enterprise of the merchant given above. The case of one of the first local men to attempt the scheme is therefore of special interest. On the local market, he purchased:

50 *mid* of millet at 6 piastres per *mid*—500 lb millet:	£3	0	0
Also, for the main work party feast, 1 goat for 40 piastres:	0	8	0
Total labour costs:	£3	8	0

He had all the labour in the tomato field performed by work parties. The value of the tomato crop, ready for sale within about 5 months, was £38—profits based entirely on production and conversions within the local economic system.

Again, one must assume that this situation is unstable: a re-evaluation as between spheres may be precipitated by this flow of value across the boundary, whereby evaluations in the two spheres are brought more closely in line. Alternatively, the critical conversions may be blocked: by a refusal to give land for cultivation to the entrepreneurs, or by the discontinuation of the beer-for-labour exchanges on anything but a reciprocal basis. There is some evidence for a trend in each of these directions, but as of 1964 no effective reaction blocked these enterprises. However, the increase in wage-labour opportunities which will probably take place will no doubt also affect this situation by making it more difficult to mobilize labour for beer on a non-reciprocal basis.

Concluding Remark

In each major section of this description of the Mountain Fur economic system I have sought to make explicit the analytical steps that I have taken, and to give the argument a general form. It should therefore be unnecessary to formulate any extensive conclusion. One general feature of this analysis might however be noted. By discussing alternative allocation in terms of 'flow', and describing the concrete factors and barriers that channel this flow, one performs an analysis that is particularly useful for the study of change, and for short-range prediction. The model is, in this respect, amenable to developments and manipulations which a more strict structural representation would not allow. This increases its adequacy for the description of what is in fact taking place in the Jebel Marra area, and should also enhance its interest to economists.

Notes

1. Based on a field visit of slightly over three months in 1964, during a year's contract with UNESCO as visiting professor at the University of Khartoum. Incidental field expenses were covered by a University of Khartoum Ford Foundation research grant; an interpreter and various other help in the field were supplied by the Jebel Marra Project of the U.N. Special Fund. I wish to thank these institutions, and the authorities and persons with which I was in contact in the Sudan, for their cooperation and help.
2. In this, I disregard the members of the craftsman caste, whose numbers are very small and whose style of life differs considerably from that of Village Fur.
3. In some cases of inheritance, when none of the heirs wishes to use the house, empty houses are indeed offered on the market and bring anywhere from 6 shillings to £2. The difficulty then is to find a buyer, since those in need of a house can call on friends and relatives to contribute towards the construction of an entirely new house, at a chosen site, through expending less than about 5 shillings-worth of their own millet on beer.

References

Barth, F. (1963), The Role of the Entrepreneur in Social Change in Northern Norway. *Acta Universitas Bergensis. Series Humaniorum Litterarum* No. 3. Bergen; Oslo: Norwegian Universities Press.

——(1966), Models of Social Organization. *Royal Anthropological Institute*, Occasional Papers, No. 23.

Bohannan, P. and Dalton, A.G. (1965), *Markets in Africa*. New York: Doubleday.

Lampen, G.D. (1950), History of Darfur. *Sudan Notes and Records* 31 (2).

Lebon, J.H.G. and Robertson, V.C. (1961), The Jebel Marra, Darfur, and its Region. *Geographical Journal* 127 (1).

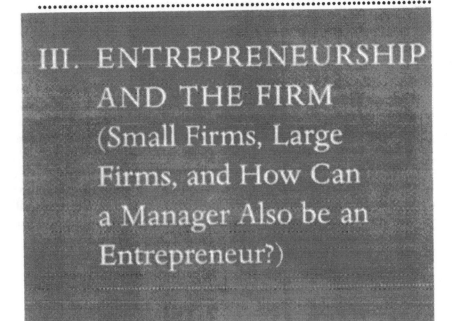

III. ENTREPRENEURSHIP AND THE FIRM (Small Firms, Large Firms, and How Can a Manager Also be an Entrepreneur?)

This section is centred around the attempt to take the mystique out of entrepreneurship and transform innovative economic behaviour into a series of skills that can be taught in the business schools. The aim, in other words, is to develop something that surely would have been an oxymoron to Schumpeter, namely 'entrepreneurial management' or 'corporate entrepreneurs'. Efforts in this direction, it should be noted, have been going on for something like fifteen years, and as long ago as 1985 Peter Drucker expressed what was at stake in a perfectly clear and unambiguous manner. 'The time has now come', he wrote, 'to do for entrepreneurship and innovation what we first did for management in general some thirty years ago: to develop the principles, the practice, and the discipline' (Drucker, *Innovation and Entrepreneurship* [New York: HarperBusiness, [1985] 1993, p. 17).

Over the years a huge number of insights have accumulated about how to go about the rationalization of entrepreneurship that Drucker talks about. Drucker, himself, for example has suggested that in order for there to be 'systematic innovation', the leadership in a firm should be on the outlook for things such as the following: the unexpected; incongruities between what is and what 'ought' to be; changes in market structures and industry structures; new knowledge; demographic changes; and changes in perceptions, mood and meaning (Drucker [1985] 1993: 35ff.). In their well-known article from 1990, 'A Paradigm of Entrepreneurship: Entrepreneurial Management' (*Strategic Management Journal*), Howard Stevenson and J. Carlos Jarillo similarly suggest what they think should characterize the behaviour of the new, entrepreneurial type of management. They emphasize especially that all people in the corporation should be trained to spot opportunities (not only the top management); that all employees and managers should be rewarded for doing so; and that the negative consequences of failing should be lessened.

When the rationalization of entrepreneurship is discussed, usually only large corporations are referred to. Most firms that exist in the world, however, are small firms, and it is legitimate to ask if also these can be changed in an entrepreneurial direction. This section of the reader makes an attempt to raise this question precisely by including readings on the problems of small firms and innovation. My sense is that the social sciences are well placed to be of assistance in this effort, since they have developed quite a bit of sophisticated knowledge about small firms: what their social structure looks like and how they operate. Two of the readings in this section are on small firms, including one that looks at the relationship between small, innovative firms and large, innovative firms.

The first reading, "When A Thousand Flowers Bloom: Structural, Collective, and Social Conditions for Innovation in Organization" by Rosabeth Moss Kanter, contains a theory of how innovations are made within the modern business firm. Kanter starts out by arguing that the typical kind of innovation, which is produced in the modern business firm, goes through several stages: (1) an innovative idea has to be produced; (2) support for the idea has to be generated; (3) the idea has to be turned into a finished product; and (4) the finished product has to be diffused to the consumer. These four stages may happen haphazardly; and one then relies on luck, intuition and the like for innovations to emerge. But, as Kanter argues, it is also possible to intervene at each of the four stages and design the corporation in such a way that the whole process is considerably facilitated. One can, for example, design jobs so that people do not feel constricted but instead are free to experiment with new ideas and tasks. Contacts with the customers—and these are known to be extremely important for generating innovative ideas—can also be built into the job. It is possible to make funds available for innovative projects and, finally, to speed up the diffusion of the finished product in various ways.

In discussing the practical implications of Kanter's analysis, it must first of all be stressed that she herself has developed a style of writing that attempts to meld analytical thought with a discussion of what can be done in practice. Kanter was trained as a sociologist and when she writes for an academic audience, as in this essay, the analytical element is dominant. This, however. does not mean that she pays no attention to the practical implications of her ideas. On the contrary, throughout her essay one can find a number of interesting and useful suggestions for what to do in concrete cases.

But even if Kanter makes an effort to bring out the practical implications of her argument in "When A Thousand Flowers Bloom", it is possible to add to these. Kanter, for example, is well aware that she is talking about a different type of entrepreneur than Schumpeter's individualistic and wilful creature; her 'corporate entrepreneur' is decidedly less original, cooperates more, and is also active within an already existing organization. But what is perhaps less clear, and needs to be discussed somewhat more than she does, is what drives this new breed of intrapreneurs. How, for example, can they be made to work harder and produce more profit? And what do you do in order to turn a non-innovative firm into a firm that has a positive attitude towards innovations and entrepreneurship? How do you break down the resistance to innovations that has been built up during many years? Kanter also stresses the interpersonal skills of the corporate entrepreneur, especially his or her capacity to lead teams and get individuals to participate in these. This would seem correct—but can these social skills also be taught? And if so, how? And by whom—through mentorship in corporations or through business schools?

Howard Aldrich is a sociologist at the University of North Carolina at Chapel Hill and does work on organizations and management issues. In "Entrepreneurial Strategies in New Organizational Populations", Aldrich mainly discusses what conclusions can be drawn for entrepreneurship from the perspective of a special school in sociology, known as population ecology. Aldrich notes, for example, that for new organizational forms founding rates are low at the beginning, while the rate of failure is high. In general, he adds, old organizations also have a tendency to do better than new ones ('the liability of newness'). And while organizations which entered the population at an early stage typically mobilize resources at a very quick pace and can survive only in a limited number of environmental conditions, organizations who enter at a later stage of the cycle mobilize resources at a considerably slower speed, but do well in a wide range of environmental conditions.

One immediate practical consequence of Aldrich's argument has to do with the question of when it is to the advantage of the entrepreneur to enter an organizational cycle: at the beginning, when the risks are high (as well as the profits and the chance to dominate the future of an industry) or later, when the risks are smaller and the field has settled down a bit? Can one counter the disadvantages of a late entry by closing off a sector of the market—by engaging, in other words, in what the economists call 'monopolistic competition'? Aldrich also mentions the problem of getting accepted, which all novel types of organizational forms have *vis-à-vis* authorities ('sociopolitical legitimation'); and here one wonders if there exists no way of speeding up this process? Should, for example, entrepreneurs follow Aldrich's suggestion and create trade associations?

The two remaining readings in this section are exceptionally lucid in their argumentation. One is written by Kenneth Arrow, Nobel laureate and active at the economics department at Stanford University, and the second by Mark Granovetter, a sociologist, also at Stanford University. In "Innovations in Large and Small Firms", Arrow notes that the decision-making structure tends to differ between firms, depending on their size. At one end there are small firms, where decisions about research and decisions about whether to go ahead economically with the research in question tend to be close (they may even be made by the same persons). And at the other end there are large firms, where research decisions and development decisions are not only separate but also far from each other. These different structures, Arrow continues, mean that small firms and large firms tend to be good at different kinds of innovations. Since there is little distance in small firms between knowledge about what research looks promising and decisions about the economic feasibility of the research in question, these tend to specialize in original research. Large firms, on the other hand, have access to huge amounts of relatively cheap money, but are less inclined to invest in original research since this is more risky and ideally demands little distance between decisions about research and finance.

Arrow's argument, it should be stressed, is exclusively based on logic and needs to be empirically tested. One would expect, for example, that it fits some industries better than others and also that it fits some societies better than others. None the less, Arrow's argument raises some extremely interesting questions. Is it possible, for example, as Arrow suggests, to develop a market in research outcomes, where large firms buy original research from small firms and develop it further? Does such a market already exist in some industries? Would it be possible for a large firm to own a number of small, innovative firms or have a share in these—or must small firms be totally autonomous in order to produce original research? Is it possible to envision other organizational forms in this context than simply small firms and large firms, perhaps a mixture of ordinary organizations and networks?

The last text in this section of the reader is authored by Mark Granovetter and entitled, "The Economic Sociology of Firms and Entrepreneurship". What Granovetter says here is part of a larger argument that economists tend to disregard the role of social relations in economic behaviour, and when they do take such interaction into account, they view it as something negative. According to economists, *homo economicus* is not hampered by any loyalties to family, friends or business acquaintances and has no personal networks whatsoever. Granovetter himself has a very different view of the role that social relations play in the economy, and he argues that while economic behaviour is *always* embedded in social relations, these sometimes have negative consequences for economic performance and sometimes positive consequences. He exemplifies this by looking at small firms in developing countries and notes that for such a firm to come into being, there has to exist some solidarity between people—but not too much solidarity. You have to be able to trust people, if you are going to hire them to work in your firm; but at the same time you do not want a number of distant relatives to show up on your doorstep and ask to be taken care of when your business is doing well. In Granovetter's terminology, there has to be a proper balance between 'the coupling' and 'the decoupling' of social relations, for a firm to come into being and to continue to exist.

Granovetter's article abounds with practical implications, and not only for developing countries. It is, for example, clear that a strategy needs to be developed in many countries for how to decouple the nuclear family from the extended kin in order to encourage small firms to come into being and flower. If this is not done, small firms will have to fight an uphill battle to survive and expand. Granovetter also argues that the process of finding a proper balance between coupling and decoupling has usually taken place by accident in history. Some minority, for example, may have been cut off from the majority of the population (*decoupling*), which has led to an intensification of its internal solidarity (*coupling*). Granovetter's argument, however, also raises the question of whether it would be possible to produce this type of effect in a conscious manner, that is by design, and perhaps even invent small economic organizations of a new kind which are better fit for economic performance and entrepreneurship. And thus we return to one of the key questions that was raised at the very beginning of this introduction, namely if the process of rationalizing entrepreneurship can also be extended to small firms.

8 When a Thousand Flowers Bloom: Structural, Collective, and Social Conditions for Innovation in Organization

Rosabeth Moss Kanter

Abstract

Innovation consists of a set of tasks carried out at the micro-level by individuals and groups of individuals within an organization. These microprocesses are in turn stimulated, facilitated, and enhanced—or the opposite—by a set of macro-level conditions. Some of these structural and social factors are more important at certain stages than at others. This paper suggests that a dynamic model of innovation is needed which connects the major tasks in the innovation process to those structural arrangements and social patterns which facilitates each. Four major innovation tasks are discussed: (1) idea generation; (2) coalition building; (3) ideal realization; and (4) transfer, or diffusion. The importance of flexibility, breadth or reach, and, particularly, integration are emphasized.

"Let a thousand flowers bloom." This slogan, designed to awaken an entire nation to new ideas, offers an apt metaphor for innovation. Innovations, like flowers, start from tiny seeds and have to be nurtured carefully until they blossom; then their essence has to be carried elsewhere for the flowers to spread. And some conditions—soil, climate, fertilizer, the layout of the garden— produce larger and more abundant flowers.

Innovations can grow wild, springing up weed-like despite unfavorable circumstances, but they can also be cultivated, blossoming in greater abundance under favorable conditions. If we understand what makes innovations grow— the microprocess by which they unfold—we can see why some macro-conditions are better for their cultivation.

It is increasingly common among writers to emphasize the nonlinear, slightly chaotic, usually sloppy, sometimes random, and often up-and-down nature of innovation (Quinn, 1985). Taken to an extreme though, as some popular writers have done, it might be tempting to conclude that it is impossible to plan for innovation, manage it, or design an organization structure to support it. This extreme viewpoint holds individual variables like creativity and leadership to be more important than structural variables and, indeed, tends to see organizations in general as negative forces, with innovations generally occurring *despite* the organization, through accidents, lucky breaks, and bootlegged funds.

My own conclusion, after systematic comparative research (Kanter, 1983), in depth fieldwork, and literature review, is more moderate. Organizational conditions—structure and social arrangements—can actively stimulate and produce innovation, as long as those conditions take into account the "organic," "natural," and even the "wild" side of innovation. Innovation is the creation and exploitation of new ideas. At its very root, the entrepreneurial process of innovation and change is at odds with the administrative process of ensuring repetitions of the past. The development of innovation requires a different set of practices and different modes of organization than the management of ongoing, established operations where the desire for or expectation of change is minimal. Stevenson and Gumpert (1985) have cast this management difference in terms of the contrast between the "promoter" type stance of the entrepreneur, driven by perception of opportunity, and the "trustee"-like stance of the administrator, driven to conserve resources already controlled (see also Hanan, 1976). Structures and practices that may work well for the perpetuation of the known tend to be at odds with innovation.

Innovation—whether technological or administrative, whether in products or processes or systems—tends to have four distinctive characteristics (Kanter, 1985).

1. The innovation process is uncertain. The source of innovation or the occurrence of opportunity to innovate may be unpredictable. The innovation goal may involve little or no precedent or experience base to use to make forecasts about results. Hoped-for timetables may prove unrealistic, and schedules may not match the true pace of progress. "Progress on a new innovation," Quinn (1979) wrote, "comes in spurts among unforeseen delays and setbacks . . . in the essential chaos of development." Furthermore, anticipated costs may be overrun and ultimate results are highly uncertain. Indeed, analysts have variously estimated that it takes an average of 10 to 12 years before the return on investment of new ventures equals that of mature

businesses (Biggadike, 1979); 7 to 15 years from invention to financial success (Quinn, 1979); and 3 to 25 years between invention and commercial production (Quinn, 1985).

2. The innovation process is knowledge-intensive. The innovation process generates new knowledge intensively, relying on individual human intelligence and creativity and involving "interactive learning" (Quinn, 1985). New experiences are accumulated at a fast pace; the learning curve is steep. The knowledge that resides in the participants in the innovation effort is not yet codified or codifiable for transfer to others. Efforts are very vulnerable to turnover because of the loss of this knowledge and experience. There need to be close linkages and fast communication between all those involved, at every point in the process, or the knowledge erodes.

3. The innovation process is controversial. Innovations always involve competition with alternative course of action. The pursuit of the air-cooled engine at Honda Motor, for example, drew time and resources away from improving the water-cooled engine. Furthermore, sometimes the very existence of a potential innovation poses a threat to vested interests—whether the interest is that of a salesperson receiving high commissions on current products, or of the advocates of a competing direction. (Fast, 1979, for example, argues that "political" problems are the primary cause for the failure of corporate New Venture Departments.)

4. The innovation process crosses boundaries. An innovation process is rarely if ever contained solely within one unit. First, there is evidence that many of the best ideas are interdisciplinary or interfunctional in origin—as connoted by the root meaning of entrepreneurship as the development of "new combinations"—or they benefit from broader perspective and information from outside of the area primarily responsible for the innovation. Second, regardless of the origin of innovations, they inevitably send out ripples and reverberations to other organization units, whose behavior may be required to change in light of the needs of innovations, or whose cooperation is necessary if an innovation is to be fully developed or exploited. Or there may be the need to generate unexpected innovations in another domain in order to support the primary product, like the need to design a new motor to make the first Apple computer viable.

If innovation is *uncertain, fragile, political,* and *imperialistic* (reaching out to embrace other territories), then it is most likely of flourish where conditions allow flexibility, quick action and intensive care, coalition formation, and connectedness. It is most likely to grow in organizations that have integrative structures and cultures emphasizing diversity, multiple structural linkages both inside and outside the organization, intersecting territories, collective pride and faith in people's talents, collaboration, and teamwork. The organizations producing more innovation have more complex structures that link people in multiple ways and encourage them to "do what needs to be done" within strategically guided limits, rather than confining themselves to the letter of their job. Such organizations are also better connected with key external resources and operate in a favorable institutional environment.

Not all *kinds* of innovation appear everywhere in equal proportions of course. Product innovations are more likely in new entrant organizations and process innovations in established ones. Product innovations are more common in earlier stages of a product's history; process innovations in later stages (Abernathy & Utterback, 1978). Technological innovations are more frequent when resources are abundant; administrative innovations when resources are scarce (Kimberley, 1981). Evolutionary innovations (modest, incremental changes) are more likely in organizations that are more formalized and "centralized"; more revolutionary innovations in organizations that are more complex and "decentralized" (Cohn & Turyn, 1984). But in general, the overall rate of innovation across types should be associated with the circumstances I have outlined.

Some of these structural and social conditions are more important at some points in the innovation process than at others. Like the flowers whose cultivation requires knowledge of its growth pattern, so does the understanding of innovation benefit from examining structural and social facilitators as they wax and wane with the innovation development process. This requires a dynamic model, a combination of a "variance" model of the factors influencing innovation and a "process" model showing how innovation unfolds (Mohr, 1978).

Recent research examining sets of innovations as they unfold over time (Schroeder *et al.*, 1986; Van de Ven, 1986) has discredited the usual process models of innovation that posit discrete stages through which an innovation idea progresses. I agree that stage models do not always adequately capture the give-and-take of innovation, and they risk artificially segmenting the process. But I propose that the structural and social conditions for innovation can be understood best if the innovation process is divided into its major tasks.

There are four major innovation tasks, which correspond roughly (but nowhere near exactly) to the logic of the innovation process as it unfolds over time and to empirical data about the history of specific innovations. These tasks are: (a) *idea generation* and activation of the drivers of the innovation (the "entrepreneurs" or "innovators"); (b) *coalition building* and acquisition of the power necessary to move the idea into reality; (c) *idea realization* and innovation production, turning the idea into a model—a product or plan or prototype that can be used; (d) *transfer* or diffusion, the spreading of the model—the commercialization of the product, the adoption of the idea.

While sometimes occurring in sequence, these tasks also overlap. But by understanding the nature of each task, we can see more easily why certain properties of organizations are related to the success of innovation. This, in turn, contributes to our knowledge of the relationship between structure and behavior, between macro-context and micro-process.

Idea Generation and Innovation Activation

Innovation begins with the activation of some person or persons to sense or seize a new opportunity. Variously called "corporate entrepreneurs" (Kanter, 1983), "intrapreneurs," "idea generators," or "idea champions" (Galbraith, 1982), such individuals are able to initiate a process of departing from the organization's established routines or systems.

Innovation is triggered by recognition of a new opportunity. Once the opportunity is "appreciated," as Van de Ven (1986) put it, someone needs to supply the energy necessary to raise the idea over the threshold of consciousness, much as Schon (1971) described the emergence of new public policies as a result of being pushed into awareness. The first key problem in the management of innovation, then, is how to get people to pay attention—how to trigger the action thresholds of individuals to appreciate and pay attention to new ideas, needs, and opportunities.

Drucker (1985) has argued that the opportunities that give rise to innovation lie in incongruities and discontinuities—things that do not fit expected patterns or that provide indications that trends may be changing. But unless we are to assume these are purely individual cognitive abilities, it is important to look at the structural conditions that facilitate the ability to see new opportunities.

Close Connection with Need Sources

Opportunity exists because need exists, so it is not surprising that close customer or user contact is an important innovation activator. An often cited national study found that over three-fourths of a set of 500 important industrial innovations owed their origins to user suggestions and even user inventions; only one-fifth originated in technical ideas looking for a home (Marquis & Myers, 1969). Users had originated 81% of the innovations in scientific instruments in another study, and 60% of those in process machinery (von Hippel, 1981).

Effective innovation thus derives from active awareness of changing user needs and sometime from direct user demands or solutions. Therefore, structural arrangements and social patterns that facilitate contact across boundaries, between potential innovators and their "market," help produce more innovation. Potential innovators benefit from being linked directly to the market, to gain a fuller personal appreciation for what users need, as well as from being connected with those functions inside the organization that manage the interface with the outside. Quinn (1985) found that high innovation companies in the United States, Japan, and Europe were characterized by a strong market orientation at the top of the company and mechanisms to ensure interaction between technical and marketing people at lower levels. At Sony, for example, new technical hires were assigned to weeks of retail selling as part of their orientation. In the prosperous years for People Express Airlines, the incentive system was designed to ensure that all executives spend at least some time each year flying as crew on their planes.

Van de Ven (1986) hypothesized that direct personal confrontations with problem sources are needed to reach the threshold of concern and appreciation required to motivate people to act. Perhaps this is why it has been observed that well-managed companies search out and focus on their most demanding customers, not the ones who are easily satisfied. Similarly, successful examples of innovations offered by managers in high technology firms tended to involve radical redefinition of the product or service as a result of encounter with the "real world" of customers or users—direct, first-hand experience of their need (Delbecq & Mills, 1985).

Raytheon's New Products Center demonstrates this principle in action. The center services a series of consumer products division, and also it has two levels of "users" and need sources: its internal divisional customers and the ultimate external consumer. Center practices involve frequent visits and tours to all of these need sources. Technical staff routinely attend trade shows, tour manufacturing facilities, and browse at retail outlets, striking up conversations with consumers.

Extra-organizational ties with users can be formalized, to ensure continuing close connection. Many computer and software companies have formed user groups, which allow them to gather ideas for new products and product improvements. Some manufacturing application laboratories solicit proposals from their customers of things they might work on (von Hippel, 1981).

These principles apply to internal administrative or organizational innovations as well as technological or product innovations. I propose, based on field observations, that those staff groups successful at creating innovations are the ones with the closest connections with the needs in the field; Honeywell's corporate human resources staff, for example, has created "councils" of key executives to ensure the continuing relevance of its offerings to the changing needs of users.

In general, then, innovation activation benefits from structural or social connections between those with the technical base (potential innovators) and those with the need (potential users). Indeed, one research group found that a higher proportion of new products failed for "commercial" reasons (misreading the need) rather than technical ones, indicating a poor interface between developers and users (Mansfield et al., 1981).

"Kaleidoscopic Thinking": Cross Fertilization

Awareness of need is one element; ability to construct new ways to address the need is a second. I have come to refer to the creativity involved in activating innovation as "kaleidoscopic thinking" (Kanter, 1986).

The kaleidoscope is an apt metaphor for the creative process, because the kaleidoscope allows people to shake reality into a new pattern. In a kaleidoscope a set of fragments form a pattern. But the pattern is not locked into place. If the kaleidoscope is shaken or twisted, or the angle of perspective is changed, the same fragments form an entirely new pattern. Often, creativity consists of rearranging already existing pieces to create a new possibility. For example, Malcolm McLean did this about 30 years ago when he developed the concept for Sea-Land, the first company to offer containerized shipping. Before Sea-Land, shipping was a tedious matter of packing and unpacking crates in order to move objects from one form of transportation to another. McLean's innovation was simple: move the whole container.

Contact with those who see the world differently is a logical prerequisite to seeing it differently ourselves. "Cosmopolitan" rather than "local" orientations—seeing more of the world—has been identified by many researchers as a factor in high rates of innovation (Rogers & Shoemaker, 1971). So the more innovative organizational units who face outward, as well as inward, take in more of the world around them, and take better advantage of "boundary spanners" to bring them intelligence about the world beyond (Robertson & Wind, 1983; Tushman, 1977). High-performing research and development (R&D) project groups have far greater communication with organizational colleagues outside the group than low-performing teams (Allen, 1984); sometimes this communication occurs in two steps, mediated by certain communication "stars" who then transmit it to the rest of the group (Tushman, 1979).

One classic set of studies of research scientists found that the most productive and creative ones were those who had more contacts *outside* their fields, who spent more time with others who did not share their values or beliefs (Pelz & Andrews, 1966). At the same time, the dangers of closing off were also clear. It took only 3 years for a heterogeneous group of interdisciplinary scientists who worked together every day to become homogeneous in perspective and approach to problems. Sociologists have used the terms "occupational psychosis" and "trained incapacity" to describe the tendency for those who concentrate on only one area and interact only with those who are similar in outlook to become less able over time to learn new things.

The "twists" on reality causing creativity may derive from uncomfortable situations where basic beliefs are challenged and alternatives suggested. It is not surprising, then, that the patterns in most large, established bureaucracies inhibit rather than activate innovation. Once people enter a field, they spend most of their time (especially their discretionary time) with other people just like them who share their beliefs and assumptions. At the top, leaders are increasingly insulated from jarring experiences or unpleasant occurrences that cause them to confront their assumptions about the world, and they spend an increasing portion of their time with people exactly like themselves. And if corporate culture encourages an orthodoxy of beliefs and a nonconfrontational stance, then idea generation is further discouraged.

Cross-fertilization of ideas instead comes from cross-disciplinary contact. Creativity often springs up at the boundaries of specialties and disciplines, rather than squarely in the middle. It is often a matter of combining two formerly separate ideas—wafers and ice cream making the world's first ice cream cone. A large oil company considers one of its greatest innovations the development of a new, highly useful chemical compound that was created because researchers from two distinct fields collaborated. Ocean Spray staged a comeback for cranberry juice because a marketing executive spent time learning about packaging; the company was the first in its industry to put juice in paper bottles. Some organizations actively facilitate cross-disciplinary exchange through product fairs or cross-division "show and tell" meetings or cross-functional teams that visit customers together (Tushman & Nadler, 1986).

But when departments of specialties are segmented and prevented from contact, when career paths confine people to one function or discipline for long periods of time, and when communication between fields is difficult or excessively formal, creativity is stifled. Huge buildings consisting of all those in one field, physically separated from people in another field, make contact impossible.

Under that kind of circumstance, outsiders may be better able to see the big picture and take a new angle on the pattern, because they are not yet aware of all the details the "experts" see that inevitably confirm the view that no change is possible. People too close to a situation often become hopeless about change, blind to the possibilities.

Thus, a great deal of important industrial innovation comes from what Schon (1967) called "innovation by invasion": a new player enters the game, bringing a new method or technique. For example, half of all major innovations in pharmaceuticals from 1935 to 1962 were based on discoveries made outside the firm that later exploited them (Mansfield *et al.*, 1981). It was Apple that first successfully commercialized the personal computer; IBM was a latecomer—and it is hard to imagine more outsiderlike amateurs than Steve Jobs and Steve Wozniak. Similarly, in my study of leading companies, newly appointed managers who came from a different field by an unusual career route—in a word, outsiders—were somewhat more likely to innovate those who rose by orthodox means (Kanter, 1983).

In general, then, contact with those who take new angles on problems facilitates innovation.

Structural Integration: Intersecting Territories

Activation of innovation is encouraged by structural integration across fields—by intersecting territories. Researchers have long observed that "communication integration" (closer interpersonal contact or connectedness via interpersonal communication channels in an organization) is positively related to the innovation rate (Rogers & Shoemaker, 1971; Tushman & Nadler, 1986). Isolation of individuals and units tends to reduce innovation at the idea generation stage by limiting awareness of opportunity, alternative approaches, and the perspective of those functions who need to contribute other "parts" to make the innovation add up to a "whole." (Van de Ven, 1986, considered the management of part–whole relationships one of the four critical innovation tasks.) These who are isolated, in short, are less attuned to alternatives than those who are well-connected.

"Matrix" organization structures (Davis & Lawrence, 1977) are highly integrative, and it is not accidental that they were first developed to aid technological innovation—the large-scale development projects in the aerospace industry—and are found more frequently in rapidly changing, highly innovating organizations (Kanter, 1983). Matrix organizations, in which mid-level employees report to both a project boss and a functional boss, force integration and cross-area communication by requiring managers from two or more functions to collaborate in reaching a decision or taking some action. This is frequently characterized as a "dotted line" relationship for those in one department to another department, signifying a working relationship but not always direct authority.

By requiring extensive cross-functional consultation, the matrix diffuses authority among a group of managers. In many instances, this opportunity can be used in a positive manner by particularly entrepreneurial managers who are able to envision alternatives and assume responsibility for pursuing them—alternatives that cut across territories.

In general, measures of complexity and diversity in an organization are positively related to initial development of innovations (though they are sometimes negatively related to eventual acceptance of the same innovation by the rest of the organization). Diversity gives the individual more latitude for discovery, but may make it difficult later to get agreement on which many proposals or demonstration projects should be implemented on a wider scale. Similarly, innovation is aided by low formalization at the initiation stage, when freedom to pursue untried possibilities is required.

Therefore, to produce innovation, more complexity is essential: more relationships, more sources of information, more angles on the problem, more ways to pull in human and material resources, more freedom to walk around and across the organization (also see Burns & Stalker, 1968; Mintzberg, 1981). One does not need a formal matrix structure to this. Indeed, it is the general characteristics of an integrative structure that make a difference in terms of encouraging innovation: looser boundaries, crosscutting access, flexible assignments, open communication, and use of multidisciplinary project teams. So specifying multiple links between managers in a formal sense (through showing more than one solid-line or dotted-line reporting relationship on an organization chart) is merely a way of acknowledging the interdependencies that complex products and innovative projects require.

Dividing the organization into smaller units based on a common end use goal but not around function or specialty also aids activation of innovation by producing structural integration at micro-level. When it comes to innovation, "small is beautiful," and flexible is even better (see Quinn, 1985). Or at least small is beautiful as long as the small unit includes all functions or disciplines and forces contact across them. Cross-fertilization across disciplines and a focus on users is built into the structure.

The idea of dividing into smaller but complete business units has been appealing to organizations seeking continual innovation. In smaller business units it is possible to maintain much closer working relationships across functions than in larger ones—one of the reasons for Hewlett-Packard's classic growth strategy of dividing divisions into 2 when they reached more than 2,000 people or $100,000,000 in sales. Even where economies of scale push for larger units, the cross-functional project or product team within a single facility (captured in such ideas as the factory-within-a-factory) helps keep the communication and the connection alive.

Broad Jobs

Idea generation is also aided when jobs are defined broadly rather than narrowly, when people have a range of skills to use tasks to perform to give them a view of the whole organization, and when assignments focus on results to be achieved rather than rules or procedures to be followed. This, in turn, gives people the mandate to solve problems, to respond creatively to new conditions, to note changed requirements around them, or to improve practices, rather than mindlessly following procedures derived from the past.

Furthermore, when broader definitions of jobs permit task domains to overlap rather than divide cleanly, people are encouraged to gain the perspective of others with whom they must now interact and therefore to take more responsibility for the total task rather than simply their own small piece of it. This leads to the broader perspectives that help stimulate innovation.

In areas that benefit from more enterprise and problem solving on the part of job holders, broader jobs seem to work better. This is the principle behind work systems that give employees responsibilities for a major piece of a production process and allow them to make decisions about how and when to divide up the tasks. Pay-for-skill systems similarly encourage broader perspective by rewarding people for learning more jobs (Tosi & Tosi, 1986).

Does this argument conflict with the numerous findings that adoption of innovation is more likely in organizations with more specialists and professionals? (e.g., Hage and Aiken's [1967] conclusion that the rate of innovation is higher when there are occupational specialties, each with a greater degree of professionalism.) No, because while specialized knowledge is an asset, confinement to a limited area and minimal contact with other professionals inhibits the ability for experts to use their knowledge in the service of change.

Potential innovators can become interested in a particular issue that develops into an innovation for several reasons. The initial impetus for innovation activation can stem from (a) an obligation of his or her position (March & Olsen, 1976); (b) a direct order; (c) a stimulus from the environment or "galvanizing event" (Child, 1972; Kanter, 1983); (d) self-motivated, entrepreneurial behavior; (e) organizational rewards and payoffs; or (f) accidental conditions (Perrow, 1981).

While much of the literature emphasizes the random, spontaneous, or deviant aspects of idea generating, some research has found that the nature of job assignments can be an activating force—either directly, because the assignment requires a new solution, or indirectly by allowing a scanning process to occur beyond what is programmed into the position. Job assignments (new ones or simply those understood as part of the job) stimulated a high proportion (51%) of the innovations in one study (Kanter, 1983). Managers did not necessarily have to think up projects by themselves to begin acting as organizational entrepreneurs; their enterprise came from accepting the responsibility and finding a way to build something new while carrying out an assigned task.

What is important is not whether there is an assignment, but its nature: broad in scope, involving change, and leaving the means unspecified, up to the doer. In my study, a manager's *formal* job description often bore only a vague or general relationship to the kinds of innovative things the manager accomplished (Kanter, 1983). Indeed, the more jobs are "formalized," with duties finely specified and "codified," the less innovation is produced in the organization. An emphasis on the "numbers" (a quantitative versus a qualitative thrust in jobs) and on efficiency also depresses the amount of innovation. "Low formalization," on the other hand, is associated with more innovativeness (Hage & Aiken, 1967).

Broad assignments are generally characteristics of staff managers in problem solving or bridging positions who have a general change mandate to "invent something" or "improve something." The innovation-producing companies are often marked by a large proportion of problem solvers in operating departments who float freely without a "home" in the hierarchy and thus must argue for a budget or find a constituency to please. The incentive to enterprise is the *lack* of defined tasks (Kanter, 1983). Thus, organizational slack (Galbraith, 1982) and slack in assignments enables the activation of innovation.

The more routinized and rules-bound a job is, the more it is likely to focus its performers on a few already-known variables and to inhibit attention to new factors. Starbuck (1983) argued that highly programmed jobs are like superstitious learning, recreating actions that may have little to do with previous success or future success. Overly elaborate and finely detailed structures and systems make organizational participants unable to notice shifts in their environment and the need for innovation, especially if they are required to send "exceptions" somewhere else for processing.

Where jobs are narrowly and rigidly defined, people have little incentive to engage in either "spontaneous" innovation (self-generated, problem solving attempts with those in neighboring tasks) or to join together across job categories for larger top-directed innovation efforts—especially if differences in job classification also confer differential status or privilege. Companies even lose basic efficiency as some tasks remain undone while waiting for the person with the "right" job classification to become available—even though others in another classification may have the skills and the time. And people tend to actively avoid doing any more work than the minimum, falling back on the familiar excuse, "That's not *my* job"—a refrain whose frequent repetition is a good sign of a troubled company.

Organizational Expectations for Innovation

Even if people are *able* to generate new ideas in the innovation activation stage, they must also feel confident that their attempts at innovation will be well received. The signals they receive about the *expectations* for innovation play a role in activating or inhibiting innovation.

One way organizations signal an expectation for innovation is by allocating funds specifically for it. In one study comparing innovation successes with failures, it was found that the failures were handicapped by a lack of resources anywhere other than in already committed operating budgets, while the successes benefited from the existence of special innovation funds (Delbecq & Mills, 1985). Despite all the heroic glamour of associating innovation with "bootlegging" funds spent on the sly, it is clearly easier to innovate when funds exist for this purpose.

Since innovations generally require resources beyond those identified in operating budgets (Kanter, 1983) for reasons that are logical—the exact nature and timing of innovation is often unpredictable—the existence of multiple sources of loosely committed funds at local levels makes it easier for potential innovators to find the money, the staff, the materials, or the space to proceed with an entrepreneurial idea. Because no one area has a monopoly on resources, there is little incentive to hoard them as a weapon; instead, a resource holder can have more influence by being one of those to *fund* an innovative accomplishment than by being a nay sayer. Thus, managers at one computer company could go "tin-cupping" to the heads of the various product lines in their facility who had big budgets, collecting a promise of a little bit of funding from many people (Kanter, 1983). This process reduced the risk on the part of all "donors" at the same time that it helped maintain the "donee's" independence.

Sheer availability of resources helps, of course. Research shows that richer and more successful organizations innovate more than poorer and less successful ones, especially in technology areas (Kimberly & Evanisko, 1979; Kimberly, 1981; Zaltman et al., 1973).

There are a variety of ways that high innovation companies make resources accessible locally or give middle-level people alternatives to tap when seeking money or materials for projects. One is to have formal mechanisms for distributing funds outside the hierarchy. 3M has put in place "innovation banks" to make "venture capital" available internally for development projects. Honeywell divisions have top-management steering committees guiding their organizational-change activities. The original steering committee solicited proposals quarterly from any employee for the formation of a problem-solving task team; the teams may receive a small working budget as needed. Also, "decentralization" keeps operating units small and ensures that they have the resources with which to act, and thus makes it more likely that managers can find the extra they need for an innovation locally.

Of course, some innovations, particularly organization ones, can be handled without money at all. Instead, the most common resource requirement in one study was staff time (Kanter, 1983). This was also decentralized in the form of "slack" and local control: people locally available with uncommitted time, or with time that they could decide to withdraw from other endeavors to be attached to an appealing project. Because mid-level personnel, professionals. and staff experts had more control over the use of their time in the more frequently innovating companies, it was easier to find people to assist in a project, or to mobilize subordinates for a particular activity without needing constant clearances from higher-level, nonlocal bosses.

A second general source of expectations for innovation lies in whether the organization's culture pushes "tradition" or "change." Innovators and innovative organizations generally come from the most modern, "up-to-date" areas rather than traditional ones with preservationist tendencies, and they are generally the higher-prestige "opinion leaders" that others seek to emulate (Rogers & Shoemaker, 1971; Hage & Dewar, 1973). But opinion leaders are innovative only if their organizations' norms favor change; this is why the values of the leaders are so important. Most people seek to be culturally appropriate, even the people leading the pack. There is thus more impetus to seek change when this is considered desirable by the company.

Pride in company, coupled with knowing that innovation is mainstream rather than countercultural, helps to stimulate innovation (and occurs as a *result* of innovation as well). A feeling that people inside the company are competent leaders, that the company has been successful because of its people, supports this. For instance, of the companies in one study, Polaroid Corporation knew that it is the technological leader in its field; Hewlett-Packard prided itself on its people-centered corporate philosophy, the H-P way, as well as on its reputation for quality, important in its retention of customers (Kanter, 1983).

Such cultures of pride stand out in sharp distinction to the cultures of inferiority that lead less innovating companies to rely on outsiders for all the new ideas, rather than on their own people.

Success breeds success. Where there is a "culture of pride," based on high performance in the past, people's feeling of confidence in themselves and others goes up. They are more likely to take risks and also to get positive responses when they request cooperation from others. Mutual respect makes teamwork easier. High performance may *cause* group cohesion and liking for workmates as well as result from it (Staw, 1975); pride in the capacity and ability of others makes teamwork possible. In an extension of the "Pygmalion Effect" to the corporation, supervisors who hold high expectations of subordinate's abilities (based on independent evaluations) may enhance that person's productivity (Wortman & Linsenmeier, 1977).

Thus, organizations with "cultures of pride" in the company's achievements and in the achievements and abilities of individuals will find themselves more innovative. This is why formal awards and public recognition make a difference—sometimes less for the person receiving them (who has, after all, *finished* an achievement) than for the observers in the same company, who see that the things they might contribute will be noticed, applauded, and remembered.

It is a self-reinforcing upward cycle—*performance stimulating pride stimulating performance*—and is especially important for innovation Change requires a leap of faith, and faith is so much more plausible on a foundation of successful prior experiences.

Finally, feeling valued and secure helps people relax enough to be creative, as Amabile's (1983) experiments on the conditions facilitating creative problem solving indicate. Groups were asked to solve problems in one of two conditions, and the creativity of their solutions was rated. In condition I, they were paid for their participation before they began to work. In condition II, which tended to resemble the corporate norm, they were paid on a contingency basis, depending on how well their group performed. In which condition were groups more creative? The first, the one that can be called a high security/high value condition. Knowing that they were already paid, members could relax, and they could assume that they were with a set of talented people. Without the tension that worry about paycheck might have caused, they could free themselves to be much more creative. Furthermore, they "rose to the occasion"; because expectations for innovation were set by advance pay, they innovated.

Integration versus Isolation

Overall, I argue that the generation of new ideas that activates innovation is facilitated by organizational complexity: diversity and breadth of experience, including experts who have a great deal of contact with experts in other fields; links to users; and outsiders, openness to the environment; and integration across fields via intersecting territories, multiple communication links, and smaller interdisciplinary business units. Conversely, isolation, or what can be termed "segmentalism" (Kanter, 1983), inhibits this critical first phase of innovation.

It is important to explain an apparent contradiction in the literature here. Some analysts appear to argue that innovation does indeed require isolation, a special organization separated from the rest and dedicated to innovation. For example, Galbraith (1982) argued that innovation requires an organization specifically designed for that purpose, with a structure, processes, rewards, and people combined in a special way; he also made clear that his focus was on "good ideas that do not quite fit into the organization's current mold." But note that the "good idea" already *exists* and the special organization is designed to focus on developing and elaborating it without distraction *once it has been identified.* Thus, isolation of the innovator group appears appropriate *later in the process,* when project ideas have been formulated.

To generate ideas in the first place, a great deal of diverse outreach is involved. R&D units that remain isolated are less creative than those that maintain close integration in the search of exploration stage. Recall the example of the

Raytheon new products department, a unit with an unusually strong track record of creative outputs. It is indeed physically isolated from the rest of the organization to allow it to work on projects undistracted. But to generate ideas and activate innovation in the first place, department members immerse themselves in the world outside the lab, wandering around the organization, seeking problems to work on from their dense network of ties in other units, attending professional conferences in scientific fields other than their own, going to trade shows to view the exhibits, etc.

Coalition Building

Once a specific project idea has taken shape, it must be sold—a necessity even when the innovator was initially handed the area as an assignment. It must be sold because the initial assignment, though bearing some legitimacy, may contain no promises about the availability of resources or support required to do something of greater magnitude than routine activities (Kanter, 1982; 1983). Thus, the second task of the innovation process involves coalition building, acquiring power by selling the project to potential allies.

Overwhelmingly, studies of innovation show the importance of backers and supporters, sponsors and friends in high places, to the success of innovation (Quinn, 1979; Maidique, 1980). Galbraith (1982) distinguished the roles of "sponsor"—those who discover and fund the increasingly disruptive and expensive development and testing efforts that shape an innovation—and "orchestrator"—managers of the politics surrounding a new idea. Observing that sponsors were usually middle managers and orchestrators were higher level executives, he argued that these informal roles could be formalized, with sponsors given resources earmarked for innovation, and orchestrators allocating time to protecting innovation-in-progress.

While most studies emphasize single roles (the "champion," the "sponsor"), detailed accounts of the history of innovations reveal the importance of a whole coalition, embryonic and informal or assembled and formal (Summers, 1986). Van de Ven (1986), in a similar vein, focuses not on a single sponsor but on the importance of transactions or "deals" in the innovation process, and he sees the management of the innovation process as managing increasing bundles of transactions over time. Indeed, he and his colleagues found, in a comparative study of seven very different large scale innovations in different sectors, that "much more than sponsorship" was involved; higher management, one or two levels removed from the innovation was directly involved in making major decisions about the project and often "ran interference" for it as well as securing necessary resources (Schroeder *et al.*, 1986). Furthermore, a comparison of over 115 innovations found in the successful ones a set of allies, often peers from other areas as well as more senior managers, behind successful innovations, ranging from the "stakeholders" who would be affected if the project was implemented to the "power sources" who contributed the tools to ensure that implementation (Kanter, 1983).

Thus, it is more appropriate to conceptualize the second major innovation task as coalition building, a broader notion that ties in more of the organization, rather than as seeking sponsorship, a narrower concept. In general, the success of an innovation is highly dependent on the amount and kind of power behind it. In contrast, innovation failures are characterized by ambivalent support; inadequate resources during the initial fragile stages of development; constant efforts to "sell" and "justify"; and personalized infighting over resources (Delbecq & Mills, 1985).

Thus, the effectiveness of the political activity the innovation entrepreneur engages in, coupled with structural conditions conducive to power acquisition and coalition building, may largely account for whether an idea ever moves into the later phase of innovation production. Social and political factors, such as the quality of the coalition building, may account for as much or more than technical factors, such as the quality of the idea, in determining the fate of innovation.

Research shows that there are some kinds of ideas that are inherently better able to attract support. The most salable projects are likely to be *trialable* (can be demonstrated on a pilot basis—see especially Delbecq & Mills, 1985); *reversible* (allowing the organization to go back to pre-project status if they do not work); *divisible* (can be done in steps or phases); consistent with sunk costs (build on prior resource commitments); concrete (tangible, discrete); *familiar or compatible* (consistent with a successful past experience and compatible to existing practices); *congruent* (fit the organization's direction); and have *publicity value* (visibility potential if they work) (Kimberly, 1981; Zaltman *et al.*, 1973). When these features are not present, as they are unlikely to be in more "radical" innovations, then projects are likely to move ahead if they are either *marginal* (appear off-to-the-side-lines so they can slip in unnoticed) or *idiosyncratic* (can be accepted by a few people with power without requiring much additional support) (Zaltman *et al.*, 1973; Kanter, 1983).

The features of successful ideas have more to do with the likelihood of gathering political support than with the likelihood of the idea to produce results. In general, the relative economic advantage of a new idea, as perceived by members of an organization, is only weakly related to its rate of adoption (Rogers & Shoemaker, 1971). Instead, "political" variables may play a larger role, especially the acquisition of "power tools" to move the idea forward.

Power Tools

Organizational power tools consist of supplies of three "basic commodities" that can be invested in action: *information* (data, technical knowledge, political intelligence, expertise); *resources* (funds, materials, space, time); and *support* (endorsement, backing, approval, legitimacy) (Kanter, 1983).

To use an economic strategy, it is as though there were three kinds of "markets" in which the people initiating innovation must compete: a "knowledge market" or "marketplace of ideas" for information; an "economic market" for resources; and a "political market" for support or legitimacy. Each of the "markets" is shaped in different ways by conditions in the environment (e.g., critical contingencies, resource scarcity; Pennings & Goodman, 1977; Pfeffer & Salancik, 1977), and by organizational structure and rules (e.g., how openly information is exchanged, how freely executives render support). And each gives the person a different kind of "capital" to invest in a "new venture" (also see Pfeffer & Salancik, 1977).

We can hardly speak of "market" at all, of course, where the formal hierarchy fully defines the allocation of all three commodities, for example, when money and staff time are available *only* through a predetermined budget and specified assignments, when information flows *only* through identified communication channels, and when legitimacy is available *only* through the formal authority vested in specific areas with no support available for stepping beyond official mandates. In organizations where there is really no market for exchanging or rearranging resources and data, for acquiring support to do something outside the formal structure, because it is tightly controlled either by the hierarchy or by a few people with "monopoly" power, then little innovative behavior is likely. Indeed, when people feel "powerless" through structural locations that limit them access to the tools, they become more controlling and conservative (Kanter, 1977; Kanter & Stein, 1979).

While some portion of the power innovators need may be already attached to their positions and available for investing in an innovation, the rest must be sought through allies. Thus, the organization's structure determines the amount and availability of power via both the distribution of power tools and the ease with which coalitions can be formed. Access to external and internal sources of power increases an innovation entrepreneur's chances of successfully creating an innovation.

Coalition Structure

Which parties are potential coalition members? Principally those on whom the innovator may be dependent—where there is interdependency affecting the fate of the idea. The concept of organizational interdependency has both a technological (Thompson, 1967) and a political (Pfeffer, 1981) component.

First, people often form interdependent relationships because of mutual task dependence. For example, a manager in a finance department may require financial information on operations costs from a production manager, who in turn receives back the financial information in some evaluated or analyzed form and uses it to assess production efficiency. The timeliness and quality of the information provided by each manager affects the other's work.

Second, interdependencies may be political in nature, since organizations are tools for "multiple stakeholders" (Kanter, 1980); managers identify and seek out others with complementary and sometimes competing interests for the purpose of trading resources, demands, etc. (March 1962; Cyert & March, 1963). Networks of interdependent members also form where people are joined by a variety of links through which goods, services, information, affect and influence flow (Tichy & Fombrun, 1979; also see Kaplan & Mazique, 1983).

In short, there are many types of interdependent relationships: *hierarchical* (Weber, 1978; Schilit & Locke, 1982); *lateral* (Thompson, 1967; Burns & Stalker, 1968); *oblique* (Kaplan & Maidique, 1983). In addition, people also work in the midst of multiple constituencies that are defined by common political or organizational interests and include persons outside the formal boundaries of the organization (Pennings & Goodman, 1977; Connolly *et al.*, 1980). Constituencies may form around task, issues, attempts to create change or block change, or salient values.

The size of the coalition is affected by how many territories the innovation crosses. The broader the ramifications of the issues involved in the proposed innovation and the greater the attendant uncertainties, the larger the coalition of supporters needs to be if the idea for innovation is to result in product action (Thompson, 1967).

Mobilizing a few potential members into an active, visible coalition also mirrors a classic dilemma in organization theory, that of finding the appropriate mix of inducements to obtain the desired contributions and work behavior from employees (Barnard, 1938). The inducements an innovator can offer to participate in a coalition include a variety of payments, such as financial incentives, resources, information, policy promises, learning experience, personal development, or emotional satisfaction (March, 1962; Riker, 1962; Gamson, 1968). The exchange of inducements for coalition participation can also extend across both vertical and lateral levels of an organization (e.g., Dalton, 1959; Blau, 1963).

Mobilizing coalition members through exchange assumes that "commodities" are available for trade, and the organizer had some control over their distribution (managers we interviewed often referred to this process as one of "horse trading"). Such commodities used to mobilize coalition members can also serve as the basis of organizational power; e.g., resources, slack, information, and political support (Mechanic, 1962; Kanter, 1977).

Access to these commodities depends to a large degree on their distribution within the firm; their munificence increases the ability to draw people into coalition that can work on an innovation.

Because corporate entrepreneurs often have to pull in what they need for their innovation from other departments or areas, from peers over whom they have no authority and who have the choice about whether or not to ante up their knowledge, support, or resources, to invest in and help the innovator, their work is facilitated by integrative devises that aid network formation and collaboration across areas: open communication; frequent mobility, including lateral career moves; extensive use of formal team mechanisms; and complex ties permitting crosscutting access.

Communication Density

Innovation flourishes where "communication integration" is high (Rogers & Shoemaker, 1971). Open communication patterns make it easier to identify and contact potential coalition members and to tap their expertise.

Examples of "open communication" systems from innovating companies stress access across segments. "Open door" policies mean that all levels can, theoretically, have access to anyone to ask questions, even to criticize. At several high innovation companies examined in one study, there were policies barring *closed* meetings. In others, the emphasis was on immediate face-to-face verbal (not written) communications (Kanter, 1983), unlike "mechanistic," low innovation organizations where written communications prevail (Burns &

Stalker, 1968). Such open communication norms acknowledge the extent of interdependence—that people in all areas need information from each other.

"Openness" at such organizations is reflected in physical arrangements as well. There may be a few "private" offices, and those that do exist are not very private. One manager had a "real" office enclosed by chest-high panels with opaque glass, but people dropped by casually, hung over the walls, talked about anything, and looked over his desk when he was not there. In general, people walk around freely and talk to each other; meetings and other work are easily interrupted, and it is hard to define "private" space. They often go to the library or conference room to "hide" to get things done, especially on "sensitive" matters like budgets (Kanter, 1983).

Open communication serves a very important function for the potential innovator. Information and ideas flow freely and were accessible; technical data and alternative points of view can be gathered with greater ease than in companies without these norms and systems. And thus both the "creative" and the "political" sides of innovation are facilitated.

Network Density

Coalition formation in the interest of innovation is also aided by conditions that facilitate dense ties through networks. Circulation of people is a first network-facilitating condition. Mobility across jobs means that people rather than formal mechanisms are the principal carriers of information, the principal integrative links between parts of the system. Communication networks are facilitated (see Thurman, 1979), and people can draw on first-hand knowledge of each other in seeking support. Knowledge about the operations of neighboring functions is often conveyed through the movements of people into and out of the jobs in those functions. As a set of managers or professionals disperse, they take with them to different parts of the organization their "intelligence," as well as the potential for the members to draw on each other for support in a variety of new roles. In just a few moves, a group that has worked together is spread around, and each member now has a close colleague in any part of the organization to call on for information or backing.

A second network-forming device is more explicit: the frequent use of integrative team mechanisms at middle and upper levels. These both encourage the immediate exchange of support and information and create contacts to be drawn on in the future. The organizational chart with its hierarchy of reporting relationships and accountabilities reflects only one reality in innovating organizations; the "other structure," not generally shown on the charts, is an overlay of flexible, ad hoc problem-solving teams, task forces, joint planning groups, and information-spreading councils.

It is common at innovating, entrepreneurial companies to make the assignments with the most critical change implications to teams across areas rather than to individuals or segmented units for example, at one company a team of mixed functional managers created a five-year production and marketing plan for a new product. This was a model of the method that top management endorsed for carrying out major tasks and projects. At a computer company, the establishment of formal interdepartmental or cross-functional committees was a common way managers sought to improve the performance of their own unit (Kanter, 1983).

The legitimacy of crosscutting access promotes the circulation of all three of the power tools: resources, information, and support. This allows innovators to go across formal lines and levels in the organization to find what they needed—vertically, horizontally, or diagonally—without feeling that they are violating protocol. Thy can skip a level or two without penalty. This is essential if there is to be hands-on involvement of managers up several levels, as Schroeder et al. (1986) found characteristic of large-scale innovations.

Matrix designs, though not essential for crosscutting access, can be helpful in legitimizing it, for the organization chart shows a number of links from each position to others. There is no "one boss" to be angered if a subordinate manager goes over his head or around to another area; it is taken for granted that people move across the organization in many directions; and there are alternative sources of power. Similarly, formal cross-area and cross-hierarchy teams may provide the occasion and the legitimacy for reaching across the organization chart for direct access (Kanter, 1983).

....

Idea Realization and Innovation Production

The third task of the innovation process involves assembling a working team to "complete" the idea by turning it into a concrete and tangible object (physical or intellectual) that can be transferred to others. The idea becomes a reality; a prototype or model of the innovation is produced that can be touched or experienced, that can now be diffused, mass-produced, turned to productive use, or institutionalized.

There are a number of critical organizational issues related to the ability to move an innovation through this phase. These issues join with social psychological (intragroup) variables to account for the performance of the group responsible for producing the innovation model.

Physical Separation

While structural isolation is a liability for idea generation or innovation activation, it is an asset for idea completion or innovative production.

Differentiated innovation units, separated from ongoing operations in both a physical and an organizational sense, are not necessary to *stimulate* or activate innovation (a task for which isolation is counter-productive), but they do appear helpful for ensuring that the working out of the innovation, the production of the initial model, actually occurs. Lockheed's term, "skunkworks," (taken from a Peanuts cartoon) has been used to refer to the special setting where innovation teams can create new things without distractions.

Galbraith (1982) has argued for the importance of "reservations"—organizational units, such as R&D groups, totally devoted to creating new ideas for future businesses—havens for "safe learning" managed by a full-time sponsor. Reservations can be internal or external, permanent or temporary. Galbraith found that some innovations, including the new electronics product he studied, were perfected at a remote site before being discovered by management; thus "the odds [for innovation] are better if early efforts to perfect and test new 'crazy' ideas are differentiated—that is, separated—from the function of the operating organization" (Galbraith, 1982).

High innovation companies in the United States, Europe, and Japan have flatter organizations, smaller operating divisions, and smaller project teams (Quinn, 1985). Small teams of engineers, technicians, designers, and model makers are placed together in "skunkworks," with no intervening organizational or physical barriers to developing the idea to prototype stage. Even in Japanese organizations supposedly known for elaborate (and slow) consensus-building processes, innovation projects are given autonomy, and top managers often work directly on projects with young engineers, including the founder of Honda himself. This approach eliminates bureaucracy, allows fast and unfettered communication, enables rapid turnaround time for experiments, and instills a high level of group loyalty and identity by maximizing communication and commitment among team members.

Boundary Management

If small, separate units aid idea model production, then boundary management is a particular problem. The team must continue to procure information and resources and return output to the rest the organization (Gladstein & Caldwell, 1984), but without becoming so outwardly focused that ability to do the job is jeopardized.

Success in building the innovation may be a function of how well external relations are handled as much as the technical feasibility of the idea. On the one hand, those who are prone to interfere must be kept from distracting the focus of the working team; on the other hand, the stakeholders, coalition members, and others whose support will be required at the transfer phase must be communicated with and involved, to ensure their support. The group must both buffer itself against too much input from its environment (Thompson, 1967) as well as manage the demand for what it is producing so that it has an appropriate level of exchange with the world around it—not too much, and not too little.

While many analysts have argued that "gatekeeping" is an important function in the management of innovation, Gladstein and Caldwell (1984) have gone further by identifying four boundary management roles in the new product teams they studied, roles that can all be played by one person or distributed throughout the group:

- Scouts, bringing in information or resources needed by the groups;
- Ambassadors, carrying out items that the group wants to transmit to others;
- Sentries, controlling the transactions that occur at the boundaries, deciding how much can come in;
- Guards, controlling how much goes out of the group.

Whereas scouts and ambassadors keep extragroup relationship smooth and get the group its needed supplies, sentries and guards buffer the group from outside interference. But note that all of these roles may be played by one person or just a few people, allowing the rest of the group to work on tasks without paying any attention to the world outside the project team. In the much publicized case of the building of a new computer at Data General, the project manager and his two aides handled all of the boundary tasks, allowing the team members to focus on completing the project in what proved to be record time (Kidder, 1981).

Boundary management is important not merely to get the working group what it needs and save it from unnecessary interference but also to handle any subtle threats to the continued existence of the innovation project. In one study, it was striking how little *overt* opposition is encountered by entrepreneurial managers—perhaps because their success at coalition building determines whether a project starts at all. Opposition or resistance seemed to take a more passive form instead: criticism of specific details of the plan, foot-dragging, low response to requests, unavailability, or arguments for preferential allocation of scarce time and resources to other pet projects. Early opposition was likely to take the form of skepticism and therefore reluctance to commit time or resources. Later opposition was likely to take the form of direct challenge to specific details of the plan that is unfolding (Kanter, 1983).

The nature of the opposition becomes clearer at the idea production points in the innovation process for several reasons. First, the very act of contacting others in the course of realizing an idea may mobilize what would otherwise have been latent or unorganized opposition. Most people will not spend their fund of political capital by overtly opposing a new idea right away, especially if it has the support of someone who is powerful, because it may never "get off the ground." Political capital would have been depleted unnecessarily. It is when it looks as though the project might actually happen that the critics begin to surface, generally arguing at the project's most vulnerable point that it has had enough time to prove itself; time to move on to something else (usually the critic's own pet project) (Kanter, 1983).

At the same time, many new ventures or innovation projects tend to be relatively invisible in the beginning, occurring in hidden corners of the organization or not significant enough to warrant their rivals' or competitors' attention. But as the effort gets closer and closer to results, it becomes more of a threat, and rivals begin to take action to crush it. At Apple, for example, a start up company by an employee was passively tolerated by chairman Jobs, but when it looked like that group might actually have a rival technology, he threatened suit, saying that it had been developed on Apple time and Apple owned it (Moritz, 1984).

My research identified a number of tactics that innovators used to disarm opponents: *waiting it out* (when the entrepreneur has no tools with which to directly counter the opposition); *wearing them down* (continuing to repeat the same arguments and not giving ground); *appealing to larger principles* (tying the innovation to an unassailable value or person); *inviting them in* (finding a way that opponents could share the "spoils" of the innovation); *sending emissaries to smooth the way and plead the case* (picking diplomats on the project team to periodically visit critics and present them with information); *displaying support* (asking sponsors for a visible demonstration of backing); *reducing the stakes* (deescalating the number of losses or changes implied by the innovation); and *warning the critics* (letting them know they would be challenged at an important meeting—with top management, for example). Note that many of these are more likely to succeed when the innovation group has a strong coalition backing it. The effectiveness of interpersonal processes depends on structural conditions.

Because of the controversy that surrounds many innovations, it is important for the working team to continue to send information outward. For example, when the project nears completion and there are things to see, they may begin to bring important people in to view the activities. Successful innovators have been observed to "manage the press," working to create favorable and up-to-date impressions in the minds of peers and key supporters (Kanter, 1983). Similarly, Friedlander and Scott (1981) found that activities of change teams were given more legitimation and were more likely to be implemented when there was a great deal of communication with top management, including two-way dialogue about particular project ideas.

Continuity

Structural and social conditions within the innovation team also make a difference in success. Because "interactive learning" (Quinn, 1985) is so critical to innovation, innovation projects are particularly vulnerable to turnover. Continuity of personnel, up to some limits (Katz, 1982), is an innovation-supporting condition.

There are sometimes good reasons, from the project's standpoint, for people to leave: inadequate performance, interpersonal tensions, the wrong skills. But every loss-and-replacement can jeopardize the success of the innovation process, in three different ways:

1. Each person leaving removes knowledge from the pool, that has not yet been routinized or systematized. In a sense, everyone leaving an innovation project does indeed take "secrets" with them—private knowledge they may have gained that has not yet been shared with the rest of the team because of the intensity with which everyone is gathering knowledge.
2. Each person entering deflects the energies and attention of the others from knowledge development to education—to try to duplicate the experience

base of current staff and avoid reinventing the wheel. But telling about it is not only time consuming; it is indeed no substitute for having been there.

3. Each person entering in a key position may wish to change course in order to exercise his or her own power, thereby failing to take advantage of accumulated knowledge. So every new boss is indeed a new beginning.

Turnover in key positions outside the project team can also create problems, though not necessarily as severe: The division is reorganized, for example, and the new management does not "understand" the venture. The coalition is disrupted and needs to be rebuilt. An organization can easily undermine an innovation without "officially" stopping it simply by reorganizing and changing its reporting relationships.

In one case, the problems of turnover are illustrated. A senior executive of a major instruments manufacturing company was recalling one of the company's venture failures—a new product start-up in one of the divisions. He knew this project well, because he had been the venture manager for the first 6 months. "I think about this often," he said, "because if I had stayed I think I could have made it work." Six months into the project, he was offered a promotion up several levels, from managing 15 people in the start-up to managing 6,000 in an established division. The career implications were clear: take it now or lose his place in line. The rewards were also clear: "The corporation was set up to reward the person running a stable $200 million business more than someone growing a business from zero to $10 million to $200 million, which is much, much harder." Even so, he remembered, "I wanted a week to think about it; I felt torn." Eventually he took the promotion. The start-up team understood the corporate career message, but they still felt abandoned. And the new manager sent in to replace him simply did not have "the feel" for what it would take to get his business going. Even more than loss of leadership, it was loss of experience that hurt this project.

Ironically, creating *change* requires *stability*—continuity of people especially during the information-rich, knowledge-intensive development stage. But established corporations often exacerbate the vulnerabilities of their new ventures and innovation efforts by the instability they encourage in and around them. Lock-step career systems that tie rewards to promotions, thus requiring job changes in order to "advance," or that put more value on the "safer" jobs in already-established businesses, encourage people to abandon development efforts before their knowledge has been "captured." Thus, organizational structures and cultures that allow *continuity* on innovation teams by facilitating unusual or "off-line" career paths, allocating human resources on a project basis rather than a time basis, and rewarding completion are helpful ingredients for successful innovation production.

Continuity is also supported where strong commitment is generated, so that people *want* to stay and *want* to contribute. Three kinds of commitment mechanisms are relevant to innovation efforts:

- Conditions encouraging a rational calculation of the benefits of continuing participation;
- Those encouraging strong social and emotional ties with the group;
- And those encouraging a strong belief in the fundamental values or purposes of the efforts (Kanter, 1972).

Structural and social facilitators of commitment to innovation teams would thus include these kinds of things, among others: A sense of "investment" might be produced by a financial stake in outcomes which grows with time spent, as AT&T's new venture teams have. A sense of "communion" might come from clear group identity and sense of specialness through team names, rituals, and celebrations like those in Data General's new computer development group (Kidder, 1981). A sense of strong values might come from reminders of the connection to user needs. At the same time, where there is also physical isolation of the team and very long working hours, energies have to focus inward, and the lure of competing ties is diminished. (See the discussion of "renunciation" in Kanter, 1972.)

It is important to note, however, that if too much time goes by before innovation completion, then team loyalty and stability can become a liability instead of an asset. Katz (1982) found that the "ideal" longevity of R&D teams is between 2 and 5 years. It takes 2 years to begin to work well together, but after 5 years the group becomes stale.

Flexibility

Flexibility is another requirement for idea realization. It is quite common for innovations to fail to proceed as planned but instead to encounter unexpected roadblocks or obstacles that require replanning and redirection if the innovation is ever to be produced. Cost overruns and missed deadlines are common, due to the inherent high uncertainty of the development process. For example, in one pharmaceutical company the ratio of actual to expected cost of new products was 2.11; the ratio of actual to expected time was 2.95 (Mansfield *et al.*, 1981).

Numerous cases in numerous fields illustrate the unpredictable nature of innovation, and therefore the need for flexibility in order to persist with a project. For example:

- GTE's Telemessenger would not show returns fast enough because, like most innovation, the product employed technology so unknown in the marketplace that prospective customers were not receptive to it, and several rounds of replanning were necessary to get the right configuration. Even assumptions about the scope of the test market had to be changed in the light of experience. What the team had originally imagined was a local test had to be rethought when the product was reconceived (successfully) as an aid to communication across the time zones, thus necessitating a national test. This change in tactics paid off. Though only 6 units were sold after a local mailing of 60,000 letters, 200 were sold at one crack to a multi-national company immediately after the test went national (Powell, 1985).
- The historic town of Alexandria, Virginia, now has an important factory redevelopment project on its waterfront, a project that seemed simple and straightforward when it was first voted on 10 years earlier but required several changes of direction midstream. But the city-owned Alexandria Torpedo Factory and Art Center almost didn't happen. Among a number of unexpected obstacles that nearly killed the project and required additional entrepreneurial effort to resolve was the fact that it threatened a small building used by a public school rowing program. Without the flexibility to make changes in order to persist with the project, the city would never have seen the results: a rise in the value of its property from $4 million to $31 million.

Thus, as Quinn (1985) found across three countries, multiple approaches, flexibility, and quickness are required for innovation of the advance of new ideas through random and often highly intuitive insights and because of the discovery of unanticipated problems. Project teams need to work unencumbered by formal plans, committees, board approvals, and other "bureaucratic delays" that might act as constraint against the change of direction.

Furthermore, innovations often engender secondary innovations, a number of other changes made in order to support the central change (Kanter, 1983). As necessary, new arrangements might be introduced in conjunction with the core tasks. Methods and structure might be reviewed and when it seems that a project is bogging down because everything possible has been done and no more results are on the horizon, then a change of structure or approach, or a subsidiary project to remove road-blocks, can result in a redoubling of efforts and a renewed attack on the problem. This is why Van de Ven (1986), among others, argued for the lack of utility of distinctions between technical and organizational innovations; in practice, one often entails the other. Indeed, restructuring of the organization often occurs during the innovation process, including joint ventures, changes in organizational responsibility, use of new teams, and altered control systems (Schroeder *et al.*, 1986).

Flexibility is an organizational rather than a purely individual variable. Those organizations that permit replanning, give the working team sufficient operating autonomy, and measure success or allocate rewards for results rather than adherence to plan are likely to have higher rates of innovation production. Because of the inherent uncertainty of innovation, advance forecasts about time or resource requirements are likely to be inaccurate; it is difficult to budget or to forecast when lacking an experience base by definition, in the case of a new idea. The GTE telemessenger was almost aborted when the project manager's first market test failed, because he had not brought in the results he promised, and he went through several rounds of argument to get an original "15 days to fix it" extended to 2 months (Powell, 1985). Requiring commitment to a predetermined course of action interferes with the flexibility needed for innovation.

Balancing Autonomy and Accountability

Some analysts argue that innovation production occurs better when the working team is left completely alone, freed from all bureaucratic procedural demands and allowed total concentration, total focus on its work. But there is a middle ground between the extreme of so many reporting requirements that the team spends more of its time preparing reports than doing the work, and the other extreme of no controls or measures until the end.

If some innovation projects fail because they are *overly constrained* by the need to follow bureaucratic rules and seek constant approvals, others may equally fail because they are *overfunded and undermanaged* by top leaders, which can remove the incentive to produce results efficiently. Indeed, Bailyn (1985) learned from her studies of R&D labs that many engineers were subject to overly constraining operational controls while permitted too much "strategic autonomy" to set their own research goals—just the opposite of the combination needed for success.

This can be a particular problem in large new ventures. In one case in a leading corporation, top management generously funded a new project development effort and then left it alone, assuming that they had done the right thing by providing abundant resources. Because they were so rich, the team wasted money on dead-ends and intriguing but unnecessary flourishes and failed to replan when early results were disappointing. The team did not need to justify their actions to anyone, and the project eventually failed. This is one reason why Stevenson and Gumpert (1985) argued that successful entrepreneurship involves *multi-stage commitments*—smaller amounts of money at more frequent intervals.

The ideal structural context surrounding an innovation project, then, should offer procedural autonomy coupled with multiple milestones that must be reached in order for the project to continue. These milestone points represent the major interface with organizational decision makers and perhaps coalition members. They also help maintain team members' own commitment by giving them targets to shoot for and occasions to celebrate.

Transfer and Diffusion

The culmination of innovation production is transfer to those who will exploit the innovation or embed it in ongoing organizational practice. Transfer needs to be handled effectively, if new products are to be successfully commercialized or new organizational practices or techniques to be successfully diffused. Isolated in its development, the innovation must again be connected with the actors and activities that will allow it to be actually used.

Social arrangements, from organization structures to patterns of practice, again make the principal difference, even more than the technical virtues of the innovation (Rogers & Shoemaker, 1971).

Strategic Alignment and Structural Linkages

Whereas creation and development—production of the innovation model—can occur with few resources, little visibility, modest coalitions, and the isolated activity of relatively small teams, *use* of the innovation is a different matter. If creation is an *intensive* process; diffusion is an *extensive* process. Use requires many other people, activities, patterns and structures to change to incorporate the innovation.

Thus, a first condition for effective transfer is minimal new change requirements because the innovation is aligned with strategy or direction and linked to the other parts of the structure, so that adjustments and changes have already been made in *anticipation* of the innovation.

It is not surprising that innovations are more successfully transferred, commercialized, or diffused where the organization or market is already receptive to the idea and prepared for its use. This is almost tautological. Where there is stronger organizational commitment in the development process, signified by funding, visibility, coalition support, and so forth, there are more "side bets" placed on the idea (that is, staking of reputations in the outcome) as well as greater "sunk costs." Thus, there will be more pressures to use the innovation in more ways and make it more central to the organization's strategy. Organizational arrangements will already have begun to bend in anticipation of the successful development, often through the negotiations among departments, the "logical incrementalism" through which new strategies are adopted (Quinn, 1980).

On the other hand, those innovations that begin life as random deviance, or unofficial bootlegging in a hidden corner of the organization, or the idiosyncratic dream of a tolerated-but-marginal actor, have a harder time getting adopted regardless of their virtues. Other actors, other departments have already made their plans without taking the possible availability of an innovation into account. Therefore, structures and practices have already been established that would have to be rearranged. These structural constraints to diffusion or transfer may be matched by political constraints: controversy over the innovation or refusal to use it by those uninvolved in its development. The latter is the common NIH (not invented here) problem; this problem particularly plagues organizational innovations (Kanter, 1983; Walton, 1975).

It has long been a cliche in the innovation literature (primarily because most scholars cite the same handful of studies) that diffusion or adoption of an innovation, once developed, is aided by formalization and centralization in the organization, by a concentration of power and a set of employees accustomed to following orders. The *opposite* structural features, then, from those that are conducive to a free flow of many new ideas are held to be necessary for ensuring the rapid acceptance of anyone.

Recent evidence, however, makes this a much more contingent proposition (Kimberly, 1980). Cohn and Turyn (1984), in a quantitative comparison of innovations in the domestic footwear industry, found that formalization and centralization were associated with adoption of *evolutionary* innovations but *not* with *revolutionary* ones.

A concentrated source of power is needed to *impose* the innovation on the organization or move it quickly through preexisting formal channels whenever the innovation has *not already been appropriately linked* to the units to which it will be transferred. Indeed, strong central authority can be argued to be just a functional alternative to strong direct links between an innovation project and those to whom its product is handed-off.

If an innovation development project is structurally well-integrated as it comes to completion, rather than segmented and isolated from the rest of the organization (Kanter, 1983), then it does not require the power of centralized authority to ensure its effective transfer. Other units have readied themselves to receive the innovation. Indeed, the hand-off or diffusion process is more difficult in organizations where interdepartmental rivalries and lack of integration cause friction when anything comes from a sister unit; then only "orders" from central authority are attended to. Perhaps this is why evidence indicates that successful new ventures in large corporations are more likely to be the ones sponsored by operating line executives rather than by corporate executives (Hobson & Morrison, 1983); the line-sponsored ventures are already closely connected with implementors.

Of course, effective transfer also requires a strategic decision that this innovation should get resources allocated to it, resources necessary to exploit its potential. For product and technical process innovations, and even for some organizational innovations, the greatest financial requirements *begin* after the model has been developed. Thus, the nature of the strategic decision process and how top management is linked to the innovation project is another critical structural element in an innovation's success or failure (Burgelman, 1984).

At the transfer point, when resources to exploit the innovation are allocated, visible and well-connected projects already aligned with the organization's strategic objectives are likely to fare better. In turn, the degree of investment the project gets, as it is moved into commercialization, routine production, or institutionalization affects its prospects for success as an ongoing product or practice. "Thinking small" and not providing adequate investment is often identified as a reason for new venture failures (Drucker, 1985). Research on the first 4 years of operation of 117 corporate ventures in established markets in manufacturing found that the businesses above the median in success began with capacity that could meet twice the current total market demands, whereas those below the median began with a capacity that could meet only 6% of the current total market demands. Furthermore, the "winning" ventures initially set higher market share objectives, had R&D spending levels twice those of the other ventures in the first 2 years and marketing expenditures about 1.5 those of the other ventures in the same period (Hobson & Morrison, 1983).

Interface Structures: Active Agents and Communication Channels

The transfer or diffusion issue should be conceptualized as a continuum. At one extreme there is perfect identity between the developers and the ultimate users, so that the innovators are essentially producing the innovation for themselves, to their own specifications, with foreknowledge that they will be using whatever it is that they make. Organizations can come close to replicating this condition in customized development work for specific clients already internally committed to use, in which client representatives actually sit on the development team. In this case, transfer or diffusion is nonproblematic; it is an inevitable part of successful development.

At the other extreme, there is little or no connection between developers and those to whom the innovation could potentially be transferred, nor is there an established transfer process. There is high uncertainty (an information issue) and controversy (a political issue) about what the next step is to get anyone to use the innovation, who should take it, and whether there are identifiable customers for the idea, whether anyone does or should want the innovation.

A variety of interface or bridging structures can reduce both the uncertainty and the controversy, thus making it more likely that successful transfer will occur.

One method for diffusing new ideas is to establish a group whose formal responsibility is to move new ideas into active use (Engel *et al.* 1981). Members serve as active agents of diffusion, managing the process by which the realized idea is transferred to those who can use it. Part of their mandate is to gather the information to make systematic the process of getting the innovation to users.

Inside organizations, such bridging structures might take the form of product managers, whose job is to manage the successful entry of a new product into the marketplace, drawing on every function in the organization that might contribute, from continuing work on the design to the manufacturing process to the sales effort. Or, in the case of organizational or work innovations, the bridging structure might be a transition team or "parallel organization" (Stein & Kanter, 1980) that concentrates on the change process as a management task in and of itself.

Agents of diffusion may also exist outside the organization. Indeed, it can be argued that external agents are even more important in diffusion than champions inside the organization, for they add real or imagined legitimacy to the idea, why Rogers and Shoemaker (1971) found contact with consultants such an important part of the diffusion of innovation. What is important is not only the cloak of respectability in which the external party clothes the innovation, but also the communication service provided. Thus, Walton (1987) found that the diffusion of work innovations in shipping in eight countries was aided by formal organizations set up to study and write about those innovations. They served as a necessary communication channel to transfer innovations to other users.

How well organized the environment is for the transfer of ideas can account for how rapidly a particular innovation is diffused. By "organized" I mean the ease with which those with common interests can find each other, and therefore how easily connections can be made between innovations and users. Thus, the existence of conferences, meetings, and special interest associations should all be valuable in diffusing innovations, even product innovations, which have to be brought to the attention of specific groups. Again, this can occur within as well as outside a particular organization. 3M and Honeywell both organize a large number of internal conferences and "idea fairs" to connect ideas with those who can use it or help take it the next step.

Trade associations, professionals and societies, and specialist consulting organizations are among those serving this purpose more broadly. The Food Marketing Institute, trade association for grocers and supermarkets, was largely responsible for facilitating the spread of universal price codes on packages from manufacturers and hence the spread of scanners in stores.

The Institutional Environment

The last issue in transfer and diffusion is a receptive and social and legal environment. The institutional environment, I propose, is so often taken for granted in the study of innovation that it tends to be visible mostly when it impedes. But the institutional environment is one of the most important factors distinguishing between eight nations in their overall record of diffusion of work innovations in shipping (Walton, 1987). Among the specific elements making a difference are patterns of labor organization and government policy and regulations. In the United States, for example, where innovation diffusion has been low, a series of fragmented labor unions bargaining independently with shipowners, with no vehicles for industry-wide collaboration by either party, accounted in part for the low diffusion rate.

The role of government in influencing innovation transfer can be a strong one. Hollomon and colleagues (1981) identified specific ways in which government policies and programs directly affect innovation adoption patterns:

- Assessment of new and existing specific technologies
- Direct regulation of the research or development of new products and processes

- Direct regulation of the production, marketing, and use of new or existing products
- Programs to encourage the development and utilization of technology in and for the private goods and services sector
- Government support of technology for public services for consumers
- Policies to affect industry structure that may affect the development and use of innovation
- Policies affecting supply and demand of human resources having an impact on technological change
- Economic policies with unintended or indirect effect on technological innovation
- Policies affecting international trade and investment
- Policies intended to create shifts in consumer demand
- Policies responding to worker demand having impact on technological change.

Whether innovations are ultimately spread and used, then, may be a matter of societal as well as industry organization. This level of analysis is not common in the innovation literature, but it demands more attention, particularly with respect to innovations that themselves have organizational consequences. Unfortunately, much of the literature is shortsighted in still looking for determinants of adoption of innovations in individual attitudes or intraorganizational structures.

But as organizations themselves bump up against the institutional limits to innovation diffusion, then the issues become clearer. For example, if the use of technological innovations has implications for job security, then the institutional patterns of labor relations in the industry may be among the most important determinants of an organization's ability to use such innovations. Several major companies are now attempting to reshape the broader institutional context in order to create conditions for more rapid diffusion of innovation within their borders. General Motors, is a notable example, planning the new Saturn subsidiary jointly with the United Auto Workers Union, using a series of joint committees. Pacific Telesis is also reshaping relations with its principal unions through local common interest forums of company officers and union presidents that define many workplace policies together. But even if the unions concur, the current labor law framework may be a significant impediment; Pacific Telesis has already faced one legal challenge to institutional restructuring.

Innovation, and the spread of innovation, is also a function of industry conditions and the support an organization can draw from its larger community, as research by Ruttan and Hayami (1984) and Trist (1981) shows. The more dependent an organization is on others (Pfeffer & Salancik, 1977), the more likely that it will be shaped or constrained in its internal innovation by those portions of the environment which dominate it. But the opposite also holds. Some environments represent "fertile fields" that provide more of the surrounding conditions conductive to innovation.

"Fertile fields" include these kinds of features, associated with entrepreneurship in the form of start-ups as well as innovation in established organizations:

- Close proximity and ample communication between innovators and users
- A more highly skilled, professionalized, cosmopolitan workforce
- A flow of new technical ideas from R&D centers
- A more complex, heterogeneous environment that encourages innovation as an uncertainty-reduction strategy (Kimberly, 1981)
- Channels of communication for exchange of innovation ideas
- Competition from entrepreneurial new companies, in turn benefiting from the availability of venture capital
- More interorganization interdependence and integration (Pierce and Delbecq, 1977)
- Public encouragement of new ideas as social goods.

This brings us full circle, for many of these same conditions help activate the innovation process as well as diffuse the models later.

The ultimate set of social structural factors supporting innovation, then, comes from the nature of the environment in which an organization operates as well as its connections to various key units in that environment. Although an innovation model may be produced in one organization independently and in isolation, it takes the actions of many for the innovation to diffuse.

It is appropriate to look beyond the borders of one organization for the determinants of innovation. Indeed, some innovations can start life as the joint product of more than one organization, through joint ventures, cooperative research efforts, and strategic alliances. The reputed Japanese "edge" in technology diffusion is said to come precisely from an institutional context allowing and encouraging such interorganizational cooperation in the same industry—a strategy still largely limited by U.S. antitrust laws. Furthermore, sometimes organizations unwittingly cooperate in innovation. For example, the failure of innovation in one organization can be the trigger for the creation of a new organization designed solely to develop that same innovation, the entrepreneurial process that has led to spinoffs from larger companies that reject innovations developed and exploited successfully by start-up companies. And the contribution of some organizations to innovation is to generate new organizations (e.g., Wiewel and Hunter, 1985).

Conclusion

I have tried to connect the major tasks in the innovation process to those structural arrangements and social patterns that facilitate each. Innovation consists of a set of processes carried out at the micro-level, by individuals and groups of individuals; and these micro-processes are in turn stimulated, facilitated, and enhanced—or the opposite—by a set of macro-structural conditions. Overall, the common organizational threads behind innovation are breadth of reach, flexibility of action, and above all, integration between those with pieces to contribute, whether inside or outside a single organization.

Undeniably, innovation stems from individual talent and creativity. But whether or not individual skills are activated, exercised, supported, and channelled into the production of a new model that can be used, is a function of the organizational and interorganizational context. Throughout, I have marshalled evidence to show the importance of integration to the innovation process, close structural connections between potential innovators and users, between functions and departments, between the innovation project and the units or organizations that will move the model into production and use. I have also shown that the integrative organizational model helpful for innovation extends beyond the borders of a single organization. Innovation benefits from interorganizational ties and organization-environment linkages as well as from internal integration.

Making a thousand flowers bloom is not a fully random or accidental process, unless we are satisfied with spindly, fragile wild flowers. Instead, the flowers of innovation can be cultivated and encouraged to multiply in the gardens of organizations designed on the integrative model, organizations where the growth rhythm of innovation is well understood.

Notes

The highly competent assistance of David V. Summers and Paul Myers is gratefully acknowledged.

Funding was provided by the Division of Research of the Harvard Business School, whose generosity is appreciated.

References

Abernathy, W.J., & Utterback, J.M. (1978). Patterns of industrial innovation. *Technology Review, 80* (June/July) 41–47.

Allen, T.J. (1984). *Managing the flow of technology: Technology transfer and the dissemination of technological information within the R&D organization.* Cambridge, MA: MIT Press.

Amabile, T.M. (1983). *The social psychology of creativity.* New York: Springer-Verlag.

Axelrod, R. (1970). *Conflict of interest.* Chicago: Marham.

Bacharach, S.B., & Lawler, E.J. (1960). *Power and politics in organizations.* San Francisco: Jossey-Bass.

Bailyn, L. (1985). Autonomy in the industrial R&D lab. *Human Resource Management, 24,* 129–146.

Barnard, C.I. (1938). *The functions of the executive.* Cambridge, MA: Harvard University Press.

Biggadike, R. (1979). The risky business of diversification. *Harvard Business Review, 57* (May–June), 103–111.

Blau, P.M. (1963). *The dynamics of bureaucracy* (2nd ed.). Chicago: The University of Chicago Press.

Burgelman, R.A. (1984). Managing the internal corporate venturing process. *Sloan Management Review, 25* (Winter), 33–48.

Burns, T., & Stalker, G.M. (1968). *The management of innovation* (2nd ed.). London: Tavistock.

Child, J. (1972). Organizational structure, environment and performance: The role of strategic choice. *Sociology, 6,* 1–22.

Cohn, S.F., & Turyn, R.M. (1984). Organizational structure, decision-making procedures, and the adoption of innovations. *IEEE Transactions on Engineering Management, EM31* (November), 154–161.

Connolly, T., Conlon, E., & Deutsch, S. (1980). Organizational effectiveness: A multiple-constituency approach. *Academy of Management Review, 5,* 211–217.

Cyert, R.M., & March, J.G. (1963). *A behavioral theory of the firm.* Englewood Cliffs, NJ: Prentice-Hall.

Dalton, M. (1959). *Men who manage.* New York: John Wiley & Sons.

Davis, S.M., & Lawrence, P.R. (1977). *Matrix.* Reading, MA: Addison-Wesley.

Delbecq, A.L., & Mills, P.K. (1985). Managerial practices that enhance innovation. *Organizational Dynamics, 14* (Summer), 24–34.

Drucker, P.F. (1985). *Innovation and entrepreneurship—Practice and principles.* New York: Harper & Row.

Engel, J.F., Kollat, D.T., & Blackwell, R.D. (1981). Diffusion of innovations. In R.R. Rothberg (Ed.), *Corporate strategy and product innovation* (pp. 472–481). New York: Free Press.

Fast, N.D. (1979). The future of industrial new venture departments. *Industrial Marketing Management, 8* (November), 264–273.

Friedlander, F., & Scott, B. (1981). The use of task groups and task forces in organizational change. In C. Cooper & R. Payne (Eds.), *Groups at work* (pp. 191–217). New York: John Wiley & Sons.

Galbraith, J. (1982). Designing the innovating organization. *Organizational Dynamics,* *10* (Summer), 5–25.

Gamson, W.A. (1968). Coalition formation. *International Encyclopedia of the Social Sciences* (pp. 529–534). New York: The MacMillan Co. and The Free Press.

Gladstein, D., & Caldwell, D. (1984). Boundary management in new product teams. In *Academy of Management Proceedings* (pp. 161–165).

Hage, J., & Aiken, M. (1967). Program change and organizational properties: A comparative analysis. *American Journal of Sociology, 72,* 503–579.

Hage, J., & Dewar, R. (1973). Elite values vs. organizational structure in predicting innovation. *Administrative Science Quarterly, 18,* 279–290.

Hanan, M. (1976). Venturing corporations: Think small to stay strong. *Harvard Business Review, 54* (May–June), 139–148.

Hobson, E.L., & Morrison, R.M. (1983). How do corporate startup ventures fare? In J.A. Hornaday, J.A. Timmons, & Karl H. Vesper (Eds.), *Frontiers of entrepreneurial research* (pp. 390–410). Wellesley, MA: Babson College Center for Entrepreneurial Studies.

Hollomon, J.H. (1981). Government and the innovation process. In R.R. Rothberg (Ed.), *Corporate strategy and product innovation* (pp. 46–59). New York: Free Press.

Kanter, R.M. (1972). *Commitment and community.* Cambridge, MA: Harvard University Press.

Kanter, R.M. (1977). *Men and women in the corporation.* New York: Basic Books.

Kanter, R.M. (1980). *Power and change in and by organizations: Setting intellectual directions for organizational analysis.* Paper presented at American Sociological Association Annual Meeting.

Kanter, R.M. (1982). The middle manager as innovator. *Harvard Business Review, 61* (July–August), 95–105.

Kanter, R.M. (1983). *The change masters.* New York: Simon & Schuster.

Kanter, R.M. (1985). Supporting innovation and venture development in established corporations. *Journal of Business Venturing, 1* (Winter), 47–60.

Kanter, R.M. (1986). Creating the creative environment. *Management Review, 75* (February), 11–12.

Kanter, R.M., & Stein, B.A. (Eds.) (1979). *Life in organizations.* New York: Basic Books.

Kaplan, R.E., & Mazque, M. (1983). *Trade routes: The manager's network of relationships* (Technical Report No. 22). Grensboro, NC: Center for Creative Leadership.

Katz, R. (1982). Project communication and performance: An investigation into the effects of group longevity. *Administrative Science Quarterly, 27,* 81–104.

Kidder, T. (1981). *The soul of a new machine.* Boston: Atlantic Little, Brown.

Kimberly, J.R. (1980). Initiation, innovation, and institutionalization in the creation process. In J.R. Kimberly & R.H. Miles (Eds.), *The organizational life cycle* (18–43). San Francisco: Jossey-Bass.

Kimberly, J.R. (1981). Managerial innovations. In W.H. Starbuck (Ed.), *Handbook of organizational design* (Vol. 1, pp. 84–104). New York: Oxford University Press.

Kimberly, J.R., & Evanisko, M.J. (1979). *Organizational innovation.* Working paper A27, School of Organization and Management, Yale University.

Maidique, M.A. (1980). Entrepreneurs, champions, and technological innovation. *Sloan Management Review, 21* (Winter), 59–76.

Mansfield, E., Rapoport, J., Schnee, J., Wagner, S., & Hamburger, N. (1981). Research and innovation in the modern corporation. In R.R. Rothberg (Ed.), *Corporate strategy and product innovation* (pp. 416–427). New York: Free Press.

March, J.G. (1962). The business firm as a political coalition. *The Journal of Politics, 24*, 662–678.

Marquis, D.G., & Myers, S. (1969). *Successful industrial innovations.* Washington, DC: National Science Foundation.

Mechanic, D. (1962). Sources of power of lower participants in complex organizations. *Administrative Science Quarterly, 7*, 347–364.

Mintzberg, H. (1981). Organizational design: Fashion or fit? *Harvard Business Review, 59* (Jan.–Feb.), 103–116.

Mohr, L.B. (1978). *Explaining organizational behavior.* San Francisco: Jossey-Bass.

Moritz, M. (1984). *The little kingdom: The private story of Apple Computer.* New York: Morrow.

Pelz, D., & Andrews, F. (1966). *Scientists in organizations.* New York: John Wiley & Sons.

Pennings, J.M., & Goodman, P.S. (1977). Toward a workable framework. In P.S. Goodman, J.M. Pennings & Associates. *New perspectives in organizational effectiveness* (pp. 146–184). San Francisco: Jossey-Bass.

Perrow, C. (1981). *Normal accidents.* New York: Basic.

Pfeffer, J. (1981). *Power in organizations.* Boston: Pitman.

Pfeffer, J., & Salancik, G.R. (1977). Organization design: The case for a coalition model of organizations. *Organizational Dynamics, 6* (Autumn), 15–29.

Pierce, J.L., & Delbecq, A.L. (1977). Organization structure, individual attitudes and innovation. *Academy of Management Review, 2*, 27–37.

Powell, J. (1985). Bootstrap entrepreneurs at GTE TeleMessenger. *GTE Together.* Winter.

Quinn, J.B. (1979). Technological innovation, entrepreneurship and strategy. *Sloan Management Review, 20* (Spring), 19–30.

Quinn, J.B. (1980). *Strategies for change: Logical incrementalism.* Homewood, IL: Irwin.

Quinn, J.B. (1985). Managing innovation: Controlled chaos. *Harvard Business Review, 63* (May–June), 73–84.

Riker, W.H. (1962). *The theory of political coalitions.* New Haven: Yale University Press.

Robertson, T., & Wind, Y. (1983). Organizational cosmopolitanism and innovation. *Academy of Management Journal, 26*, 332–338.

Rogers, E.M., & Shoemaker, F.F. (1971). *Communication of innovations: A cross-cultural approach* (2nd ed.). New York: The Free Press.

Ruttan, V.W., & Hayami, Y. (1984). Toward a theory of induced institutional innovation. *Journal of Development Studies, 20*, 203–223.

Schilit, W.K., & Locke, E.A. (1982). A study of upward influence in organizations. *Administrative Science Quarterly, 27*, 304–316.

Schon, D. (1967). *Technology and change.* New York: Delacorte.

Schon, D. (1971). *Beyond the stable state.* New York: Norton.

Schroeder, R., Van de Ven, A., Scudder, G., & Polley, D. (1986). Observations leading to a process model of innovation. Discussion Paper No. 48, Strategic Management Research Center, University of Minnesota.

Starbuck, W.H. (1983). Organizations as action generators. *American Sociological Review, 48*, 91–115.

Staw, B.M. (1975). Attribution of the 'causes' of performance: A general alternative interpretation of cross-sectional research on organizations. *Organizational Behavior and Human Performance, 13*, 414–432.

Stein, B.A., & Kanter, R.M. (1980). Building the parallel organization: Toward mechanisms for permanent quality of work life. *Journal of Applied Behavioral Science, 16*, 371–388.

Stevenson, H., & Gumpert, D. (1985). The heart of entrepreneurship. *Harvard Business Review, 64* (March–April), 84–94.

Summers. D.V. (1986). Organizing in middle management: A politico-structural model of coalition formation in complex organizations. Ph.D. dissertation, Department of Sociology, Yale University.

Thompson, J.P. (1967). *Organization in action.* New York: McGraw-Hill.

Thurman, B. (1979–1980). In the office: Networks and coalitions. *Social Networks, 2*, 47–63.

Tichy, N., & Fombrun, C. (1979). Network analysis in organizational settings. *Human Relations, 32*, 923–965.

Tosi, H., & Tosi, L. (1986). What managers need to know about knowledge-based pay. *Organizational Dynamics, 14* (Winter), 52–64.

Trist, E. (1981). The evolution of sociotechnical systems as a conceptual framework and as an action research program. In A. Van de Ven & W. Joyce (Eds.), *Perspective on organization design and behavior* (pp. 19–75). New York: John Wiley & Sons.

Tushman, M. (1977). Special boundary roles in the innovation process. *Administrative Science Quarterly, 22*, 587–605.

Tushman, M. (1979). Work characteristics and subunit communication structure: A contingency analysis. *Administrative Science Quarterly, 24*, 82–98.

Tushman, M., & Nadler, D. (1986). Organizing for innovation. *California Management Review, 28* (Spring), 74–92.

Van de Ven, A.H. (1986). Central problems in the management of innovation. *Management Science, 32*, 590–607.

Von Hippel, E. (1981). Users as innovators. In R.R. Rothberg (Ed.), *Corporate strategy and product innovation* (pp. 239–251). New York: Free Press.

Walton, R. (1987). *Innovating to compete.* San Francisco: Jossey-Bass.

Weber, M. (1978). Guenther Ross and Claus Wittich, (Trans.) *Economy and society* (Vol. 2). Berkeley, CA: The University of California Press.

Wiewel, W., & Hunter, A. (1985). The interorganizational network as a resource: A comparative case study on organizational genesis. *Administrative Science Quarterly, 30,* 482–497.

Wortman, C.B., & Linsenmeier, J.A.W. (1977). Interpersonal attraction and techniques of ingratiation in organizational settings. In B.M. Staw & G. Salancik (Eds.), *New Directions in Organizational Behavior* (pp. 133–178) Chicago: St. Clair Press.

Zaltman, G., Duncan, R., & Holbek, J. (1973). *Innovations and organizations.* New York: John Wiley & Sons.

9 Entrepreneurial Strategies in New Organizational Populations

Howard E. Aldrich

Introduction

The first organization of its kind faces a different set of challenges than one which simply carries on a tradition pioneered by thousands of predecessors in the same industry. Given the conditions facing pioneering founders, are different strategies needed for them than for imitators and borrowers? Focusing on the period during which a new form emerges is a crucial theoretical issue, because the struggle to carve out a niche for a new population involves such strong forces that the events of that period may be forever imprinted on the form that persists (Boeker, 1988, Stinchcombe, 1965). Defeat of opposing populations and co-optation of institutional actors, in particular, may cement a form in place that is resistant to change.

Focusing on the early phases of a population's life also reminds us that many promising populations never realize their potential, because they fail to develop an infrastructure, are unable to defeat or come to terms with opposing populations, and never win institutional support. Ecological studies have made salient the high disbanding rate within most organizational populations, but theorists have overlooked the logical corollary of low rates of population formation. Astley (1985) implicitly raised this issue, but investigators have not followed it up. Accordingly, identifying what strategies might be effective for founders of new forms helps us understand the forces contributing to increasing or decreasing variety in organizational communities.

Entrepreneurs confront two issues of legitimacy in crafting their strategies during the initial period of a population's life. First, key actors in the new population's environment lack knowledge about the novel organizational form, and this lack of information and understanding means the form begins with low cognitive legitimacy. Second, key actors—especially cultural and political elites—may withhold approval until a form has proven itself, thus producing an early deficit of sociopolitical legitimacy. Entrepreneurs initially must work with the resources their environments make available, and so organization-centered strategies are a logical first choice. However, population survival ultimately depends on unified action by organizations, and so entrepreneurs search for effective routes to collection action.

In this chapter, I examine the social processes surrounding the creation of a new population of organizational forms. After reviewing three empirical generalizations about foundings, based on ecological and institutional studies, I discuss two kinds of legitimation problems facing entrepreneurs: Low cognitive and low sociopolitical legitimacy. Both types of legitimacy are affected by the institutional, interpopulation, and intrapopulation processes affecting the growth of a new population.[1] I discuss the strategies that founders might pursue under these conditions, focusing on trust-building activities and behaviors fostering cooperative relations.

Some Crucial Observations

I first discuss the concept of a new organizational form, and then present three empirical generalizations about the early processes of a form's development.

New Forms

What is a new organizational form? Theorists have debated this question and not resolved it, although the broad outlines of a possible answer are inherent in various definitions of organizational form. Theorists searching for an *a priori definition* have suggested that forms are polyethic groupings of competencies, which are shared by most but not necessarily all of a population's members (McKelvey and Aldrich, 1983). Theorists with a more pragmatic, open-ended definition have suggested that a form is a set of observable characteristics known (or assumed) to affect organizational fitness (Hannan and Freeman, 1986). In this more pragmatic view, forms are sustained by forces which segregate them from other forms and are dissolved by forces which cause them to blend into surrounding forms—such as internal technological developments and external institutional pressures.

If forms are viewed as pools of distinctive competencies, then new forms may arise from competence-destroying innovations (Tushman and Anderson, 1986). They may also arise, however, from the development of competencies which are totally new, rather than in an existing stream of competencies. If forms are sustained by a balance between segregating and blending pressures, then new forms may arise from forces that operate on a source of initial diversity in a population, transforming arbitrary differences into differences with significant social consequences via a new balance of blending and segregating pressures (Hannan and Freeman, 1986).

In theory, it is possible to make a distinction between forms that begin with competence destroying innovations and those that begin with innovations that create a totally new stream of competencies. In practice, however, theorists have not used this distinction or have used it inconsistently. Regardless of whether a new population arises from a radical discontinuity that severs its ties to an existing population, or from an innovation with no clear historical roots, the situation faced by early founders is unlike that faced by people simply starting one more in a long line of organizations with an enduring population.

Three Generalizations

What is different about foundings early as opposed to late in a population's history? One of the strongest empirical generalizations established by organizational ecologists is that founding rates and disbanding rates vary systematically with the size of a population. This pattern, called density dependence, has been observed in many different kinds of populations in several nations: Nonprofit voluntary associations, local businesses, national businesses, and minimalist organizations (Singh and Lumsden, 1990). Analysts assume that populations develop historically by growing in numbers, and thus ecological studies using density are implicitly historical.

Consider one likely possibility: One might imagine that when a new organizational form first appears—when, by definition, population size is zero—the rush to fill the new niche would cause an explosion in the founding rate. From this viewpoint, we might expect founding rates to be highest when the potential niche is nearly empty and opportunity-seeking entrepreneurs are scrambling for advantage. However, founding rates are lower—sometimes substantially so—in the early stages of population growth than they are later.

Net of other factors, founding rates are low in newly established, small populations, increase as a population grows in size, and then eventually turn down again after a population passes a certain point. In some populations, founding rates at the later stages of a population's history return to levels similar to those observed early in its history. At the peak of the density dependence effect, founding rate are many times what they are at lower or higher levels of population size.

We might also imagine that the earliest entrepreneurs in a new population enjoy a substantial advantage over latecomers, such that they would have lower disbanding rates than those who follow. After all, they enter when the field is underpopulated, and product or service standards are still in flux. In fact, disbanding rates are highest, net of other factors, when a population is small. In some industries, a majority of the pioneering firms exit before the population reaches a stable point. The microcomputer industry exhibits this tendency well: "Several of the early entrants filed for bankruptcy (e.g., Osborne, Computer Devices and Vector Technologies) and many others had serious trading difficulties (e.g., Vector Graphic, Fortune, Intertec Data Systems, Altos Computer Systems and Grid Systems)" (Lambkin and Day, 1989, p. 13).[2] Disbanding rates decline as populations grow, reaching an asymptote before beginning to climb again as further increases in size occur. At their low point, disbanding rates are many times lower than the rates observed earlier or later in the population's history.

A second empirical generalization, not as well-established as the first, is that most new organizations in the early years of a population's history are r-specialists. Ecologists have identified two dimensions of organizational forms that are linked to different stages in a population's life history: r-vs. K-strategies, and specialism vs. generalism (Hannan and Freeman, 1986). The distinction between r- and K-strategies rests on the difference between forms which mobilize resources quickly and jump into an opportunity, at the expense of efficiency—called an r-strategy— and forms which mobilize resources more slowly and do best when conditions in a niche have stabilized, when a more efficient form has become evident— called a K-strategy. The distinction between specialism and generalism rests on the difference between forms which concentrate their fitness on a limited range of environmental conditions, in which they do exceptionally well—called specialists—and forms which spread their fitness over a wide range of environmental conditions, doing a tolerable job in most but being best in none— called generalists.

When an opportunity opens up which existing forms cannot exploit—even generalists, with their extended fitness set—r-specialists mobilize quickly and pioneer in establishing and developing the niche. If the population succeeds in holding and expanding the niche, eventually r-specialists are succeeded as the most fit form by K-strategists (generalists and specialists). Details of the succession process need not concern us here, as I am interested in the early stages of population growth, but the central dynamic is convergence on a dominant design, increasing standardization of products or services, and widespread disbandings of r-specialists (Anderson and Tushman, 1990; Lambkin and Day, 1989; Romanelli, 1989; Tushman and Anderson, 1986).

A third empirical generalization is that organizational age and disbanding rates are negatively associated. Originally formulated as the principle of "the liability of newness" by Stinchcombe (1965), the decreasing risk of disbanding as organizations age has been observed in many different populations (Aldrich and Auster, 1986; Singh and Lumsden, 1990). Stinchcombe posited a set of factors responsible for this association: The difficulty of breaking the ties of existing organizations to crucial resources, the need to create new social relations among strangers, problems in creating administrative routines from scratch, and so forth.

A liability of newness is apparently not characteristic of all populations. Some organizations in some populations experience a liability of adolescence rather than newness, as initial endowments protect young organizations for a short period—how long is an empirical question—and then disbandings rise to a peak before dropping again. Earlier investigators evidently overlooked heterogeneity in the association between age and disbanding rates because they did not control for differences in initial endowments, such as capital or sponsorship (Fichman and Levinthal, 1991; Brüderl and Schüssler, 1990).

The liability of newness may be particularly acute in populations with new forms, whereas the liability of adolescence may be more likely in established populations. If so, then disbanding rates for young organizations would be substantially higher in new populations than in established populations, and previous research has confounded the two.

Three generalizations, then, form the backdrop to my exploration of the challenges facing entrepreneurs in new populations: Founding rates are density dependent, rising and then falling as populations grow; favored forms are also density dependent, with r-specialists favored early in a population's history and K-strategists favored later; and, foundings face a liability of newness/adolescence which older organizations do not.

Entrepreneurs and Legitimation Processes

Entrepreneurs found organizations when they succeed in mobilizing resources in response to perceived opportunities. Identifying opportunities, assembling resources, and recruiting and training employees are problems face by all entrepreneurs, regardless of historical context. Environmental conditions make them easier or harder, but they are always problematic. Issues of an organizational form's legitimacy, however, vary systematically over the lifecycle of organizational populations, and organizational ecologists have argued that they are a major force driving density dependence in founding and disbanding rates. Two aspects of legitimation have been identified (Ranger-Moore *et al.*, 1991): Cognitive, or knowledge about what form an organization takes and what is needed to succeed in a population, and sociopolitical, or the value placed on a form by cultural norms and political authorities.

Cognitive legitimation refers to the process by which an organizational form comes to be taken for granted, and to the spread of knowledge about effective forms. When a form becomes taken for granted, time and other organizing resources are conserved, and potential entrepreneurs can copy a well-understood model. *Sociopolitical legitimation* refers to the process by which forms are accepted as appropriate and right, given the norms and laws of a society. A notable example is the institutionalization of labor unions in the United States with the passage of the Wagner Act in 1935, which gave special status under federal law to unions following the form specified in the Act (Hannan and Freeman, 1986, p. 62). Clearly, cognitive legitimation may be achieved without sociopolitical approval necessarily following (e.g., gin mills and speak-easies in the United States, in the 1920s, or underground abortion clinics in the United States prior to 1973).

The context within which new organizational forms struggle for legitimacy is set by institutional, interpopulation, and intrapopulation processes. Foundings of new organizations are highly dependent upon the events experienced by the small number of already existing organizations in a population and in the larger community of populations. Intrapopulation processes—prior foundings, disbandings, density, and factors associated with density—structure the environment into which new forms are born. Interpopulation processes—the nature of relations between populations. whether competing or cooperating, and actions by dominant organizations—affect the distribution of resources in the environment and the terms on which they are available to entrepreneurs. Institutional factors—government policies, political events, cultural norms—shape the macrocontext within which other processes occur. Clearly, conditions facing entrepreneurs founding organizations with new forms are substantially different from those faced by founders who are simply reproducing old forms.

Trust and Other Entrepreneurial Strategies

The institutional, interpopulation, and intrapopulation constraints facing entrepreneurs in new populations are considerable. In these situations, entrepreneurs must go beyond the strategies used when existing forms are simply being reproduced. In the face of such difficulties, what is an entrepreneur to do? In addition to the obvious suggestion regarding hard work and diligent effort, I propose that one answer lies in the social and interorganizational relationships founders of new forms establish. In particular, following ideas developed by Axelrod (1984), Gartner and Low (1990), Fiol (1991), Van de Ven and Garud (1991) and others, I believe that successful entrepreneurs are more likely than others to work on building networks of trust and cooperative exchange governed by norms of reciprocity.

Generic Trust

Gartner and Low (1990) defined trust as "the expectation that a business relationship will be successful" and posited that trust occurs when one party in a relationship believes that "things will work out." They argued that organizations emerge when entrepreneurs are successful in achieving an understanding among the trusting parties—potential customers, creditors, suppliers, and other individuals and organizations—that things will work out, and they posited that entrepreneurs achieve this condition by engaging in trust-building activities. They explicitly linked their ideas to ecologists' and institutionalists' notions of legitimacy, noting that issues of legitimacy and trust building are most evident during the genesis of organizations.

Three conditions must be satisfied for trust to arise: The trusting party must come to believe that the two parties have shared expectations, that the other party will make reasonable efforts to meet their shared expectations, and that the other party is competent to carry out the necessary activities (Gartner and Low, 1990, pp. 8–9). In their model, each of the three conditions is necessary to ensure trust. Borrowing from Zucker's (1986) analysis, they identified three modes of trust production: Process-based, which is tied to direct personal experiences: characteristic-based which is tied to shared social characteristics; and institution-based, which stems from an external source able to guarantee that the trusting party's expectations will be met.

217

Reframed in social network terminology, they have identified two bases for joint or collective action: *Categorical* —trust produced by similarities based in sharing membership in some nominal group (ethnicity, gender, religion), and *network*—trust produced by social relationships in which the trusted and trusting parties are implicated (friendship, work group, action set). Their third mode—*institution-based* trust—is really external to the trusting parties' relationship and must be invoked by one of them to be operative.

Gartner and Low (1990), following Weick (1979), provided an extensive discussion of the interaction sequences entrepreneurs would follow as they build an organization. Its essence is a series of repeated interactions in which the parties learn what to expect from one another and discover their mutual dependencies. As the sequences stabilize, an organization emerges.

Gartner and Low (1990, p. 18) argued that the concept of trust "provides a link between factors influencing organization formation at the individual level to factors influencing formation at the organizational and environmental levels." Specifically, they believed that the social process of gaining *legitimacy* is shaped by the interpersonal processes of achieving *trust* in the organizing process. The benefits from bringing together Gartner and Low's social-psychological approach with ecology's sociological approach is more readily apparent if we follow the distinction I have made between organizational foundings that reproduce old forms and those that embody new forms.

Trusting Others

Entrepreneurs creating new organizational forms face rather different conditions than those operating in the relative security of simply reproducing old forms. The "reproducers" operate in a vast sea of trust, compared to the "innovators." With their form having achieved high cognitive legitimacy, and most likely also sociopolitical legitimacy, most founders of recognized forms face relatively minor legitimacy problems. The "trust" dilemma they are preoccupied with is a very different sort of issue than the one faced by the early founders of biotechnology firms, for example. Indeed, perhaps we should label reproducers' problems as "postlegitimacy" issues.

Founders of new forms are, in a sense, even *more* likely to need trust-building strategies than the fortunate entrepreneurs described by Gartner and Low. Without the advantages of a taken-for-granted form and without widespread sociopolitical approval, founders must first call upon whatever personal and interpersonal resources they possess. Innovating entrepreneurs are in an almost pure "bootstrapping" situation—they must learn by doing. They must interact with extremely skeptical customers, creditors, suppliers, and other resource holders. Without the comfort of being able to observe existing, long-lived forms, why should potential trusting parties "trust" an entrepreneur's claims that a relationship "will work out?"

Thus, what entrepreneurs need is a set of supplemental strategies to those enumerated by Gartner and Low (1990, p. 31) for strengthening a trusting party's beliefs in the shared expectations, reasonable efforts, and competence of the aspiring entrepreneur. Innovators must overcome low cognitive and low sociopolitical legitimacy, and I suggest the following strategies, in addition to those listed by Gartner and Low.

Beginning Strategies

The fundamental strategy for gaining cognitive and sociopolitical legitimacy is a combination of Gartner and Low's (1990) process and characteristic-based modes: Founders must conduct their transactions according to the rules of cooperative exchange identified by Axelrod (1984). Axelrod wrote of the evolution of cooperation, and sociologists have written similarly of the norm of reciprocity: A set of rules which, if followed, sustain a mutually beneficial, non-exploitative relationship between parties whose interests potentially conflict. The emergent rules arise through a sustained process of repeated interactions, in which the parties learn to trust one another. An entrepreneur's individual goal is to construct and sustain an identity as someone who can be trusted.

Cognitive Legitimacy

Consider two different contexts in which organizing activity might occur, one a community in which there are diffuse ties of obligation and trust extending directly and indirectly to nearly all participants, and the other a community in which participants are mostly strangers to each other and ties are mostly instrumental. In the first community, participants may enjoy the benefits of a generalized exchange system, in which obligations are not necessarily repaid by the party incurring them. Instead, participants who share categorical and/ or network-based solidarity may assume the obligations of one another, as in kinship or ethnic-based communities (Waldinger *et al.*, 1990). In the second community, generalized exchange is not an option, and so participants must work within a restricted exchange system, in which accounts are kept between each pair of transacting parties.

In systems of restricted exchange, the possibilities of opportunism, exploitation, and other unfavorable exchange outcomes are quite high. Under such conditions, one extreme adaptation is to write iron-clad contracts, spelling out in excruciating detail all the contingencies in a relation, whereas at the other extreme, a firm foregoes arm's-length relations in favor of handling as many matters as possible "in house" (Williamson, 1981). Gartner and Low (1990) identified a third adaptation—to create relations of trust, in which parties believe that "things will work out."

In this situation of incipient trust, in which founders are building relations of trust from scratch, Axelrod's empirically derived set of rules for producing cooperative behavior seems a likely path to entrepreneurial integrity—founders should follow a "tit-for-tat" strategy. In two-person transactions in which there is the presumption that the relation will be continued through, perhaps, an indefinite future, we would expect effective entrepreneurs to do the following:

- Never be the first to defect in the relation—always keep their word, until the other party gives them a reason not to.
- In cases where the other party defects—breaks an agreement, doesn't meet agreed-upon standards, lies, cheats, or steals—astute entrepreneurs react immediately with action, showing that they are punishing the other party. Although the original formulation of Axelrod's rule allowed no "second chance" before reacting with disciplining behavior, in practice it is sometimes difficult to interpret others' behaviors as clearly not conforming to an agreement. Uncertainty about what constitutes a defection, problems in reading the other party's behavior (Fiol, 1991), and accidental defections are conditions which may deter a spirited response to perceived defections. Indeed, negotiation over the meaning of behaviors and the creation of a context of meaning in which behaviors can be better understood are at the heart of building trusting relations.
- Keeping the strategy simple and direct—although some theories of competitive strategy suggest otherwise, Axelrod's axioms suggest that if founders follow observable and interpretable strategies, other parties will not be misled into attempting defecting behaviors.

Entrepreneurs are in a situation where they must develop a new context of meaning, and not just adapt within an existing context (Fiol and Lyles, 1985). Incremental adjustments are admirable when a population is established and environments are stable, but founders of new forms must develop insights, knowledge, and a new context of meaning that allow the collective survival of a population.

Founders must construct an image of the new form as a reality, as something that naturally should be taken for granted (Gartner *et al.*, 1992). A new vocabulary must be coined, new labels manufactured, and beliefs engendered in a form with no natural history. Founders who can behave "as if" the form were a reality—producing and directing great theatre, as it were—may convince others of the tangible reality of the new form. Self-confidence and interpersonal attractiveness are probably important, but what counts is whether others believe in the new form.

Although formulated in the context of examining behaviors and meanings *within* organizations, Fiol's (1991) proposition that *identities* link an organization's culture—consisting of unarticulated underlying beliefs and values—with the behaviors of its members illuminates the task facing new founders. The trusting parties who are the targets of entrepreneurs' legitimizing strategies attempt to make sense of entrepreneurs' behaviors by drawing on existing understandings of what they observe. This meaning-making process is mediated by what the trusting parties perceive as the identities of the founders: Gamblers, serious business leaders, cowboy entrepreneurs, high achievers, wild-eyed inventors, water-walkers, and so forth. Note that any of these labels is potentially applicable, but that their meanings differ drastically.

Entrepreneurs can take advantage of the inherent ambiguity in interpreting organizational behaviors—finding the meaning to what is observed—by skillfully framing and editing their behaviors and intentions *vis-à-vis* the trusting parties. They need to emphasize those aspects of their ventures and their own backgrounds which evoke identities that other parties will understand as risk-oriented but responsible. If any "deception" is involved, it is surely self-deception more than deceit, because founders themselves probably have to accept the identity they wish to convey if they are to give credible performances.

Sociopolitical Approval

If founders can overcome the barriers to effective collective reaction, they can rise above the individual and organizational level and run together "in packs" (Van de Ven, 1991). Such efforts are often not very effective because collective action is extremely difficult to organize early in the life of a population. Nonetheless, the returns to collective action are so high that populations which achieve an effective level of self-organization have substantial advantages over others which are not organized.

Initial collaborations begin informally, in networks of interfirm relations, but some later develop into more formalized strategic alliances, consortia, and trade associations (Powell, 1990). Van de Ven and Garud (1991) noted that studies of high-technology industries, such as the cochlear implant industry, found that new-to-the-world innovations tend to be pursued by a handful of parallel, independent actors who rapidly come to know one another through personal interaction and through traveling in similar social/technical circles, such as attending the same industry conferences and technical committee meetings. This small handful of actors can generate networks which, in the aggregate, result in institutional-legitimating events.

A first-mover in a new population may become a node in a developing network of firms, or perhaps even a central point, acting as a broker (Aldrich and Whetten, 1981). As central points, they can significantly shape the course of subsequent events. However, as competitive strategy theory points out, first-movers often make mistakes, and are thus a target for followers, as well as a central point (Teece, 1987). Thus, first-movers may find they are better off running in packs than striking out very far ahead (Van de Ven, 1991).

Widespread knowledge of effective forms of business interest associations means that trade associations sometimes *do* start early in the life of a population, such as the Association of Quick Copy Shops, which was created relatively early in that form's history (Aldrich and Staber, 1988). Lobbying state and national governmental offices is typically carried out by business interest associations, agents (often lawyers) hired by associations, and designated employees of the very largest firms in the United States. Organizations with new forms find it difficult to compete with such lobbyists unless they also form an association.

Trade associations are "minimalist organizations"—able to operate on low overheads and quickly adapt to changing conditions—and are thus fairly easy to found (Halliday et al., 1987). Many trade associations, following the example of state bar associations and many other voluntary associations, operate out of the offices of member firms in their early years, and others are administered by law firms which represent some of the larger firms in the industry. Thus, the catalyst to an association's founding is often a population champion who steps forward and volunteers to cover the cost of running the association as it recruits enough members to gain a stable dues base. Typically, the largest firms in an industry do this, and they are well represented on the association's board of directors.

Once founded, trade associations play a critical role in promoting an industry's sociopolitical legitimacy (Aldrich and Staber, 1988). They help firms formulate product/process standards via trade committees, publish trade journals, they conduct marketing campaigns to enhance the industry's standing in the eyes of the public, and they promote trade fairs at which customers and suppliers can gain a sense of the industry's stability. Trade associations represent the industry to government agencies, and play a critical role in times of crisis which may threaten an industry's public image. Within 24 hours of the chemical plant explosion in Bhopal, India, the Chemical Manufacturer's Association had prepared an extensive press kit, recruited chemical firm executives to be interviewed by the media, and was moving aggressively to control the damage suffered by the industry.

Some existing populations may have cooperative (mutualistic, symbiotic, complementary, etc.) relations with a new form, and thus actually *assist* its emergence and growth (Astley and Fombrun, 1987; Brittain and Wholey, 1988; Staber, 1989). For example, some manufacturers of microcomputers assisted software companies as a way of expanding the potential uses of their products. Computer manufacturers bundled software with the machines they sold, loaned new machines to software producers, and otherwise contributed to their growth as an industry. In biotechnology, some startups have established strategic alliances with large pharmaceutical firms to manufacture and market their products (Powell, 1990).

If a new population faces overt conflict with another population, then a trade association of industry council will probably be required to mobilize the population's strength. However, many interpopulation relations are more matters of education and negotiation than of zero-sum conflict. For example, new biomedical and health-care populations only survive if they can convince their parties (insurance companies and the government) to pay the costs that patients cannot bear, such as computerized tomography scans or cochlear implants. Thus, firms in the industry must cooperate to educate and influence these third parties to include the product or service in their payment reimbursement systems (Van de Ven, 1991).

....

Discussion and Conclusions

New organizations are always vulnerable to the liabilities of newness, but never more so than when entrepreneurs have no precedents for their actions. The first organization of its kind faces a different set of challenges than one which simply carries on a tradition pioneered by thousands of predecessors in the same industry. Given the institutional, interpopulation, and intrapopulation conditions facing pioneering founders, different strategies are called for than those used by imitators and borrowers.

Not so long ago, such questions would have been addressed by focusing on the personality traits of pioneers (Aldrich and Wiedenmayer, 1992; Gartner, 1989). Investigators would have asked what mind-sets characterize pioneers, and what can we learn from studying these people? More recently, sociologically informed theorizing has focused on the social context of behavior and on the social forces which channel and shape action (Granovetter, 1985; Tilly, 1984), rather than on the personalities of actors. However, when sociologistic thinking is carried too far, it loses sight of the social–psychological processes that create and sustain the context of meaning for social behaviors (Aldrich, 1992; Powell and DiMaggio, 1991). I have argued that, at certain stages in a new population's history, entrepreneurs may need charisma, persuasiveness, and vision, all of which require strong interpersonal skills.

Legitimation issues vary systematically over the life cycle of organizational populations, and they are a critical force driving density dependence in founding and disbanding rates. I have used two aspects of legitimation in my analysis: *Cognitive legitimation*, the process by which an organizational form comes to be taken for granted, and *sociopolitical legitimation*, the process by which forms are accepted as appropriate and right, given the norms and laws of a society. I focused on dynamics at the individual and organizational levels, suggesting how the progressive building of trust may work its way *up* the hierarchy, collectively reshaping the larger environment. An individual entrepreneur's contributions are especially visible early in a population's history, at the r-specialist stage.

Imprinting

The period during which a new form emerges deserves more theoretical attention, because the struggle to carve out a niche for a new population involves such strong forces that the events of that period may be forever imprinted on the form that persists. The greater the conflict, the more extreme the struggle, and the more radical the breaks in existing interorganizational relations, the greater the likelihood that organizations will not examine their positions again. Indeed, the model of population development implicit in my argument points toward a population that eventually is in harmony with its interorganizational and institutional environment. As a settled member of the community, the new population takes its place as a defender of the *status quo*.

My examination of the early phases of a population's life also implies that many promising populations never realize their potential, because they fail to develop an infrastructure, are unable to cope with opposing populations, and never win institutional support. Thus, understanding the strategies used by founders of new forms helps us understand the forces contributing to population variety in organizational communities.

Rushing in Regardless

In the face of all the problems confronting founders in new populations, why do entrepreneurs continue to rush in? Moshe Farjoun (personal communication) suggested five possibilities. First, the gains to succeeding are so high that founders often disregard the costs of failing. Second, founders may be unaware of the risk they are taking, because they lack information. Third, even if founders know the dangers, they may believe they can succeed regardless, and even do better than most. Fourth, some founders start new ventures because they feel driven to accomplish a mission, and nothing can dissuade them. Fifth, in spite of the risks, founders may lack viable alternatives and thus see a new business as reasonably attractive (Waldinger *et al.*, 1990).

Thus, even though founding a new organization with an unproven form is risky business under any conditions, aspiring entrepreneurs continue to found organizations. The first organization of its kind faces a different set of challenges than one which simply carries on a tradition pioneered by thousands of predecessors in the same industry. Such foundings are risky, but they should not be labeled foolish. In spite of the institutional, interpopulation, and intrapopulation conditions facing pioneering founders, strategies are available which raise the odds of survival for founders willing to take the risk.

Notes

1. The intrapopulation level refers to relations between organizations within the same population, sharing a similar form; the interpopulation level refers to relations between two populations with different forms. These relations range

from cooperation to competition to mutual indifference. The institutional level refers to the organized actors that shape the context for a population, including government, sources of disseminators of cultural norms and values such as organized religion and the mass media, and the educational system (Aldrich and Wiedenmayer, 1992).

2. In some high-technology, capital-intensive industries, such as microprocessors and minicomputers, very few firms actually disbanded in the early years of the population. This raises three questions: Were all the startups actually identified or did some go through all the necessary steps for founding except the last (Katz and Gartner, 1988); what is the proper time interval to use in judging "early"— months, years, or decades; and, is there a systematic difference across populations in the level of initial resource endowments protecting individual firms against early exit (Fichman and Levinthal, 1991).

....

References

Aldrich, H. (1992). "Paradigm Incommensurability? Three Perspectives on Organizations." In Reed, M.I. and Hughes, M.D., eds., *Rethinking Organizations: New Directions in Organizational Theory and Analysis*. Newbury Park, CA: Sage.

Aldrich, H.E. and Auster, E.R. (1986). "Even Dwarfs Started Small: Liabilities of Age and Size and Their Strategic Implications." In Staw, B. and Cummings, L.L., eds., *Research in Organizational Behavior*, Vol. VIII. Greenwich, CT: JAI Press, pp. 165–198.

Aldrich, H.E. and Staber, U.H. (1988). "Organizing Business Interests: Patterns of Trade Association Foundings, Transformations, and Deaths." In Carroll, G.R., ed., *Ecological Models of Organization*. Cambridge. MA: Ballinger, pp. 111–126.

Aldrich, H.E. and Whetten, D.A. (1981). "Organization Sets, Action Sets, and Networks: Making the Most of Simplicity." In Nystrom, P. and Starbuck, W., eds., *Handbook of Organizational Design*. New York: Oxford University Press, pp. 385–408.

Aldrich, H.E. and Wiedenmayer, G. (1992). "From Traits to Rates." In Katz, J. and Brockhaus, R., eds., *Advances in Entrepreneurship, Firm Emergence, and Growth*, Vol. I. Greenwich, CT: JAI Press.

Anderson, P. and Tushman, M. (1990) "Technological Discontinuities and Dominant Designs: A Cyclical Model of Technological Change." *Administrative Science Quarterly*, Vol. 35, pp. 604–633.

Astley, W. (1985). "The Two Ecologies: Population and Community Perspectives on Organizational Evolution." *Administrative Science Quarterly*, Vol. 30, pp. 224–241.

Astley, W. and Fombrun, C. (1987). "Organizational Communities: An Ecological Perspective." In Bacharach, S.B., ed., *Research in the Sociology of Organizations*, Vol. 5. Greenwich, CT: JAI Press, pp. 163–185.

Axelrod, R. (1984). *The Evolution of Cooperation*. New York: Basic Books.

Boeker, W. (1988). "Organizational Origins: Entrepreneurial and Environmental Imprinting at the Time of Founding." In Carroll, G.R., ed., *Ecological Models of Organization*. Cambridge. MA: Ballinger, pp. 33–51.

Brittain, J. and Wholey, D. (1988). "Competition and Coexistence in Organizational Communities: Population Dynamics in Electronic Components Manufacturing." In Carroll, G.R., ed., *Ecological Models of Organization*. Cambridge, MA: Ballinger, pp. 195–222.

Brüderl, J. and Schüssler, R. (1990). "Organizational Mortality: The Liabilities of Newness and Adolescence." *Administrative Science Quarterly*, Vol. 35, pp. 530–547.

Fichman, M. and Levinthal, D.A. (1991). "Honeymoons and the Liability of Adolescence: A New Perspective on Duration Dependence in Social and Organizational Relationships." *Academy of Management Journal*, Vol. 16, pp. 442–468.

Fiol, C. (1991). "Managing Culture as a Competitive Resource: An Identity-based View of Sustainable Competitive Advantage." *Journal of Management*, Vol. 17, pp. 191–211.

Fiol, C. and Lyles, A. (1985). "Organizational Learning." *Academy of Management Review*, Vol. 10, pp. 803–813.

Gartner, W.B. (1989). "Some Suggestions for Research on Entrepreneurial Traits and Characteristics." *Entrepreneurship: Theory and Practice*, Vol. 14, No. 1, pp. 27–37.

Gartner, W.B. and Low, M. (1990). "Trust as an Organizing Trope." Unpublished paper presented at the Academy of Management Meetings, San Francisco, CA, August.

Gartner, W.B., Starr, J. and Bird, B. (1992). "Organizational Behavior/Entrepreneurial Behavior." *Entrepreneurship: Theory and Practice*.

Granovetter, M. (1985). "Economic Action and Social Structure: The Problem of Embeddedness." *American Journal of Sociology*, Vol. 91, pp. 481–510.

Halliday, T., Powell, M., and Granfors, M.W. (1987). "Minimalist Organizations: Vital Events in State Bar Associations, 1870–1930," *American Sociological Review*, Vol. 52, No. 4, pp. 456–471.

Hannan, M.T. and Freeman, J.H. (1986). "Where Do Organizational Forms Come From?" *Sociological Forum*, Vol. 1, pp. 50–72.

Katz, J. and Gartner, W.B. (1988). "Properties of Emerging Organizations." *Academy of Management Review*, Vol. 13, pp. 429–441.

Lambkin, M. and Day, G. (1989). "Evolutionary Processes in Competitive Markets." *Journal of Marketing*, Vol. 53, pp. 4–20.

McKelvey, B. and Aldrich, H.E. (1983). "Populations, Organizations, and Applied Organizational Science." *Administrative Science Quarterly*, Vol. 28, pp. 101–128.

Powell, W.W. (1990). "Neither Market nor Hierarchy: Network Forms of Organization." In Cummings, L.L. and Staw, B., eds., *Research in Organizational Behavior*. Greenwich, CT: JAI Press, pp. 295–336.

Powell, W.W. and DiMaggio, P. eds., (1991). *The New Institutionalism in Organizational Analysis*. Chicago, IL: University of Chicago Press.

Ranger-Moore, J., Banaszak-Holl, J., and Hannan, M.T. (1991). "Density-dependent

Dynamics in Regulated Industries: Founding Rates of Banks and Life Insurance Companies," *Administrative Science Quarterly*, Vol. 36, pp. 36–65.

Romanelli, E. (1989). "Environments and Strategies of Organization Start-up: Effects on Early Survival," *Administrative Science Quarterly*, Vol. 34, pp. 369–387.

Singh, J. and Lumsden, C.J. (1990). "Theory and Research in Organizational Ecology," *Annual Review of Sociology*, Vol. 316, pp. 161–195.

Staber, U.H. (1989). "Organizational Foundings in the Cooperative Sector in Atlantic Canada: An Ecological Perspective," *Organization Studies*, Vol. 10, pp. 383–405.

Stinchcombe, J.G. (1965). "Social Structure and Organizations." In March, J.G., ed., *Handbook of Organizations*. Chicago: Rand McNally, pp. 142–193.

Teece, D. (1987). "Profiting from Technological Innovation: Implications for Integration, Collaboration, Licensing, and Public Policy." In Teece, D., ed., *The Competitive Challenge*. Cambridge, MA: Ballinger.

Tilly, C. (1984). *Big Structures, Large Processes, Huge Comparisons*. New York: Russell Sage Foundation.

Tushman, M. and Anderson, P. (1986). "Technological Discontinuities and Organizational Environments." *Administrative Science Quarterly*, Vol. 31, No. 3, pp. 439–465.

Van de Ven, A. H. (1991). "A Systems Framework for Studying the Process of Entrepreneurship." Paper presented at a conference on Theories of Entrepreneurship, University of Illinois, Champaign-Urbana, IL, October 18.

Van de Ven, A. H. and Garud, R. (1991). "Innovation and Industry Development: The Case of Cochlear Implants." Unpublished paper, Strategic Management Research Center, University of Minnesota, MN.

Waldinger, R., Aldrich, H.E. and Ward, R.H. (1990). *Ethnic Entrepreneurs*. Newbury Park, CA: Sage.

Weick, K. (1979). *The Social Psychology of Organizing*. New York: Random House.

Williamson, O. (1981). "The Economics of Organization: The Transaction Cost Approach." *American Journal of Sociology*, Vol. 87, No. 3, pp. 548–577.

Zucker, L.G. (1986). "Production of Trust: Institutional Sources of Economic Structure, 1840–1920." In Staw, B.M. and Cummings, L., eds., *Research in Organizational Behavior*, Vol. 8, Greenwich, CT: JAI Press, pp. 53–112.

Innovation in Large and Small Firms

Kenneth J. Arrow

Introduction

This essay is intended to begin the elaboration of a theme: the interaction between the observed sizes of firms and their internal decision-making procedures. This theme is a major one in the symphony of entrepreneurial activity. The entrepreneur, as the maker and changer of economic and productive life, is usually envisaged as an individual. In the neoclassical tradition, he (or, rarely, she) is the lightning calculator, the individual who rapidly scans the field of alternative productive processes and chooses the optimum at any given set of prices. In the Austrian tradition, most notably in the work of Schumpeter,[1] he is endowed with a special psychology that makes him all the more an individual in the strict sense of the word—he cannot be replaced by a machine or by a multiplicity of individuals, who would inevitably slow him down. "He travels fastest who travels alone," says an ancient proverb.

However, the individual entrepreneur-proprietor does not loom nearly as large today as suggested by these accounts. The large—even giant—firm is a massive presence on the economic landscape. These large firms not only predominate in the static allocation of resources, but are the sources of much of the world's change. They share fully with others as the sources and users of innovations.

This is not to deny the continued importance of the relatively small firm and the individual inventor. Indeed, the coexistence of large and small firms is itself an interesting intellectual question. If, in fact, large firms do have advantages over smaller ones, why are small firms not eliminated in the competitive struggle? More generally, if there are differential advantages to one size or another of firm, why do firms not converge to the optimal size?

The presence of large firms creates logical difficulties for the concept of property and for the reward structure of the individual, as Berle and Means[2] pointed out almost fifty years ago. The sharp calculating eye of the neoclassical entrepreneur was for his own profits, and even those who gave a more psychological interpretation to entrepreneurial motives could hardly deny that revenue was essential among them. But an employee, however entrepreneurial in spirit, does not have property rights and cannot claim profits, the residual revenues after contractual claims. Much ingenuity can go into alternative compensation schemes, but the maker of decisions about innovations can no longer be simply identified with the recipient of rewards (and taker of losses) from them.

Of equal, or even greater, significance is the diffuse control structure of the large firm. Essentially, no one can make decisions without limits even within the framework of feasibility. Even a chief executive officer is restricted, partly because of the need to adhere to well-defined operating procedures, and partly because limits on span of control prevent him from making more than a limited range of decisions with limited information. In large firms, entrepreneurship has sociological as well as psychological and economic dimensions.

The remarks thus far show that entrepreneurial activity, however defined, operates in different ways in large firms than in small ones. I will concentrate here on entrepreneurship as Schumpeter conceived it—the process of innovation. The basic decisions are the recognition of promising ideas and the financing of their development. We want to discuss how these decisions operate in firms of varying sizes.

An economist would not, of course, discuss any issues of decision making by firms without taking account of market relations. Since the development of innovations is an investment, the most relevant market is the capital market. However, innovations are, by their nature, rather odd commodities from a neoclassical viewpoint. They tend to be indivisible. Their development is attended by uncertainty—if everything about an innovation were known, it would not be an innovation. What is still more, the properties and economic potential of an innovation are by its nature likely to be better known to the innovator than to a prospective source of financing.

In short, the supply of capital for innovation is not modeled well by conventional competitive market theory. Indeed, most of the analysis in this chapter will center about the methods of financing innovation and their implications.

The chapter is organized as follows: In the next section, I review in the sketchiest way the idea that large firms are really significant in the economy and constitute a phenomenon about which we cannot be indifferent. I then describe an idealized model of the process of innovation (oversimplified of course) designed to serve as a basis for subsequent discussion. The heart of the paper follows, an attempt to understand the factors in the decision to innovate and (what is essentially equivalent) the financing of the innovative activity. In particular, I stress the systematic variation of these decisions with firm size and complexity. It is concluded that there is likely to be a tendency toward specialization—less costly and more original innovations will come from small firms, and those involving higher development costs but less radical departures in principle will come from larger firms. This specialization creates opportunities for trade, as all specialization does; in this case, the trade will frequently be in firms as such—that is, takeovers and mergers.

The Significance of Large Firms

From the popular viewpoint, the concentration of economic power is one of the most obvious aspects of the economic world. In mainstream neoclassical economics, it hardly appears—especially in more abstract versions of the neoclassical system (for instance, Arrow and Hahn).[3] Of course, the presence of natural monopoly is recognized, and this is the basis for the doctrine of price regulation. Even here, many economists consider that there is sufficient competition from substitute products to make natural monopoly an unimportant concept.

The trouble is that the analytic tools of neoclassical economics are not well adapted to departures from perfect competition. There are two pillars to the edifice: the optimizing behavior of the firm and household, and the equilibrating forces of the markets that link them. Optimizing behavior can indeed be discussed under conditions of market power; the theory of monopoly is rich in implications. But the concept of imperfectly competitive markets is very hard to define. Various ad hoc constructions, such as Chamberlin's notion of monopolistic competition,[4] have appeared, but they suffer from inconsistencies. Game theory has supplied a formal framework that, in principle, replaces markets by more general forms of interactions, but it has not yet succeeded in producing a *general* theory comparable in power to the theory of general competitive equilibrium.

Hence, there is a bias toward analyzing the competitive case. As we know, this analysis requires, if taken literally, that the production possibility sets be convex. In particular, it requires constant or diminishing returns to scale. The latter case suggests a bias toward small firms—under free entry, the smaller the better. Constant returns, on the other hand, is neutral toward the size of firms. If two firms merge, the owners will (under perfect competition) be neither better off nor worse off than they were before. Under perfect markets, including perfect capital markets, the profits of two different activities will simply be additive.

A good deal of the empirical literature on firm sizes has been devoted to arguing that the competitive model is adequate in practice—that is, there are not many markets dominated by one or two firms. This may well be true; it follows that the static efficiency characteristics of competitive equilibrium can be postulated to hold in the real world. This is very far from denying the existence of very large firms or from explaining this phenomenon.

For it is certainly a fact. Depending on what measures you use, 500 firms constitute half or more of the nonagricultural economy.[5] It is frequently argued that the indices of concentration have not shown much secular rise, at least not for 75 years or so. However, this misses the point. The economy has grown enormously in this period. If it were merely a question of replication—that is, if the economy were expanding homogeneously—we would expect the number of firms to increase in the same proportion. Since firms differ in size, for whatever reason, we would expect the *proportion* of firms of a given size to be constant, while the total number increases.

To be sure, the expansion of the economy has not been merely a replication. The fact that per capita income is rising—and, more strongly, that factor productivity (output per unit input) is or was rising—implies a change in the proportions of the economy. But one component of growth in the market remains sheer size—population or total factor supply (capital and labor). One might expect, then, that the number of firms would be proportional to the extensive growth of the economy (its size in population or inputs), while the size of each firm might be expected to grow with the intensive growth (for example, output per capita or per unit factor supply). This is what has happened (roughly) to the distribution of individual income. It can be expressed as the constancy of the Lorenz curve—that is, the proportion of total income received by a given proportion of the population arrayed by income level (for example, the upper tenth of income recipients) is a constant.

But this is not what has happened with the distribution of firm sizes. The proportion of total sales or income received by a fixed *number* of firms has more or less remained constant.[6] Therefore, the proportion of income received by a fixed proportion of firms starting from the top (say, an upper decile again) has increased.

In short, we find that the size of each firm has increased more than proportionally to intensive growth. If intensive growth is identified with productivity (either of labor or of total inputs), it follows that not only the outputs but also the inputs of the average firm have risen. This implies that the forces determining the sizes of firms (in particular the economies of scale and the size of the market) have so shifted as to make larger firms more advantageous.

The increasing costs of innovation are a possible candidate, and the later analysis in this chapter implicitly makes the case for this proposition. At this point, however, I only wish to establish that there has been a significant shift to larger sizes of firms and that this shift has systematic economic consequences and causes.

One obvious feature of larger firms (as contrasted with smaller contemporary firms or even with the same firms when they were smaller) is that they are more complex. They are not simply scale expansions of smaller firms, any more than the economy as a whole is a scale expansion of its earlier historical self. Even if the added activities are similar in nature to the original ones, random fluctuations would make coordinating activities profitable. More broadly, growth usually involves disaggregation of activities and differentiation of products and activities.[7] No doubt these tendencies can ultimately be explained in terms of indivisibilities and other causes of increasing returns to scale. The complexity requires additional control functions at the central level.[8]

Coordinating activities themselves are costly; not only do they directly involve the use of resources (managerial and supporting personnel, associated equipment, space, and communication channels), but they also impose costs upon decision making at lower levels by creating delays and requiring additional communication costs. They are undertaken because the costs of coordination are exceeded by the benefits.[9] As Coase has argued, these benefits are relevant only if they are not obtainable by coordinating separate activities in the marketplace, through prices.[10]

This point can be emphasized by considering the multidivisional firm and the role of transfer pricing. A large firm is organized into profit centres, each of which operates as virtually a separate firm. Transactions between them are market transactions, and payments between them are made at current market prices or (if no suitable market exists) at transfer prices mimicing market prices.

Presumably the opportunities for direct (as opposed to market oriented) coordination of activities have been exhausted within the profit centers. What distinguishes the large firm, however, from a collection of smaller firms is that many resource-allocation decisions are still made at a central level—particularly capital formation. A profit center is responsible for its own decisions on current flows, but in general it cannot make its own investment decisions, except possibly for very trivial ones. Indeed, it is surprising how often decisions on investment require the approval of the Board of Directors, while decisions of at least equal importance relating to pricing and production are decentralized to much lower levels.

There is, in short, an internal centralized mechanism for allocating available investment funds to specific projects among the various profit centers. The internal capital-allocation mechanism is not, properly speaking, a market—that is, a profit center cannot borrow any amount at a fixed rate of interest. Rather, the project it proposes must be examined by the allocating authority for feasibility and profitability.

It would not be correct to contrast this allocation mechanism with an external capital market thought of as a true market in the textbook sense. Much, though not all, external financing is also project-specific and rationed. A bank does not lend by buying securities from anonymous sellers, but by lending to particular firms and individuals and often by looking at the particular project that lender wishes to finance.

(We will not here study why capital allocation is so largely centralized, even in an otherwise decentralized firm. Part of the reason, certainly, must be the relatively slow feedback. The head of a profit center is not personally liable for the costs of bad investments. Considering job mobility, he may not be around to take any consequences when an investment is realized.)

It is important to distinguish the existence or absence of an internal capital allocation (in this sense) from the presence or absence of external financing. The supply of capital available for internal allocation can come either from retained profits in the various profit centers or from the outside. Large firms in general have an advantage in access to the outside capital market. One reason is the principle of insurance. Investing as they do in a variety of projects, their earnings are apt to be more stable and, therefore, the riskiness of their securities is reduced. Another reason is an economy of scale in attention and information-gathering from the viewpoint of the suppliers of funds. A large firm is a greater demander, and it therefore pays potential investors to concentrate their attention on that firm's activities rather than scattering it in one-shot transactions over many firms, for each of which there will be relatively little opportunity to use the information.

Diversification of activities also implies a more stable source of internal funds. Hence, in general, large firms will have a disproportionately larger and more stable internal capital supply than smaller firms will.

A Model of the Innovation Process

Innovations are infinitely variable; indeed, they include all alterations in knowledge of current production relations between inputs and outputs. Most are very small, but those are not the ones we are concerned with here. We wish to stress those large enough that deliberate decisions are needed to proceed along the path of innovation. An innovation may never be realized as a product; if it is so realized, it may not remain in production very long. The process of innovation is, virtually by definition, filled with uncertainty; it is a journey of exploration into a strange land.

We take as a primitive of the system a stream of *concepts*—ideas for innovation. These occur to individuals both within firms and elsewhere. A concept may or may not prove to be feasible. If it is feasible, it may or may not prove to be profitable. These determinations require investment, and it is these investment decisions that we are investigating.

For simplicity, we will distinguish two further stages after the concept, those of *research* and of *development*. Somewhat arbitrarily, we will think of research as determining the feasibility of the concept and development as determining its profitability.

In this model, the concepts are random events, not controllable and unaffected by policy. They will, of course, depend on many factors, but especially on the state of knowledge in the relevant specialty. This in turn, may be influenced by previous innovations in the same intellectual area.

Decisions are made at the next two stages. First, research is needed to determine if the concept can be translated into actuality. The research may be more or less costly to carry out. When it is completed, it yields information about the prospects for development in the following sense. At the start of the development process, there will be a relation between the profitability of the innovation when it is finally introduced (possibly zero or even negative) and the amount invested in development. This relation depends on the information gathered in the research phase—that is, the profitability of the innovation at any given level of development expenditure will vary with the information obtained from research. Further, the relation of profitability to development cost is uncertain even given the research outcome.

To put it in a slightly different language, the research outcome is purchased by the research expenditure. The profitability of innovation after development is a random variable with a probability distribution conditional on both the research outcome and the decision about development expenditure. Given this distribution, the firm has the problem of choosing the optimal development expenditure. The optimal level might be (and frequently is) zero; but if it is not zero, it is frequently a very large amount.

In this simple model, there are two points at which decisions are made: (1) to engage in research and (2) to determine the optimal level of development expenditure. In the first decision, the information potentially available to the decision makers consists of the concept and publicly available information. In the second, it consists of the concept and the research outcome together with publicly available information. Of course, this oversimplifies the process in many ways. The sharp distinction between research and development is overstated: furthermore, the development process itself is sequential. Instead of a single decision establishing development expenditures for an entire project, there are repeated reassessments based on information revealed by the development process itself. However, our simplification will be adequate for our purposes here.

What must be insisted upon is the privacy of the information and its relation to the locus of decision-making. The two relevant pieces of information, to repeat, are the initial concept and the research outcome. They are received in the first instance by some particular individuals. If these individuals were the decision makers, there would be no difficulty in principle. The decisions made (to engage in research and to choose the optimal level of development expenditures) would be optimal given the information available.

But the individuals concerned are members of organizations, small or large. The decisions to be made involve the allocation of resources. Some of these decisions might be structurally delegated to them. However, as the amounts involved increase, there will be more and more need for approval at higher levels. The internal capital-allocation mechanism will become involved. The lower levels who have the relevant information cannot make the final decisions; their scope of authority is often restricted to making recommendations.

The important question then becomes, how is the information initially available communicated to the capital-allocation mechanisms? There are two classes of reasons why information cannot be conveyed without cost:

(1) communication channels have limited capacity; and (2) there are incentive effects that reduce the reliability of information transmission.

1. The specialists who have the concepts and undertake the research have more knowledge of the context than others. An engineer has had training that may not be available to the generalist who allocates resources. Thus, any information conveyed will not be understood as well by the recipient as by the sender.

Second, the specialists have spent more time with the project than any reviewing agency with many other responsibilities could. The capacity to absorb information is always limited. Hence, again there is degradation of information with transmission.

There may, to be sure, be situations in which the central mechanism has better information in some respects than the specialists. It might have better knowledge of other similar concepts and might well have better understanding of the commercial—as opposed to technical—possibilities. However, there will always be a degradation of the technical information, so that the probability distribution of outcomes of the development process (for given development costs) will on the average be wider.

2. Within a given firm it may be assumed, as a first approximation, that there is no distortion of the information; the specialist presents the information as well as he or she can. However, if information has to cross the boundaries of the firm (for instance, to attract capital from outside investors), the incentive increases to present information misleadingly. Negative aspects might be slurred over, probabilities of success exaggerated.

As a second approximation, there can be some distortion even within the firm. There is some incentive to increase the importance of one's work, to make it appear more valuable in potentiality and thereby earn material and nonmaterial rewards. As in any investment activity, the individual bears limited financial responsibility for failure. Furthermore, for research and development over extended periods of time, the feedback is so slow that the individual is not apt to be in the same position when the program shows results. Finally, the responsibility for success and failure in any position—but especially in one involving such uncertainties as those of research and development—is very hard to assess. That a project failed by no means proves that it should not have been undertaken.

From these considerations, the following implications may be drawn: (1) When responsibility for decisions on research and development is shared because of a need for approval of capital expenditures, the information used in making these decisions is apt to be degraded from its initial state. (2) The longer the chain of communication involved in the approval of projects, the more the information is apt to be degraded. (3) When the chain of communication crosses the boundary of the firm, the degradation of information is apt to be much more severe.[11]

....

The Decision to Innovate and Firm Size

We can now draw the threads of the analysis together. In particular, the different strategic responses of small firms and large firms to the emergence of research concepts will be analyzed. For simplicity, I speak as if there were just two discrete sizes of firm; of course, there is a continuum of firm sizes and a parallel continuum of innovation strategies.

Innovation has been described as a two-stage decision process. As usual, the appropriate analysis must proceed in reverse order of time. That is, we must first study the decision on development expenditure given the research concept and the research outcome, then analyze the decision to engage in research.

Suppose, then, that we compare a large and a small firm, both of which engaged in research starting from the same concept and observed the same research outcome. The small firm is well informed about the development possibility function—that is, the function relating expected profitability to a given level of development expenditures. It can therefore calculate an optimal level of development expenditures. However, if the amount is large enough, it will not be able to finance it from its own capital funds. It could seek capital from outside. Assume, however, that it has fully utilized whatever general borrowing power it has. Then it has to seek financing based on the project itself. However, for reasons adduced in the last section, the transmission of information across the boundary of the firm will be accompanied by considerable degradation. It follows that capital will be available from the outside only on unfavorable terms (if at all) so that the scale of development expenditures will be less than optimal. Indeed, if the amount of development funds required is very large, it will be essentially impossible to finance the project by borrowing.

A small firm can in many cases obtain outside financing by sale of equity. When the amounts involved are large relative to the initial size of the firm, the transaction amounts to selling the development prospects and is likely to be accompanied by a change in control. (I will take up the possibility of sale of research findings in the next section)

A large firm facing the same research concept and research outcome will have much less severe restrictions on funding. However—as usual in economic affairs—there is no pure gain without offsets. The difficulties of communicating with an external capital market are replaced by those of communicating with the internal capital-allocation mechanism. As we have seen, the information loss in the large firm is greater than that in the small firm, but less than that involved in reaching the external market. Therefore, the large firm will tend to invest suboptimally in development expenditures. However, it will do better than the small firm for large development expenditures that the larger firm can finance but the small firm cannot; it will do less well on expenditures small enough that the small firm can also finance them.

As an additional hypothesis, it might be supposed that the information loss in the large firm is greater for proposals with greater novelty. The prior information of the internal capital-allocation mechanism may not equip it to evaluate novelties very well. The smaller firm, having less information loss, may be able to accept greater novelty more easily (provided it can finance the development process). Hence, there may be a bias against greater originality in large firms.

It may be objected that a large firm is not more capable of financing large expenditures than a small one. It has larger resources, but it also has larger demands of all kinds. Hence, it is no more capable of financing a given large expenditure for development than the small firm, as it has other large development expenditures competing for the scarce funds. This is an important point. But there are at least two reasons why we would expect the financing ability of large firms to grow more than proportionately to their size: (1) as we have already seen, large firms have disproportionate access to the external capital market without reference to specific projects. Hence, the pool of available capital is more than proportionately larger. Further (as also noted) the size of the financing available is likely to be statistically steadier, decreasing the probability that a demand for a large amount of development expenditures will coincide with a transient shortage of capital funds. (2) If there are a number of potential demands for development expenditures, the demand will also be statistically steadier. There is a high probability that an above-average demand for development expenditures in one area will be offset by a below-average demand in another. This potential offsetting is less available in small firms.

Basically, then, the superiority of large firms in financing rests on the operations of the insurance principle, though it is aided by economies of information to companies that supply capital to the large firms.

We have first analyzed in dynamic programming form the effects of firm size on the development decision, given the outcome of the research phase. From the above reasoning, for each research concept and each research outcome there is an expenditure on development and a probability distribution of profitabilities in production. These will be affected (as indicated) both by the development profitability function and by the availability of capital, which, in turn, is conditioned by the problems of information transmission. Hence, there will be a probability distribution of anticipated profitabilities taking account of both development expenditures and subsequent profitabilities in production. It has been argued that, on the average, small firms will be superior if the optimal development costs are low and large firms will be superior if costs are large.

Now consider the decision to engage in research. (Again, for the time being, ignore the possibility that the research outcome can be sold.) Before engaging in research, the development profitability function is itself unknown; nevertheless there will be expectations of it. In probability language, the development profitability function (itself a random variable expressing the distribution of profitability in production conditional on development expenditures) is taken as conditional on research outcome after that is known and as unconditional (more precisely, conditional on research concept but not on outcome) before research is undertaken.

Given the research concept, it may be expected (though without certainty) that subsequent development expenditures will be low if the project is at all feasible. In that case, it follows that small firms will be more likely to undertake the research than large firms. The opposite is the case if the unconditional distribution implies that development expenditures are likely to be high. Already at the point where the decisions to undertake research are made, there is differential selection among firms of differing sizes.

Thus, on the average one would expect firms to specialize in projects whose optimal development scales are correlated with the size of the firm. Projects anticipated to lead to large expenditures will on the whole be less than optimally funded, because large firms have higher transmission losses for information.

If the supplementary hypothesis advanced above is correct (that larger firms will find it harder to allocate capital to very novel ventures), then it is also true that very novel research concepts will be less likely to lead to research projects in large firms than in small.

Finally, it must be pointed out that the correlation in research undertaken between firm size and optimal level of development expenditures, though positive, will be far from perfect. The level of development expenditures, as repeatedly emphasized, will depend on the research outcome. Research, by its nature, is uncertain. It can easily happen that a research program is undertaken with a probability distribution of optimal development expenditures whose expectation is relatively small before the research outcome is observed. The distribution conditional on research outcome may be quite different, possibly with a large expectation. This is a far from rare event. Of course, the opposite can also occur; if the correct distributions are held, it must occur comparably frequently.

It can therefore happen that a small firm undertakes a line of research whose outcome would optimally involve a much larger development expenditure than it is prepared to undertake. It will either pursue the development on a much smaller scale than optimal, or it will discontinue it altogether if there are sufficient increasing returns to scale in the development process.

....

A Market for Research Outcomes

This concluding section seeks to remove one limitation of the preceding. The research outcome may itself be the object of a market transaction. Selling ideas is not entirely as simple as selling goods, but they are valuable to at least some potential buyers. Establishment and transfer of property rights can take several forms. The research outcome might be patentable, in which case the sale is straightforward. Alternatively, the buyer might value a whole constellation of working knowledge embodied in the firm. In that case, the sale of the research outcome could be equivalent to the sale of the whole firm.

From the discussion thus far, the natural sellers of research outcomes would be small firms that, after observing the outcome, determine that optimal expenditures on development exceed the financial capacity of the firm. In view of the uncertainty about development costs at the moment of the research concept, such situations can arise easily. The buyers might be individuals or groups of individuals in the external capital market who wish to secure their investment in such an uncertain situation by equity acquisition rather than bonds. More likely, however, it is the large firms in similar fields who constitute the natural demand side of the innovation market, whether research outcomes are sold in the form of patents or of whole firms.

The existence of markets for research outcomes alters the incentive structures for undertaking research within both large and small firms. For small firms, it lessens the inhibition on starting research for which large development expenditures are likely. If this came to pass, they do not find the research useless— they can sell the outcome to a large firm. One must still reckon with a loss of information as it passes across the boundaries between the large and small firms. Hence, the incentives for the research are less than they would be within the large firm. Since the large firm is well informed, it is also true that the loss of information is less than it would be between the small firm and the general external-capital market, so that the possibility of sale to large firms is not negligible, as we have assumed the external financing of expensive developments by small firms to be.

The existence of markets for research outcomes also alters the incentives for research within large firms—for the worse. For now the firm has an alternative supply of research outcomes on which to base its development of innovations. The constraints on its total development expenditures imply that anticipated availability of research outcomes on the market will reduce the incentive to use only internally generated research outcomes.

There are limits to relying on the market for research inputs into the development process. For example, internal research capability is complementary to externally purchased research outcomes. It is needed to evaluate them and to synthesize them with other research outcomes, whether internal or external. But clearly some substitution takes place.

If this analysis is meaningful, it suggests a division for labor according to firm size. Smaller firms will tend to specialize more in the research phase and in smaller development processes; larger firms will devote a much smaller proportion of their research and development budget to the research phase. They will specialize in the larger developments and will buy a considerable fraction of the research basis for their subsequent development of innovations.

While anecdotes are no substitute for good statistical analysis, a striking number of innovations have been produced by giant corporations on the basis of ideas (and perhaps some production) by small firms.

....

Notes

1. J.A. Schumpeter, *Business Cycles*, vol. I (New York and London: McGraw-Hill, 1939), pp. 94–109.
2. A.A. Berle, Jr., and G.C. Means, *The Modern Corporation and Private Property* (New York: Macmillan, 1932).
3. K.J. Arrow, and F.H. Hahn, *General Competitive Analysis* (San Francisco and Edinburgh: Holden-Day and Oliver & Boyd, 1971).
4. E.H. Chamberlin, *The Theory of Monopolistic Competition*, 6th ed. (Cambridge, Mass.: Harvard University Press, 1950).

5. See, for example, table 3.1, p. 40, in F.M. Scherer, *Industrial Market Structure and Economic Performance* (Chicago: Rand McNally, 1970).

6. For the period from 1899 to 1939, see G.W. Nutter, *The Extent of Enterprise Monoply in the United States 1899–1939* (Chicago: University of Chicago Press, 1951). For more recent trends or lack thereof, see W.F. Mueller and L.G. Hamm, "Trends in Industrial Market Concentration 1947 to 1970." *Review of Economics and Statistics* 56 (1974): 511–520.

7. G.J. Stigler, "The Division of Labor is Limited by the Extent of the Market," *Journal of Political Economy* 56 (1951): 185–193.

8. A. Chandler, Jr., *The Visible Hand: The Managerial Revolution in American Business* (Cambridge, Mass.: Harvard University Press, 1977).

9. For more complete discussion, see K.J. Arrow, *The Limits of Organization* (New York: Norton, 1974): Ch. 2.

10. R.H. Coase, "The Theory of the Firm." *Economica N.S.* 4 (1937): 368–405.

11. In order not to interrupt the main line of the argument, I have left rather vague the concept of the profitability of the innovation, which appears as an output of the development process. It is not necessary that the innovation give rise to market power—that is, that it be a commodity with some distinct differentiation from others and on which, therefore, a monopoly profit can be earned. (Of course, this possibility is not excluded either.) But even if the product, or a close substitute, is one already produced, an innovation may amount to a cost reduction. Hence, the firm will earn a rent on the superior productivity induced by the innovation. It must be recognized, however, that the knowledge embodied in an innovation cannot fully be made property. It is apt to be copied by others, and, as the knowledge spreads, the price of the product will decline. Hence, the anticipated profitability must take account of the declining rent from the innovation.

11 The Economic Sociology of Firms and Entrepreneurs

Mark Granovetter

The central issue I want to address is how it is possible for entrepreneurs to assemble the capital and labor required to sustain the cooperative venture we call a "firm." Although firms will find it difficult to survive in an economic environment that affords them no profit, I argue that the possibility of profits—that is, profits above and beyond those available in other uses of resources, or what are sometimes called "excess profits"—is also not a sufficient condition for such emergence; instead, one must study the social structure within which individuals and groups attempt the construction of firms.

Homo Economicus and the Problem of Trust in Entrepreneurship

The New Institutional Economics leads us to expect that the scale of economic operations in any system will be just the one appropriate to the transaction costs and types found there. But the literature on economic and political development is quite different in this respect, implying that the existing scale is too small in many less-developed settings so that one must find the "obstacles" to the organization of firms and larger-scale activity.

The view of traditional development theory that embeddedness of economic action in noneconomic obligations inhibits economic expansion implies that the problem is a deficiency in the numbers of *homines economici*, individuals whose motivations are unalloyedly economic and thereby not entangled in kinship or other social obligations. But empirical studies of settings with many such individuals make clear that where the undersocialized model of human action[1] actually does approximate reality, the problems of trust that I have argued it implies become paramount and have a profoundly chilling effect on the expansion of economic activity.[2]

I shall catalogue a series of striking examples from Java[3] and from the Philippines[4] and speculate on their theoretical significance. Dewey notes that in the Javanese town (dubbed "Modjokuto") studied by her and also by Geertz, commercial relations typically did not overlap with those of kinship or neighborhood but were almost purely economic in nature.[5] Though most of the urban traders are from rural backgrounds, the population density is so high that few have carried previous relations from the village over to the urban setting. Contracts are correspondingly difficult to enforce given the absence of support from mutual kin, neighbors, or other social groupings.[6] Modjokuto is lacking in persisting ties between buyers and sellers. The same is true for ties among the merchants themselves. There are a few crops, like onions, that lend themselves to large-scale trade, and then Javanese traders do form groups, pooling capital and labor to buy in quantity at lower prices. But the groups are formed to handle a single transaction only, and then dissolve; each trader belongs to more than one group at a time, which spreads the risk.[7] Credit is difficult to find in part because information about credit risks is scarce and costly in this atomized setting.[8] Geertz puts more stress than Dewey on the frequency of alliances between small traders, but affirms also their short-lived character.[9] He argues that what is lacking here among the (typically) Islamic small businessmen "is not capital, for... their resources are not inadequate; not drive, for they display the typically 'Protestant' virtues of industry, frugality, independence, and determination in almost excessive abundance; certainly not a sufficient market... What they lack is the power to mobilize their capital and channel their drive in such a way as to exploit the existing market possibilities. They lack the capacity to form efficient economic institutions; they are entrepreneurs without enterprises."[10]

The rugged individualism characteristic of traders in the Modjokuto bazaar economy leads to some attempts at enterprise but "also involves very important limitations on the capacity to grow, by limiting the effective range of collective organization. Modjokuto enterprises seem to grow so large and then no larger, because the next step means widening the social base of the enterprise beyond the immediate family connections to which, given that lack of trust which is the inverse of individualism, they are limited.[11]

In the bazaar economy Geertz studied in Morocco, buyer-seller relations are by comparison quite long-term; cooperation among *sellers*, however, is still minimal. Correspondingly, vertical integration between merchants and artisans is absent; there are no integrated craft-commercial enterprises or permanent connections between the two, and the artisans are concerned to avoid such connections, fearing the dependence this would involve. This is so despite the sharp division of labor between the roles: artisans almost never market their own products, but rather sell them to merchants who then resell them to other merchants or consumers.[12] Even craft workshops where a group of artisans work together are conceived as a cluster of two-person arrangements.[13]

In the Philippines, the city of Estancia shows that a pattern empirically very similar to that found in Modjokuto and Morocco can arise from a very different cultural and social-structural situation.[14] As in Modjokuto, there are partnerships in buying, where a group pools its resources; these are also short-lived, shifting arrangements. But despite rapid economic growth in Estancia, spearheaded especially by the fishing industry, small family enterprises have not given way to larger corporate institutions. Even in the largest enterprises, everyone is totally dependent on the owner, and the operation rises and falls with that individual. Why? In Estancia, one of the

most powerful and obvious impediments to corporate economic activities is a pervasive mistrust of others, fortified by innumerable accounts of economic double-dealing in the town. Even within a nuclear family, when it comes to business matters, trust between individuals is often limited. The common assumption is that people are primarily concerned with their own personal welfare or short-term benefit and will take advantage of a situation of trust, whenever possible... The leaders of large organizations—economic or other—are always suspected of using the position, members, or resources for their own personal purposes, and they often do. This of course justifies similar action by lower-echelon members. The expectation that others work only for their own advantage is so powerful that even partnerships between kinsmen or close friends rarely last more than a few weeks or months... Groups larger than a simple partnership are obviously all the more vulnerable. Given this atmosphere of distrust, the most circumstantial and unfounded charges are likely to be accepted.[15]

This sounds very much like the problems of mistrust in Modjokuto. But unlike the highly individualistic Moslem traders of that Javanese city, Estancia residents are predominantly Catholic, live in a small city where there are elaborate networks of noneconomic relations overlaid on the economic ones, and have well-developed personalized ties between clients and customers and among vendors.[16] A sense of "moral economy" operates in Estancia among subsistence vendors, so this is a setting where at least within a well-defined local group people have a feeling of responsibility for one another.[17] But a broader look at the culture and social structure shows that despite this strong sense of the "right to survive", and despite an elaborate network of horizontal linkages, there is also a marked sense of competitiveness among individuals at the *same* hierarchical level. In Modjokuto a similar competitiveness comes from the absence of social connections. In Estancia it seems instead to arise from a social structure that is densely connected, but in a way that stresses vertical, hierarchical, patron-client relations. This lowland Philippine system was originally oriented to landlord-tenant relations, and the pattern has continued with local politicians taking the superior's role. Culturally, interaction in such a system is smooth, Szanton argues, where status differences are clearcut and mutual obligations clearly understood. But then, among the "relatively poor, be they tenants or other traditional workers, horizontal ties to others of similar status are of limited value both because they usually have few resources to spare, and more important, because they are often in competition with one another for support and aid from the same higher status figures... Horizontal solidarity is not characteristic of traditional [Philippine] lowland society."[18] In times of crisis it is vertical ties that will make the difference for you. Basically, economic goods move down the hierarchy and social and political support move up. Thus, the "most significant solidarities, cleavages, and oppositions in the social pyramid tend to be vertical (and factional) rather than horizontal (and ideological) as they are in class-structured societies."[19]

So far we see that social systems with a lack of horizontal solidarity—*which can arise in various ways*—are deficient in the trust required to build enterprises larger than those run by individuals or families. The Philippine example is an important contrast to that of Java because it shows that the lack of trust among individuals need not be the result of an atomized social structure that isolates individuals from one another, but may occur instead because of the particular way even a dense structure is connected.

Does it follow that a high level of horizontal solidarity is the prescription for expansion? This would be the exact reverse of what traditional development theory claimed, and even the most inadequate theories rarely give way to their exact opposites. Consider Geertz's account of economic enterprise in a small (population 12,000) Balinese town.[20] Though Tabanan is, like Modjokuto, administratively part of Indonesia and the two towns are not far apart geographically, they are light-years apart in culture and social structure. Not so long ago, Tabanan was ruled by princes and aristocrats, and though deprived of political power in the new regime, they continue to be involved in a "complex network of specific and explicit ties both with one another and with the great mass of commoners they once ruled."[21] This matters a great deal because it is from this group of displaced rulers that the entrepreneurial class in Tabanan is almost entirely drawn.

The strong vertical solidarities here are similar to those of the lowland Philippines. But Bali is quite different in that there is strong horizontal solidarity as well. Balinese social structure is characterized by social groups called *seka*, formed on the basis of religious, political, economic, or other criteria. "Every Balinese belongs to from three or four up to nearly a dozen of these groups, and the value of *seka* loyalty, putting the needs of one's group above one's own, is, along with caste pride, a central value in Balinese social life. This *seka* pattern of organization gives to Balinese village social structure both a strongly collective and yet a peculiarly complex and flexible pattern. Balinese do almost everything, even the simplest of undertakings, in groups which... almost invariably involve personnel clearly far in excess of what is technically necessary."[22] Given the centrality of these groups, "almost the whole of Balinese economic life is realized through one or another of these *seka*, strictly individual activity being rather rare."[23]

From this description, it sounds as if the problems of Modjokuto and of Estancia are nicely overcome in Tabanan. The entrepreneurs are highly prestigious in local eyes. They are aristocrats and thus "have at their disposal a quantity of cultural capital in the form of traditional social loyalties and expectations which Modjokuto's selfmade shopkeepers entirely lack."[24] Adding to this the horizontal solidarity of Balinese culture, how can enterprises lose? And in fact, enterprises start fairly readily in Tabanan and even undergo some moderate level of expansion. But there is a fly in the ointment, and it is just what traditional development theory highlighted—that the firm anchored in noneconomic loyalties "has a tendency to behave uneconomically because of the 'social welfare' pressures of its members who, for the most part, are not basically growth-minded. Not only is there great pressure to divide profits rather than reinvest them, but there is also a tendency to employ overly large staffs in an attempt by the directorate to appease the rank and file... The trouble with Balinese-owned concerns', the abdicated king of Tabanan, who runs his hotel by himself, said to me with some shrewdness, 'is that they turn into relief organizations rather than businesses."[25] There is, here, a kind of moral economy that militates against the rationalization of firms if this appears to be at the expense of the community. Both commoners and nobles expect and demand that economic decisions "will lead to a higher level of welfare for the organic community as a whole and not just to an enrichment of a self-interested, emergent managerial class."[26] Thus, whereas Modjokuto's firms cannot expand to the most economic level, those in Tabanan tend to expand beyond that point because of their noneconomic commitments.

But this account raises the question of why a system with strong hierarchical but weak horizontal solidarity, as in the Philippines, does not use the vertical ties to build enterprises that can then be rationalized because there is less pressure to operate them as social welfare programs than there is in a Balinese-type system. And in fact there is some evidence from Estancia that this is a real possibility. Szanton reports that the Filipino vertical model of relations has been applied to all economic enterprises. Thus, in commercial, fishing outfits, the owner "was cast in the role of the landlord/politician responsible for the maintenance of his crewmen and their families. The crew were structurally equivalent to the tenants, and provided political support to the owners."[27] But given the lack of horizontal solidarity, such a pattern may work better in a firm like a fishing outfit, where the level of horizontal cooperation and complexity required is low, than in one with a more elaborate division of labor, which requires cooperation and trust rather than competition for the patron's favor. This in itself would be a severe limitation.

But it turns out also that even the fishing outfit pattern is more vulnerable than it might seem. Szanton indicates that such operations worked well before World War II, but since then the sense of mutual obligation has declined between owners and workers; the former now feel less responsibility and correspondingly get less political and other kinds of support from their workers. What has led to this has been an increase in the proportion of young, mobile, migrant fishermen without families. The patron-client system, as with other vertically oriented moral economy systems, is highly personalized and localized. It is easier for patrons to decline their traditional responsibilities to young, single newcomers than it would be to known individuals with long-standing local family connections. Although there is no systematic data over time as to what has caused this, it appears from Szanton's account[28] that an unravelling process has taken place: After the war, the owners' costs began to increase, especially the costs of capital investment. This led them to reduce the sharing of profits that they had previously practiced. The worsened situation for the workers led to an outflux of those with local family connections and an influx of young newcomers with little sense of obligation to the owner, with less concern regarding aid from above in a possible crisis and more for maximizing personal incomes. But this change in workers' attitudes, and correspondingly in their practices—for example, surreptitiously selling fish at sea without the owner's knowledge—put more pressure on the owner's practice of moral economy, which in turn led to further shift in the composition of crews, in a process of mutual feedback. What this shows is that the old pattern was stable as long as the set of individuals involved remained localized; but when forces arose that brought in new workers who did not belong to the old set of social arrangements that held the operation together, the system broke down. It could be sustained only in the context of a working ideology approximating that of "moral economy."

....

Conditions for Entrepreneurial Success:
The Case of the Rotating Credit Association

So far we see that individuals and groups attempting to assemble firms may face on the one hand the problem of insufficient solidarity among themselves, which produces a failure of trust, and on the other hand the problem of uncontrolled solidarity, which produces excessive noneconomic claims on an enterprise. Under what conditions can these mirror-image problems be overcome? We can gain further insight into this issue from examination of one of the most successful informal institutions for raising capital in many parts of the world: the rotating credit association.

In developing and developed countries alike, small new firms have always had difficulty raising capital from formal institutions such as banks, which have no good way to assess the risks of these ventures and, given their small scale, would not find it economical to invest in acquiring such information. Thus it is commonplace to observe the raising of capital from family and friends. But the amount of capital that can be so raised is always small, and this creates a comparative advantage for the rotating credit association.

Such associations are spread widely over the world, and have received special attention in Japan, China, Southeast Asia, India, West Africa, and the Caribbean. They occur with many variations, but as Geertz indicates,

[the] basic principle upon which the rotating credit association is founded is everywhere the same: a lump sum fund composed of fixed contributions from each member of the association is distributed, at fixed intervals and as a whole, to each member of the association in turn. Thus, if there are ten members of the association, if the association meets weekly, and if the weekly contribution from each member is one dollar, then

each week over a ten-week period a different member will receive ten dollars . . . If interest payments are calculated . . . the numerical simplicity is destroyed, but the essential principle of rotating access to a continually reconstituted capital fund remains intact. Whether the fund is in kind or in cash; whether the order the members receive the fund is fixed by lot, by agreement, or by bidding; whether the time period over which the society runs is many years or a few weeks; whether the sums involved are minute or rather large; whether the members are few or many; and whether the association is composed of urban traders or rural peasants, of men or women, the general structure of the institution is constant.[29]

From the description it is obvious that the rotating credit association is a way to save money and raise capital. Compared to individual savings at home, it has the macroeconomic advantage of always keeping money in circulation, and compared to schemes in which a designated individual acts as a banker and treasurer, holding deposits from others, it has the advantage that at each periodic meeting the fund is distributed to a member and cannot therefore be embezzled.[30] Because each meeting is typically a social occasion, often at the home of a member, and members are usually in some way socially connected to one another, this form of saving has a personal and social element that carries its own rewards, increases social solidarity, and provides additional incentives to participate. Unlike most other situations where one receives a loan and is thereby in the position of supplicant, in a rotating credit association "the recipient of a fund, far from suffering a loss of dignity, is often the member of honour or host at a feast or some other form of entertainment."[31]

Ardener notes that such an arrangement will fail unless all members meet their obligations, but suggests that the

pressure of public opinion within the membership may be enough to ensure this. It is interesting to note the very great importance placed upon these obligations in some communities . . . . The member who defaults in one association may suffer to such an extent that he may not be accepted as a member of any other. In some communities the rotating credit institution has become so rooted in the economic and social system that exclusion would be a serious deprivation . . . . A member may go to great lengths, such as stealing . . . or selling a daughter into prostitution . . . in order to fulfill his obligations to his association; failure to meet obligations can even lead to suicide.[32]

These pressures nicely illustrate what Portes calls "enforceable trust"—in which transactions among members of a community are "undergirded by certainty that no one will shirk in their eventual repayment."[33]

Ardener also points out that such associations may function as money markets, since members who have not yet received funds can obtain loans from those who have.[34] This and other banking aspects of these associations raise the natural question of where such associations stand with respect to banks in communities that may contain both. Geertz, writing in a period when development theory pointed to impersonal institutions as the most efficient possible mode of economic functioning, described the rotating credit association as a "middle rung" in economic development, since it is

obviously limited in the scale and complexity of commercial activity which it can support . . . . In the more developed cases, the traditional elements weaken and the stress comes to be placed on . . . bureaucratic organization and the like . . . . In this sense, the form is . . . self-liquidating, being replaced ultimately by banks, cooperatives, and other economically more rational types of credit institutions. But these latter can only function when the differentiation of a specific economic pattern of norms has occurred—when courts will enforce contracts, when managers worry about their business reputations and keep honest books, and when investors feel safe in giving cash resources to debtors to whom they are not related. Cultural change of this sort takes place, however, in steps rather than all at once, and in the intermediary stages the association fulfills a valuable function in organizing traditional and rational economic attitudes in such a way that the process continues rather than stultifies or breaks down into anomie.[35]

But Ardener was critical of this argument, noting that purely economic or rational aspects do not always predominate in the larger or more sophisticated associations of this kind and that even when the rotating credit associations are professionally organized, such aspects as feasting and conviviality may be important. She reports:

In Vietnam, for instance, where associations are comparatively businesslike (with government registration, the keeping of books, and so forth), feasting is still required and meetings must be "gay" and "elegant" . . . . The persistence of the institutions in communities in which banks and co-operatives exist, such as in Great Britain, Japan, and South Africa, and the recent formation of an association by bank employees in the Sudan, suggests that there is still a place for these institutions alongside "other more economically rational" types of institution.[36]

Even in countries such as Cameroon, where rotating credit associations are illegal, they are widely supported by large segments of the community, including those who are actively involved in more formal varieties of banking. This is an example of the persistence of institutions based on personal relations long past the point of demise predicted by the argument that optimally efficient markets must be based on impersonal transactions.

We note also that because rotating credit associations include many individuals who would not normally be considered creditworthy by formal banking institutions, in part because the investigation required to support small loans would be uneconomical, they efficiently serve an important share of the credit market that would otherwise be without funds for entrepreneurship. For this reason, some formal institutions have explicitly copied the techniques of the rotating credit association, creating a new set of institutions often called "peer lending" or "micro-lending," in which loans are collateralized not by goods but by a set of other individuals, assembled by the borrower, who take corporate responsibility for the loan and who cannot themselves receive loans until the books are at least partially cleared on the original loan. The Grameen Bank of Bangladesh has made the largest number of such loans, and this movement appears to be spreading rapidly.[37] In this light the rotating credit association, rather than being a transient middle rung to be replaced by more advanced institutions, turns out to be more advanced in certain respects than the usual impersonal models, in that it makes use of naturally occurring social capital,[38] a low-cost strategy.

The importance of rotating credit associations for entrepreneurship in the advanced industrial societies was highlighted by the work of Ivan Light on the comparative entrepreneurial performance in the United States of Chinese, Japanese, and blacks.[39] Chinese and Japanese (especially before World War II), and to some extent West Indian blacks, successfully developed small businesses by raising capital through rotating credit associations. But blacks who migrated to industrial cities from the southern United States did not make use of rotating credit associations and had great difficulty in raising capital for businesses. What explains this difference?

We know that rotating credit associations require, for their successful operation, a set of members who are sufficiently solidary with one another that they scrupulously avoid defaulting on their obligations to contribute regularly. Those who organize the associations must have enough information about potential members to make accurate judgments of this solidarity. In countries where members of rotating credit associations are natives, local kinship and friendship networks suffice to assure this. Among immigrants, some other form of assurance is required. The key, Light argues, was that Japanese and Chinese who immigrated to the United States before World War II came from just a few areas of their home countries. Eighty-nine percent of Japanese emigrated from eleven southern prefectures, and virtually all Chinese from one of seven districts in Kwangtung province, whose main city is Canton (now Guangdong).[40]

Both groups erected an elaborate structure of organizations based on the exact locale of emigration. These organizations were ascriptive (that is, geographic origins and not preferences determined membership) so there was no possibility of the different organizations competing for members or of the dilution of loyalty through multiple memberships. Moreover, the obligations owed to one another by those from the same home area were matched by the reluctance of those from other areas to help (in finding employment, for example, or giving financial assistance). In addition to performing other functions, such associations became the nuclei of rotating credit associations which thereby flourished and provided the capital needed for opening small businesses and investing in real estate. Light's discussion of West Indian blacks is much briefer, but a similar pattern appears in which home area in the West Indies formed the core for their version of rotating credit associations, which had reached the islands from West Africa with slaves who were transported there.

American blacks, on the other hand, had lost this organizational arrangement from their "cultural repertoire."[41] They had lost touch with their particular African origins and had no opportunity during slavery, as did West Indians, to set up independent businesses which they financed on their own; nor was there much chance to acquire such businesses after emancipation. Moreover, black migrants to northern cities did not especially identify with their home areas in the south and, like white migrants, had virtually no organizations based on these origins. Light explains this difference between the black and the Asian experience by suggesting that "[i]nternational migration is a more drastic form of uprooting than is interstate migration . . . [so] it is not surprising that neither black nor white interstate migrants have felt it necessary to erect organizational monuments to their state of origin."[42] Also, whereas the Chinese and Japanese were nostalgic about their background and often intended (at least in principle) to return someday, southern-born blacks were happy to leave their background behind.

This is not to say that northern blacks had no organizational life. On the contrary, there was a rich variety of voluntary organizations, but to Light this is precisely the problem: these organizations did not have the hold of moral solidarity over their members and had to compete among themselves for membership. Many fraternal organizations had overlapping membership, which diluted any special hold any single one might have. Then any businesses based in one such organization would have to cope with noneconomic claims from co-members of the many overlapping organizations. It was simply too difficult to create moral solidarity "among a voluntary membership which was ascriptively unrelated."[43] Ethical discipline and solidarity would have been facilitated by the social isolation of the membership in the community, so that members would always be in one another's company. Asian groups could do so because they had a putative cultural differentiation: "Cantonese from Toishan spontaneously spent their waking hours in one another's company. In part this pattern reflected a preference . . . but it also reflected the unwillingness of non-Toi-shanese to associate with Toi-shanese (and vice-versa) and the subsequent necessity for Toi-shanese to band together."[44]

Thus the black community did not generate the localized solidarities required to sustain such institutions as rotating credit associations, even if these had been in their cultural repertoire. Instead, large and impersonal organizations like the Urban League and the National Negro Business League, staffed by the black elite, tried to recruit poor blacks to the idea of small business; but since the "league chapters were structurally isolated voluntary associations of the wealthy, they were unable to reach lower-class black youth."[45]

And beyond the matter of raising capital, the Japanese and Chinese organizations offered assistance of all sorts to ethnic businesses, including regulation of competition and price supports. This was possible because of the nonoverlapping, clearly organized structure of these groups; no such assistance could arise from the black community. The only exceptions to the general underrepresentation of blacks in business occurred when organizations were formed that could create ascriptive-like solidarities. Since territoriality could not be used in this way, an alternative was the religious sect; Father Divine, a black religious leader who emerged in the Great Depression, mobilized at least a half-million blacks as his followers and by the 1950s had erected a large network of small businesses which they owned and operated. The "secret of Father Divine's miracles was his special ability to induce sect members to cooperate."[46] But this all depended on belief in his divinity, which was necessarily fragile; thus when he died in 1965, his "kingdom" evaporated.

The Balance between Coupling and Decoupling: The Case of the Overseas Chinese

The discussion of rotating credit associations shows that the solidarity required for assembling coherent combinations of economic activity depends on a well-defined collection of people who identify one another as belonging to the same collectivity by ethnic or even more specific markers such as place of origin. This indicates that at least as important as the intensity of interaction is the clearly defined boundary beyond which such intensity and trust falls off sharply. Such a boundary is required in order to sustain trust internally, but also to limit the extent of the group that can make claims on the economic organization that has been constructed.

This is illustrated especially well by the overseas Chinese—the one group that has successfully put together efficient firms in South-east Asia, an achievement notable for its rarity in the context of the Philippine and Indonesian difficulties I have catalogued. Empirically this success is well documented.[47] The temptation is great to explain it in terms of Chinese culture, and indeed it would be hard to argue that the culture of overseas Chinese is not in fact importantly different in ways that facilitate business success. But cultural understandings and practices do not emerge out of thin air; they are shaped by and in turn shape structures of social interaction.

All accounts agree that Chinese businesses experience dramatically lower operating costs because of the existence of trust within that community. Credit is extended and capital pooled with the expectation that commitments will be met; delegation of authority takes place without fear that agents will pursue their own interests at the expense of the principal's. Rotating credit associations are just one mechanism successfully used for these purposes.

Why is this so among the Chinese? Overseas Chinese constitute small, cohesive minorities with extensive family and organizational connections that shape noneconomic and economic activities alike. In Modjokuto, for example, Dewey reports that Chinese families organize themselves into bangsa, groups based on common descent from some specific area of China. "Such a group speaks the same Chinese dialect and for the most part marries endogamously. The relations between the members are formalized in various associations, burial societies, sports groups, commercial associations, and the like."[48] There is a tendency for members of one bangsa all to be in the same business and to deal mostly with one another. Within these groupings, and to some extent (not clearly specified by Dewey) across them in the Chinese community as a whole, "ties of kinship and comembership in the various types of associations reinforce and are reinforced by the commercial relationships so that a series of closely knit communities is created, with connections reaching all over Java and often beyond."[49] In building these structures, local Chinese are making use of classical Chinese culture as a "tool kit":[50] "old Chinese models of family, secret society, and association are used as a basis for extending commercial relations beyond the nuclear family and the local group.[51] In this close-knit, cohesive community, norms of proper behavior become clearly crystallized and internalized; deviance cannot be hidden and will be swiftly dealt with if it does occur. Given the enormous advantages of dealing within the closed bangsa community of businesspeople, the penalty of having to move outside of it in one's dealings is very stiff.

But the Chinese social structure that facilitates their business relations sounds suspiciously similar to that of the Balinese described by Geertz,[52] who run up against the problem that the diffuse claims of friends and relatives against the economic resources of business organizations prevent those businesses from being run efficiently. Yet Chinese businesses do not seem to suffer from this problem. The abdicated king of Tabanan commented to Geertz that if you go into a Balinese business, "there are a half-dozen directors, a book-keeper or two, several clerks, some truck drivers and a hoard (sic) of semi-idle workers; if you go into a Chinese concern of the same size there is just the proprietor, his wife, and his ten-year-old boy, but they are getting even more work done."[53] What then shields Chinese businesses from the excessive claims of friends and relatives? Dewey suggests about Java that "one factor which may be important is the minority position of the Chinese . . . . In relation to the Javanese they are a small community. (In Modjokuto they numbered about 1,800 out of a total of approximately 18,000.) The number of people who will call on a given merchant for favored treatment is limited by the size of the community, and further by the split between *Peranakan* [Chinese in Java for several generations] and *Totok* [recent immigrants] and by the division of the latter into *bangsa*. This limitation keeps demands from becoming so burdensome as to nullify the economic advantage. . . . [By contrast] for the Javanese . . . the lack of focused groupings would open a merchant to demands from an unlimited number of other Javanese."[54] The Balinese also have well-defined groupings, the *seka* mentioned above. But unlike Chinese *bangsa* members, each Balinese (like the northern blacks described by Ivan Light) belongs typically to numerous *seka*,[55] and though these groupings do organize economic life, the overlap in membership among these groupings means that if one *seka* is the core of a business, members of that group may still be subject to diffuse claims from fellow members of other *seka*.

A related argument is made by Davis, based on his observations in Baguio City in the Philippines. Trying to explain why Chinese merchants are so much more successful than Filipino ones, he provides evidence *against* the general propositions that Chinese sellers work harder or that they are more clever businessmen. He then notes that Filipino kinship is bilateral so that kin groups are not well defined. Since you inherit some relatives from each parent, your own kin group is different from that of either parent and is exactly the same only for full siblings. In this context, Omohundro, in his study of the Filipino Chinese merchant community, observes that "employees and suppliers operated on the not-unfounded assumption that a man who married a Filipino was either already financially shaky or soon would be, when Filipino relatives made their demands on him," and so would not give him credit any more.[56]

Chinese, by contrast, have corporate kinship groups traced through the male line—a well-defined set of relatives that makes collective action and the mobilization and management of resources easier. The eldest male is in charge, whereas in Filipino kinship groups no one is obviously in charge. "Therefore the Chinese kin group has several important features like those of stock corporations, with perhaps the greatest difference being that kinship limits participation."[57] The better-defined kinship groups of the Chinese, therefore, not only limit the diffuse noneconomic claims that may be made of the business but also provide a stronger base for collective action and a more effective structure of authority. One Chinese informant told Davis that "[m]embers of Filipino families are always fighting among themselves, but we put someone in charge."[58]

What we must look for then, in understanding successful entrepreneurial activity, is some combination of social cohesion sufficient to enforce standards of fair business dealing and an atmosphere of trust, along with circumstances that limit the noneconomic claims on a business that prevent its rationalization. The relative small size and cohesive social structure of groups that are minorities in their location (and if they are beleaguered and despised minorities, they are that much more likely to pull together socially and culturally) may often provide just the right combination of these factors, thus helping to explain the often-noted economic success of expatriate minority groups.[59] Even in settings where hardly any integrated enterprises exist we may expect that those that do exist have such origins—for example, the very few integrated craft-commercial enterprises reported by Geertz in Sefrou, Morocco, are Jewish in origin.[60]

More generally, immigrants have an advantage over natives in achieving the right balance between what might be called "coupling" and "decoupling." Chinese in China, despite the obvious presence of Chinese culture, can suffer from excessive claims. Thus Wong suggests that it has been typical of entrepreneurs in China to "leave their native homes to conduct business" so that "relatives will not be abundant in the communities in which they work."[61] In moving to regions where they have fewer ties, they gain some of the advantages of immigrants.[62]

Conversely, immigrant minorities rarely suffer from the problem of excessive claims, in part because their solidarity is emergent and constructed and thus likely to have clear boundaries.[63] It may also be the case that immigrant enterprises, especially in the early stages, are sufficiently fragile that claims on their resources are muted; then once they are successful, especially in a multiethnic environment, claims can be warded off by hiring employees from other ethnic groups, to whom no special allegiance is owed.[64]

Intergroup Relations and the Advantages of Minorities

Thus far I have discussed the characteristics of groups that succeed or fail in constructing enterprises. But this level of argument must be supplemented with an analysis of how such groups relate to others. One aspect of this analysis involves cultural differences among groups. For the overseas Chinese, for example, there was no stigma in lending or borrowing money it merely demonstrated one's high level of ambition.[65] For other groups such as Thais and Malays, however, to be in debt was a source of shame, so indigenous producers preferred to borrow secretly from Chinese traders rather than from local institutions or families, where the debt could become public knowledge.[66] Debtor-creditor relations are stigmatized in these cultures by moral economy norms, or what Gosling refers to as a "distributive ethic" reinforced by Buddhism and Islam: If you have a surplus, you share it. Status results from distributing this surplus to achieve "social capital." You are then owed obligations that could be discharged with labor—creating, in effect, a patron-client system.[67]

There are other practical reasons why locals like to deal with Chinese businessmen. One is the distance it provides from bureaucratic control systems such as tax collection agencies, which would enter the picture in the case of a loan from a bank.[68] Another is that the contact with a member of a different group, who is attuned to a wide outside network, provides valuable information that is not redundant with that available within one's own group and may be useful for understanding the current business environment.[69]

If there are reasons why native-born prefer to deal with merchants and businesses from outside their own group, there are also reasons why this preference is reciprocated by the outsiders. One such important reason is that it is difficult to pursue commercial roles *within* a community that is close-knit and stresses a norm of mutual help and obligation. Foster, writing on Thailand, notes that

a trader who was subject to the traditional social obligations and constraints would find it very difficult to run a viable business. If, for example, he were fully part of the village society and subject to the constraints of the society, he would be expected to be generous in the traditional way to those in need. It would be difficult for him to refuse credit, and it would not be possible to collect debts . . . . The inherent conflict of interest in a face-to-face market transaction would make proper etiquette impossible or would at least strain it severely, which is an important factor in Thai social relations . . . . If, however, a person is not a member of the society, his obligations may be different, as may the power of the society over his behavior; this has important implications for the conduct of trade. Members of different ethnic groups are in many ways outside the community . . . . [E]xpectations of generosity decrease markedly for members of other ethnic groups in contrast with one's own.[70]

This theme is echoed in other cultures. Waldinger and his coauthors[71] cite Wong's study of Chinese grocers in the Watts section of Los Angeles as showing that "social distance from their black customers allows . . . competitive practices that black storekeepers, with social ties to the community, cannot follow."[72] Or in Amsterdam, Boissevain and Grotenberg note that more than three-quarters of clients of Chinese and Hindustani Surinamese merchants "come from outside their ethnic group, [thus] it is far easier for them to deny credit and to be more strict and businesslike about collecting debts."[73] Though the trading group may be less wedded to moral economy norms than its customers, their advantage is fundamentally based on social-structural decoupling from customers rather than on a different ideology; it thus appears to retain its force even in situations where the traders and their customers are members of separate ethnic groups that are virtually identical culturally, such as the Mons minority trading with Thai customers.[74]

Indeed, there is no special reason why a local minority must be *ethnically* different at all from the majority in order to experience some of these advantages, and Szanton reports that in Estancia the Protestant minority, divided into four sects, is more successful in business than the Catholic majority. He points out that "whereas a Roman Catholic entrepreneur may have difficulty denying requested favors from the great bulk of the similarly Catholic townspeople, the Protestant businessman with more limited social ties to relatively like-minded persons can more easily say no, and maintain more narrowly contractual relations with others."[75] Migrants to Estancia, also less entangled in local obligations, are disproportionately represented among successful entrepreneurs.[76] Thus, any cultural device that can decouple one group from another may facilitate commerce.

Because of the advantages of separation, groups may retain their ethnic distinction to a degree that they would not otherwise undertake. As against the sociologically naive idea that ethnicity is a primordial characteristic of individuals determined by nature and biology, many recent writers have stressed the "construction of ethnicity" for political and economic purposes.[77] The extreme version of this view is proposed in the New Institutional Economics—that groups "choose" to emphasize ethnic traits as the optimal strategy to maximize income in certain situations. La Croix, for example, suggests that groups solve their economic problems by choosing "a common ('homogeneous') asset—a collection of characteristics—that is less costly for the group to acquire than outsiders, that yields a stream of utility or income generating a normal rate of return to the asset, and that is sufficiently specific and valuable to generate the appropriately large stream of quasi-rents. The choice of ethnic, religious, and genealogical characteristics fulfills these criteria . . . ."[78]

A more prudent analysis would take account of the historical, cultural, and social-structural constraints on such "choices" and of the circumstances that may generate strong ethnic identities for noneconomic reasons. But there is certainly some evidence that ethnic separateness is cultivated in situations where it is of economic value. Foster reports that the minority Mons of Thailand are far more likely to preserve their distinctive ethnic traits when they are engaged in commerce, where the traits pay off, than when in farming, where they do not.[79] Gosling observes that the Chinese in Thailand and Malaysia must retain their Chinese identity because it "permits the antisocial behavior required in commerce and stresses the fact that the game must be played by the dealer-shopkeeper's rules. Once the Chinese acts like a Malay or Thai, he is expected to behave like a Malay or Thai and loses the advantage of ethnic difference.[80] This "chosenness" of cultural difference can be closely attuned to situations. Gosling observed a Chinese shopkeeper in a Malay village who "appeared to be considerably acculturated to Malay culture, and was scrupulously sensitive to Malays in every way, including the normal wearing of sarong, quiet and polite Malay speech, and a humble and affable manner. However, at harvest time when he would go to the field to collect crops on which he had advanced credit, he would put on his Chinese costume of shorts and undershirt, and speak in a much more abrupt fashion, acting, as one Malay farmer put it, 'just like a Chinese.' This behavior was to insure that he would not be treated like a fellow Malay who might be expected to be more generous on price or credit terms."[81]

While it is illuminating to think of the keeping and manipulating of ethnic identity as a matter of rational choice, such analysis usually takes as given the most interesting part of the problem—the factors that make it cost-effective to do so in the first place, for a particular group. Thus, one reason why overseas Chinese pay a stiff penalty for malfeasance within their own group is that in most of Southeast Asia, their opportunities outside of business are limited. In the Philippine city studied by Omohundro, "to cease to be a merchant is to cease to be Chinese."[82] This is partly because native groups disdain commerce, partly because the Chinese do not have the contacts required to enter other fields, and partly because official policy actively prevents their entry. Thus, even if Chinese settlers wanted to enter agriculture, it would have been difficult for them to do so.

Compare the situation of overseas Chinese to that of the Kenyan businessmen studied by Marris and Somerset, who "seldom find a way to assimilate kinship successfully within a hierarchy of managerial authority" which, contrary to the precepts of development theory, puts them at a massive disadvantage in relation to Asian and especially Indian businesses, which are built along kinship lines.[83] This results in part because the Asians, "as a minority excluded from agriculture by colonial policy, could bring much stronger sanctions to bear in their business relationships. A man who cheated his family or caste could be ostracized from commercial employment and had few other sources of livelihood to turn to."[84]

But business is a peripheral activity in African communities, so the sanctions for malfeasance or intransigence that one can mobilize against a relative are weak, since there are usually alternative lines of work available. Indeed, many of the African businessmen interviewed in this study thought that jealousy and insubordination were more likely with relatives than strangers. Marris and Somerset suggest that as business becomes more and land less important, so that a commercial class consolidates, the family may become more significant in African businesses. Note the nicely ironic reversal: rather than family involvement reflecting an early stage of development in the economic process, such involvement is difficult at this early stage and can only be constructed once the process of development has reached a certain plateau.

The discrimination that minority groups face can actually generate an advantage in constructing family businesses, since even if the children of successful business owners become well educated, their opportunities outside the ethnic business sector will be severely limited and the likelihood of their remaining in a family business and putting their talents to work there is much higher. Once this discrimination fades, intergenerational continuity in businesses is harder to sustain, since in most times and places the educated children of entrepreneurial parents seek occupations more associated with their level of education, such as the independent professions.[85] Indeed, Marion Levy has argued that one reason Japan industrialized more successfully than China was that in China the class system was more open, so merchants' and industrialists' sons could rise into the more esteemed social roles of officials and landowners, whereas in Japan the incumbents of these economic roles were assigned ethnic-like traits as a group, in a feudal hierarchy, and prevented from moving into other institutional spheres. Talent was thus confined within the business community and a level of cohesion achieved that was less accessible under Chinese conditions, where both talent and resources were continuously drained from business.[86]

In modern settings we also see numerous instances where discrimination against a group served as a double-edged sword, preventing them from entering most occupations but pushing them into a niche that they were able to dominate, in part by virtue of the enforced ethnic cohesion within that niche. The general point is that conditions "that raise the salience of group boundaries and identity, leading persons to form new social ties and action-sets, increase the likelihood of entrepreneurial attempts by persons within that group and raise the probability of success."[87] This is clear in the case of Japanese domination of truck farming and gardening in California between the two world wars.[88] Thus, the optimal balance between coupling and decoupling may ironically be forced on a group by circumstances beyond its control.

Local decoupling of a group from other groups may actually facilitate a network of weak ties to similar groups in other areas, by freeing time and energy for such relations. Thus successful entrepreneurial groups, compared to other groups, often have a wider network of relationships with individuals—typically of their own group—in other locations. Geertz points out, for example, that both the Moslem entrepreneurs of Modjokuto and the Hinduized aristocratic ones of Tabanan "stand outside the immediate purview of village social structure, as did the traditional groups from which they have emerged. Further, both groups are primarily interlocal in their outlook, some of their most important ties being with groups and individuals in areas other than their own, and this too is a heritage from their progenitors."[89] Extensive connections into other communities are also characteristic of the Chinese in Indonesia and the Philippines,[90] and minority groups such as Parsees and Marwaris who dominate the industrial economy of India.[91] This wider network can be both cause and effect of vertical integration in an economic sector controlled by one group, as for the Japanese hold on truck farming at the levels of production, wholesaling, and retailing in interwar California.[92]

Such interlocal connections can arise in several different ways. The Islamic entrepreneurs of Modjokuto are descended from itinerant market-circuit traders who, hundreds of years ago, maintained commercial ties all over Java, a pattern they have continued. In Bali, "horizontality grew out of the sophisticated court culture . . . . Tabanan's aristocracy not only formed a regional ruling group, but had and still has important and intimate social relationships with similar groups in the other regional capitals of the island."[93] Both groups are "insulated by occupation or by rank from the localized bonds of village society,"[94] which then must be both cause and consequence of their extensive ties to other areas. Chinese minorities are all the more insulated, typically occupying a very low, disdained social status in the local village or town, and so have some of their social energies freed for more long-distance relationships—relationships that may also be facilitated by being able to identify kinsmen and migrants from one's home region of China in other towns and cities.

The ability to call on personalized contacts over a wide geographic area affords considerable advantage in smoothing backward and forward transactions. There are information advantages as well, as Davis tells us of Chinese wholesale grocers in Baguio City, Philippines, whose "commercial relationships with the large Manila supply houses . . . provide them with better price information than is available to Filipino stallholders with whom they deal . . . . [T]hey are able to take advantage of impending price increases by withholding items in order to obtain higher future prices."[95] And not being locally rooted can be a great advantage when economic opportunities shift: "In the early 1960s when the expansion of motorization brought commercial fishing to the more distant islands and the southern coast of Masbate, and Estancia became a major marketing and transshipping point, . . . Chinese quickly reestablished themselves in these newly developing areas, often as the sole merchant buying the local catch in exchange for marine and household goods . . . . Since their most important ties were to other Chinese merchants in the urban areas, they could more easily set aside temporary local relationships to shift operations to more profitable locales. Filipino merchants, with overlapping social, political, and economic ties in their home communities, seem more likely to remain in them even if somewhat larger profits beckon elsewhere.[96]

....

The Conditions for Ethnic Group Advantage

The discussion thus far suggests that in settings where firms first emerge from more undifferentiated economic activity, certain well-defined social groups have special advantages that resolve the dual and somewhat opposite problems of trust and of diffusion of business success into the provision of community welfare. It has been especially (though not exclusively) immigrant and other minority groups that have appeared in such accounts.

A close look at economic history suggests, however, that although we can pick out many striking cases where such groups have an advantage and dominate economic activity and the construction of firms, there are also settings where economic activity is beginning but no such groups can be identified. There are a number of possible explanations of this.

One is that although conditions exist that would give advantage to a group of the sort I have discussed, no such group is able to construct its distinctive ethnic or other markers in a way that allows it to play this role. Functionalist arguments suggest that good solutions can always be constructed, but this neglects the requirement that solutions be constructed out of existing materials. The Chinese in Southeast Asia and the Indians of East Africa were already present in the locales where they came to dominate certain lines of economic activity, partly because they saw the opportunities and migrated there and partly because colonial powers intentionally used those groups as buffers between themselves and local groups, in order to soften the impact of domination (this was especially clear in the British policy of "indirect rule"). In other words, what Portes has called the "mode of incorporation" of these groups created the potential for economic advantage.[97] But even where minority groups are present in a promising situation, there is no guarantee that they will be able to manage their social structure in a way that optimizes their opportunities.

Another possibility is that although no group is clearly identified by analysts or perhaps even by contemporaries, there nevertheless exists in that setting some group of families whose social structure approximates that which solves the dual problems cited here. Analysis of business success has not been oriented to such social structural considerations so groups like this, if not clearly flagged by ethnic markers, may be missed in attempts to explain the economic situation.

In these first two explanations of the apparent absence of coherent minorities from their frequently strong role in economic activity, I supposed that conditions in fact were favorable for minorities to play such a role, which they may not always be. For example, one favorable—and historically common—condition is cultural: it occurs when the majority group disdains the search for profit. This disdain is evident when those who trade in subsistence goods are seen as not belonging to the moral community if their trade is oriented to profit and carried out at prices arrived at outside the local moral economy. Where such separation is in place, only outsiders who do not partake of the moral economy and suffer relatively little from its sanctions can be effective entrepreneurs. Thus Ortiz notes that among the Paez, only the most marginal in the community sold food for profit at market prices, violating local mores.[98] In Southeast Asia, as I have noted above, the Chinese filled this role.

The economic historian Gerschenkron, opposing the sociological argument of the 1950s and 1960s which posited that values would have to change before development could take place, noted that this is "in obvious conflict with the facts," since there were European instances "where magnificent entrepreneurial activities were conducted in the face of a dominant value system that was violently opposed to such activities and continued regarding the working of the land . . . as the only economic activity that was pleasing in the eyes of the Lord."[99]

Even if such values don't *prevent* entrepreneurial activity, they may still impose serious *costs* on it, and I suggest that it is under just such circumstances that minority ethnic groups have a comparative advantage.

Conversely, in seventeenth century Philadelphia where entrepreneurs were *not* drawn from any particular ethnic background, Doerflinger reports that the setting was distinguished, as few in history have been, by a "spirit of enterprise, a driving compulsion to swiftly develop a powerful dynamic economy,"[100] and that making a fortune was considered quite a respectable ambition. We may thus propose that in settings where the dominant system of values is broadly favorable to profit-making and economic pursuits, immigrant and minority groups will be less likely to find advantage.

We need also to inquire whether the advantages of groups such as those I have discussed obtain equally under all *economic* circumstances. The usual undifferentiated macroeconomic argument would suggest that a "rising tide lifts all boats."[101] Then we would expect minority groups, like others, to have difficulty in hard times but to succeed during an economic boom. I want to argue the opposite: that minority or other groups whose patterns of coupling and decoupling solve the problems I have described find their main advantage under difficult economic conditions.

This appears to be the case for the Javanese and Philippine examples I have cited, where Chinese dominate commerce. In her account of Estancia, in the Philippines, M. Szanton notes that market conditions worsened considerably after World War II; there was a considerable influx of traders and thus "subsistence vending" provided economic security for those who might otherwise be unemployed. "The marketplace," she suggests, "seems so devised as to be able to continuously absorb more persons and provide them with at least minimal income for survival."[102]

In the Javanese town of Modjokuto, Geertz and Dewey document the advantage of Chinese over local Moslem traders.[103] This was not always the case: before the Depression, there existed large, well-integrated, Moslem-dominated trade organizations that were able to "pool resources, distribute routes and enforce debts within the groups . . . . After the Depression, the combination of a weakened economy and an overcrowding of the market network with an increasing number of marginal traders sapped the dynamic of the merchant class" and now, "the few outstanding efforts by members of the old merchant class to create more efficient productive and distributive institutions in the town are nearly swamped by the hundreds of small-scale petty traders trying to squeeze a marginal living out of traditional commerce."[104]

In Doerflinger's account of Philadelphia wholesale merchants in the eighteenth and nineteenth centuries, it seems clear that no particular ethnic group dominated trade, although there were some real ethnic and quasi-ethnic divisions. What is common to this case and the case of Modjokuto in the 1920s is a highly favorable macroeconomic situation in which entry of firms is relatively easy, capital can be raised without difficulty, and profits have not yet been squeezed. Doerflinger notes, for example, that much of the trade in Philadelphia was in imports and exports and that capital was available from English merchants who extended it freely even without knowing much about the borrowers.[105]

This general argument may help us also to see in what *sectors* of an economy groups will have an advantage. Wong, in his study of Shanghainese textile firms in Hong Kong, argues that it is in industries with especially low entry barriers, like textiles—where there are few economies of scale, proprietary technologies, or product differentiations—that one may expect the use of particularistic criteria to form solidary groups that fend off intruders.[106] In other words, ties of group solidarity can substitute for "natural" factors that create barriers to entry, and so we may expect to see solidary groups in markets that on purely economic grounds would be expected to be competitive, but empirically are not.

Another factor is that the advantage of ethnic businesses seems most robust where the most problematic commodity required is trust. On the other hand, where it is technical knowledge, the ethnic advantage may fade. This is one reason why "middleman" occupations present a special opportunity for the visiting ethnic.[107] Not that there is no technical aspect to these occupations: certainly there are complex bookkeeping and other matters that must be mastered before businesses like these can be run. But such knowledge is relatively static, and once acquired within the group is no longer problematic; trust in one's coworkers is the main problem. Where technical knowledge of a constantly changing variety is required in employees, the advantages of ethnically closed kinship networks may diminish, and Lim thus argues that Chinese firms in Hong Kong that specialize in high-tech areas no longer find an advantage in traditional Chinese management practices; this is confirmed by her empirical study of Chinese export-oriented electronics firms in Singapore and Malaysia, where access to capital, technology, labor, and overseas marketing outlets are determined "by the relationship of Chinese business, not to other Chinese organizations but to foreign firms on the one hand and local government on the other."[108] But few sectors of any modern economy fit this requirement of constant technical change, so the ethnic advantage may be quite substantial over a large area of economic life.

So it appears that the advantages of immigrant or minority ethnic groups are especially pertinent where profit is disdained, under difficult economic conditions, where credit is tight and the industry barely under way, in industries with low barriers to entry, and where trust rather than technical knowledge is the most valuable commodity. Under such conditions, even temporary setbacks may sink a firm, and there is no margin for error. In more favorable conditions, the ethnic advantage fades. An ethnic group may even become underrepresented in such a case since its ability to monopolize under adverse circumstances is eliminated, and without such a monopoly, its status as a group of second-class citizens may then be highlighted and militate against successful enterprise.

It does not follow that majority groups in good economic times have no problems of trust or of noneconomic claims. These problems appear under all conditions, and can be dealt with only at a cost. Under sufficiently favorable macroeconomic conditions, as in Java in the 1920s, the difficulties and costs of getting credit, building an organization, and finding ways to either trust subordinates or monitor their behavior without a cohesive social grouping can be borne. But even in that setting I would argue that these still *are* difficulties and costs, and that under more difficult conditions they simply cannot be borne, and will sink altogether any attempt to expand economic activity; then, only groups who can manage these problems at lower cost can sustain commerce.

Conclusion

While my analysis points clearly to the importance of noneconomic and institutional factors as determinants of entrepreneurship, it adds to the study of norms and values the more concrete issue of how social structure and exchange are patterned. I take these factors not as competing with economic variables, but rather as part of an account that must consider both.

I have especially highlighted patterns of group solidarity that give immigrants and other minorities advantage in the construction of enterprise. The argument is that even if external conditions are favorable to their playing this role, such groups must also be characterized by a complex balance of internal coupling with decoupling from outside groups. This balance is determined in large part by historical and economic conjunctures outside of individuals' control, though it is subject to some manipulation at the margins. This manipulation is the subject of rational choice arguments offered by institutional economists, and must not be ignored; it is useful only, however, if supplemented by the type of historical and contextual analysis I have suggested.

I have focused on the small scale of enterprise formation, neglecting some of the larger problems in the study of economic development, such as the way enterprises agglomerate into large-scale business groups and how they interact with other institutional sectors such as labor, government, and consumers. The important topic of agglomeration, though beyond the scope of the present analysis, is an especially natural extension of the discussion of immigrants and minority groups in the economy, since such groups may form large industrial conglomerates or sets of loosely affiliated firms that dominate the most modern industrial sector of an economy, as did the Chinese in Indonesia or the Marwaris in India.[109]

To explain how this occurs requires an argument beyond that advanced here. I have so far outlined as a solution to the problem of enterprise a strategy based on trust and limited liability that seems to be very well-suited to the successful construction of small firms, but would appear thereby to have a built-in barrier to expansion. The number of family members or co-ethnics whom the entrepreneur can know well enough to trust implicitly must necessarily be small. Rather than expanding a business to its most profitable size, many owners whose enterprise is based on family or co-ethnics expand instead by putting some trusted individual in charge of *another* business, sometimes a branch but sometimes unrelated. This is one reason for the frequent observation that entrepreneurs in developing countries have a number of irons in the fire—often in different branches of economic activity.[110]

But it does not follow from this that the road to progress away from small enterprise and toward more familiar large-scale capitalistic units is best traversed by moving to "modern," impersonal economic institutions. Instead, many large industrial empires, including very substantial financial institutions, have been built out of smaller personalized arrangements based on family and friends. Quite elaborate structures of alliance and control have been built by ethnic minorities who have used ties of kin and friendship in artful combination with bureaucratic structures which provide the scaffolding for much larger-scale operations than could be mounted by family alone.[111] It suffices to conclude here by noting that as we progress in our understanding of the sociology of the economy, we will find a surprisingly large role for the supposedly archaic categories of ethnicity and kinship; the idea that these are superseded in the economy of the modern world by efficient and impersonal institutions is a wishful vestige of Enlightenment idealism that careful analysis does not sustain.

....

Notes

This chapter is drawn largely from draft chapters of my book-in-progress, which will be published by Harvard University Press as *Society and Economy: The Social Construction of Economic Institutions*. I am grateful to Alejandro Portes, Patricia Fernández Kelly, Bryan Roberts, and Saskia Sassen for their critical comments on the earlier draft.

1. Cf. Mark Granovetter, "Economic Action and Social Structure: The Problem of Embeddedness," *American Journal of Sociology* 91, no. 3 (November 1985): 481–510.

2. The concept of trust deserves a more explicit theoretical discussion, which space limitations preclude here. See pp. 38–47 of my "Problems of Explanation in Economic Sociology," in N. Nohria and R. Eccles, eds., *Networks and Organizations: Structure, Form and Action* (Boston: Harvard Business School Press, 1992).

3. Alice Dewey, *Peasant Marketing in Java* (Glencoe. Ill.: Free Press, 1962); Clifford Geertz, *Peddlers and Princes* (Chicago: University of Chicago Press, 1963).

4. William G. Davis, *Social Relations in a Philippine Market: Self-Interest and Subjectivity* (Berkeley: University of California Press, 1973); David L. Szanton, *Estancia in Transition: Economic Growth in a Rural Philippine Community* (Quezon City. Philippines: Ateneo de Manila University Press, 1971).

5. Dewey, *Peasant Marketing,* p. 31.

6. Ibid., p. 42.

7. Ibid., p. 88.

8. Ibid., p. 92.

9. Geertz, *Peddlers,* p. 40.

10. Ibid., p. 28.

11. Ibid., p. 126.

12. Clifford Geertz, "Suq: The Bazaar Economy in Sefrou," in C. Geertz, H. Geertz. and L. Rosen, eds., *Meaning and Order in Moroccan Society* (New York: Cambridge University Press, 1979), pp. 183–185.

13. Ibid., p. 191.

14. D. Szanton, *Estancia.*

15. Ibid., p. 51.

16. See Maria C.B. Szanton, *A Right to Survive: Subsistence Marketing in a Lowland Philippine Town* (University Park, Penn.: Penn State University Press, 1972).

17. The concept of "moral economy" is used in this chapter in the sense introduced by E.P. Thompson's landmark essay on English collective action in the eighteenth century, "The Moral Economy of the English Crowd in the Eighteenth Century," *Past and Present* 50 (February 1971): 76–136. It denotes a situation where there is widespread agreement in a population that economic processes must meet certain specified moral standards in order to be legitimate. This is a special

case of the postulate of "socially oriented economic action" proposed by Alejandro Portes, 1995. 'Economic Sociology and the Sociology of Immigration', in Portes, A. (ed.), *The Economic Sociology of Immigration*. New York: Russell Sage Foundation.

18. D. Szanton, *Estancia*, p. 87.

19. Ibid., p. 89n. Such a pattern is widely reported for Mediterranean countries, but also in other widely separated parts of the world, such as Holland and Thailand, where Hanks refers to factions as "entourages." See L.M. Hanks, "The Corporation and the Entourage: A Comparison of Thai and American Social Organization," in S. Schmidt, L. Guasti, C. Lande, and J. Scott, eds., *Friends, Followers and Factions* (Berkeley: University of California Press, 1977), pp. 161–167.

20. Geertz, *Peddlers*.

21. Ibid., p. 83.

22. Ibid., p. 84.

23. Ibid., p. 85.

24. Ibid., p. 106.

25. Ibid., p. 123.

26. Ibid., p. 125.

27. D. Szanton, *Estancia*, p. 89.

28. Ibid., pp. 89–91.

29. Clifford Geertz, "The Rotating Credit Association: A 'Middle-Rung' in Development," *Economic Development and Cultural Change* 10, no. 3 (1962): 243.

30. Shirley Ardener, "The Comparative Study of Rotating Credit Associations," *Journal of the Royal Anthropological Institute* 94, Part 2 (1963): 217.

31. Ibid., p. 221.

32. Ibid., p. 216.

33. Portes, op.cit.

34. Ardener, "Comparative Study," p. 220.

35. Geertz, "Rotating Credit," pp. 262–263.

36. Ardener, "Comparative Study," p. 222.

37. Marguerite Holloway and Paul Wallich, "A Risk Worth Taking," *Scientific American* 267, no. 5: (November 1992): 126.

38. See Portes, op.cit.

39. Ivan Light, *Ethnic Enterprise in America: Business and Welfare Among Chinese, Japanese and Blacks* (Berkeley: University of California Press, 1972).

40. Ibid., pp. 62, 81.

41. Ibid., p. 36.

42. Ibid., p. 102.

43. Ibid., p. 131.

44. Ibid., p. 133.

45. Ibid., p. 117.

46. Ibid., p. 148.

47. For Indonesia see Dewey, *Peasant Marketing*, pp. 42–50 and Geertz, *Peddlers*; for

the Philippines see Davis, *Social Relations*, pp. 198–202 and D. Szanton, *Estancia*, pp. 97–99.

48. Dewey, *Peasant Marketing*, pp. 44–45.

49. Ibid., p. 45.

50. Ann Swidler, "Culture in Action: Symbols and Strategies," *American Sociological Review* 51, no. 2 (1986): 273–286.

51. Dewey, *Peasant Marketing*, p. 45.

52. Geertz, *Peddlers*.

53. Ibid., p. 123.

54. Dewey, *Peasant Marketing*, p. 46.

55. Geertz, *Peddlers*, pp. 84–85.

56. John Omohundro, *Chinese Merchant Families in Iloilo: Commerce and Kin in a Central Philippine City* (Athens, Ohio: Ohio University Press 1981).

57. Davis, *Social Relations*, p. 200.

58. Ibid., p. 200.

59. See, for example, Landa, "Homogeneous Middleman."

60. Geertz, "Suq," p. 252 no. 101.

61. Siu-Lun Wong, "Industrial Entrepreneurship and Ethnicity: A Study of the Shanghainese Cotton Spinners in Hong Kong" (Ph.D. diss., Wolfson College, Oxford, 1979), p. 284.

62. He argues also that it is humiliating in China for a kinsman to make claims on an entrepreneur (Ibid., p. 284).

63. See Portes, op. cit.

64. These points were impressed upon me by Alejandro Portes and Bryan Roberts, in discussion at the Russell Sage Foundation meetings on economic sociology of immigration.

65. Peter Gosling, "Chinese Crop Dealers in Malaysia and Thailand: The Myth of the Merciless Monopsonistic Middleman," in Linda Y.C. Lim and L.A. Peter Gosling, eds., *The Chinese in Southeast Asia*, Vol. I, *Ethnicity and Economic Activity* (Singapore: Maruzen Asia, 1983), p. 143, and Maurice Freedman, "The Handling of Money: A Note on the Background to the Economic Sophistication of Overseas Chinese" *Man* 59, item no. 89 (1959): 64–65.

66. Linda Lim, "Chinese Economic Activity in Southeast Asia: An Introductory Review," in Lim and Gosling, eds., *The Chinese in Southeast Asia*, Vol. I, *Ethnicity and Economic Activity*, p. 9. One informant observed to Gosling that borrowing from local cooperatives was "better than the radio if you want everyone to know how much money you owe" (Gosling, "Crop Dealers," p. 144). Not only was borrowing from the Chinese merchants a less formal procedure in the sense of not involving paperwork, but the entire transaction could be carried out with exquisite sensitivity to the cultural need to avoid the *appearance* of a loan. Gosling's account is worth citing in detail: "I have watched Malays borrow from a Chinese shopkeeper without ever knowing that a financial transaction was in progress. A

cigarette is shared; the shopkeeper asks if there is anything the client wants. The client makes vague humorous remarks about how his wife pesters him for a sewing machine and his children like sweets and they exchange some common remarks about the jump in prices, the high costs of living and the wasteful ways of their wives and children. The shopkeeper then suggests that he has not yet banked the proceeds from the store and that if the client needs something to tide him over, he is welcome to it. The client usually buys a pack of cigarettes (which is put on his account) and takes the money folded into a small wad with the cigarettes, an invisible transaction unless one is watching closely. After the client has left the shop, the shopkeeper writes the loan and the pack of cigarettes in his ledger" (p. 166).

67. Gosling, "Crop Dealers," p. 143–144.

68. Aram Yengoyan, "The Buying of Futures: Chinese Merchants and the Fishing Industry in Capiz, Philippines," in Lim and Gosling, eds., *The Chinese in Southeast Asia*, Vol. I, *Ethnicity and Economic Activity*, pp. 117–130.

69. Gosling, "Crop Dealers," p. 138; cf. Mark Granovetter, "The Strength of Weak Ties," *American Journal of Sociology* 78, no. 6 (May 1973): 1360–1380.

70. Brian Foster, "Ethnicity and Commerce," *American Ethnologist* 1, no. 3 (1974): 441.

71. Roger Waldinger, Robin Ward, and Howard Aldrich, "Ethnic Business and Occupational Mobility in Advanced Societies," *Sociology* 19 (1985): 586–597.

72. Charles Choy Wong, "Black and Chinese Grocery Stores in Los Angeles' Black Ghetto," *Urban Life* 5 (1977): 439–464.

73. Jeremy Boissevain and Hanneke Grotenberg, "Culture, Structure and Ethnic Enterprise: The Surinamese of Amsterdam," *Ethnic and Racial Studies* 9 (January 1986): 13.

74. Brian Foster, "Minority Traders in Thai Village Social Networks," *Ethnic Groups* 2 (1980): 223.

75. D. Szanton, *Estancia*, p. 97.

76. Ibid., p. 95. Szanton reports that in addition to migrants, Protestants and Chinese, one other group in Estancia provides more than its share of entrepreneurs: women. The local cultural pattern is such that women more easily than men can limit the diffuse claims against their businesses that might prevent them from running efficiently. Men are judged "largely on their adherence to the traditional hierarchical interpersonal role behavior patterns demanding generosity and magnanimity towards others in the larger society," but women are judged mainly on how well they manage their family's internal economic aaffairs. Thus they are "expected to be thrifty and to haggle in the marketplace which is, in a culturally real sense, beneath a man's dignity." So if you ask a woman for a loan or for rice, she can more easily say no or request repayment of a loan, on the grounds of her family's needs. Wives, in this setting, are thus often the marketing agents for fishermen or farmers (D. Szanton, *Estancia*, p. 94). Furthermore, women are less likely than men, when provoked, to engage in physical violence. Thus it is "literally

safer for a woman to enter 'hard,' narrowly contractual economic relationships with others. Their ability to deny credit or demand payment of debts without fear of violence is essential to commercial enterprises in which goods produced elsewhere . . . are purchased from dealers outside the town, dealers who similarly demand payment in full and on time" (Ibid., p. 95). It is hard to know how widespread such a cultural pattern is, but with the exception of the Middle East, where women's roles are severely limited by Islamic culture, most reports of marketing and commerce in less developed settings show a preponderance of women in the most important roles. Whether they have as distinct entrepreneurial advantages in these other settings as in Estancia seems to me hard to establish on the basis of existing studies.

77. See, for example, the essays in Susan Olzak and Joanne Nagel, eds., *Competitive Ethnic Relations* (Orlando, Fla.: Academic Press, 1986).

78. Summer La Croix, "Homogeneous Middleman Groups: What Determines the Homogeneity?" *Journal of Law, Economics and Organization* 5, no. 1 (1989): 219.

79. Brian Foster, "Minority Traders in Thai Village Social Networks," *Ethnic Groups* 2 (1980): 223, 239.

80. Gosling, "Crop Dealers", p. 156

81. Peter Gosling, "Changing Chinese Identities in Southeast Asia," in Gosling and Lim, eds., *The Chinese in Southeast Asia*, Vol. II, *Identity, Culture and Politics* (Singapore: Maruzen Asia, 1983), p. 4.

82. Omohundro, *Merchant Families*, p. 12.

83. Peter Marris and Anthony Somerset, *The African Businessman: A Study of Entrepreneurship and Development in Kenya* (London: Routledge and Kegan Paul, 1971), p. 135

84. Ibid., p. 145.

85. Cf. Edna Bonacich and John Modell, *The Economic Basic of Ethnic Solidarity: Small Business in the Japanese American Community* (Berkeley: University of California Press, 1980).

86. Levy, "Contrasting Factors," p. 187.

87. Howard Aldrich and Catherine Zimmer, "Entrepreneurship Through Social Networks," in Raymond Smilor and Donald Sexton, eds., *The Art and Science of Entrepreneurship* (Cambridge, Mass.: Ballinger, 1985), p. 14.

88. Leonard Broom and Ruth Riemer, *Removal and Return: The Socio-Economic Effects of the War on Japanese Americans* (Berkely: University of California Press, 1949); Bonacich and Modell, *Economic Basis;* and Robert Jiobu, "Ethnic Hegemony and the Japanese of California," *American Sociological Review* 53 (June 1988): 353–367.

89. Geertz, *Peddlers*, p. 148.

90. Dewey, *Peasant Marketing*, p. 45; D. Szanton, *Estancia*, p. 99; Davis, *Social Relations*. p. 203.

91. Thomas Timberg, *The Marwaris: From Traders to Industrialists* (New Delhi: Vikas, 1978).

92. Broom and Riemer, *Removal*.
93. Geertz, *Peddlers*, p. 149.
94. Ibid., p. 149.
95. Davis, *Social Relations*, pp. 202–203.
96. D. Szanton, *Estancia*, p. 99.
97. See Portes, op. cit.
98. Sutti Ortiz, *Uncertainties in Peasant Farming: A Colombian Case* (New York: Humanities Press, 1973).
99. Alexander Gerschenkron, "The Modernization of Entrepreneurship," in Myron Weiner, ed., *Modernization: The Dynamics of Growth* (New York: Basic Books, 1966), p. 253.
100. Thomas Doerflinger, *A Vigorous Spirit of Enterprise: Merchants and Economic Development in Revolutionary Philadelphia* (Chapel Hill: University of North Carolina Press, 1986), p. 5.
101. Ivan Light and Carolyn Rosenstein Light, "Demand Factors in Entrepreneurship" (Department of Sociology, University of California, Los Angeles, 1989, mimeographed).
102. M. Szanton, *Right to Survive*, p. 138.
103. Geertz, *Peddlers*; Dewey, *Peasant Marketing*.
104. Geertz, *Peddlers*, pp. 13, 17.
105. Doerflinger, *Spirit*, p. 68.
106. Siu-Lun Wong, "Individual Entrepreneurship," p. 254.
107. See Edna Bonacich, "A Theory of Middleman Minorities," *American Sociological Review* 38 (October 1973): 583–594.
108. Linda Lim, "Chinese Business, Multinationals and the State: Manufacturing for Export in Malaysia and Singapore," in Lim and Gosling, eds., *The Chinese in Southeast Asia*, Vol. I, *Ethnicity and Economic Activity*, p. 246.
109. Richard Robison, *Indonesia: The Rise of Capital* (Sydney: Allen & Unwin, 1986); Timberg, *Marwaris*.
110. See for example, Norman Long, "Multiple Enterprises in the Central Highlands of Peru," in S. Greenfield, A. Strockon, and R. Aubey, eds., *Entrepreneurs in Cultural Context* (Albuquerque: University of New Mexico Press, 1979).
111. A fuller account of these processes can be found in Mark Granovetter, "Business Groups," in Neil Smelser and Richard Swedberg, eds., *Handbook of Economic Sociology* (New York: Russell Sage Foundation and Princeton University Press, 1994), Chap. 22.

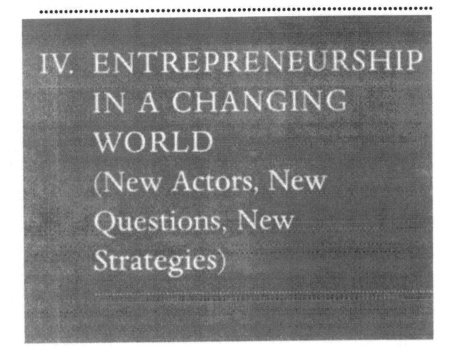

IV. ENTREPRENEURSHIP IN A CHANGING WORLD (New Actors, New Questions, New Strategies)

From a Weberian perspective, it may well seem that the current attempt to transform the mythical and individualistic entrepreneur of Schumpeter into a clonable kind of entrepreneur at business schools all over the world represents a form of disenchantment and rationalization of the world. Another way of presenting this whole development, however, would simply be to say that the study of entrepreneurship has advanced quite a bit during the last ten–fifteen years, and that it today is possible to teach something that earlier many people thought could not be taught.

This fourth and last part of the volume attempts to give a sense of the richness and creativity that can be found in current social science research on entrepreneurship. Two articles, for example, discuss entrepreneurship in relation to networks. In "The Network Entrepreneur", a general theory of entrepreneurship based on networks is presented; and in "The Origins and Dynamics of Production

Networks in Silicon Valley" the role of industrial networks in Silicon Valley is studied. "Entrepreneurship and Culture: The Case of Freddy, the Strawberry Man" uses an anthropological approach to study entrepreneurship and adds an existentialist twist to the analysis. *Ethnic Entrepreneurs*, the last article, finally, differs from the others in that it summarizes many years of research on a specific topic: ethnicity and entrepreneurship. The richness of this last article gives a sense of what sustained academic attention can lead to; and it thereby also gives a sense of the kind of empirical sophistication we can look forward to in many other areas, if the current boom in entrepreneurial studies continues.

The first reading, "The Network Entrepreneur" by Ronald Burt, provides a general introduction to network theory and also contains a special theory of entrepreneurship, based on this perspective. The author notes that networks are central to the notion of social capital and suggests that they can be conceptualized in two different ways. According to the first, networks are seen as important because they lead the actor to certain resources; and according to the second, the networks themselves are seen as a resource, since they allow the actor better access, better timing and a better chance for referrals. Burt follows the second approach and suggests a theory of entrepreneurship which is purely structural in nature. A person, he says, can act as an entrepreneur to the extent that he or she is in a position to mediate between different groups of actors in his or her network. If there is no link between two groups in an actor's network, Burt explains, there exists a so-called structural hole; and this means that the actor can intervene between the two groups as a *tertius gaudens* ('the third who benefits'). A practical example would be someone who knows one group of people who want to buy something, and another group of people who want to sell something. He or she is then in a position to mediate between the two groups and charge a commission for doing so.

Burt is the author of a practical guide on how to use networks, "The Network Entrepreneur" (1987), and well aware of the practical implications of his theories. In the article reproduced in this volume, for example, he explains very carefully how a person should arrange his or her network in order to maximize information about opportunities. The idea of locating or creating a *tertius gaudens* position in one's network is also easy to translate into practice. Burt's article can, furthermore, be taken as a point of departure for a more general discussion of networks and entrepreneurship. Networks, for example, often play a crucial role for ethnic entrepreneurs. Women in many countries are today trying to build up their own networks to counter exclusively male or 'old boys' networks', and different strategies can be used in this effort. Networks are also often created to counter the rigidities of formal organizations and to create new types of interconnections between organizations. Further practical questions to discuss, include the following two: In what other areas, besides female and ethnic entrepreneurship, can networks play a positive role? and, When do networks play a negative role and impede entrepreneurship?

The next article, "The Origins and Dynamics of Production Networks in Silicon Valley" by AnnaLee Saxenian, is a study of Silicon Valley. The focus is on the new kind of relationship between computer system firms and their main suppliers, which has developed after a severe crisis hit the region in the mid-1980s. Instead of arm's length relationships, industrial networks have emerged which are characterized by deep, long-lasting and equal relationships. This way, the computer system firms have become free to specialize and to compete more effectively, and the suppliers free to develop into more sophisticated and less labor-intensive outfits. Working so closely together has also facilitated the emergence of many new products—the result of 'complementary innovation', in the author's terminology. According to Saxenian, this type of collaboration has made it possible for Silicon Valley to once again become a world leader in an industry, which is extremely volatile.

Saxenian's text touches on many interesting issues, including one that has not been mentioned until now (and which is further discussed in her exciting book *Industrial Advantage*), namely the role of industrial regions in furthering entrepreneurship. For the average entrepreneur, this issue translates, for example, into the question of where to locate—in place X or in a place with a more developed industrial system? (I do not dare to say that Saxenian's article also raises the question for the individual entrepreneur whether to develop a whole new industrial region—although this is exactly what Frederic Terman did in the case of Silicon Valley!). It is clear that the actors in the industrial networks that Saxenian describes are very careful not to become totally dependent on one single party, but try to spread the risks. Is this a wise strategy—or is it possible to imagine situations where this type of behavior can be counterproductive? Finally, it appears that the collaboration between producers of computer systems and their suppliers have developed against the background of a very intense social life in Silicon Valley. Is it possible to encourage social interaction and an entrepreneurial spirit among people in some area by introducing, say, afterwork facilities—bars, gyms and so on? Or can this type of interaction and spirit only develop in a spontaneous manner?

In the next reading, Monica Lindh de Montoya's "Entrepreneurship and Anthropology: The Case of Freddy, the Strawberry Man", an argument is made that anthropology has a distinct contribution to make to the modern study of entrepreneurship and, more precisely, that some of the activities of the entrepreneur are to be understood as a reading of the different cultural codes that exist in society. These different codes state, for example, when and how credit can be given, what is allowed in a negotiation between buyer and seller, and so on; and the entrepreneur is someone who is extra-sensitive to these codes and knows how to read them in an expert fashion. What is so often referred to as simply 'spotting an opportunity', is, in other words, part of a much more complicated cultural process. Lindh de Montoya's argument is illustrated by a fascinating case study of a dealer in strawberries in Bailadores, Venezuela, 'Freddy, the Strawberry Man'. The reader gets to know Freddy's background and his various business enterprises, from his days as a student of economics until some years later, when he is a family man and on his way to some success.

The practical implications of Lindh de Montoya's argument are interesting to discuss. For one thing, it is clear that a good entrepreneur, from this perspective, needs to know his or her culture in great detail. The argument of the author actually gets very close to that of Hayek about 'practical knowledge', which is discussed in the introduction to this volume: only by having a special kind of very detailed and concrete knowledge is it possible to become an entrepreneur. But how is this knowledge to be acquired, and also, how is one to develop that special sensitivity to a reading of one's culture that the author talks about? Can, for example, an immigrant develop the same kind of knowledge of a country as someone who has grown up in this culture? The practical case that Lindh de Montoya presents is one of small business; and it may be of some interest to discuss whether a detailed knowledge of a local culture is as important for big business. One may also wonder how globalization affects the theory of entrepreneurship as a form of sensitivity to one's culture. Does there exist, for example, an emerging global economic culture? And if so, how has this global economic culture come into being—and how can one spot opportunities in it?

As mentioned in the introductory essay, research on ethnicity and entrepreneurship tends to be of a very practical nature, and the insights that have accumulated over the years can often be translated directly into advice on how to proceed for the entrepreneur-to-be. The observation that there typically exists a market for ethnic goods among the members of a minority group is an example of this, and also the fact that this market has definite limits, unless people outside the group happen to like the ethnic good as well. The authors of the very last reading in this anthology, "Ethnic Entrepreneurs", note that it is common for members of a particular ethnic group, which has just moved to a new locality, to try to buy up the businesses of an older ethnic group, if the children of the latter do not want to take over after their parents since they have better opportunities elsewhere. An interesting question to discuss, after having read "Ethnic Entrepreneurs", is whether the current level of sophistication in this type of research is such that people who belong to disadvantaged minorities can be directly trained to become more entrepreneurial. Do such programmes already exist? Another question, connected to this, is whether it is possible to generalize from research on ethnic entrepreneurs to research on entrepreneurs in general, and thereby turn advice to ethnic entrepreneurs into advice to entrepreneurs in general?

12 The Network Entrepreneur

Ronald S. Burt

My starting point is this: a player brings capital to the competitive arena and walks away with profit determined by the rate of return where the capital was invested. The market-production equation predicts profit: invested capital, multiplied by the going rate of return, equals the profit to be expected from the investment. Investments create an ability to produce a competitive product. For example, capital is invested to build and operate a factory. Rate of return is an opportunity to profit from the investment.

Rate of return is keyed to the social structure of the competitive arena and is the focus here. Each player has a network of contacts in the arena. Certain players are connected to certain others, trust certain others, are obligated to support certain others, and are dependent on exchange with certain others. Something about the structure of the player's network and the location of the player's contacts in the social structure of the arena provide a competitive advantage in getting higher rates of return on investment. This chapter is about that advantage. It is a description of the way in which social structure renders competition imperfect by creating entrepreneurial opportunities for certain players and not for others.

Opportunity and Social Capital

A player brings three kinds of capital to the competitive arena. There are more, but three are sufficient here. First, the player has financial capital—cash in hand, reserves in the bank, investments coming due, lines of credit. Second, the player has human capital. Natural abilities—charm, health, intelligence, and looks—combined with skills acquired in formal education and job experience give you abilities to excel at certain tasks. Third, the player's relationships with other players are social capital. You have friends, colleagues, and contacts more generally through whom you receive opportunities to use your financial and human capital. I refer to opportunities broadly, but I certainly mean to include the obvious examples of job promotions, participation in significant projects, influential access to important decisions, and so on. The social capital of people aggregates into the social capital of organizations. In a firm providing services—for example, advertising, brokerage, or consulting—there are people valued for their ability to deliver a quality product. Then there are the "rainmakers," valued for their ability to deliver clients. The former do the work and the latter make it possible for all to profit from the work. The former represent the financial and human capital of the firm; the latter represent its social capital. More generally, property and human assets define the firm's production capabilities. Relations within and beyond the firm are social capital.

Distinguishing Social Capital

Financial and human capital are distinct in two ways from social capital. First, they are the property of individuals. They are owned in whole or in part by a single individual defined in law as capable of ownership, typically a person or corporation. Second, they concern the investment term in the market production equation. Whether held by an actual person or the fictive person of a firm, financial and human capital gets invested to create production capabilities. Investments in supplies, facilities, and people serve to build and operate a factory. Investments of money, time, and energy produce a skilled manager. Financial capital is needed for raw materials and production facilities. Human capital is needed to craft the raw materials into a competitive product.

Social capital is different on both counts. First, it is a thing owned jointly by the parties to a relationship. No one player has exclusive ownership rights to social capital. If you or your partner in a relationship withdraws, the connection dissolves with whatever social capital it contained. If a firm treats a cluster of customers poorly and they leave, the social capital represented by the firm-cluster relationship is lost. Second, social capital concerns rate of return in the market production equation. Through relations with colleagues, friends, and clients come the opportunities to transform financial and human capital into profit.

Social capital is the final arbiter of competitive success. The capital invested to bring your organization to the point of producing a superb product is as rewarding as the opportunities to sell the product at a profit. The investment to make you a skilled manager is as valuable as the opportunities and the leadership positions to which you get to apply your managerial skills. The investment to make you a skilled scientist with state-of-the-art research facilities is as valuable as the opportunities and the projects to which you get to apply those skills and facilities.

More accurately, social capital is as important as competition is imperfect and investment capital is abundant. Under perfect competition, social capital is a constant in the production equation. There is a single rate of return because capital moves freely from low-yield to high-yield investments until rates of return are homogeneous across alternative investments. Where competition is imperfect, capital is less mobile and plays a more complex role in the production equation. There are financial, social, and legal impediments to moving cash between investments. There are impediments to reallocating human capital, both in terms of changing the people to whom you have a commitment and in terms of replacing those people with new. Rate of return depends on the relations in which capital is invested. Social capital is a critical variable. This is all the more true where financial and human capital are abundant—which in essence reduces the investment term in the production equation to an unproblematic constant.

These conditions are generic to the competitive arena, making social capital a factor as routinely critical as financial and human capital. Competition is never perfect. The rules of trade are ambiguous in the aggregate and everywhere negotiable in the particular. The allocation of opportunities is rarely made with respect to a single dimension of abilities needed for a task. Within an acceptable range of needed abilities, there are many people with financial and human capital comparable to your own. Whatever you bring to a production task, there are other people who could do the same job; perhaps not as well in every detail, but probably as well within the tolerances of the people for whom the job is done. Criteria other than financial and human capital are used to narrow the pool down to the individual who gets the opportunity. Those other criteria are social capital. New life is given to the proverb of success being determined less by what you know than by who you know. As a senior colleague once remarked, "Publishing high-quality work is important for getting university resources, but friends are essential." Only a select few of equally qualified people get the most rewarding opportunities. Only some of comparably high-quality products come to dominate their markets. So, the question is how.

The Who and the How

The competitive arena has a social structure; players trust certain others, are obligated to support certain others, are dependent on exchange with certain others, and so on. Against this backdrop, each player has a network of contacts: everyone you now know, everyone you have ever known, and everyone who knows you even though you don't know them. Something about the structure of the player's network and the location of the player's contacts in the social structure of the arena form a competitive advantage in getting higher rates of return on investment.

There are two routes into the social capital question. The first describes a network as your access to people with specific resources, creating a correlation between theirs and yours; the second describes social structure as capital in its own right. The idea for the first approach has circulated as power, prestige, social resources, and more recently, social capital. Nan Lin and his colleagues provide an exemplar for this line of work, showing how the occupational prestige of a person's job is contingent on the occupational prestige of a personal contact leading to the job (Lin 1982; Lin *et al.* 1981; Lin and Dumin 1986). Related empirical results appear in Campbell *et al.* (1986); De Graaf and Flap (1988); Flap and De Graaf (1989); and Marsden and Hurlbert (1988). Coleman (1988) discusses the transmission of human capital across generations. Flap and Tazelaar (1989) provide a thorough review with special attention to social network analysis.

Empirical questions in this line of approach concern the magnitude of association between contact resources and your own resources, and variation in the association across kinds of relationships. Granovetter's (1973) weak-tie metaphor, discussed in detail shortly, is often invoked to distinguish kinds of relationships.

Network analysis will recognize this as an example of social contagion analysis. Network structure does not predict attitudes or behaviors directly. It predicts similarity between attitudes and behaviors. The research tradition is tied to the Columbia Sociology survey studies of social influence conducted during the 1940s and 1950s. In one of the first well-known studies, for example, Lazarsfeld *et al.* (1944) show how a person's vote is associated with the party affiliations of friends. Persons claiming to have voted for the presidential candidate of a specific political party tend to have friends affiliated with that party. Social capital theory developed from this approach describes the manner in which resources available to any one person in a population are contingent on the resources available to individuals socially proximate to that person.

Empirical evidence is readily available. People develop relations with people like themselves (see, for example, Fischer 1982; Marsden 1987; Burt 1990). Wealthy people develop ties with other wealthy people. Educated people develop ties with one another. Young people develop ties with one another. There are reasons for this. Socially similar people, even in the pursuit of independent interests, spend time in the same places. Relationships emerge. Socially similar people have more shared interests. Relationships are maintained. Further, we are sufficiently egocentric to find people with similar tastes attractive. Whatever the etiology for strong relations between socially similar people, it is to be expected that the resources and opinions of any one individual will be correlated with the resources and opinions of their close contacts.

A second line of approach describes social structure as capital in its own right. Where the first line describes the network as a conduit, the second line describes how networks are themselves a form of social capital. This approach is much less developed than the first. Indeed, it is little developed beyond intuitions in empirical research on social capital. Network range, indicated by size, is the primary measure. For example, Boxman et al. (1991) show that people with larger contact networks obtain higher paying positions than people with small networks. A similar finding in social support research shows that persons with larger networks tend to live longer (Berkman and Syme 1979).

Both lines of approach are essential to a general definition of social capital. Social capital is at once the structure of contacts in a network and resources they each hold. The first term describes *how* you reach. The second describes *who* you reach.

For two reasons, however, I ignore the question of "who" to concentrate on "how." The first is generality. The question of "who" elicits a more idiographic class of answers. Predicting rate of return depends on knowing the resources of a player's contacts. There will be interesting empirical variation from one kind of activity to another, say job searches versus mobilizing support for a charity, but the empirical generalization is obvious: doing business with wealthy clients, however wealth is defined, has a higher margin than doing business with poor clients. I want to identify parameters of social capital that generalize beyond the specific individuals connected by a relationship.

The second reason is correlation. The two components in social capital should be so strongly correlated that I could reconstruct much of the phenomenon from whichever component more easily yields a general explanation. To the extent that people play an active role in shaping their relationships, a player who knows how to structure a network to provide high opportunity knows who to include in the network. Even if networks are passively inherited, the manner in which a player is connected within social structure says much about contact resources. I will show that *players with well-structured networks obtain higher rates of return*. Resources accumulate in their hands. People develop relations with people like themselves. Therefore, how a player is connected in social structure indicates the volume of resources held by the player and the volume to which the player is connected.

The nub of the matter is to describe network benefits in competition so as to be able to describe how certain structures enhance those benefits. The benefits are of two kinds, information and control. I describe information benefits first because they are more familiar; then control benefits, showing how both kinds of benefits are enhanced by the same element of social structure.

Information

Opportunities spring up everywhere: new institutions and projects that need leadership, new funding initiatives looking for proposals, new jobs for which you know of a good candidate, valuable items entering the market for which you know interested buyers. The information benefits of a network define who knows about these opportunities, when they know, and who gets to participate in them. Players with a network optimally structured to provide these benefits enjoy higher rates of return to their investments because such players know about, and have a hand in, more rewarding opportunities.

Access, Timing, and Referrals

Information benefits occur in three forms: access, timing, and referrals. Access refers to receiving a valuable piece of information and knowing who can use it. Information does not spread evenly through the competitive arena. It is not that players are secretive, although that too can be an issue. The issue is that players are unevenly connected with one another, are attentive to the information pertinent to themselves and their friends, and are all overwhelmed by the flow of information. There are limits to the volume of information you can use intelligently. You can only keep up with so many books, articles, memos, and news services. Given a limit to the volume of information that anyone can process, the network becomes an important screening device. It is an army of people processing information who can call your attention to key bits—keeping you up to date on developing opportunities, warning you of impending disasters. This secondhand information is often fuzzy or inaccurate, but it serves to signal something to be looked into more carefully.

Related to knowing about an opportunity is knowing who to bring into it. Given a limit to the financing and skills that we possess individually, most complex projects will require coordination with other people as staff, colleagues, or clients. The manager asks, "Who do I know with the skills to do a good job with that part of the project?" The capitalist asks, "Who do I know who would be interested in acquiring this product or a piece of the project?" The department head asks, "Who are the key players needed to strengthen the department's position?" Add to each of these the more common question, "Who do I know who is most likely to know the kind of person I need?"

Timing is a significant feature of the information received by a network. Beyond making sure that you are informed, personal contacts can make you one of the people informed early. It is one thing to find out that the stock market is crashing today. It is another to discover that the price of your stocks will plummet tomorrow. It is one thing to learn the names of the two people referred to the board for the new vice-presidency. It is another to discover that the job will be created and your credentials could make you a serious candidate for the position. Personal contacts get significant information to you before the average person receives it. That early warning is an opportunity to act on the information yourself or invest it back into the network by passing it on to a friend who could benefit from it.

These benefits involve information flowing from contacts. There are also benefits in the opposite flow. The network that filters information coming to you also directs, concentrates, and legitimates information about you going to others.

In part, this does no more than alleviate a logistics problem. You can only be in a limited number of places within a limited amount of time. Personal contacts get your name mentioned at the right time in the right place so that opportunities are presented to you. Their referrals are a positive force for future opportunities. They are the motor expanding the third category of people in your network, the players you do not know who are aware of you. I am thinking of that remark so often heard in recruitment deliberations: "I don't know her personally, but several people whose opinion I trust have spoken well of her."

Beyond logistics, there is an issue of legitimacy. Even if you know about an opportunity and could present a solid case for why you should get it, you are a suspect source of information. The same information has more legitimacy when it comes from someone inside the decision-making process who can speak to your virtues. Speaking about my own line of work, which I expect in this regard is typical, candidates offered the university positions with the greatest opportunity are people who have a strong personal advocate in the decision-making process, a person in touch with the candidate to ensure that all favorable information, and responses to any negative information, get distributed during the decision.

Benefit-Rich Networks

A player with a network rich in information benefits has: 1) contacts established in the places where useful bits of information are likely to air, and 2) a reliable flow of information to and from those places.

The second criterion is as ambiguous as it is critical. It is a matter of trust, of confidence in the information passed and in the care with which contacts look out for your interests. Trust is critical precisely because competition is imperfect. The question is not whether to trust, but who to trust. In a perfectly competitive arena, you can trust the system to provide a fair return on your investments. In the imperfectly competitive arena, you have only your personal contacts. The matter comes down to a question of interpersonal debt. If I do for her, will she for me? There is no general answer. The answer lies in the match between specific people. If a contact feels that he is somehow better than you—a sexist male dealing with a woman, a racist white dealing with a black, an old-money matron dealing with an upwardly mobile ethnic—your investment in the relationship will be taken as your proper obeisance to a superior. No debt is incurred. We use whatever cues can be found for a continuing evaluation of the trust in a relation, but really don't know it until the trusted person helps when you need it. With this kind of uncertainty, players are cautious about extending themselves for people whose reputation for honoring interpersonal debt is unknown. The importance of this point is illustrated by the political boundary that exists around senior management for outsider managers trying to break through the boundary (Burt 1992: Ch. 4).

We know from social science research that strong relations and mutual relations tend to develop between people with similar social attributes such as education, income, occupation, and age (e.g. Fischer 1982; Burt 1986, 1990; and Marsden 1987).

This point is significant because it contradicts the natural growth of contact networks. Left to the natural course of events, a network will accumulate redundant contacts. Friends introduce you to their friends and expect you to like them. Business contacts introduce you to their colleagues. You will like the people you meet in this way. The factors that make your friends attractive make their friends attractive because like seeks out like. Your network grows to include more and more people. These relations come easily, they are comfortable, and they are easy to maintain. But these easily accumulated contacts do not expand the networks so much as they fatten it, weakening its efficiency and effectiveness by increasing contact redundancy and tying up time. The process is amplified by spending time in a single place; in your family, or neighborhood, or in the office. The more time you spend with any specific primary contact, the more likely you will be introduced to their friends. Evidence of these processes can be found in studies of balance and transitivity in social relations (see Burt 1982: 55–60, for review), and in studies of the tendency for redundant relations to develop among physically proximate people (e.g., the suggestively detailed work of Festinger *et al.* 1950; or the work with more definitive data by Fischer 1982, on social contexts; and Feld 1981, 1982, on social foci).

Whether egocentrism, cues from presumed shared background and interests, or confidence in mutual acquaintances to enforce interpersonal debt, the operational guide to the formation of close, trusting relationships seems to be that a person more like me is less likely to betray me. For the purposes here, I put the whole issue to one side as person-specific and presumed resolved by the able player.

That leaves the first criterion, establishing contacts where useful bits of information are likely to air. Everything else constant, a large, diverse network is the best guarantee of having a contact present where useful information is aired.

Size is the more familiar criterion. Bigger is better. Acting on this under-standing, a person can expand their network by adding more and more con-tacts. They make more cold calls, affiliate with more clubs, attend more social functions. Numerous books and self-help groups can assist you in "network-ing" your way to success by putting you in contact with a large number of potentially useful, or helpful or like-minded people. The process is illustrated by the networks at the top of Figure 12.1. The four-contact network at the left expands to sixteen contacts at the right. Relations are developed with a friend of each contact in network A, doubling the contacts to eight in network

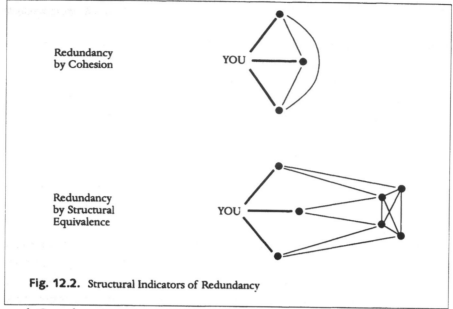

Fig. 12.2. Structural Indicators of Redundancy

work C, and so on.

Size is a mixed blessing. More contacts can mean more exposure to valuable information, more likely early exposure, and more referrals. But increasing network size without considering diversity can cripple the network in significant ways. What matters is the number of nonredundant contacts. Contacts are redundant to the extent that they lead to the same people, and so provide the same information benefits.

Consider two four-contact networks, one sparse the other dense. There are no relations between the contacts in the sparse network, and strong relations between every contact in the dense network. Both networks cost whatever time and energy is required to maintain four relationships. The sparse network provides four nonredundant contacts, one for each relationship. No one of the contacts gets you to the same people reached by the other contacts. In the dense network, each relationship puts you in contact with the same people you reach through the other relationships. The dense network contains only one nonredundant contact. Any three are redundant with the fourth.

The sparse network provides more information benefit. It reaches information in four separate areas of social activity. The dense network is a virtually worthless monitoring device because the strong relations between people in the network means that each person knows what the other people know, so they will discover the same opportunities at the same time.

The issue is opportunity costs. At minimum, the dense network is ineffi-cient in the sense that it returns less diverse information for the same cost as the sparse network. A solution is to put more time and energy into adding nonredundant contacts to the dense network. But time and energy are limited, which means that inefficiency translates into opportunity costs. Taking four relationships has an illustrative limit on the number of strong relations that a player can maintain, the player in the dense network is cut off from three-fourths of the information provided by the sparse network.

Structural Holes

It is convenient to have a term for the separation between nonredundant contacts. I use the term *structural hole*. Nonredundant contacts are connected by a structural hole—a structural hole is a relationship of nonredundancy between two contacts. The hole is a buffer, like an insulator in an electric circuit. As a result of the hole between them, the two contacts provide network benefits that are in some degree additive rather than overlapping.

Empirical Indicators

Nonredundant contacts are disconnected in some way—either directly in the sense that there is no direct contact between them or indirectly in the sense that one has contacts that exclude the others. The respective empirical conditions that indicate a structural hole are *cohesion* and *structural equivalence*. Both conditions define holes by indicating where they are absent.

Under the cohesion criterion, two contacts are redundant to the extent that they are connected to each other by a strong relationship. A strong relationship indicates the absence of a structural hole. Examples would be father and son, brother and sister, husband and wife, close friends, people who have been partners for a long time, people who frequently get together for social occasions, and so on. You have easy access to both people if either is a contact. Redundancy by cohesion is illustrated at the top of Figure 12.2. The three contacts are connected to one another, and so provide the same network benefits. The presumption here—routine in network analysis since Festinger *et al*'s (1950) analysis of information flowing through personal relations and Homans' (1950) theory of social groups—is that the likelihood of information moving from one person to another is proportional to the strength of their relationship.

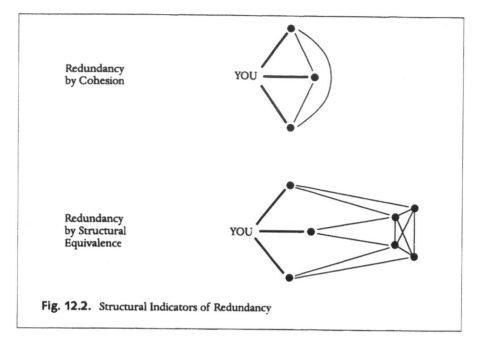

Fig. 12.2. Structural Indicators of Redundancy

Empirically, strength has two independent dimensions: frequent contact and emotional closeness (see Marsden and Hurlbert 1988; Burt 1990).

Structural equivalence is a useful second indicator for detecting structural holes. Two people are structurally equivalent to the extent that they have the same contacts. Regardless of the relation between structurally equivalent people, they lead to the same sources of information and so are redundant. Where cohesion concerns direct connection, structural equivalence concerns indirect connection by mutual contact. Redundancy by structural equivalence is illustrated at the bottom of Figure 12.2. The three contacts have no direct ties with one another—they are nonredundant by cohesion. But each leads you to the same cluster of more distant players. The information that comes to them, and the people to whom they send information, are redundant. Both networks in Figure 12.2 provide one nonredundant contact at a cost of maintaining three.

The indicators are neither absolute nor independent. Relations deemed strong are only strong relative to others. They are our strongest relations. Structural equivalence rarely reaches the extreme of complete equivalence. People are more or less structurally equivalent. Also, the criteria are correlated. People who spend a lot of time with the same other people often get to know one another. The mutual contacts responsible for structural equivalence set the stage for the direct connection of cohesion. The empirical conditions between two players will be a messy combination of cohesion and structural equivalence, present to varying degrees, at varying levels of correlation.

Cohesion is the more certain indicator. If two people are connected with the same people in a player's network (making them redundant by structural equivalence), they can still be connected with different people beyond the network (making them nonredundant). But if they meet frequently and feel close to one another, then they are likely to communicate and probably have contacts in common. More generally, and especially for fieldwork informed by attention to network benefits, the general guide is the definition of a structural hole. There is a structural hole between two people who provide nonredundant network benefits. Taking the cohesion and structural equivalence conditions together, redundancy is most likely between structurally equivalent people connected by a strong relationship. Redundancy is unlikely, indicating a structural hole, between total strangers in distant groups. I return to this issue again, to discuss the depth of a hole, after control benefits have been introduced.

The Efficient-Effective Network

Balancing network size and diversity is a question of optimizing structural holes. The number of structural holes can be expected to increase with network size, but the holes are the key to information benefits. The optimized network has two design principles: efficiency and effectiveness.

EFFICIENCY. The first principle concerns efficiency, and it says that you should maximize the number of nonredundant contacts in the network to maximize the yield in structural holes per contact. Given two networks of equal size, the one with more nonredundant contacts provides more benefits. There is little gain from a new contact redundant with existing contacts. Time and energy would be better spent cultivating a new contact among previously unreached people.[1] Maximizing the nonredundancy of contacts maximizes the structural holes obtained per contact.[2]

Efficiency is illustrated by the networks in Figure 12.3. These reach the same people reached by the networks in Figure 12.1, but in a different way. What expands in Figure 12.1 is not the benefits, but the cost of maintaining the network. Network A provides four nonredundant contacts. Network B provides the same number. The information benefits provided by the initial four contacts are redundant with benefits provided by their close friends. All that has changed is the doubled number of relationships maintained in the

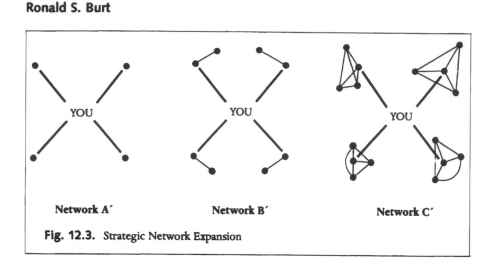

Fig. 12.3. Strategic Network Expansion

network. The situation deteriorates even further with the sixteen contacts in network C. There are still only four nonredundant contacts in the network, but their benefits are now obtained at a cost of maintaining sixteen relationships.

With a little network surgery, the sixteen contacts can be maintained at a fourth of the cost. As illustrated in Figure 12.3, select one contact in each cluster to be a primary link to the cluster. Concentrate on maintaining the primary contact, and allow direct relationships with others in the cluster to weaken into indirect relations through the primary contact. Those players reached indirectly are secondary contacts. Among the redundant contacts in a cluster, the primary contact should be the one most easily maintained and most likely to honor an interpersonal debt to you in particular. The secondary contacts are less easily maintained or less likely to work well for you (even if they might work well for someone else). The critical decision obviously lies in selecting the right person to be a primary contact. That is the subject of trust discussed above. With a good primary contact, there is little loss in information benefits from the cluster and a gain in the reduced effort needed to maintain the cluster in the network.

Repeating this operation for each cluster in the network recovers effort that would otherwise be spent maintaining redundant contacts. By reinvesting that saved time and effort in developing primary contacts to new clusters, the network expands to include an exponentially larger number of contacts while expanding contact diversity. The sixteen contacts in network C of Figure 12.1, for example, are maintained at a cost of four primary contacts in network C' of Figure 12.3. Some portion of the time spent maintaining the redundant other twelve contacts can be reallocated to expanding the network to include new clusters.

EFFECTIVENESS. The second principle for the optimized network requires a further shift in perspective. Distinguish primary from secondary contacts and focus resources on preserving the primary contacts. Here contacts are not people on the other end of your relations; they are ports of access to clusters of people beyond. Guided by the first principle, these ports should be nonredundant so as to reach separate, and therefore more diverse, social worlds of network benefits. Instead of maintaining relations with all contacts, the task of maintaining the total network is delegated to primary contacts. The player at the center of the network is then free to focus on properly supporting relations with primary contacts, and expanding the network to include new clusters. Where the first principle concerns the average number of people reached with a primary contact, the second concerns the total number of people reached with all primary contacts. The first principle concerns the yield per primary contact. The second concerns the total yield of the network. More concretely, the first principle moves from the networks in Figure 12.1 to the corresponding networks in Figure 12.3. The second principle moves from left to right in Figure 12.3. The target is network C′ in Figure 12.3; a network of few primary contacts, each a port of access to a cluster of many secondary contacts.

Figure 12.4 illustrates some complexities inherent in unpacking a network to maximize structural holes. The BEFORE network contains five primary contacts and reaches a total of fifteen people. However, there are only two clusters of nonredundant contacts in the network. Contacts 2 and 3 are redundant in the sense of being connected with each other and reaching the same people (cohesion and structural equivalence criteria). The same is true of contacts 4 and 5. Contact 1 is not connected directly to contact 2 but he reaches the same secondary contacts, so contacts 1 and 2 provide redundant network benefits (structural equivalence criterion). Illustrating the other extreme, contacts 3 and 5 are connected directly, but they are nonredundant because they reach separate clusters of secondary contacts (structural equivalence criterion). In the AFTER network, contact 2 is used to reach the first cluster in the BEFORE network, and contact 4 is used to reach the second cluster. The time and energy saved by withdrawing from relations with the other three primary contacts is reallocated to primary contacts in new clusters. The BEFORE and AFTER networks are both maintained at a cost of five primary relationships, but the AFTER network is dramatically richer in structural holes, and so the network benefits.

Network benefits are enhanced in several ways. There is a higher volume of benefits because more contacts are included in the network. Beyond volume, diversity enhances the quality of benefits. Nonredundant contacts ensure exposure to diverse sources of information. Each cluster of contacts is an independent source of information. One cluster, no matter how numerous its members, is one source of information because people connected to one another tend to

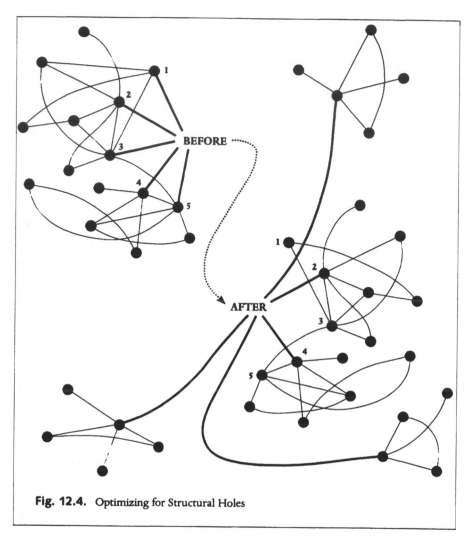

Fig. 12.4. Optimizing for Structural Holes

know about the same things at about the same time. The information screen provided by multiple clusters of contacts is broader, providing better assurance of the player being informed of opportunities and impending disasters. Further, since nonredundant contacts are only linked through the central player, you are assured of being the first to see new opportunities created by needs in one group that could be served by skills in another group. You become the person who first brings people together, giving you the opportunity to coordinate their activities. These benefits are compounded by the fact that having a network that yields such benefits makes you even more attractive as a network contact to other people, easing the task of expanding the network to serve your interests best.

Control and the Tertius Gaudens

I have described how structural holes can determine who knows about opportunities, when they know, and who gets to participate in them. Players with a network optimized for structural holes enjoy higher rates of return on their investments because they know about, and have a hand in, more rewarding opportunities.

They are also more likely to secure favourable terms in the opportunities they choose to pursue. The structural holes that generate information benefits also generate control benefits, giving certain players an advantage in negotiating their relationships. To describe how this is so, I break the negotiation into structural, motivational, and outcome components. The social structure of the competitive arena defines opportunities, a player decides to pursue an opportunity, and is sometimes successful.

Tertius Gaudens

Beginning with the outcome, sometimes you will emerge successful from negotiation as the *tertius gaudens*. Taken from the work of Georg Simmel, the *tertius* role is useful here because it defines successful negotiation in terms of the social structure of the situation in which negotiation is successful. The role is the heart of Simmel's later (1922) analysis of the freedom an individual derives from conflicting group affiliations (see Coser 1975 for elaboration).[3] The *tertius gaudens* is "the third who benefits" (Simmel 1923: 154, 232).[4] The phrase survives in what I am told is a well-known Italian proverb: *Fra i due litiganti, il terzo gode* (Between two fighters, the third benefits), and it has moved north to a more jovial Dutch phrase; *de lachende derde* (the laughing third).[5] *Tertius, terzo*, or *derde*— the phrase describes an individual who profits from the disunion of others.

There are two *tertius* strategies: being the third between two or more players after the same relationship, and being the third between players in two or more relations with conflicting demands. The first, and simpler, strategy is the familiar economic bargaining between buyer and seller. Where two or more players want to buy something, the seller can play their bids against one another to get a higher price. The strategy extends directly to social commodities: a woman with multiple suitors, or a professor with simultaneous offers of positions in rival institutions.

The control benefits of having a choice between players after the same relationship extends directly to choice between the simultaneous demands of players in separate relationships. The strategy can be seen between hierarchical statuses in the enterprising subordinate under the authority of two or more superiors: for example, the student who strikes her own balance between the simultaneous demands of imperious faculty advisors.[6] The bargaining is not limited to situations of explicit competition. In some situations, emerging as the *tertius* depends on creating competition. In proposing the concept of a role-set, for example, Merton (1957: 393–394) identifies this as a strategy designed to resolve conflicting role demands. Make simultaneous, contradictory demands explicit to the people posing them, and ask them to resolve their—now explicit— conflict. Even where it does not exist, competition can be produced by defining issues in a way that contact demands become contradictory and must be resolved before you can meet their requests. Failure is possible. You might provide too little incentive for the contacts to resolve their differences. Contacts drawn from different social strata need not perceive one another's demands as carrying equal weight. Or you might provide too much incentive. Now aware of one another, the contacts could discover sufficient reason to cooperate in forcing you to meet their mutually agreed upon demands (Simmel 1902: 176, 180–181, calls attention to such failures). But if the strategy is successful, the pressure on you is alleviated and replaced with an element of control over the negotiation. Merton states the situation succinctly: the player at the center of the network "... originally at the focus of the conflict, virtually becomes a more or less influential bystander whose function it is to highlight the conflicting demands by members of his role-set and to make it a problem for them, rather than for him, to resolve *their* contradictory demands" (1957: 430).

The strategy holds equally well with large groups. Under the rubric "divide and rule", Simmel (1902: 185–186) describes institutional mechanisms by which the Incan and Venetian governments obtained advantage by creating conflict between subjects. The same point is illustrated more richly in Barkey's (1990) comparative description of state control in early seventeenth-century France and Turkey. After establishing the similar conditions in the two states at the time, Barkey asks why peasant–noble alliances developed in France against the central state while no analogous or substitutable alliances developed in Turkey. The two empires were comparable in many respects that scholars have cited to account for peasant revolt. They differed in one significant respect correlated with revolt— not in the structure of centralized state control, but in control strategy. In France, the king sent trusted representatives as agents to collect taxes and affect military decisions in provincial populations. The intrusion by these outside agents, *intendants*, affecting fundamental local decisions was resented by the established local nobility. Local nobility formed alliances with the peasantry against the central state. In Turkey, the sultan capitalized on conflict between leaders in the provinces. When a bandit became a serious threat to the recognized governor, a deal was struck with the bandit making him the legitimate governor. As Barkey puts it, "At its most extreme, the state could render a dangerous rebel legitimate overnight. This was accomplished by the striking of a bargain which ensured new sources of revenue for the rebel and momentary relief from internal warfare and perhaps, an army or two for the state" (1990: 18). The two empires differed in their use of structural holes. The French king ignored them, assuming he had absolute authority. The Turkish sultan strategically exploited them, promoting competition between alternative leaders. Conflict within the Turkish empire remained in the province, rather than being directed against the central state. As is characteristic of the control obtained via structural holes, the resulting Turkish control was more negotiated than the absolute control exercised in France. It was also more effective.

The Essential Tension

There is a presumption of tension here. Control emerges from *tertius* brokering tension between other players. No tension, no *tertius*.

It is easy to infer that the tension presumed is one of combatants. There is certainly a *tertius*-rich tension between combatants. Governors and bandits in the Turkish game played for life-or-death stakes. Illustrating this inference, a corporate executive listening to my argument expressed skepticism. Her colleagues, she explained, took pride in working together in a spirit of partnership and goodwill. The *tertius* imagery rang true to her knowledge of many firms, but not her own.

The reasoning is good. But the conclusion is wrong. I referred the skeptical executive to an analysis of hole effects that by coincidence was an analysis of managers at her level, in her firm (Burt 1992: Ch. 4). Promotions are strongly correlated, illuminatingly so for women, with the structural holes in a manager's network.

The tension essential to the *tertius* is merely uncertainty. Separate the uncertainty of control from its consequences. The consequences of the control negotiation can be life or death in the extreme situation of combatants, or merely a question of embarrassment. Everyone knows you made an effort to get that job, but it went to someone else. The *tertius* strategies can be applied to control with severe consequences or to control of little consequence. What is essential is that control is uncertain, that no one can act as if they have absolute authority. Where there is any uncertainty about whose preferences should dominate a relationship, there is an opportunity for the *tertius* to broker the negotiation for control by playing demands against one another. There is no long-term contract that keeps a relationship strong, no legal binding that can secure the trust necessary to a productive relationship. Your network is a pulsing swirl of mixed, conflicting demands. Each contact wants your exclusive attention, your immediate response when a concern arises. Each, to warrant their continued confidence in you, wants to see you measure up to the values against which they judge themselves. Within this preference web, where no demands have absolute authority, the *tertius* negotiates for favorable terms.

The Connection with Information Benefits

The negotiating of the *tertius* brings me back to information benefits. Structural holes are the setting for *tertius* strategies. Information is the substance. Accurate, ambiguous, or distorted information is moved between contacts by the *tertius*. One bidder is informed of a competitive offer in the first *tertius* strategy. A player in one relationship is informed of demands from other relationships in the second *tertius* strategy.

The two kinds of benefits augment and depend on one another. Application of the *tertius* strategies elicits additional information from contacts interested in resolving the negotiation in favor of their own preferences. The information benefits of access, timing, and referrals enhance the application of strategy. Successful application of the *tertius* strategies involves bringing together players who are willing to negotiate, have sufficiently comparable resources to view one another's preferences as valid, but will not negotiate with one another directly to the exclusion of the *tertius*. Having access to information means being able to identify where there is an advantage to bringing contacts together and is the key to understanding the resources and preferences being played against one another. Having that information early is the difference between being the one who brings together contacts versus being just another person who hears about the negotiation. Referrals further enhance strategy. It is one thing to distribute information between two contacts during negotiation. It is another thing to have people close to each contact endorsing the legitimacy of the information you distribute.

Entrepreneurs[7]

Behavior of a specific kind converts opportunity into higher rates of return. Information benefits of structural holes might come to a passive player, but control benefits require an active hand in the distribution of information. Motivation is now an issue. The *tertius* plays conflicting demands and preferences against one another, building value from their disunion. You enter the structural hole between two players to broker the relationship between them. Such behavior is not to everyone's taste. A player can respond in ways ranging from fully developing the opportunity to ignoring it. When you take the opportunity to be the *tertius*, you are an entrepreneur in the literal sense of the word—a person who generates profit from being between others. Both terms will be useful in these precise meanings: *entrepreneur* refers to a kind of behavior, the *tertius* is a successful entrepreneur.

Motivation is often traced to cultural beliefs and psychological need. For example, in *The Protestant Ethic and the Spirit of Capitalism*, Weber (1905: especially 166ff) describes the seventeenth-century bourgeois Protestant as an individual seeking—in his religious duty, his Calvinist "calling"—the profit of sober, thrifty, diligent exploitation of opportunities for usury and trade. Psychological need is another motive. McClelland (1961) describes the formation of a need to achieve in childhood as critical to later entrepreneurial behavior (a need that can be cultivated later if desired—McClelland 1975). Schumpeter stresses non-utilitarian motives: "First of all, there is the dream and the will to found a private kingdom, usually, though not necessarily, also a dynasty. . . . Then there is the will to conquer: the impulse to fight, to prove oneself superior to others, to succeed for the sake, not of the fruits of success, but of the success itself. . . . Finally, there is the joy of creating, of getting things done, or simply of exercising one's energy and ingenuity" (Schumpeter 1912: 93).[8]

Opportunity and Motivation

These are powerful frameworks for understanding competition, but I do not wish to detour into the beliefs behind entrepreneurial behavior. I propose to leap over the motivation issue by taking, for three reasons, a player's network as simultaneously an indicator of entrepreneurial opportunity and motivation.

First, there is the clarity of an opportunity. Players can be pulled to entrepreneurial action by the promise of success. I do not mean that players are rational creatures expected to calculate accurately and act in their own interest. Nor do I mean to limit the scope of the argument to situations in which players act as if they were rational in that way. I mean simply that between two opportunities, any player is more likely to act on the one with the clearer path to success. The clarity of opportunity is its own motivation. As the number of entrepreneurial opportunities in a network increases, the odds of some being clearly defined by deep structural holes increases, so the odds of entrepreneurial behavior increase. To be sure, a person whose abilities or values proscribe entrepreneurial behavior is unlikely to act, and someone inclined to entrepreneurial behavior is more likely to act, even taking the initiative to create opportunities. Regardless of ability or values, however, within the broad range of acceptable behaviors, a person is unlikely to take entrepreneurial action if the probability of success is low. You might question the propriety of a scholar negotiating between universities offering a position, but the question is not an issue for the player with one offer.

There are also network analogues to the psychological and cultural explanations of motive. Beginning with psychological need, a person with a taste for entrepreneurial behavior is prone to building a network configured around such behavior. If I find a player with a network rich in the structural holes that make entrepreneurial behavior possible, I have a player willing and able to act entrepreneurially. But it is the rare person who is the sole author of his or her network. Networks are more often built in the course of doing something else. Your work, for example, involves meeting people from very different walks of life, so your network ends up composed of contacts who, without you, have no contact with one another. Even so, the network is its own explanation of motive. As the volume of structural holes in a player's network increases—regardless of the process that created them—the entrepreneurial behavior of making and negotiating relations between others becomes a way of life. This is a network analogue to the cultural explanation of motive. If all you know is entrepreneurial relationships, the motivation question is a nonissue. Being willing and able to act entrepreneurially is how you understand social life.

I will treat motivation and opportunity as one and the same. Because of a clear path to success, or the tastes of the player as the network's author, or the nature of the player's environment as author of the network, a network rich in entrepreneurial opportunity surrounds a player motivated to be entrepreneurial. At the other extreme, a player innocent of entrepreneurial motive lives in a network devoid of entrepreneurial opportunity.

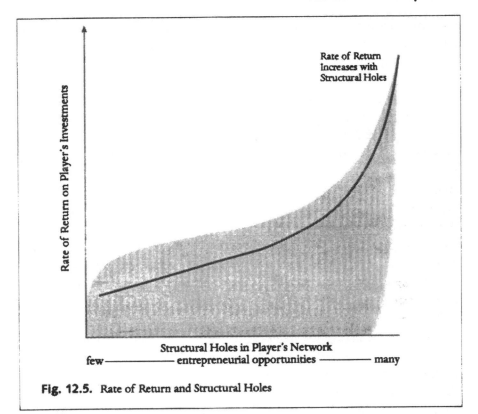

Fig. 12.5. Rate of Return and Structural Holes

Measurement Implications

Entrepreneurial motivation highlights a complexity that might otherwise obscure the association between structural holes and rates of return. Consider the graph in Figure 12.5. Players are defined by their rate of return on investments (vertical axis) and the entrepreneurial opportunities of structural holes in their networks (horizontal axis).

The sloping line in the graph describes the hole effect of players rich in structural holes (horizontal axis) getting higher rates of return on investments (vertical axis). The increasingly positive slope of the line captures the increasing likelihood of *tertius* profit. A player invests in certain relationships. They need not all be high-yield relationships. The higher the proportion of relationships enhanced by structural holes, the more likely the player is an able entrepreneur, and so the more likely that the player's investments are in high-yield relationships. The result is a higher aggregate rate of return on investments.

I have shaded the area in the graph to indicate how I expect data to be distributed around the line of association. There is no imperative that says players have to take advantage of the benefits provided by structural holes. Players rich in entrepreneurial opportunity may choose to develop opportunities (and so appear in the upper-right corner of the graph) or ignore them (and so appear in the lower-right corner of the graph). Some players in Figure 12.5 are above the line. Some are below. If players were perfectly rational, observations would be clustered around the line. Players would take advantage of any entrepreneurial opportunity presented to them. A control for differences in player motivation, such as a McClelland measure of need for achievement, would have the same effect. The point is not the degree of deviation from the line of association; it is the greater deviation below the line. Variable motivation creates deviations below the true hole effect on rate of return.

This emphasizes the relative importance for empirical research of deviations above and below the line of association. Observations in the lower-right corner of the graph, players under-utilizing their entrepreneurial opportunities, might be due to variation in motivation. Observations in the upper-left corner are a severe test of the argument. Players who have opportunities can choose whether to develop them. Players without opportunities do not have that choice. Within the limits of measurement error, there should be no observations in the upper-left corner of the graph.

....

Notes

1. For the purpose here, I ignore the many day-to-day tactical issues critical to maintaining a network. Thorough treatment requires considerable discussion and didactic devices. This is the function of the seminars offered by the Denver firm, Strategic Connections. I discuss tactical issues in a short book, *The Network Entrepreneur*, written in 1987 for distribution from the firm.

2. The number of structural holes is not increased directly, but is likely to increase. The presumption through all this is that the time and energy to maintain relationships is limited and the constant pressure to include new contacts will use all time and energy available (as in the preceding footnote). Although structural holes are not increased directly by maximizing nonredundant contacts, they can be expected to increase indirectly from the reallocation of time and energy from maintaining redundant contacts to acquiring new nonredundant contacts (as illustrated in Figure 12.4).

3. This theme is often grouped with Durkheim's (1893) argument for the liberating

effect of a division of labor, but it is useful to distinguish the two arguments for the purposes here. Simmel focuses on the liberating quality of competition between multiple affiliations, which is the concern here. Durkheim focuses on the liberating quality of interdependent affiliations. Integration, rather than competition, is Durkheim's theme. That theme continues in Blau's (1977) analysis of cross-cutting social circles, in which he argues that conflict between strata becomes increasingly difficult as affiliations provide people with alternative stratification hierarchies. Flap (1988) provides a network-oriented review of such work, building from anthropology and political science, to study the "crisscross" effect inhibiting violence.

4. Georg Simmel introduced this phrase in papers on the importance of group size, translated and published by Albion Small in the *American Journal of Sociology* (Simmel 1896: 393–394; 1902: 174–189). A later version was translated by Wolff (Simmel 1923: 154–169; 232–234).

5. I am grateful to Anna di Lellio for calling my attention to the Italian proverb and to Hein Schreuder for calling my attention to the Dutch expression. The idea of exploiting a structural hole is viscerally familiar to all audiences, but interestingly varied across cultures in phrasing the profit obtained (an interesting site for a Zelizer 1989 kind of analysis).

6. This point is nicely exemplified in Simmel's discussion of subordination comparing the freedom of two medieval subordinate positions, the bondsman ("unfree") and the vassal: "An essential difference between the mediaeval 'unfree' men and the vassals consisted in the fact that the former had and could have only one master, while the latter could accept land from different lords and could take the oath of fealty to each. By reason of the possibility of placing themselves in the feudal relation to several persons the vassals won strong security and independence against the individual lords. The inferiority of the position of vassalage was thereby to a considerable degree equalized" (1896: 394).

7. In the interests of saving space, a substantial block of material was deleted between here and the next section, on: (1) the literal meaning of entrepreneurs, (2) the importance of structural holes within the clusters of secondary contacts, (3) market boundaries, and (4) a more thorough discussion of holes defined by cohesion versus structural equivalence. If the leap to structural autonomy seems awkward here, consider looking at the full discussion (Burt 1992: Ch. 1).

8. I am grateful to Richard Swedberg for giving me the benefit of his careful study of Schumpeter in calling my attention to these passages. Their broader scope and context are engagingly laid out in his biography of Schumpeter (Swedberg 1991). The passages can also be found in the Schumpeter selection included in Parsons et al.'s *Theories of Society* (1961: 513). See also Swedberg, Richard 1993. 'On the Relationship between Economic Theory and Economic Sociology in the Work of Joseph Schumpeter', in R. Swedberg (ed.), *Explorations in Economic Sociology*. New York: Russell Sage Foundation, pp. 42–61.

References

Barkey, Karen. (1990). "Rebellious Alliances; The State and Peasant Unrest in Early Seventeenth Century: France and the Ottoman Empire." Paper presented at the 1989 annual meeting of the American Sociological Association.

Berkman, Lisa F., and S. Leonard Syme. (1979). "Social Networks, Host Resistance, and Mortality: A Nine-Year Follow-Up Study of Alameda County Residents." *American Journal of Epidemiology* 109: 186–204.

Blau, Peter M. 1977. *Heterogeneity and Inequality*. New York: Free Press.

Boxman, Ed A.W., Paul M. De Graaf, and Hendrik D. Flap. (1991). "The Impact of Social and Human Capital on the Income Attainment of Dutch Managers." *Social Networks* 13: 51–73.

Burt, Ronald S. (1982). *Toward a Structural Theory of Action*. New York: Academic Press.

—— (1986). "A Note on Sociometric Order in the General Social Survey Network Data." *Social Networks* 8: 149–174.

——(1990). "Kinds of Relations in American Discussion Networks." In C. Calhoun, M.W. Meyer, and W. Scott eds., *Structures of Power and Constraint*. New York: Cambridge University Press, pp. 411–451.

—— (1992). *Structural Holes*. Cambridge, MA: Harvard University Press.

Campbell, Karen E., Peter V. Marsden, and Jeanne S. Hurlbert. (1986). "Social Resources and Socioeconomic Status." *Social Networks* 8: 97–117.

Coleman, James S. (1988). "Social Capital in the Creation of Human Capital." *American Journal of Sociology* 94: S95–120.

Coser, Rose Laub. (1975). "The Complexity of Roles as a Seedbed of Individual Autonomy." In L.A. Coser ed., *The Idea of Social Structure*. New York: Harcourt, Brace, Jovanovich, pp. 237–263.

De Graaf, Nan D., and Hendrik D. Flap. (1988). "With a Little Help from My Friends." *Social Forces* 67: 453–472.

Feld, Scott. L. (1981). "The Focused Organization of Social Ties." *American Journal of Sociology* 86: 1015–1035.

——(1982). "Social Structural Determinants of Similarity." *American Sociological Review* 47: 797–801.

Festinger, Leon, Stanley Schachter, and Kurt W. Back. (1950). *Social Pressures in Informal Groups*. Stanford: Stanford University Press.

Fischer, Claude S. (1982). *To Dwell Among Friends*. Chicago: University of Chicago Press.

Flap, Hendrik D. (1988). *Conflict, Loyalty, and Violence*. New York: Verlag Peter Lang.

Flap, Hendrik D., and Nan D. De Graaf. (1989). "Social Capital and Attained Occupational Status." *Netherlands' Journal of Sociology* 22: 145–161.

Flap, Hendrik D., and F. Tazelaar. (1989). "The Role of Informal Social Networks on the Labor Market: Flexibilization and Closure." In H. Flap ed., *Flexibilization of the Labor Market*. Utrecht, Holland: ISOR, University of Utrecht, pp. 99–118.

Granovetter, Mark S. (1973). "The Strength of Weak Ties." *American Journal of Sociology* 78: 1360–1380.

Homans, George C. (1950). *The Human Group*. New York: Harcourt, Brace and World.

Lazarsfeld, Paul F., Bernard Berelson, and Hazel Gaudet. (1944). *The People's Choice*. New York: Columbia University Press.

Lin, Nan. (1982). "Social Resources and Instrumental Action." In P.V. Marsden and Nan Lin eds., *Social Structure and Network Analysis*. Beverly Hills, CA: Sage, pp. 131–145.

Lin, Nan, and Mary Dumin. (1986). "Access to Occupations Through Social Ties." *Social Networks* 8: 365–385.

Lin, Nan, Walter M. Ensel, and John C. Vaughn. (1981). "Social Resources and Strength of Ties." *American Sociological Review* 46: 393–405.

Marsden, Peter V. (1987). "Core Discussion Networks of Americans." *American Sociological Review* 52: 122–131.

Marsden, Peter V., and Jeanne S. Hurlbert. (1988). "Social Resources and Mobility Outcomes: A Replication and Extension." *Social Forces* 67: 1038–1059.

McClelland, David C. (1961). *The Achieving Society*. Princeton: Van Nostrand.

Merton, Robert K. (1957) (1968). "Continuities in the Theory of Reference Group Behavior." In *Social Theory and Social Structure*. New York: Free Press, pp. 335–440.

Schumpeter, Joseph A. (1912) (1961). *The Theory of Economic Development*. Translated by R. Opie. Cambridge, MA: Harvard University Press.

Simmel, Georg. (1896). "Superiority and Subordination as Subject-Matter of Sociology, II." Translated by A. Small. *American Journal of Sociology* 2: 392–415.

——(1902). "The Number of Members as Determining the Sociological Form of the Group, II." Translated by A. Small. *American Journal of Sociology* 8: 158–196.

——(1922) (1955). *Conflict and Web of Group Affiliations*. Translated by K.H. Wolff and R. Bendix. New York: Free Press.

——(1923) (1950). *The Sociology of Georg Simmel*. Translated by K.H. Wolff. New York: Free Press.

Stigler, George J. (1957) (1965). "Perfect Competition, Historically Contemplated." In George J. Stigler ed., *Essays in the History of Economics*. Chicago: University of Chicago Press, pp. 234–267.

Swedberg, Richard (1991). *Schumpeter—A Biography*. Princeton: Princeton University Press.

Weber, Max. (1904–1905) (1930). *The Protestant Ethic and the Spirit of Capitalism*. Translated by T. Parsons. New York: Charles Scribner's Sons.

Zelizer, Viviana A. (1989). "The Social Meaning of Money: 'Special Monies'". *American Journal of Sociology* 95: 342–377.

13 The Origins and Dynamics of Production Networks in Silicon Valley

AnnaLee Saxenian

Computer systems firms in Silicon Valley are responding to rising costs of product development, shorter product cycles and rapid technological change by focusing and building partnerships with suppliers, both within and outside of the region. Well-known firms like Hewlett-Packard and Apple Computers and lesser known ones like Silicon Graphics and Pyramid Technology are organized to combine the components and sub-systems made by specialist suppliers into new computer systems. As these firms collaborate to both define and manufacture new systems, they are institutionalizing their capacity to learn from one another. Three cases—a contract manufacturer, a silicon foundry, and the joint development of a microprocessor—illustrate how inter-firm networks help account for the sustained technological dynamism of the regional economy.

This essay analyzes the origins and dynamics of production networks in Silicon Valley from the perspective of the region's computer systems firms. Students of Silicon Valley have focused almost exclusively on the evolution of the semiconductor industry; when that industry fell into crisis in the mid-1980s, most assumed that the region itself would decline. Yet by the end of the decade, the regional economy had rebounded, as hundreds of new computer producers and suppliers of microprocessors, specialty chips, software, disk drives, networking hardware and other components generated a renewed wave of growth.

This revitalization is evident in regional output and employment figures. In spite of the worst recession in the region's history during 1985–86, the shipments of Silicon Valley high technology manufacturers and software enterprises grew 60 percent between 1982 and 1987 (from $15 billion to $24 billion), and employment in these firms expanded more than 45 percent during the decade. While there were only 69 establishments in the region producing computers in 1975, by 1980 there were 113, and by 1985 the number had more than doubled to 246.[1]

These new computer systems firms are at the hub of Silicon Valley's expanding production network. Well-known companies such as Tandem and Apple Computers, and lesser known ones such as Silicon Graphics and Pyramid Technology are organized to recombine components and sub-systems made by specialist suppliers—both within and outside of the region—into new computer systems. As they collaborate with key suppliers to define and manufacture new systems, they are reducing product development times and institutionalizing their capacity to learn from one another. These production networks help account for the sustained technological dynamism of the Silicon Valley economy.

Geographers and other social scientists have documented the emergence of flexible systems of production in regions such as Silicon Valley [22, 28, 32, 2, 31]. Most of the research on these regions, however, overlooks the changing nature of inter-firm and inter-industry relationships. In their detailed study of the location of the U.S. semiconductor industry, for example, Scott and Angel document the vertical disaggregation of production and the dense concentration of inter-firm transactions in Silicon Valley, but do not explore the nature of the relations between semiconductor firms and their customers and suppliers.

When Florida and Kenney argue that Silicon Valley's flexibility derives from arm's length exchanges and atomistic fragmentation—and thus provides no match for Japan's highly structured, large-firm dominated linkages—they, too, overlook growing evidence of the redefinition of supplier relations among U.S. technology firms [8,17]. Moreover, it is difficult to reconcile their bleak predictions with the continued dynamism of the Silicon Valley economy.

Students of business organization, by contrast, have focused on the emergence of network forms of industrial organization—intermediate forms which fall between Williamson's ideal types of market exchange and corporate hierarchy. In the two decades since Richardson [26] observed the pervasive role of cooperation in economic relations, the literature on inter-firm networks and alliances has burgeoned [23, 20, 16, 10, 14, 15, 29]. Nonetheless, there has been little attention to the emergence of inter-firm networks in America's high technology regions.

The case of the computer systems business in Silicon Valley demonstrates how inter-firm networks spread the costs and risks of developing new technologies and foster reciprocal innovation among specialist firms. This paper begins by describing how the region's systems firms are responding to the rising costs of product development, shorter product cycles and rapid technological change by remaining highly focused and relying on networks of suppliers. In so doing, they are rejecting the vertically integrated model of computer production which dominated in the postwar period, in which a firm manufactured most of its technically sophisticated components and sub-systems internally.

The paper's second section analyzes the redefinition of supplier relations among Silicon Valley computer firms and their vendors. The creation of long-term, trust-based partnerships is blurring the boundaries between interdependent but autonomous firms in the region. While this formalization of inter-firm collaboration is recent, it builds on the longstanding traditions of informal information exchange, inter-firm mobility and networking which distinguish Silicon Valley [1, 3, 27].

The final section of the paper presents three cases which illustrate how inter-firm collaboration fosters joint problem-solving between Silicon Valley systems firms and their specialist suppliers. These cases—of a contract manufacturer, a silicon foundry and the joint development of a microprocessor—demonstrate how the process of complementary innovation helps to account for Silicon Valley's technological dynamism.

This paper draws on the findings of more than 50 in-depth interviews with executives and managers in Silicon Valley-based computer systems firms and suppliers during 1988, 1989 and 1990. The sample includes the region's leading computer systems firms, many computer firms started during the 1980s, and a wide range of producers of semiconductors, disk drives, and other components.

....

Creating Production Networks

Competitive conditions in the computer systems business changed dramatically during the 1970s and 1980s. The cost of bringing new products to market increased at the same time that the pace of new product introductions and technological change accelerated. Hewlett-Packard's Vice-President of Corporate Manufacturing, Harold Edmondson, claims that half of the firm's orders in any year now come from products introduced in the preceding three years, and notes that:

In the past, we had a ten year lead in technology. We could put out a product that was not perfectly worked out, but by the time the competition had caught up, we'd have our product in shape. Today we still have competitive technology, but the margin for catch up is much shorter—often under a year[2]

Computer makers like HP must now bring products to market faster than ever before, often in a matter of months.

The cost of developing new products has in turn increased along with growing technological complexity. A computer system today consists of the central processing unit (CPU) which includes a microprocessor and logic chips, the operating system and applications software, information storage products (disk drives and memory chips), ways of putting in and getting out information (input-output devices), power supplies, and communications devices or networks to link computers together. Although customers seek to increase performance along each of these dimensions, it is virtually impossible for one firm to produce all of these components, let alone stay at the forefront of each of these diverse and fast changing technologies.

Systems firms in Silicon Valley are thus focusing on what they do best, and acquiring the rest of their inputs from the dense infrastructure of suppliers in the region as well as outside. This represents a fundamental shift from the vertically integrated approach to computer production characterized by IBM, DEC and other established U.S. computer firms.[3] In this model, which survived in an era of slower changing products and technologies, the firm designed and produced virtually all of the technologically sophisticated components and sub-systems of the computer in-house. Subcontractors were used as surge capacity in times of boom demand, and suppliers were treated as subordinate producers of standard inputs.

When Sun Microsystems was established in 1982, by contrast, its founders chose to focus on designing hardware and software for workstations and to limit manufacturing to prototypes, final assembly and testing. Sun purchases application specific integrated circuits (ASICs), disk drives, and power supplies as well as standard memory chips, boxes, keyboards, mice, cables, printers and monitors from suppliers. Even the printed circuit board at the heart of its workstations is assembled by contract manufacturers. Why, asks Sun's Vice-President of Manufacturing Jim Bean, should Sun vertically integrate when hundreds of specialty shops in Silicon Valley invest heavily in staying at the leading edge in the design and manufacture of microprocessors, disk drives, printed circuit boards (PCBs), and most other computer components and sub-systems? Relying on outside suppliers reduces Sun's overhead and insures that the firm's workstations use state-of-the art technology.

This unbundling also provides the flexibility to introduce new products and rapidly alter the product mix. According to Sun's Bean: "If we were making a stable set of products, I could make a solid case for vertical integration.[4] He argues, however, that product cycles are too short and technology is changing too fast to move more manufacturing in-house. Relying on external suppliers allowed Sun to introduce four major new product generations in its first five years of operation, doubling the price-performance ratio each successive year. Sun eludes clone-makers by the sheer pace of new product introduction.

The guiding principle for Sun, like most new Silicon Valley systems firms, is to concentrate its expertise and resources on coordinating the design and assembly of a final system, to advance critical technologies which represent the firm's core capabilities [24], and to spread the costs and risks of new product development through partnerships with suppliers. Tandem Computers manufactures its own PCBs, but purchases all other components externally. Mips Computer Systems set out to manufacture the microprocessors and PCBs for its workstations, but quickly sold its chipmaking and board assembly operations in order to focus on system design and development.

Some of the region's firms explicitly recognize their reliance on supplier networks and foster their development. Apple Computers' venture capital arm makes minority investments in promising firms which offer complementary technology. In 1984, for example, Apple invested $2.5 million in Adobe Systems, which produces the laser printer software critical to desktop publishing applications. Tandem Computers similarly invested in a small local telecommunications company, Integrated Technology Inc, and the two firms have jointly developed networking products to link together Tandem non-stop systems.

Companies like Sun, Tandem, and Mips recognize that the design and production of computers can no longer be accomplished by a single firm: it requires the collaboration of variety of specialist firms, none of which could complete the task on its own. This reliance on outsourcing is reflected in the high level of sales per employee of Silicon Valley firms: compare Apple's $369,593 and Silicon Graphics $230,000 per employee to IBM's $139,250 and DEC's $84,972 [25].

These highly focused producers depend on the unparalleled agglomeration of engineers and specialist suppliers of materials, equipment and services in Silicon Valley, and on the region's culture of open information exchange and interfirm mobility, which foster continual recombination and new firm formation [1,3,27]. This infrastructure supports the continued emergence of new producers, while allowing them to remain specialized and helps explain the proliferation of new computer systems producers in the region during the 1980s—even as costs of developing and producing systems skyrocketed.

The decentralization of production and reliance on networks is not limited to small or new firms seeking to avoid fixed investments. Even Hewlett-Packard, which designs and manufactures chips, printed circuit boards, disk drives, printers, tape drives, and many other peripherals and components for its computer systems, has restructured internally to gain flexibility and technical advantage.

During the 1980s, HP consolidated the management of over 50 disparate circuit technology units into two autonomous divisions, Integrated Circuit Fabrication and Printed Circuit Board Fabrication. These cross-cutting divisions now function as internal subcontractors to the company's computer systems and instrument products groups. They have gained focus and autonomy which they lacked as separate units tied directly to product lines. Moreover, they must now compete with external subcontractors for firm business, which has forced them to improve service, technology, and quality. These units are even being encouraged to sell to outside customers in some instances. In short, HP appears to be creating a network within the framework of a large firm.

The networks extend beyond the system firms and their immediate suppliers. Silicon Valley's suppliers of electronic components and sub-systems are themselves vertically disaggregated—for the same reasons as their systems customers. Producers of specialty and semi-custom integrated circuits, for example, have focused production to spread the costs and risks of chipmaking. Some specialize in design, others in process technology, and still others provide fabrication capacity for both chip and systems firms [30].

The same is true in disk drives. Innovative producers like Conner Peripherals and Quantum have explicitly avoided vertical integration, relying on outside suppliers not only for semiconductors but also for the thin-film disks, heads and motors which go into hard drives. Facing the pressures of rapidly changing product designs and technologies, they rely heavily on third party sources for most components and perform only the initial design, the final assembly, and testing themselves.

The costs and risks of developing new computer systems products are thus spread across networks of autonomous but interdependent firms in Silicon Valley. In an environment which demands rapid new product introductions and continual technological change, no one firm can complete the design and production of an entire computer system on its own. By relying on networks of suppliers—both within the region and more distant—Silicon Valley systems firms gain the flexibility to introduce increasingly sophisticated products faster than ever before.

The New Supplier Relations

Silicon Valley's systems makers are increasingly dependent upon their suppliers for the success of their own products. Sun founder Scott McNealy acknowledges that "the quality of our products is embedded in the quality of the products we purchase"—which is no understatement, since so much of a Sun workstation is designed by its suppliers.[5] The highly focused systems producer relies on suppliers not only to deliver reliable products on time put also to continue designing and producing high quality, state-of-the-art products.

While many systems firms begin as Sun did, integrating standard components from different suppliers and distinguishing their products with proprietary software, virtually all now seek specialized inputs to differentiate their products further. These computer makers are replacing commodity semiconductors with ASICs and designing customized disk drives, power supplies, keyboards and communication devices into their systems.[6] As specialist suppliers continue to advance technologies critical to their own products, they reproduce the technological instabilities that allow this decentralized system to flourish. And there is little evidence that the pace of innovation in computers will stabilize in the near future.

Competition in computers is thus increasingly based on the identification of new applications and improvements in performance rather than simply lower cost. Silicon Valley firms are well known for creating new product niches such as Tandem's fail-safe computers for on-line transaction processing, Silicon Graphics' high performance super workstations with 3-D graphics capabilities, and Pyramid Technology's mini-mainframe computer systems. Nonetheless, even the producers of general purpose commodity products such as IBM-compatible personal computers ("clones") are being driven to source differentiated components in order to reduce costs or improve the performance of their systems. Everex Systems, for example, designs custom chip sets to improve the performance of its PC clones.

The more specialized these computers and their components become, the more the systems firms are drawn into partnerships with their suppliers. And as they are increasingly treated as equals in a joint process of designing, developing and manufacturing innovative systems, the suppliers themselves become innovative and capital-intensive producers of differentiated products.

This marks a radical break with the arm's length relations of a mass production system, in which suppliers manufactured parts according to standard specifications and competed against one another to lower price, and in which portions of production were subcontracted as a buffer against fluctuations in market demand, output and labor supply [12]. In this model, suppliers remained subordinate and often dependent on a single big customer. IBM was notorious for managing its suppliers in this fashion during the early 1980s, and Silicon Valley systems firms today explicitly contrast their supplier relations with those of IBM [19].[7]

Silicon Valley systems firms now view relationships with suppliers more as long-term investments than short-term procurement relationships.[8] They recognize collaboration with suppliers as a way to speed the pace of new product introductions and improve product quality and performance. Most firms designate a group of "privileged" suppliers with whom to build these close relationships. This group normally includes the 20 percent of a firm's suppliers that account for 75–80 percent of the value of its components: typically between 15 and 30 producers of integrated circuits, printed circuit boards, disk drives, power supplies, and other components which are critical to product quality and performance.

These relationships are based on shared recognition of the need to insure the success of a final product. Traditional supplier relations are typically transformed by a decision to exchange long-term business plans and share confidential sales forecasts and cost information. Sales forecasts allow suppliers to plan investment levels, while cost information encourages negotiation of prices that guarantee a fair return to the supplier while keeping the systems firm competitive. In some cases these relationships originate with adoption of Japanese just-in-time (JIT) inventory control systems, as JIT focuses joint attention on improving product delivery times and quality. It often requires a reduction in the number of suppliers and the creation of long-term supplier relations as well as the sharing of business plans and technical information.[9]

Reciprocity guides relations between Silicon Valley's systems firms and their suppliers. Most of these relationships have moved beyond the inventory control objectives of JIT to encompass a mutual commitment to sustaining a long-term relationship. This requires a commitment not to take advantage of one another when market conditions change and can entail supporting suppliers through tough times—by extending credit, providing technical assistance or manpower, or helping them find new customers.

Businesses commonly acknowledge this mutual dependence. Statements like "our success is their success" or "we want them to feel like part of an extended family" are repeated regularly by purchasing managers in Silicon Valley systems firms, whose roles have changed during the past decade from short-term market intermediaries to long-term relationship-builders. Managers describe their relationships with suppliers as involving personal and moral commitments which transcend the expectations of simple business relationships. In the words of one CEO:

In these partnerships, the relationship transcends handling an order. There is more than a business relationship involved. In addition to the company's commitment, there are personal commitments by people to make sure things happen. Furthermore, there are moral commitments: not to mislead the other party, to do everything possible to support the other party, and to be understanding.[10]

Suppliers are being drawn into the design and development of new systems and components at a very early stage; and they are typically more closely integrated into the customer's organization in this process. A key supplier is often consulted during the initial phases of a new computer system's conception—between two and five years prior to actual production—and involved throughout the design and development process. Some Silicon Valley firms even include suppliers in their design review meetings.

This early cooperation allows a supplier to adapt its products to anticipated market changes and exposes the systems engineers to changing component technologies. In the words of HP Manufacturing VP Harold Edmondson

We share our new product aspirations with them and they tell us the technological direction in which they are heading . . . We would never have done it this way 10 years ago.[11]

Tandem's Materials Director, John Sims, similarly describes how information is shared early in the firm's product development process:

There is a lot of give and take in all aspects of these relationships . . . We have a mutual interest in each other's survival. We share proprietary product information, and we work jointly to improve designs and develop the latest technologies. We continually push each other to do better.[12]

According to an executive at Silicon Valley contract manufacturer Flextronics:

In the early stages of any project, we live with our customers and they live with us. Excellent communication is needed between design engineers, marketing people, and the production people, which is Flextronics.[13]

Once production begins, the relationship between the two firms continues at many different levels. Not only does the customer firm's purchasing staff work with the supplier, but managers, engineers, and production staff at all levels of both firms meet to redefine specifications or to solve technical or manufacturing problems. In many cases, the flow of information between the two firms is continuous.

These relationships represent a major departure from the old practice of sending out precise design specifications to multiple sources for competitive bids. In fact, price is rarely considered as important as product quality and reliability in selecting a key supplier. Most firms choose a reliable, high quality supplier for a long-term relationship, recognizing that the price will be lower over the long-term because unpredictable cost fluctuations will be reduced.

As these relationships mature, it is increasingly difficult to speak of these firms as bounded by their immediate employees and facilities. This blurring of firm boundaries is well illustrated by the case of Adaptec, Inc., a Silicon Valley based maker of input–output controller devices. When it was formed in 1981, Adaptec management chose to focus on product design and development and to rely on subcontractors for both semiconductor fabrication and board assembly. The key to this strategy is the investment Adaptec has made in building long-term partnerships with its core suppliers—including Silicon Valley start-up International Microelectronic Products (IMP), Texas Instruments (TI), and the local division of the large contract manufacturer SCI. Adaptec's Vice-President of Manufacturing, Jeffrey Miller, describes the high degree of trust which has evolved through continuing interaction between engineers in both organizations, claiming:

Our relations with our vendors is not much different than my relationship was at Intel with our corporate foundry—except now I get treated as a customer, not as corporate overhead . . . It really is very hard to define where we end and where our subcontractors begin: Adaptec includes a portion of IMP, of TI, and of SCI.[14]

In the words of HP's Edmondson, the partners in these relationships cooperate in order to "pull one another up relative to the rest of the industry."[15] This blurring of the boundaries of the firm transcends distinctions of corporate size or age. While many Silicon Valley start-ups have allied with one another and "grown up" together, others have benefitted from relationships with large established firms, both in and outside of the region.

Moreover, while non-disclosure agreements and contracts are normally signed in these alliances, few believe that they really matter (especially in an environment of high employee turnover like Silicon Valley). Rather the firms accept that they share a mutual interest in one another's success and that their relationship defies legal enforcement. According to Apple Computers' Manager of Purchasing, Tom McGeorge:

We have found you don't always need a formal contract . . . If you develop trust with your suppliers, you don't need armies of attorneys . . . In order for us to be successful in the future, we have to develop better working relationships, better trusting relationships, than just hounding vendors for price decreases on an annual basis.[16]

Of course, truly collaborative relationships do not emerge overnight or function flawlessly. There is a constant tension between cooperation and control. It may take years before trust develops or a supplier is given more responsibility. As with any close relationship, misunderstandings arise. Some relationships are terminated—in industry lingo, they result in "divorce"—while others languish temporarily and are revitalized with joint work. What is striking is how many of these relationships appear to not only survive but to flourish.

Although these relationships are often remarkably close, both parties are careful to preserve their own autonomy. Most Silicon Valley firms will not allow their business to account for more than 20 percent of a supplier's product and prefer that no customer occupy such a position. Suppliers are thus forced to find outside customers, which insures that the loss of a single account will not put them out of business. This avoidance of dependence protects both supplier and customer, and it promotes the diffusion of technology across firms and industries. One local executive suggests the ideal situation is to hold a preferred position with suppliers, but not an exclusive relationship. "Dependence," he notes, "makes both firms vulnerable."[17]

Regional proximity facilitates collaborative supplier relations. Materials Director at Apple Computers, Jim Bilodeau, describes the firm's preference for local suppliers:

Our purchasing strategy is that our vendor base is close to where we're doing business . . . We like them to be next door. If they can't, they need to be able to project an image like they are next door.[18]

Sun's Materials Director Scott Metcalf similarly claims that:

In the ideal world, we'd draw a 100 mile radius and have all our suppliers locate plants, or at least supply depots, into the area.[19]

These managers agree that long-distance communication is often inadequate for the continuous and detailed engineering adjustments required in making technically complex electronics products. Face-to-face interaction allows firms to address the unexpected complications in a supplier relationship that could never be covered by a contract. The president of a firm which manufactures power supplies for computers and peripherals, explains:

I don't care how well the specifications are written on paper, they are always subject to misinterpretation. The only way to solve this is to have a customer's engineers right here. There is no good way to do it if you are more than fifty miles away.[20]

Nor is this desire for geographic proximity reducible to cost considerations alone. The trust, information exchange and teamwork which are the basis of collaborative supplier relations require continued interaction which is difficult to achieve over long distances.

This is not to suggest that all Silicon Valley systems firms are tightly integrated into cooperative relationships with all of their suppliers. Traditional arm's length relations persist, for example, with suppliers of such commodity inputs as raw materials, process materials, sheet metal, and cables. Nor is it to imply that all of a firm's key suppliers are located in the same region. Many Silicon Valley firms purchase components such as commodity chips or disk drives from Japanese vendors.

Systems firms in Silicon Valley are, however, redefining their relationships with their most important suppliers. A network of long-term, trust-based alliances with innovative suppliers represents a source of advantage for a systems producer which is very difficult for a competitor to replicate. Such a network provides both flexibility and a framework for joint learning and technological exchange.

Production Networks and Innovation

Silicon Valley today is far more than an agglomeration of individual technology firms. Its networks of interdependent yet autonomous producers are increasingly organized to grow and innovate reciprocally. These networks promote new product development by encouraging specialization and allowing firms to spread the costs and risks associated with developing technology-intensive products. They spur the diffusion of new technologies by facilitating information exchange and joint problem solving between firms and even industries. Finally, the networks foster the application of new technologies because they encourage new firm entry and product experimentation.

Three cases demonstrate how these production networks promote techno-logical advance in Silicon Valley. The first is the relationship of systems firms to their contract manufacturers, which are changing from sweatshops into technologically sophisticated, capital-intensive businesses as they assume more responsibility for product design and process innovation. The second case in-volves a foundry relationship between a large systems firm and a small design specialist in which each contributes distinctive, state-of-the-art expertise to a process of complementary innovation. In the third case, a systems firm spreads the costs of perfecting a state-of-the-art microprocessor through joint product development with a semiconductor producer.

Taken together, these cases demonstrate how collaboration fosters joint problem solving and how Silicon Valley's firms are learning to respond collectively to fast changing markets and technology.

Contract Manufacturers

Printed circuit board assembly has historically been among the most labor-intensive and least technically sophisticated phases of electronics manufacturing. Contract assembly was traditionally used by systems firms in Silicon Valley to augment in-house manufacturing capacity during periods of peak demand. Commonly referred to as "board stuffing", it was the province of small, undercapitalized and marginal firms which paid unskilled workers low wages to work at home or in sweatshops. Many of these assemblers moved to low-wage regions of Asia and Latin America during the 1960s and early 1970s.

This profile changed fundamentally during the 1980s. Systems firms like IBM, HP and Apple expanded their business with local contract manufacturers in order to lower their fixed costs and respond to shorter product cycles. This enabled the region's PCB assemblers to expand and upgrade their technology. As small shops received contracts and assistance from larger systems firms, they invested in state-of-the-art manufacturing automation and assumed more and more responsibility for the design and development of new products.

Flextronics Inc. was one of Silicon Valley's earliest board stuffing firms. During the 1970s it was a small, low value-added, "rent-a-body" operation which provided quick turnaround board assembly for local merchant semiconductor firms. By the late 1980s it was the largest contract manufacturer in the region and offered state-of-the-art engineering services and automated manufacturing.

This transformation began in 1980 when Flextronics was purchased by new management. The company expanded rapidly in the subsequent years, shifting the bulk of its services from consignment manufacturing, in which the customer provides components which the contract manufacturer assembles according to the customer's designs, to "turnkey" manufacturing, in which the contract manufacturer selects and procures electronic components as well as assembling and testing the boards.

The shift from consignment to turnkey manufacturing is a shift from a low risk, low value-added, low loyalty subcontracting strategy to a high risk, high value-added, high trust approach because the contract manufacturer takes responsibility for the quality and functioning of a complete subassembly. This shift greatly increases the systems firm's dependence on its contract manufacturer's process and components. Flextronics' CEO Robert Todd describes the change:

With turnkey they're putting their product on the line, and it requires a great deal of trust. This kind of relationship takes years to develop and a major investment of people time.[21]

Todd claims that whereas a consignment relationship can be replicated in weeks, it can take years to build the trust required for a mature turnkey relationship in which the design details of a new product are shared. These relationships demand extensive organizational interaction and a surprising amount of integration.[22] As a result, firms which consign their manufacturing typically have six or seven suppliers which compete on the basis of cost, while those relying on turnkey contractors build close relations with only one or two firms, selected primarily for quality and responsiveness.

The shift to turnkey manufacturing has clear implications for a firm's location. Flextronics CEO Robert Todd claims:

We've never been successful for any length of time outside of a local area. We might get a contract initially, but the relationship erodes without constant interaction. Sophisticated customers know that you must be close because these relationships can't be built over long distances.[23]

This explains why the US contract manufacturing business is highly regionalized. During the 1980s, Flextronics established production facilities in Massachusetts, South Carolina, Southern California, Hong Kong, Taiwan, Singapore, and the People's Republic of China.[24] SCI Systems, the largest US contract manufacturer, is based in Alabama where costs are very low, but has a major facility in high-cost Silicon Valley in order to build the relationships needed to serve the local market.

By 1988 over 85 percent of Flextronics' business was turnkey; in 1980 it had been entirely consignment. This growth was initially due to a close relationship with rapidly expanding Sun Microsystems which by 1988 accounted for 24 percent of Flextronics business. The two firms have explicitly sought to limit this share in order to avoid dependency. Flextronics has diversified its customer base by developing customers in a wide range of different industries. The firm now also serves firms in the disk drive, tape drive, printer, and medical instruments industries.

Two recent trends in contract manufacturing illustrate how specialization breeds technological advance and increasing interdependence. On one hand, Silicon Valley systems companies are relying on contract manufacturers for the earliest phases of board design. Flextronics now offers engineering services and takes responsibility for the initial design and layout of Sun's circuit boards as well as the pre-screening of electronic components. The use of contract manufacturers for board design implies a radical extension of inter-firm collaboration because systems firms must trust subcontractors with the proprietary designs which are the essence of their products. When successful, such a relationship increases the agility of the systems firms while enhancing the capabilities of the contract manufacturers. In fact, Flextronics is now capable of manufacturing complete systems, although this accounts for only 5 percent of their business.

The second trend, the increasing use of surface mount technology (SMT), is transforming printed circuit board assembly into a capital-intensive business. While the traditional through-hole assembly technique involves soldering individual leads from an integrated circuit through the holes in circuit boards, SMT uses epoxy to glue electronic components onto the board. The new process is attractive because it produces smaller boards (components can be mounted on both sides of the board) and because it is cheaper in volume than through-hole.

SMT is, however, far more complex and expensive than through-hole assembly. It requires tight design rules, high densities, and a soldering process which demands expertise in applied physics and chemistry and takes years of experience to perfect. Industry analysts describe SMT as 5 to 10 times more difficult a process than through-hole. Moreover, a single high speed SMT production line costs more than $1 million.

Contract manufacturer Solectron Corporation has led Silicon Valley in the adoption of SMT, investing more than $18 million in SMT equipment since 1984.[25] It has captured the business of IBM, Apple, and HP (as well as many smaller Silicon Valley firms) by automating and emphasizing customer service, high quality, and fast turn-around. According to one venture capitalist and industry veteran, Solectron's manufacturing quality is superior to that found in any systems firms in Silicon Valley.[26]

This manufacturing excellence is due in part to Solectron's investment in state-of-the-art equipment. It is also the result of their expertise accumulated by applying lessons learned from one customer to the next. All of Solectron's customers thus benefit from learning that would formerly have been captured by individual firms. Moreover, lessons learned in manufacturing for firms in one sector are spread to customers in other sectors, stimulating the inter-industry diffusion of innovations.

The use of contract manufacturers, initially an attempt to spread risks, focus resources, and reduce fixed costs in an era of accelerating new product introductions, is thus producing mutually beneficial technological advance. While many of Silicon Valley's contract assemblers remain small and labor intensive, some, such as Flextronics and Solectron, are no longer subordinate or peripheral units in a hierarchical production system. Rather, they have transformed themselves into sophisticated specialists which contribute as equals to the vitality of the region's production networks.

Silicon Foundries

Silicon foundries are the manufacturing facilities used for the fabrication of silicon chips, or semiconductors. The use of external foundries grew rapidly in the 1980s as semiconductor and systems firms began designing integrated circuits themselves but sought to avoid the cost of the capital intensive fabrication process [30]. Like contract manufacturers, foundries offer their customers the cumulative experience and expertise of specialists. Unlike contract assemblers, however, silicon foundries have always been technologically sophisticated and highly capital intensive—and they have thus interacted with customers as relative equals offering complementary strengths. This relationship can be an exchange of services with limited technical interchange, or it can offer significant opportunities for reciprocal innovation.

The collaboration between Hewlett-Packard and semiconductor design specialist Weitek illustrates the potential for complementary innovation in a foundry relationship. Weitek, which has no manufacturing capacity of its own, is the leading designer of ultra-high speed "number crunching" chips for complex engineering problems. In order to improve the performance of the Weitek chips, HP opened up its state-of-the-art 1.2 micron wafer fabrication facility, historically closed to outside firms, to Weitek for use as a foundry.

This alliance grew out of a problem that HP engineers were having with the development of a new model workstation. They wanted to use Weitek designs for this new product, but Weitek (which had supplied chip-sets to HP for several years) could not produce chips which were fast enough to meet HP's needs. Realizing that the manufacturing process at the foundry Weitek used slowed the chips down, the HP engineers suggested fully optimizing the

Weitek designs by manufacturing them with HP's more advanced fabrication process.

This culminated in a three-year agreement which allows the two firms to benefit directly from each other's technical expertise. The agreement guarantees that HP will manufacture and purchase at least $10 million worth of the Weitek chip-sets in its foundry and it provides Weitek the option to purchase an additional $20 million of the chip-sets from the foundry to sell to outside customers.

This arrangement assures HP a steady supply of Weitek's sophisticated chips and allows them to introduce their new workstation faster than if they designed a chip in-house and it provides Weitek with a market and the legitimacy of a close association with HP, as well as guaranteed space in a state-of-the-art foundry. Moreover, the final product itself represents a significant advance over what either firm could have produced independently.

Both firms see the real payoff from this alliance in expected future technology exchanges. According to an HP program manager who helped negotiate the deal: "We wanted to form a long-term contact (sic) with Weitek—to set a framework in place for a succession of business opportunities."[27] By building a long-term relationship, the firms are creating an alliance which allows each to draw on the other's distinctive and complementary expertise to devise novel solutions to common problems. HP now has greater access to Weitek's design talent and can influence the direction of these designs. Weitek has first-hand access to the needs and future plans of a key customer as well assured access to HP's manufacturing capabilities. Both are now better positioned to respond to an unpredictable and fast changing market.

In spite of this increased interdependence, HP and Weitek have preserved their autonomy. Weitek sells the chip-sets they produce on HP's fab to third parties, including many HP competitors, and continues to build partnerships and collect input from its many other customers (in fact, Weitek deliberately limits each of its customers to less than 10 percent of its business). Meanwhile, HP is considering opening its foundry to other outside chip design firms, and it still maintains its own in-house design team. The openness of such a partnership insures that design and manufacturing innovations that grow out of collaboration diffuse rapidly.

Both firms see this relationship as a model for the future. While HP does not intend to become a dedicated foundry, it is looking for other partnerships that allow it to leverage its manufacturing technology using external design expertise. Weitek, in turn, depends upon a strategy of alliances with firms which can provide manufacturing capacity as well as insights into fast evolving systems markets.

Collaborative Product Development

Joint product development represents the ultimate extension of interdependence in a networked system. The collaboration between Sun Microsystems and Cypress Semiconductor to develop a sophisticated version of Sun's RISC (reduced instruction set computing) microprocessor is a classic example. A RISC chip uses a simplified circuit design that increases computing speed and performance of a microprocessor.

Sun's first workstations were based entirely on standard parts and components. The firm's advantage lay in proprietary software and its ability to introduce new products quickly. Over time, the firm began to distinguish its products by adding new capabilities, enhancing its software, and purchasing semicustom components. Sun's most significant innovation was to design its own microprocessor to replace the standard Motorola microprocessors used in its early workstation. This RISC based microprocessor, called Sparc, radically improved the speed and performance of Sun's products—and simultaneously destabilized the microprocessor market.

Sun further broke with industry tradition by freely licensing the Sparc design, in contrast with Intel and Motorola's proprietary approach to their microprocessors. The firm established partnerships with five semiconductor manufacturers, which each use their own process technology to produce specialized versions of Sparc.[28] The resulting chips share a common design and software, but differ in speed and price. After supplying Sun, these suppliers are free to manufacture and market their versions of Sparc to other systems producers.

As a result, Sun has extended acceptance of its architecture while recovering some of its development costs and avoiding the expense of producing and marketing the new chip. Its suppliers, in turn, gain a guaranteed customer in Sun and a new and promising product—which they are jointly promoting. Collaboration allowed Sun to reduce significantly the cost of producing a new microprocessor. The firm spent only $25 million developing the Sparc chip, compared to Intel's $100 million investment in its 80368 microprocessor. In the words of one computer executive:

The real significance of Sparc and of RISC technology is that you no longer have to be a huge semiconductor company, with $100 million to spare for research development, to come up with a state-of-the-art microprocessor.[29]

Mips Computer Systems has similarly designed its own RISC chip and licensed it to three Silicon Valley semiconductor vendors.

Sun's partnership with Cypress Semiconductor extends such collaboration the furthest. In 1986, the two firms agreed to develop jointly a high speed, high performance version of Sparc. A team of approximately 30 engineers from both companies worked at a common site for a year—thus combining Sun's Sparc architecture and knowledge of systems design and software with Cypress' integrated circuit design expertise and advanced CMOS fabrication process. This core team was supported through constant feedback from the product development, marketing, and testing specialists in each firm. Cypress Vice-President of Marketing, Lowell Turriff, describes the collaboration as an "ideal marriage" characterized by "an amazing environment of cooperation."[30]

The two firms benefit from complementary expertise: Sun gained access to Cypress' advanced design capabilities and its state-of-the-art CMOS manufacturing facility to produce a very high speed microprocessor; Cypress gained an alliance with a rapidly growing systems firm, insights into the direction of workstation technology and a new, high performance, product. Cypress executives envision similar partnerships with customers in other industrial markets, including telecommunications and automobiles.

By building a network of collaborative relationships with suppliers like Cypress, Sun has not only reduced the cost and spread the risks of developing its workstations, but has been able to bring new products with innovative features and architectures to market rapidly. These relationships prevent competitors from simply imitating Sun's products, and represent a formidable competitive barrier.

This explains Sun's championing of systems which rely on readily available components and industry standard technologies (or "open systems"). Under this approach, computers made by different firms adhere to standards which allow them to use the same software and exchange information with one another. This marks a radical break from the proprietary systems approach of industry leaders IBM, DEC and Apple. Open standards encourage new firm entry and promote experimentation because they force firms to differentiate their products while remaining within a common industry standard. Proprietary systems, by contrast, exclude new entrants and promote closed networks and stable competitive arrangements.

As Silicon Valley producers introduce specialized systems for a growing diversity of applications and users, they are fragmenting computer markets. The market no longer consists simply of mainframes, minicomputers and personal computers: it is segmented into distinct markets for super-computers, super minicomputers, engineering workstations, networked minicomputers, personal computers, parallel and multiprocessor computers and specialized educational computers [19]. As long as this process of product differentiation continues to undermine homogeneous mass markets for computers, Silicon Valley's specialist systems producers and their networks of suppliers will flourish.

....

Conclusions

Technical expertise in Silicon Valley today is spread across hundreds of specialist enterprises, enterprises which continue to develop independent capabilities while simultaneously learning from one another. As computer systems firms and their suppliers build collaborative relationships, they spread the costs and risks of developing new products while enhancing their ability to adapt rapidly to changing markets and technologies.

This is not to suggest that inter-firm networks are universally diffused or understood in Silicon Valley. The crisis of the region's commodity semiconductor producers in the mid-1980s is attributable in part to distant, even antagonistic, relations between the chipmakers and their equipment suppliers [30, 33]. Other examples of arm's length relationships and distrust among local producers can no doubt be identified [6]. However, these failures of coordination do not signal inherent weaknesses in network forms of organization, but rather the need for the institutionalization of inter-firm collaboration in the U.S.

Proposals to replace Silicon Valley's decentralized system of production with an "American keiretsu"—by constructing tight alliances among the nation's largest electronics producers and suppliers [5]—would sacrifice the flexibility which is critical in the current competitive environment. Such proposals also misread the changing organization of production in Japan, where large firms increasingly collaborate with small and medium-sized suppliers and encourage them to expand their technological capabilities and organizational autonomy [13, 21, 7]. In Japan, as in Silicon Valley, a loosely integrated network form of organization has emerged in response to the market volatility of the 1970s and 1980s.

The proliferation of inter-firm networks helps to account for the continued dynamism of Silicon Valley. While the region's firms rely heavily on global markets and distant suppliers, there is a clear trend for computer systems producers to prefer local suppliers and to build the sort of trust-based relationships which flourish with proximity. The region's vitality is thus enhanced as inter-firm collaboration breeds complementary innovation and cross-fertilization among networks of autonomous but interdependent producers.

....

Notes

Special thanks to Christopher Freeman, David Teece, Chris DeBresson and two anonymous reviewers for helpful comments and encouragement on earlier drafts of this paper.

1. High technology manufacturing and services include: computers and office equipment (SIC 357), communications equipment (SIC 366), electronic components (SIC 367), guided missiles (367), instruments (SIC 38), and data processing (SIC 737). Data on the value of shipments is from the U.S. Census of Manufactures and Census of Service Industries; employment figures are from the California Employment Development Department, ES202 Series; and the number of establishments is from U.S. Bureau of the Census, County Business Patterns.
2. Interview, Harold Edmondson, Vice-President of Corporate Manufacturing. Hewlett-Packard Corporation, 5 February 1988.
3. IBM was forced to rely on outside vendors to an unprecedented extent in the early 1980s in order to bring a personal computer to market rapidly enough to compete with Apple.
4. Cited in: "For flexible, quality manufacturing, don't do it yourself," *Electronic Business*, 15 March 1987. In 1990, Sun introduced limited printed circuit board assembly operations, however the firm remains committed to a highly focused strategy.
5. Cited in W. Bluestein, "How Sun Microsystems buys for quality," *Electronics Purchasing*, March 1988.
6. On the trend to customize inputs such as disk drives and power supplies, see R. Faletra and M. Elliot, "Buying in the Microcomputer Market," *Electronics Purchasing*, October 1988.
7. See, for example, E. Richards, "IBM pulls the strings", *San Jose Mercury News*, 31 December 1984.
8. D. Davis, "Making the Most of Your Vendor Relationships", *Electronic Business*, 10 July 1989. Collaborative supplier relations have been documented in a wide range of industries, including the US and German auto industries [11, 28], the French machine tool industry [18], and the Japanese electronics and auto industries [7, 21].
9. When HP introduced JIT in the early 1980s, for example, the firm's cost reductions and improvements in manufacturing efficiency were widely publicized in Silicon Valley. JIT has since been widely adopted in the region. See "Hewlett-Packard swears by 'Just-in-Time' System". *San Jose Business Journal*, 10 June 1985.
10. Cited in M. Cohodas, "What makes JIT work", *Electronics Purchasing*, January 1987.
11. Cited in S. Tierston, "The Changing Face of Purchasing," *Electronic Business*, 20 March 1989.
12. Interview, John Sims, Director of Materials, Tandem Computers, 13 April 1988.
13. Cited in *The San Jose Mercury News*, 25 July 1988.

14. Interview with Jeffrey Miller, Vice-President of Marketing, Adaptec Corporation, 10 May 1988.

15. Interview, Harold Edmondson, Vice-President of Corporate Manufacturing, HP, 5 February 1988.

16. Cited in M. Cohodas, "How Apple buys electronics," *Electronics Purchasing,* November 1986.

17. Interview, Henri Jarrat, President and Chief Operating Officer, VLSI Technology, 10 May 1988.

18. Cited in M. Cohodas, "How Apple Buys Electronics," *Electronics Purchasing,* November 1986.

19. Interview, Scott Metcalf, Director of Materials, Sun Microsystems, 30 March 1988.

20. In order to improve its responsiveness, the firm recently moved part of its manufacturing from Hong Kong to Silicon Valley. Sun Microsystems, which is its neighbor, in turn increased its purchases of the firm's power suppliers from $500,000 to more than $8 million a year. Interview, Robert Smith, President, Computer Products/Boschert, 1 September 1988.

21. Interview, Robert Todd, CEO, Flextronics Inc., 2 February 1988.

22. Flextronics' CEO meets with Sun's Senior Vice-President of Operations for breakfast once a month to insure that trust is maintained at the top and high-level problems are addressed. Meanwhile planning, engineering, purchasing and marketing personnel from the two firms meet still more frequently—often weekly, and in some cases daily—to solve problems and plan for the future. This involves an immense amount of sharing and typically results in highly personalized relationships between the two firms. Interview, Dennis Stradford, Vice-President of Marketing, Flextronics, 3 March 1988.

23. Interview, Robert Todd, CEO, Flextronics, Inc., 2 February 1988.

24. This expansion was too rapid. In 1989, Flextronics was forced to restructure its worldwide business because of significant excess manufacturing capacity and operating losses which began with a downturn in the disk drive business. To eliminate excess capacity, the production facilities in Massachusetts, South Carolina, Southern California, and Taiwan were sold or closed.

25. G. Lasnier, "Solectron to acquire 10 advanced Surface Mount Systems," *San Jose Business Journal*, 8 February 1988.

26. Interview, William Davidow, Partner, Mohr Davidow Ventures, 21 April 1988.

27. Cited in S. Jones, "Hewlett-Packard inks Major Chip Deal," *San Jose Business Journal*, 18, May 1987.

28. The firms are Fujitsu Ltd. (the first to manufacture the Sparc chip because the leading US semiconductor firms refused to accept external designs), LSI Logic, Bipolar Integrated Technologies, Cypress Semiconductor and Texas Instruments.

29. B. Schlender, "Computer Maker aims to transform Industry and become a Giant," *The Wall Street Journal*, 18 March 1988.

30. Interview, Lowell Turriff, Vice-President Marketing, Cypress Semiconductor, 7 March 1988.

References

[1] D. Angel, The Labor Market for Engineers in the US Semiconductor Industry, *Economic Geography* 65 (2) (1989) 99–112.

[2] M. Best, *The New Competition: Institutions of Industrial Restructuring* (Harvard University Press, Cambridge, MA, 1990).

[3] A. Delbecq and J. Weiss, The Business Culture of Silicon Valley: Is it a Model for the Future? in: J. Weiss (ed.), *Regional Cultures, Managerial Behavior and Entrepreneurship* (Quorom Books, New York, 1988).

[4] R. Dore, Goodwill and the Spirit of Market Capitalism, *The British Journal of Sociology* XXXIV (4) (1983) 459–482.

[5] C. Ferguson, The Coming of the U.S. Keiretsu, *Harvard Business Review* (July–August 1990).

[6] R. Florida and M. Kenney, Why Silicon Valley and Route 128 Won't Save Us, *California Management Review* 33(1) (1990) 68–88.

[7] M. Fruin, Cooperation and Competition: Interfirm Networks and the Nature of Supply in the Japanese Electronics Industry, Euro-Asia Center, INSEAD (1988).

[8] R. Gordon, Growth and the Relations of Production in High Technology Industry, Paper presented at Conference on New Technologies and New Intermediaries, Stanford University (1987).

[9] M. Granovetter, Economic Action and Social Structure: The Problem of Embeddedness, *American Journal of Sociology* 91 (1985) 481–510.

[10] H. Hakansson, *Industrial Technological Development: A Network Approach* (Croom Helm, Beckenham, 1987).

[11] S. Helper, Supplier Relations at a Crossroads: Results of Survey Research in the US Auto Industry, Boston University, Department of Operations Management (1990).

[12] J. Holmes, The Organization and Locational Structure of Production Subcontracting" in: A. Scott and M. Storper (eds.), *Production, Work and Territory* (Allen and Unwin, Boston, 1986).

[13] K. Imai, Evolution of Japan's Corporate and Industrial Networks, in: B. Carlsson (ed.), *Industrial Dynamics* (Kluwer, Dordrecht, 1988).

[14] J. Jarillo, On Strategic Networks, *Strategic Management Journal* 9 (1988) 31-41.

[15] J. Johanson and L. Mattson, Interorganizational Relations in Industrial Systems: A Network Approach Compared with the Transactions Cost Approach, *International Studies of Management and Organization* XVII (1) (1987) 34-48.

[16] R. Johnston and P. Lawrence, Beyond Vertical Integration—the Rise of the Value-Adding Partnership, *Harvard Business Review* (July–August 1988) 94-101.

[17] A. Larson, Cooperative Alliances: A Study of Entrepreneurship, PhD dissertation, Harvard University, Sociology and Business Administration (1988).

[18] E. Lorenz, Neither Friends nor Strangers: Informal Networks of Subcontracting in French Industry, in: D. Gambetta (ed.), *Trust* (Basil Blackwell, New York, 1988).

[19] R. McKenna, *Who's Afraid of Big Blue?* (Addison Wesley, New York, 1989).

[20] R. Miles and C. Snow, Organizations: New Concepts for New Forms, *California Management Review* XXVIII (3) (1986) 62–73.

[21] T. Nishiguchi, Strategic Dualism: An Alternative in Industrial Societies, Ph.D. dissertation, Oxford University, Nuffield College (1989).

[22] M. Piore and C. Sabel, *The Second Industrial Divide* (Basic Books, New York, 1984).

[23] W. Powell, Neither Market nor Hierarchy: Network Forms of Organization, *Research in Organizational Behavior* 12 (1990) 295–336.

[24] C. Prahalad and G. Hamel, The Core Competence of the Corporation, *Harvard Business Review* (May–June 1990).

[25] J. Quinn, T. Doorley and P. Paquette, Technology in Services: Rethinking Strategic Focus, *Sloan Management Review* (Winter 1990) 79–87.

[26] G. Richardson, The Organisation of Industry, *The Economic Journal* (Sept. 1972) 3883–896.

[27] E. Rogers, Information Exchange and Technological Innovation, in: D. Sahal (ed.), *The Transfer and Utilization of Technical Knowledge* (Lexington Books, Lexington, MA, 1982).

[28] C. Sabel, Flexible Specialization and the Reemergence of Regional Economies, in: P. Hirst and J. Zeitlin (eds.), *Reversing Industrial Decline* (Berg, Oxford, 1988).

[29] C. Sabel, H. Kern and G. Herrigel, Collaborative Manufacturing: New Supplier Relations in the Automobile Industry and the Redefinition of the Industrial Corporation, Massachusetts Institute of Technology (1989).

[30] A. Saxenian, Regional Networks and the Resurgence of Silicon Valley, *California Management Review* 33 (1) (1990) 89–112.

[31] A. Scott and D. Angel, The U.S. Semiconductor Industry: A Locational Analysis, *Environment and Planning* A19 (1987) 875–912.

[32] M. Storper and A. Scott, The Geographical Foundations and Social Regulation of Flexible Production Complexes, in: J. Wolcher and M. Dear (eds.), *Territory and Social Reproduction* (Allen & Unwin, London, 1988).

[33] J. Stowsky, The Weakest Link: Semiconductor Equipment, Linkages, and the Limits to International Trade, Working Paper No. 27, Berkeley Roundtable on the International Economy, University of California, Berkeley, 1988.

Entrepreneurship and Culture: The Case of Freddy, the Strawberry Man

Monica Lindh de Montoya

This article discusses the contribution that anthropology, and especially the notion of culture, can make to the study of entrepreneurship.[1] In it, I will draw on ethnographic material I collected about a rural-urban entrepreneur dealing in strawberries, and try to show how anthropology can illuminate fundamental issues in entrepreneurship, and some of the processes involved in starting and running a business. Because of the nature of my data I am concerned with small-scale businesses, primarily in the developing world, but I believe that the phenomena I observed have their counterparts in modern economies, and that my discussion therefore has a general relevance.

Anthropological studies of economies have tended to center on exchange in non-market economies or on trade in developing areas, where markets begin to penetrate and sometimes coexist with other forms of exchange. Anthropologists have shown how integration into the larger economy has led to the disappearance of indigenous models of trade, and how modern and traditional, western and nonwestern economic practices articulate; often to the detriment of the weaker partner. Yet recent years have seen the emergence of new directions in economic anthropology. Perhaps the collapse of plan economies and the subsequent hegemony of the free market worldwide have made anthropologists anxious to probe the nature of 'the economic.' The world of business, and the market in all its guises, is rapidly gaining territory in all peoples' life-worlds as non-capitalist alternatives fail or disappear, and states relinquish an increasing portion of their responsibilities to the free market.

In view of the trend in anthropology to direct the discipline's analytical eye towards Western cultures and to foment a cultural critique (Marcus and Fischer 1986), a reconsideration of the possibilities of the field of economic anthropology is overdue. Studies such as those of Abolafia (1996), Carrier (1995, 1997) and some of those included in Dilley (1992) are a handful of recent works that have begun to focus on the modern marketplace, using anthropological tools to decipher the meanings of the activities carried out there.

The phenomenon of entrepreneurship has always held an interest for students of business and for the general public. The success stories of well-known entrepreneurs fascinate and inspire people from all walks of life. Yet entrepreneurship has not been much examined by anthropologists; which is not to say that entrepreneurs do not figure in many anthropological texts. There have been numerous studies of traders, particularly in the context of marketing in developing countries, such as those of Babb (1989), Beals (1975), Clark (1988, 1994), Cohen (1969), Cook and Diskin (1976), Geertz (1963, 1979), Mintz (1961), and Plattner (1975, 1985).[2] People involved in business operations of many different kinds cross the pages of studies that do not focus on their entrepreneurial or business abilities as such. For example, studies of peasants (Cancian 1972, Cook 1990, Mitchell 1991, Stonich 1993) show how they often combine agricultural and/or craft production, labor-migration and petty trade to earn a living in ways that require considerable negotiation, calculation and entrepreneurial ability.

Anthropological research on traders typically deals with trading networks, strategies, the circulation of goods, the relationships between traders themselves, and relations between these actors and the outside world, be it with their competition, clients, or with government efforts to encourage, curb or channel commerce. In most cases, however, traders are discussed as traders, as if they were born as such; and there is little scrutiny of the process of entrepreneurship: of innovation, the discovery of profit opportunities, and the psychology of entrepreneurship—in short, of how a trader becomes a trader. Rather, studies center on how enterprises are 'put together' and maintained within a cultural context.

Much of the emphasis in economic anthropology has been on production and circulation, and more recently, on consumption; there has been less detailed attention to negotiation, and to the complex issues of risk and trust, which are a crucial part of entrepreneurship. And unfortunately, few anthropological studies of entrepreneurs in modern economies have been undertaken.[3] It seems that once profit motives and money-earning that parallel our own are observed 'in the field,' we assume that the economy runs on a logic similar to our own, a logic which we tend to give economists and other specialists the territorial rights over.[4]

Barth was the first of the anthropologists to have concerned themselves specifically with entrepreneurship. He approached the subject in his work on Norway (Barth 1963) and on Darfur (Barth 1967). Greenfield produced an edited volume (Greenfield *et al.* 1979) containing interesting close-up snapshots of entrepreneurs across times and cultures; and with Strickon (Greenfield and Strickon 1981: 497–99), pointed out the virtues of Barth's actor-oriented, decision-making approach in a programmatic article calling for the examination of the selective factors that determine the fate of entrepreneurial decisions. Geertz has discussed entrepreneurship in *Peddlers and Princes* (1963) and his work on the *suq* in Sefrou (1979) also provides important insights on negotiation. But perhaps it could be said that entrepreneurship is usually a non-problem for anthropologists, since the discipline currently has little ambition of being a predictive social science. Anthropologists go out into the world to describe and explain, but have, on the whole, been less interested in developing theories to predict or shape future behavior.

Much of the concern of the social sciences in respect to entrepreneurship has been with how best to define it, and more recently, how to encourage it; particularly in the context of economic development or in the wake of economic downturns in developed countries. The entrepreneur goes about his business bearing a mythical aura—he is a special person with a particular talent, who does a special thing, creating products, employment, and prosperity. The goal is to define and synthesize his actions or talents into a formula that can be applied where needed—entrepreneurship as a specific tool to be implemented against poverty.[5] Anthropologists working to further development have been more interested in encouraging community-based remedies such as broad agricultural programs, cooperatives and so on, focusing on group, rather than individual economic solutions. In this context, the individual entrepreneur may be seen as more of a villain, than a hero. Additionally it should be mentioned that anthropologists have uncompromisingly criticized the ethnocentricity and limitations of development programs (Long 1989; Hobart 1993).

In the introduction to this volume, Swedberg makes a case for the usefulness of the social sciences in the study of entrepreneurship, pointing out that the disciplines of sociology, anthropology, psychology and economic history have all produced studies of relevance to scholars involved in unravelling the mysteries of the subject. I agree with his argument, and further believe that despite the hitherto relative dearth of such studies, anthropology is particularly well suited to the exploration of questions associated with entrepreneurship. One of the discipline's strengths is its method of gathering data—through the observation of and interaction with the subject of the study—and another is its holistic approach, focused on culture. While economists have theorized about growth and progress and the nature of entrepreneurship within the larger economic system, they more seldom undertake concrete case studies of entrepreneurial action. And despite prevailing ideas about cold rationality and the cutthroat world of business, this world is an intensely social one[6] the functioning of which requires shared cultural understandings and the constant cooperation of a myriad of actors. The kinds of 'bright ideas' and nascent economic ventures that become established depend to a great extent on what is socially possible within a particular society, and issues such as trust, risk, and the relationship between individual gains and social responsibility are inherent in the process of developing a business. Anthropology can profitably turn its attention to the ways in which such questions are faced and negotiated, and how their solution shapes the entrepreneur and the nature of his enterprise.

Freddy the Strawberry Man

Some of the issues involved in entrepreneurial processes to which an anthropological discussion may contribute can be illuminated by taking a look at the case of Freddy, an entrepreneur active in trading strawberries. The data was collected on various opportunities between 1986 and 1990, while I was conducting fieldwork on vegetable traders in the Venezuelan Andes.

Bailadores, a village located in the upper Mocoties valley of the Venezuelan Andes lies at an altitude of circa 1700 meters above sea level in one of the *valles altos*, or cool valleys, where horticultures such as potatoes, cabbage, carrots, beets, garlic—and strawberries—are grown. Vegetables are cultivated on small, independently owned family farms scattered throughout the valley. The area is one of the country's largest producers of vegetables for the wholesale markets of the major cities of the nation, and has been producing considerable quantities since the 1970s. Since cash-crop production began, the farmers of the valley have been highly involved with marketing entrepreneurs, on whom they depend for the sale of their crops. The first traders came from outside the community, but have been displaced by local entrepreneurs, many of them farmers' sons who started small enterprises on a shoestring. Freddy's activities make an interesting example because he worked entirely within the region, and because his small strawberry venture demonstrates many of the points I wish to examine.

I first met Freddy at *Las Delicias*, an informal restaurant at the valley's farmers' cooperative. The restaurant was a meeting point where farmers, traders and villagers who came to the cooperative on errands, or did their shopping in the grocery in the complex, often stopped to catch up on the latest happenings in the valley. One morning when I arrived for breakfast it was crowded and I shared a table with Freddy. He did not look like most of the people who frequented *Las Delicias*; but was dressed more like a city man than the workers and farmers of the valley. I still remember the pink-and-gray-striped short-sleeved shirt he was wearing; so well ironed that I could see the sharp creases in the sleeves. He had very straight, stiff black hair, and black eyes, a bit unusual in the valley, where many people had more European features. He had a twitch in his right shoulder, which he would hunch and roll forwards now and then as he spoke. A slight man, he stood about five foot eight in his well-polished, heeled leather boots.

As we ate breakfast on the open-air patio of *Las Delicias*, Freddy began to talk about his life. He told me he was originally from Bailadores, but that he now lived in the city of Mérida[7] with his wife and son in a rented apartment. He had moved there to study economics at the university, and had taken most of the courses he needed for his degree. But had not finished his studies because of his involvement in business activities, which had taken so much of his time that he could not keep up with the coursework. And also, he pointed out, the salaries that university graduates were earning were not very fat, and he could make more money running his own business.

Freddy explained that he operated a business dealing in strawberries. Every Monday and Thursday he came to Bailadores to pick up berries that he sold in Mérida and in the neighbouring states of Trujillo and Barinas. He had an oral agreement with certain farmers to pick up all their berries twice a week, regardless of how much their plants were producing. Occasionally, when he needed more than they could provide, he would buy from others. He sold the strawberries to bakeries, small supermarkets, ice-cream parlors, *fruterias*,[8] and to restaurants. It was not profitable for him to sell to large businesses such as food processors, he said, because they paid for deliveries in 30 to 90 days, and he had to pay the farmers right away—or at the latest, when he returned for the next load. Industries were riskier to deal with, he said; when times were tough, they might not be able to pay you, or only paid a part of their debt. He reasoned that since an industry is a large and important customer, it would be easy to fall into the situation where one gave them more berries on credit, hoping they would manage to pull through and cancel their previous debt; and in this vicious cycle, one's time, energy and profits would be lost. "*Mi trabajo se pierde,*" he said—my work is lost.

It was far better to have many small customers than a handful of big ones, Freddy continued. He had several suppliers, too; from some he bought strawberries for up to 5–6,000 *bolívares* a week, at 10 *bolívares* the kilo; from others, he bought much less. He was in a difficult branch because strawberries were so perishable and he had no refrigeration. On his way to Barinas, a hot city in the plains southeast of the Andes, he drove through the *páramo*, the cold zone of the mountains—but nevertheless, the bumpy road tended to make the berries mushy. Once he arrived in Barinas he had to deliver fast; and anything he could not sell would be lost, spoiled by the heat.

Another problem was that strawberry plants did not produce the same amount of berries year-round, and the market also fluctuated, sometimes in the opposite way. Just now, there was a bit of a scarcity, he explained, but in a month there would be a boom in production. He was managing because in Mérida the university—which brought a lot of business to the city—was on strike and students had left, so the local businesses were almost at a standstill. In a month, though, there would be tourists in town because the nation's schools would close for the summer; and since Mérida was a popular place for vacationing, the demand for berries would rise.

Freddy's business was to provide his clients with the berries they needed, which varied by season, but his commitments to the strawberry producers were unchanging—he had to take their berries even if he was not able to sell all of them. And in times of scarcity, when plants were not producing much, he had to scrounge up extra berries from somewhere, in order not to disappoint his customers.

He believed that he could sell more than he did, but said he lacked the time to expand the business. An assistant could not help him make his rounds, he thought, because only he knew how to treat his customers—an important part of the business. His customers depended on his deliveries, and did not buy from others who came by sporadically, offering cheaper berries, because his regular deliveries were vital for them. Freddy knew exactly what kind of berries each client wanted; some needed ripe ones, some greener ones, some would take smaller berries while others needed impressively big ones for decorating fancy baked goods. No employee would ever pay attention to such details, and consequently, it was difficult to expand the business beyond the area he was capable of serving himself, he said; his personal contact with the clients was a key to the business. 'They know when I'm coming, and they're waiting for me. '*Aquí viene el fresero*'—here comes the strawberry man—I hear them say when I walk in the door.'[9]

....

What Does an Entrepreneur Do?

Freddy, then, was one of the local entrepreneurs profiting from the upsurge in cash crop production in the valley by developing a business strategy of his own. How shall one define entrepreneurship? On the whole, economic theory has neglected the role of the entrepreneur in economic development, something Cosgel (1996) suggests has to do with the metaphors and stories used in the construction of economic thought, which frame thinking and can hide as many aspects of reality as they illuminate. Among those economic theorists that have turned their attention to the entrepreneur, there has been considerable difference of opinion about how to correctly define entrepreneurship and the profit resulting from entrepreneurial activity. What, actually, is an entrepreneur—what does he do?

Cantillon, an Irish banker living in France in the 1700s, was the first to use the term. His theory of the entrepreneur stresses function, rather than personality or social status; Cantillon's (1931) entrepreneur is someone who engages in exchanges for profit, using business judgement in a situation of uncertainty, buying at one price to sell at another, uncertain price in the future (Hébert and Link 1988). This view of the entrepreneur as a risk-taker was subsequently developed in the works of other theorists such as Knight (1921), and Mises (1949) and Mill (1965). Cantillon also spoke of business judgement, or decision-making, as important to entrepreneurship; a theme echoed by Marshall (1925), Mises (1951) and Schultz (1980) among others such as Kirzner, who writes of the entrepreneur as someone who discovers profit opportunities and is an allocator of resources among alternative possible uses (Kirzner 1985).

According to Hébert and Link, early English economic theorists did not make a distinction between the capitalist and the entrepreneur, nor make important contributions to the development of a theory of entrepreneurship. For Adam Smith the ownership of capital was a prerequisite, and the roles of entrepreneur and capitalist were thus entwined. Following scholars did little to develop the theory, and as the authors point out, British classical economics leaves the impression that businesses practically run themselves; there is little sense of a dynamic agent involved in business development (Hébert and Link 1988).

It was the Frenchman Jean Baptiste Say (1845) who first expanded the idea of entrepreneurship to include not only risk bearing, but also the act of combining different elements into a profitable enterprise, and providing management. This is a definition of entrepreneurship elaborated by many subsequent theorists, including Mill, Marshall, Clark (1907), Davenport (1913) and Schumpeter (1934), and it meshes well with the concept as used in anthropological studies, where traders often operate between distinct social spheres, bringing together diverse cultural or economic resources into a business operation.

Schumpeter is the economist most often associated with the modern theories of entrepreneurship, which often depart from his writings. For Schumpeter, the human agent is at the center of the process of economic development; change comes from within the system, and the agent of change is the entrepreneur. His function is solely innovation, although this essential function is often, by coincidence, interlaced with others; including risk bearing, management, and so on. But it is the capacity for innovation that sets him apart. Schumpeter defined innovation rather broadly, as the making of new combinations. An innovator could create a new kind of, or quality of, good; introduce a new method of production, a new market, a new source of supply, or he could change the organization of an industry, such as by creating or destroying a monopoly. However, once the new combination had been carried out, and the business was functioning according to plan, the entrepreneurial phase was over. Departing from Schumpeter, Gudeman (1992) has pointed out that in his role as innovator, the entrepreneur makes a cultural contribution, a new combination which did not exist until he brought it into being. He also notes, however, that it is not necessarily the innovator who is able to make a profit from these cultural contributions by bringing them to the market in a saleable form.

Influenced by Schumpeter's work, contemporary Austrian theorists have brought the discussion of the act of entrepreneurship more into the realm of mental processes. Mises saw entrepreneurship as action, which was by nature always speculative, since the future can not be known. Entrepreneurs made decisions, which could bring profit or loss—but it was in the mental act of decision making by the entrepreneur that profit originated: 'Profit is a product of the mind, of success in anticipating the future state of the market' (Mises 1951: 21).

Kirzner, Mises' student, has in turn emphasized entrepreneurship as a creative act of discovery. He describes the entrepreneur as someone with a heightened sense of alertness to profit opportunities. Shackle (1966) tries to reconcile the creativity and imagination of the entrepreneur with risk-bearing activities— the entrepreneur, he says, characteristically gambles on his imagination (Hébert and Link 1988).

Writers on the history of entrepreneurial theory offer their own definitions, which try to synthesize others' contributions. Hébert and Link suggest that the entrepreneur is 'someone who specializes in taking responsibility for and making judgement decisions that affect the location, the form, and the use of goods, resources, or institutions' (Hébert and Link 1988: 155). Kilby, in his discussion of entrepreneurship in undeveloped economies, favors conceptualizing it as 'the performance of services that are required but not available in the market' (Kilby 1971: 29). He further points out the usefulness of describing actual entrepreneurial activities, rather than attributes, such as risk-taking or innovation, that may not be relevant to a particular activity.

Definitions of entrepreneurship thus vary a good deal and are colored by particular economists' larger views of economic life and processes. Definitions of what is happening on the ground go hand in hand with attempts to fit the phenomenon into a larger scheme of things, a theory. By collecting first-hand observations of entrepreneurial activity, anthropology can contribute to defining the activity from the bottom-up.

....

Discovery: Freddy's story

Freddy was one of the first businessmen I got to know during my fieldwork. He was married to Ana, a law student, and they had a five-year old son, Chucho. The oldest of five children, Freddy was an only son. He had grown up in a house on Bailadores' main street, and his father had founded the local *linea* of minibuses that transported passengers from Bailadores to Tovar, the nearest town. Together, his parents had also run a business producing and selling eggs. When his father had died of a heart attack several years ago, Freddy had helped to put his oldest sister through university—she studied medicine, had graduated recently, and was working in a hospital in Barinas. His mother lived there with her, as did his youngest sister, who was about to graduate from high school. His two other sisters were also studying in the university.

This is what he told me when I asked him how he got involved in the strawberry business:

My friends call me 'Freddy *el turco*' because I'm always selling something.[10] When I was studying at the university I had few economic resources, and I wanted to become economically independent. I looked for part-time jobs but I didn't have much luck. An uncle of mine worked selling clothes in Mérida, and one day he gave me some pants to sell to my friends. I sold them easily, and he gave me another dozen. I sold more and more for him, and decided to go into business on my own. I borrowed 500 *bolívares* from my father, and another 500 from my grandfather, and went to Colombia, to Cúcuta[11] to buy my first load of merchandise. Boy, was I scared the first time I tried to smuggle goods through the customs—I was so scared I wouldn't get through that I only bought eight pairs of pants. The second time, I passed a dozen through. But before long I got to know the ropes, and I started taking big loads of pants and jeans through.

I also used to take the boat to Curazao to buy tee shirts. I'd buy 200 at a time, and get them through customs without paying duties—no problem. I was making good money, and set up a little boutique in my student room—I had a carpenter make shelves and organized it really well. But then the owner of the house I was living in became jealous of my business, and made me close it. I started to sell wholesale to the local stores instead, and that was better, really; it left me with more free time. You can see my mind wasn't much on study in those days, though; I was making lots of money when things were at their best. I'd been working at it for about 8 years all together when Black Friday and the currency devaluation shut me down. Overnight, it was all over.

I was used to spending money like crazy—when I think of how I lived, it's hard to believe. I'd been moving lots of money and lost most of it on the devaluation. After selling off everything and paying my debts, I only had 50.000 left. I was really depressed. For six months, I didn't work. I just didn't know what to do next. My father-in-law offered to get me a job as a bureaucrat—he has political connections—but I didn't want to work like that, just couldn't imagine working for someone else, and living on a fixed salary. Finally I took my 50.000 and planted a crop on land in San Lazáro, in Trujillo,[12] where Ana was born—and with that crop I managed to earn another 30.000.

With this money Freddy started his strawberry business. Since contraband was no longer profitable he had to find a new product, and turned to commercializing local products. It was his mother who suggested he try selling flowers in Barinas, where she was living. Freddy would travel to Bailadores and buy a load of flowers, truck them home in the cool of the evening, pass the night in Mérida, then head for his mother's house in Barinas before dawn, making the four-hour drive along the twisting Transandean highway. He tried to establish a clientele for flowers from Bailadores in Barinas, but it was discouraging. There were few florists, and they bought in small quantities. Then he tried bringing strawberries, too, and did better with them, selling to *fruterias*, bakeries, and a few restaurants. This was heartening, but a weekly trip to Barinas could not provide him with enough to live on—and he did not sell enough to make a second weekly trip worthwhile. Instead, he began to take flowers and berries up to San Lazáro in Trujillo, where he knew people through his wife's family, and from the time he had recently spent planting there. He also sold what he could to the scattering of hotels and restaurants along the Transandean highway, and to a few businesses in the villages he passed.

Gradually, he expanded his operation. When I met him, he had been working with strawberries for over two years, and was buying between 200 and 350 kilos, twice a week, for a network of clients in Barinas, Trujillo, and in Mérida.

His weeks were gruelling. He would pick up berries in Bailadores on Mondays to distribute to his customers in Mérida in the late afternoon. By four the next morning he was on the road to Barinas, stopping *en route* to deliver to rural restaurants and storekeepers. By nine he would reach the city and make deliveries around town before heading up the mountains again in the early afternoon, in order to be home before nightfall. Wednesdays were free of travel, but often spent doing errands at the bank, or visiting clients to get paid for back deliveries. Thursdays he picked up berries in Bailadores again, and delivered in town, and Fridays were spent on the road travelling to San Lázaro.

Freddy summed up his account of his weeks by saying that he was working very hard, now, to make enough money to be able to set up an ice-cream shop in Mérida; a profitable and stable business which he could run in the future when he was older and less able to travel. So, his work had a concrete goal. Several times he emphasized that he liked being his own boss, that he preferred to work alone. In his work he did many of the things which entrepreneurs have been defined as doing; he combined different elements—his knowledge of agricultural production in Bailadores, and the possible needs of urban clients— with management skills, using them to avoid risk. As much as possible, he tried to match his berry purchases with clients' needs, and when forced to accept more berries than he could sell, he cleaned them with the help of his wife, added sugar, and froze them in his home freezer to sell in times of scarcity. By providing regular deliveries of fresh berries to small businesses in the region, he had opened up new markets for strawberries, and was, in this way, an innovator. Within a very limited market, he had created a competitive enterprise.

As I have noted, the entrepreneur has been seen from many perspectives; as capitalist, risk-taker, decision-maker, manager, innovator of business combinations, and of new technologies. Popular representations seldom make distinctions between these roles. However, certain particular elements seem to define entrepreneurship in the public imagination; that of the discovery of new opportunities, and of the entrepreneur as the unusual person with an unique, all-consuming vision or dream. The entrepreneur is someone who sees possibilities others fail to see, and who acts confidently on these perceptions. This 'discovery', or alertness to profit opportunities, as Kirzner has described it, takes place prior to subsequent risk taking, decision-making, resource combination, technological development, and so on. One might argue that ideally, it continues throughout the life of an enterprise, since in a competitive and constantly changing business milieu discovery must by nature be an ongoing process; a continuous evolution in which a business changes form and function in response to demands and possibilities presented by its environment.

In an interesting article, Don Lavoie (1991) presents ideas on entrepreneurship that should be of interest to anthropologists. He begins with the idea that culture is a complex of meanings that makes action comprehensible, an open-ended process of communication which shapes development in economics, politics and social institutions, and is, in turn, shaped by them. He goes on to criticize social scientists for discussing entrepreneurship in a way that disregards the role of culture in entrepreneurial activities. Most often creative processes are disregarded; for example, entrepreneurial action is presented as simply being the act of taking advantage of profit opportunities neglected by others—they are 'out there' to be 'found'. Lavoie argues that culture has everything to do with the entrepreneurial process, and focuses on the discovery and interpretation of opportunities, which he says are matters of genuine creativity and of cultural interpretation; there is nothing mechanic about them. 'Profit opportunities,' writes Lavoie, 'are not so much like road signs to which we assign an automatic meaning as they are like difficult texts in need of a sustained effort of interpretation.' When an entrepreneur notices niches overlooked by others, 'he is reading selected aspects of a complex situation others have not read.' And it is culture that gives pre-direction to the entrepreneur's vision, enabling him to read certain things (Lavoie 1991: 46).

Criticizing economists' dependence on the isolated individual to create the framework for analyzing human action in general, Lavoie uses Gadamer's work on language (Gadamer 1989) to argue that as much as society consists of individuals, through their use of language, individuals consist of society. Although the entrepreneur is depicted as a loner or dreamer bucking a crowd—a maverick— his ability to 'read' opportunities can not be due to isolation or separateness, but is rather due to a higher degree of sensitivity to what others are looking for. Highly successful entrepreneurs, he believes, are especially well plugged into the culture.

'What gives them the ability to sense what their customers will want is not some kind of mysterious alertness that gets 'switched on' but their capacity to read the conversations of mankind. They can pick up the sense of where their fellows in the cultures stand, what values they adhere to, what purposes they pursue, what they consider beautiful, and what they deem profane (Lavoie 1991: 49–50).

Entrepreneurial acts then, Lavoie concludes, are readings of and contributions to different conversations, and successful entrepreneurs can join these conversational processes and move them in particular directions.

This is a vision of entrepreneurship that I find very useful when looking at particular processes in which Freddy was involved. He was certainly very much in tune with the 'conversations' going on around him. Brought up in a family where commercial activity was part of the daily household routine, he easily started an enterprise of his own as a student in Mérida, capitalizing on the proximity of the Colombian border and the price and popularity of contraband clothing. He specialized in student clothing, where he knew the market and his clientele. When the venture disintegrated, he turned to other niches in whose language he was conversant—that of planting, and then of commercializing rural products. What should be elaborated, I think, is the idea of 'discovery' as a search, and as a creation of opportunity, more than a sudden inspiration. Freddy did not discover strawberries as a product until he began with flowers and realized they alone could not support him, and it was his family, particularly his mother, who encouraged him to try these new activities. His entrance into the strawberry business was as much a conscious battle to create a viable business, as much a belief that this project could be success, as it was the 'discovery of opportunity.'

....

Access to the Market

When I met Freddy, I already knew quite a bit about local strawberry production. Nearly all of the berries being produced in the valley were being grown under contract to Simón, an immigrant from the Canary Islands,[13] who had come to Bailadores twelve years earlier and planted strawberries on land he rented just outside the village. He had experimented with different varieties of plants to find one well suited to the local climate, and then expanded, importing a large amount of strawberry plants from the U.S.A.

Simón devised a system under which he leased plants to other farmers, who sold the production to him for an agreed-upon price for a determined period, after which the plants belonged to the producer. Because vegetable prices had fluctuated a great deal, some farmers were interested in a crop that had a fixed price and eagerly dedicated part of their fields to strawberry production. In this way, Simón gained access to thousands of kilos of strawberries—5–6,000 kilos a day during production peaks. The entire crop, except for small quantities that Simón retailed in a shop in his home, was sold to industrial buyers. Since all—or nearly all—the berries grown in Bailadores were produced under contract, I wondered where Freddy was getting his supply.

I had the opportunity to ask him a few weeks later, when I travelled with him to Mérida. As we got to know each other, I often caught a ride with him to or from the city when I had errands there. He would pick me up just before heading home with the pickup truck full of boxes of berries, and seemed pleased to have company on his trip. I was always eager to hear his version of the news and gossip circulating among the farmers of the valley. The two hours on the road to Mérida would fly by, as he commented on the goings-on in the village. When I asked him where he bought his berries, when they were all under contract to Simón, he explained that Simón was seriously in arrears with his payments to many of the producers. He said:

It's tough selling to industries. They pay late—after 90 days—and if they're seeing hard times and you're unlucky, they might not even pay you cash. Maybe they'll try to get you to accept a used vehicle or something like that, instead of cash. What do you do then? You've got to sell it, and you'll probably take a loss. The producers don't want to wait three months for their money. They need it now, for the next planting, to pay their costs. That's why some of them will sell to me even if they're still supposed to be bringing their berries to Simón. They're afraid they'll never see their money. They figure since he owes them so much, they have the right to sell to whomever they want. And you know, I heard Simón just bought a coffee farm, in Santa Cruz de Mora. That's where the producer's money is going, if you ask me. He owes 60.000 *bolívares* to one of the farmers who sells to me—so now I get half of the production. And he owes another guy over 100.000. If Simón has a heart attack, he's going to take a lot of others with him.

Freddy concluded with a laugh.

I was interested to hear that Simón's enterprise was falling apart. "So you're buying from Simón's producers?"

When I started out, I bought from Francisco, he's another guy from Bailadores who sells berries in Mérida. No one would sell to me because I didn't have a reputation as a businessman, not as someone who bought strawberries. I knew most of the producers—I grew up here, after all, but I didn't have a commercial relationship with them, and I didn't know how to begin that relationship. So, I bought from Francisco in Mérida, paying a *bolívar* more, and staying out of his territory—I only travelled to Barinas and up into Trujillo at first. When you're starting out, you got to let people take advantage of you, it's the way you learn. After a while I found out where Francisco was buying, and people found out that I was buying berries. Francisco wanted to keep on supplying me, making me pay that *bolívar* extra. One day I refused. I'd made my own contacts. Francisco was angry, began to call me a *tramposo*,[14] and he spread word that I was a real *tracalero*,[15] he tried to make the producers afraid to sell to me. By then I'd started to find new clients in Mérida, and of course he didn't like that. But after a while things settled down, the market was big enough for both of us. Now we have the Mérida market covered between the two of us, most of the time we respect each other's clients, but now and then, when sales are bad, we don't. Sometimes, Francisco will try to sell his berries at a *bolívar* less, but I give my customers better berries, I let them return them if they're bad, and I promise a constant supply. Even when there's almost nothing to be had, I'm out, trying to get a hold of enough for everybody. And I give my clients credit. When I first started I didn't have enough capital to give anybody credit, but once I could do it, I did. It's a good way to keep clients. They're not as likely to buy from somebody who happens to come by with cheaper berries.

I let customers pay when it suits them. Only those who buy the least pay when I deliver. Others, I bring them a bill when their account gets up to 1,000 Bs., or so. Some pay at the end of the month, or every two weeks. Most of them give me a check to be cashed on some date in the future. That way they have time to sell and get the money in the bank. If the check bounces, I don't go back and make a fuss right away, I wait a few days and try to cash it again. If it bounces a second time I tell the client—I do it in a friendly way—that payments are no problem, I can wait for the money, but that I don't want any bouncing checks because of all the time and energy it takes to go to the bank. I got to wait in the line, fill out forms, go to the other line, and then wait some more. The way I look at it, it's better to have a few good clients than a lot of bad ones.

Freddy said he paid his suppliers in cash, when he came to get the next delivery. Sometimes, if he had many clients with payments outstanding, he would ask to take berries on credit; and since the producers knew him and his family, and he had a good record of paying them on time, they gave him credit without any problems. They had confidence that he would pay, and always received their money much faster than they did when they sold to Simón. And, Freddy added, he was very careful with his best suppliers. He had two producers whose entire production he bought, and he bought from several others periodically, when there were peaks in demand. Now and then, he bought from a fellow in Mérida who was trying to get into the marketplace and was having trouble— but this was only as a last resort, in a scarcity.

Credit, then, was an important part of Freddy's business operation. He both offered credit to his clients to keep them faithful, and requested it from his suppliers when he needed it. Along with his offers of steady supply, regular deliveries, and selected quality berries, credit relationships tightened the social bonds between him and his clients and producers, and was one way of insuring continued commerce as well as making business possible at all, in some cases. Acheson (1985) has written of long-term trading relationships as a way of evening out inequalities or dissatisfactions in a future trade. They do serve this purpose, and are also a way of dealing with uncertainty and a lack of information about market conditions, as noted by Mintz (1961) and Geertz (1979). Credit is an important aspect of a trading relationship, and bears complex moral overtones. In Bailadores I eventually became aware that few trades were immediate cash transactions. Entrepreneurs routinely took produce from farmers on credit. Complaints of abuses were frequent.[16] Farmers, in turn, were dependent on a variety of forms of credit in order to carry out production. Formal credit—bank loans—were used only by the well-off, who had property they were willing to mortgage; most farmers felt too economically vulnerable to consider loans.

Trust and Community

Ways of gaining access to products, or of extending goods via credit relationships, speak to an entrepreneur's embeddedness in the ongoing social relations within communities where he carries out his business (Granovetter 1985). It should be pointed out that taking and offering credit required not only knowledge and actively maintained social relationships of different sorts on Freddy's part. Credit possibilities may be 'out there,' but quite a bit of talented negotiation is necessary to obtain them, and likewise, offering credit requires sacrifice—the temporary postponement of gratification—and the extension of trust.

Relationships involving risk and trust are obviously an integral part of Freddy's business. Without them, he would have more difficulty both finding berries and keeping his clients loyal. Berry producers no longer trusted Simón to pay them for their berries, and thus risked trading with Freddy; but he had to buy berries from Francisco, until he established a reputation for being a berry trader. Now he is anxious to maintain his contacts by keeping up his reputation for promptly settling his accounts. It was the ability to identify farmers whose trust in Simón had lapsed, that gave Freddy (and Francisco, before him) access to products for trade—these rips in the social fabric allowed them to move in and refigure local commerce in strawberries. But trust relationships are constantly in flux. As I came to know people in the village better, I began to hear stories about Freddy—a few producers told me that they had sold to him for a time, but had stopped because he had not treated them fairly. I also heard Freddy's comments on these disagreements; for as our acquaintance turned into a friendship, he seemed to know what stories I would hear, and slip in his version of the events into our discussions.

Although trust gained through embeddedness provides business opportunities, being embedded in the life of a community also puts reins on the entrepreneurs' plans and ambitions. During my time in Bailadores, I saw Freddy's business evolve as activities in the community changed. When, after a protracted period of paying his suppliers sporadically, Simón went bankrupt owing most of them considerable sums, this had dire consequences for Freddy. Nearly all of the producers eliminated their strawberry plants rather than renewing them, which threatened his supply of berries. It was a time of rising crop prices, and farmers preferred to plant vegetables, which they now deemed more profitable than the berries that had proven to have such a frustrating market.

Freddy's solution was to begin planting strawberries on a sharecropping basis. He worked with marginal producers—people still considerably involved in subsistence agriculture—in remote areas of the valley, where cash-crop agriculture had still not penetrated because of poor roads and limited possibilities for irrigation. Like Simón, he provided the plants, and offered to buy their entire production at a fixed price. Through sharecropping, however, he became involved in the daily life of his producers in a different way.

One of the problems with going to work on the plants we've got *a medias*[17] is that every time I go, they invite me to eat. I told Luis [his sharecropper] I couldn't eat every time I went up to check the plants, but he said that since they made food for the workers anyway, I might as well eat, too. I argued no, *eso da pena*,[18] anyone could think that I was just going up there for the meals. Luis said that of course he knew that wasn't true, and that if I didn't eat, his wife would be offended. And then there's his son, he's named Chucho, like my boy. When I show up he follows me all over the farm—he's become my number-one fan. So now Luis's taken to calling me *compadre*,[19] although we're not really *compadres*.

Freddy's uneasiness about his relationship with Luis and his family reflected more than a concern with violating social codes. The meals, and little Chucho's affection for him, are elements that increasingly compromise the business nature of his relationship with his *medianero*. Freddy's sharecropping relationships, as well as his verbal agreements with producers and clients, have their formal obligations, established by moral codes and tradition, but they exist within an ongoing process of renegotiation and redefinition. The help and kindness, the innocence and servility of the partner without capital asks to be translated into flexibility on the part of the 'capitalist,' who though aware of, and disturbed by, this gradual change in the essence of their relationship is unable to withdraw from the social tentacles which draw him into a more intimate relationship than he had intended. To do so would be to signal a reluctance to share social closeness, would be interpreted as a slight, and could be the first step in the destruction of the mutual confidence important to all business dealings; it would be a declaration that the kinds of obligations established through sociality were unwelcome and unlikely to be honored.

Indeed, one might speculate that the community tries to hold the entrepreneur within its realm of influence, knowing that while it has fetters on him, it may benefit from his ability to create wealth. This takes place between individuals, but occurs at another level when a community prevails upon business leaders to share their prosperity through investments for a more general good. This may be done by requesting 'good works' of a philanthropic nature, or through a more regulated levy. In Bailadores, there were ideas of imposing a local tax on the intermediaries in rural products; of making them contribute, for example, half a *bolívar* for each kilo of valley produce that they commercialized. In discussion, the middlemen were not so much against this idea as I expected, but insisted that if they were to contribute, they must have the right to determine where this contribution was to be invested. Here, then, a potential community resource began to emerge, but with a tug-of-war over its destination. Like the discovery of the profit niches themselves, the discussion over and eventual destination of these profits is culturally embedded.

While the community seeks to hold the entrepreneur and appropriate a portion of his profit, the entrepreneur seeks to distance himself and acquire a measure of independence, to disembedd himself from the network of relationships that bind him. When he gains in power, this may become possible. As Freddy's enterprise expanded with the informal contracts he established with different sharecroppers, his method of doing business changed: nowdays, he told me, a few months before I left the community, he seldom paid for a load of berries right after their sale. It was better for him to pay for a part of them, and receive another load, and his *medianeros* continued to bring him their berries because they had no alternative ways to market them. By staying in debt to the farmers he kept them on their toes, he said, assuring himself good quality produce.

If I paid them outright they'd soon be giving me all kinds of berries, tiny, green—terrible quality. So I pay a part and leave the rest for later, the more the better. That way they make sure I get what I need, and on time, too. Believe me, they want to help me please my clients in Mérida, so I can pay them someday ... they're even more concerned with my solvency than I am! So I take berries, pay a part, receive more berries, pay another part, and so it goes, with me falling more and more behind, until something happens and I have to pay up, or until it's in my interest.

And meanwhile, Freddy had begun to negotiate to buy land in a remote part of the valley, hoping to obtain a state loan and to begin production without sharecroppers, on his own. His actions seemed to parallel those of Simón four years ago, who had also allowed his debts with his suppliers to grow, and had invested in land in another area for coffee production. At that time, Freddy had taken pains to maintain his reputation as a prompt payer, because that was the only way he could get access to any strawberries at all. At the same time, he now complained about the trouble he had collecting his bills from some of his clients in Mérida; they would receive berries and pay for a part of past deliveries, in much the same way he kept his suppliers hanging on. The ability of entrepreneurs to skilfully manipulate the cultural codes of their society, balancing between the permissible and the profane, tugging moral codes into a new conformation, is, I suggest, what often makes them perceived as dangerous, and as potential hazards to the welfare of the larger community.[20]

It occurred to me that a large part of entrepreneurship, at least in the rural environment, seemed to be a matter of doing business with other people's money or resources. Capital was scarce, and if available, often too dear to be risked. Those who had to put up the goods that business was transacted over, were those without the power to withhold them; the producer who needed to sell his berries, the middleman who lived off their sale. Perhaps the best definition of an entrepreneur here is as someone who is able to put together resources that are not his own, in a combination that allows him, over time, to accumulate capital.[21] It is his embeddedness in a local culture that enables this. In the insecure rural arena, commercial gains were often invested in a more secure enterprise. Most of the middlemen in the valley who were able to capitalize invested in land, while a few tried ventures—real estate, vehicles—outside the rural sphere. Freddy dreamt of his ice-cream shop.

What, then, can anthropology offer studies of entrepreneurship? I have tried to analyze how the activities of the would-be entrepreneur are ensconced in a cultural setting, and consist of a "reading," as Lavoie would say, of that culture. This is where anthropology has a role, in the explication of how difficult-to-elucidate understandings of culture, risk and trust, individual and community play into the shape that entrepreneurship takes in particular settings. When I think of Freddy, I remember an extraordinary trip I made with him to Mérida one rainy evening. The windshield wipers on his truck were broken, and the pane dim with condensation. He drove by peering out through a clear patch of window near the hood, gripping the wheel tightly and talking all the while. As we descended in altitude, it grew foggy, but Freddy knew the route so well that he seemed to have no need to see the road. The moments he felt unsure, he stopped and asked me to open my door a crack, just to make sure we were still on the pavement. To me, the memory of that trip has become a metaphor for his life and ventures, moving ahead with confidence, if limited visibility, playing it by ear, staying on the road. It's what we all do in our lives as we struggle to turn setbacks into opportunities; and the 'feel' an entrepreneur makes use of to advance and to survive in the business world is the knowledge and instinct that comes from experience gathered in a particular cultural milieu.

....

Notes

1. This article was written during post-doctoral studies at the University of Texas at Austin. I thank the Population Research Center for their sponsorship, and HSFR, The Swedish Council for Research in the Humanities and the Social Sciences, for a post-doctoral grant. I would also like to thank Richard Swedberg for his helpful comments on this article.

2. Sociologists have written on ethnic entrepreneurs; the works of Bonacich (1973), Wertheim (1980), and the articles collected in Evers and Schrader (1994) come to mind. For a discussion of sociologists' contributions to the study of entrepreneurship, see Swedberg's Introduction in this volume.

3. Recent exceptions are Carrier's (1997) study of Paul Hawken's book *Growing a Business*, and Stewart's (1992) study of gypsy horse-traders.

4. Interesting objections are raised by Gudeman (1986), Gudeman and Rivera (1991) and Parry and Bloch (1989).

5. For one example, see Soto (1989), whose discussion of the informal sector in Peru as a positive force representing a true market economy (in comparison with the more 'mercantilist' formal economy) and call for the reformation of the country's legal structures in the economic sphere raised considerable debate.

6. That this is so is attested by the importance business people place on learning the proper etiquette and customs of the foreign places where they do business.

7. Mérida is the capital of the state and also a tourist center and the site of the *Universidad de Los Andes*, Venezuela's second-largest public university. Its attractions include its cool climate, beautiful setting and proximity to the Pico Bolívar, the country's highest peak, which tourists can reach by cable car.

8. A small shop selling fresh fruit, fruit salad, and fruit drinks.

9. Freddy was making an important point here. There is a general shortage of qualified administrative personnel in Venezuela, as Moises Naim (then the academic director of IESA, the Instituto de Estudios Superiores de Administración) has pointed out in an interview (Sanz 1987). This problem is particularly acute in the rural setting, where wages are also lower than in urban areas. But another

important reason why Freddy avoids using employees is the fear of competition, for anyone who learnt his business might become a potential competitor in the future.

10. *Turco* means 'Turk' and refers to the peddlers and shopkeepers of middle-eastern origin who have settled in many Venezuelan towns and villages and opened dry-goods shops.

11. Cúcuta is a Colombian city across the border from Venezuela's San Antonio del Táchira. There is lively commerce between these two border towns, flowing in different directions depending on the currency exchange rate. At the time to which Freddy was referring, the Venezuelan currency was strong and the smuggling of goods from Cúcuta into the cities of the Venezuelan Andes was common. Since Colombia has a more advanced textile industry than Venezuela, clothes were in great demand. In February of 1983, the Venezuelan currency, the *bolívar*, was devalued on 'Black Friday' and contraband began to flow in the opposite direction.

12. Trujillo is one of the Venezuelan Andean states, and borders Mérida. Ana's family came from the village of San Lázaro there, and still owned land in the community.

13. Beginning in the late 1960s, a number of immigrants from the Canary Islands settled in Bailadores to undertake vegetable production. There is a sizeable number of immigrants from the Canary Islands in Venezuela as a whole. Locally, they are recognized as having had an important role in the valley's transformation from an area of subsistence production to market production.

14. A *tramposo* is a person who sets a trap, or takes advantage of someone.

15. A common expression for 'a cheat.'

16. See Lindh de Montoya (1996) for a discussion of rural credit-based trade.

17. A *medias* is the local term for crops produced on a sharecropping basis.

18. *Dar pena* means to make ashamed.

19. *Compadre* means co-parent, and is a ritual bond (godfatherhood) involving responsibilities towards a child. It is legitimized through the Catholic Church at baptism, and their mutual obligations strengthen the social bonds between *compadres*.

20. Keith Hart has explored the relationship between the entrepreneur and his community in an interesting article (1975) using case studies from the Frafra of Ghana. He suggests that perceptions of entrepreneurial accumulation are related to the form of the economic and social exchanges which link the entrepreneur and the community.

21. In this context, see Ann Swidler's suggestion (1986) that culture can be viewed as a 'tool kit' that provides habits, skills and styles from which people choose elements to use in solving problems and constructing 'strategies of action.' The entrepreneur puts material resources together, but is also arguably choosing and putting together cultural behaviors that serve his needs, and thereby expands his (and by extension the community's) cultural repertoire (Hannerz 1969: 186).

References

Abolafia, Mitchell (1996) *Making Markets: opportunism and restraint on Wall Street.* Cambridge, Mass.: Harvard University Press.

Acheson, J. (1985) 'Social Organizatoin of the Maine Lobster Market', in Stuart Plattner (ed.) *Markets and Marketing.* Lanham, Md.: University Press of America.

Babb, Florence (1989) *Between Field and Cooking Pot: the Political Economy of Marketwomen in Peru.* Austin: University of Texas Press.

Barth, Fredrik (1963) *The Role of the Entrepreneur in Social Change in Northern Norway.* Oslo: Universitetsforlaget.

Barth, Fredrik (1967) 'Economic Spheres in Darfur', in Raymond Firth (ed.) *Themes in Economic Anthropology.* London: Tavistock.

Beals, Ralph L. (1975) *The Peasant Marketing System of Oaxaca, Mexico.* Los Angeles: University of California Press.

Bonacich, E. (1973) 'A Theory of Middleman Minorities', *American Sociological Review* 38: 583–594.

Cancian, Frnak (1972) *Change and Uncertainty in a Peasant Economy: the Maya Corn Farmers of Zinacantan.* Stanford: Stanford University Press.

Cantillon, R. (1931) *Essai sur la nature du commerce en général.* London: Macmillan.

Carrier, James G. (1995) *Gifts and Commodities: Exchange and Western Capitalism since 1700.* London: Routledge.

Carrier, James G., ed. (1997) *Meanings of the Market: The Free Market in Western Culture.* Oxford: Berg.

Carrier, James G. (1997) 'Mr Smith, Meet Mr Hawken', in James G. Carrier (ed.) *Meanings of the Market: The Free Market in Western Culture,* pp. 129–157. Oxford: Berg.

Clark, Gracia, ed. (1988) *Traders Versus the State: Anthropological Approaches to Unofficial Economies.* Boulder, Colorado: Westview Press.

Clark, Gracia (1994) *Onions are my Husband: survival and accumulation by West African market women.* Chicago: University of Chicago Press.

Clark, J.B. (1907) *Essentials of economic theory.* New York: Macmillan.

Cohen, Abner (1969) *Custom and politics in urban Africa: a study of Hausa migrants in Yoruba towns.* Berkeley: University of California Press.

Cook, Scott (1990) *Obliging need: rural petty industry in Mexican capitalism.* Austin: University of Texas Press.

Cook, Scott and Martin Diskin, eds. (1976) *Markets in Oaxaca.* Austin: University of Texas Press.

Cosgel, Metin M. (1996) 'Metaphors, Stories and the Entrepreneur in Economics', *History of Political Economy* 28(1): 57–76.

Davenport, H. (1913) *Economics of enterprise.* New York: Macmillan.

Dilley, Roy, ed. (1992) *Contesting Markets: Analyses of Ideology, Discourse and Practice.* Edinburgh: Edinburgh University Press.

Evers, H.-D. and H. Schrader, eds. (1994) *The Moral Economy of Trade: Ethnicity and Developing Markets.* Eidos: London, Routledge.

Gadamer, H.-G. (1989) *Truth and Method.* New York: Crossroad.

Geertz, Clifford (1963) *Peddlers and Princes: Social Change and Economic Modernization in two Indonesian Towns.* Chicago: University of Chicago Press.

Geertz, Clifford (1979) 'Suq: The Bazaar Economy in Sefrou', in C. Geertz, H. Geertz and L. Rosen (eds.), *Meaning and Order in Moroccan Society.* Cambridge: Cambridge University Press.

Granovetter, Mark (1985) 'Economic Action and Social Structure: The Problem of Embeddedness', *American Journal of Sociology* 91(3): 481–510.

Greenfield, S., A. Strickon and R.T. Aubey, eds. (1979) *Entrepreneurs in Cultural Context.* Albuquerque: University of New Mexico Press.

Greenfield, S. and A. Strickon (1981) 'A New Paradigm for the Study of Entrepreneurship and Social Change', *Economic Development and Cultural Change* 29(3): 467–499.

Gudeman, Stephen (1986) *Economics as Culture: Models and Metaphors of Livelihood.* London: Routledge and Kegan Paul.

Gudeman, Stephen (1992) 'Remodeling the house of economics: culture and innovation', *American Ethnologist,* 19(1): 141–154.

Gudeman, Stephen and Alberto Rivera (1991) *Conversations in Colombia: The Domestic Economy in Life and Text.* New York: Cambridge University Press.

Hannerz, Ulf (1969) *Soulside; Inquiries into Ghetto Culture and Community.* New York: Colombia University Press.

Hart, Keith (1975) 'Swindler or Public Benefactor?' in Jack Goody (ed.) *Changing Social Structure in Ghana: Essays in the Comparative Sociology of a New State and an Old Tradition,* pp. 1–35. London: International African Institute.

Hébert, R.F. and A.N. Link (1988) *The Entrepreneur: Mainstream Views and Radical Critiques.* New York: Praeger.

Hobart, Mark, ed. (1993) *An Anthropological Critique of Development: the Growth of Ignorance.* London: Routledge.

Kilby, Peter (1971) 'Hunting the Heffalump', in Peter Kilby (ed.) *Entrepreneurship and Economic Development,* pp. 1–40. New York: The Free Press.

Kirzner, Israel (1985) *Discovery and the Capitalist Process.* Chicago: University of Chicago Press.

Knight, F.H. (1921) *Risk, Uncertainty and Profit.* New York: Houghton Mifflin.

Lavoie, Don (1991) 'The Discovery and Interpretation of Profit Opportunities: Culture and the Kirznerian Entrepreneur', in Brigitte Berger (ed.) *The Culture of Entrepreneurship,* pp. 33–51. San Francisco: ICS Press.

Lindh de Montoya, M. (1996) *Progress, Hunger and Envy: Commercial Agriculture, Marketing and Social Transformation in the Venezuelan Andes.* Stockholm: Stockholm Studies in Social Anthropology.

Long, Norman (1989) *Encounters at the Interface: A perspective on social discontinuities in rural development.* Wageningen: Agricultural University.

Marcus, George and Michael J. Fischer, eds. (1986) *Anthropology as Cultural Critique*. Chicago: The University of Chicago Press.

Marshall, Alfred (1925) *Memorials of Alfred Marshall*. London: Macmillan.

Mill, J.S. (1965) *Principles of Political Economy*. New York: Augustus M. Kelley.

Mintz, Sidney (1961) *Pratik: Haitian Personal Economic Relationships*. Proceedings of the 1961 Annual Spring Meeting of the American Ethnological Society.

Mises, Ludwig von (1949) *Human Action: A treatise on economics*. New Haven: Yale University Press.

Mises, Ludwig von (1951) *Profit and Loss*. South Holland, IL: Consumers-Producers Economic Service.

Mitchell, William P. (1991) *Peasants on the Edge: Crop, cult and crisis in the Andes*. Austin: University of Texas Press.

Parry, Jonathan and Maurice Bloch, eds. (1989) *Money and the Morality of Exchange*. Cambridge: Cambridge University Press.

Plattner, Stuart (1975) 'The Economics of Peddling', in Stuart Plattner (ed.) *Formal Methods in Economic Anthropology*. Washington D.C.: Special Publication of the American Anthropological Association.

Plattner, Stuart, ed. (1985) *Markets and Marketing*. Monographs in Economic Anthropology, No. 4. Lanham, Md.: University Press of America.

Sanz, Elvira (1987) 'Fortalezcamos Nuestras Instituciones. Tertulia con Moises Naim', in *Tertulias de la Revista de Nosotros*. Caracas: Departamento de Relaciones Públicas de Lagoven, S.A.

Say, J.-B. (1845) *A Treatise on Political Economy*. Philadelphia: Grigg & Elliot.

Schultz, T.W. (1980) 'Investment in entrepreneurial ability', *Scandinavian Journal of Economics* 82: 437–448.

Schumpeter, Joseph A. (1934) *The Theory of Economic Development*. Cambridge: Harvard University Press.

Shackle, G.L.S. (1966) *The Nature of Economic Thought*. Cambridge: Cambridge University Press.

Soto, Hendando de (1989) *The Other Path: The Invisible Revolution in the Third World*. London: I.B. Tauris & Co. Ltd.

Stewart, Michael (1992) 'Gypsies at the Horse-Fair: A Non-Market Model of Trade', in Roy Dilley (ed.) *Contesting Markets: Analysis of Ideology, Discourse and Practice*, pp. 97–114. Edinburgh: Edinburgh University Press.

Stonich, Susan (1993) *I am Destroying the Land! The Political Ecology of Poverty and Environmental Degradation in Honduras*. Boulder, Colorado: Westview Press.

Swedberg, Richard (1999) 'Introduction', in R. Swedberg (ed.) *Entrepreneurship: the Social Science View*. Oxford: Oxford University Press.

Swidler, Ann (1986) 'Culture in Action: Symbols and Strategies', *American Sociological Review*, 51: 273–286.

Wertheim, W.F. (1980) 'The Trading Minorities in Southeast Asia', in Hans Dieter Evers (ed.) *Sociology of Southeast Asia: Readings on Social Change and Development*. Kuala Lumpur: Oxford University Press.

15 Ethnic Entrepreneurs

Roger Waldinger, Howard Aldrich, and Robin Ward

The revival of small business has been widely accompanied by the infusion of new ethnic owners into the ranks of petty proprietorship. By 1980, self-employment already accounted for a substantial share of employment among those newcomers who had moved to the United States in the years since the renewal of large-scale immigration in 1965. In four of the five principal immigrant-receiving metropolitan areas—New York, Los Angeles, Miami, and San Francisco—immigrant self-employment rates among males were close to or above the 10% mark, as can be seen in Table 15.1. The immigrant imprint is most dramatic in Miami, where a 30-year influx of Cuban refugees has transformed a decaying, stagnant city into a booming economy that some analysts have called the "capital of Latin America" (Rieff 1987; Levine 1985). Elsewhere, it has been more a matter of immigrants finding niches where small businesses could thrive. In industries like garments, restaurants, petty retailing, taxis, and so on, newcomers have found a supportive environment in which entrepreneurial activity has flourished—as will be seen in the chapters that follow.

In Britain, the percentage of Indian males in self-employment increased from 6% in 1971 to about 18% in 1982, with the equivalent figures for Caribbean males at 2% and 7% (Ward and Jenkins 1984; Department of Employment 1988). Cypriots and Asians revived London's dying East End clothing trade (Saifullah Khan 1979) and created a new one in the West Midlands (Ward et al. 1986). Chinese and Cypriot immigrants have come to dominate the traditional fish and chips trade. Indian and Pakistani entrepreneurs are now prominent in several other areas of retailing (chemist's shops, small grocery stores, discount

Table 15.1. Self-Employment Rates in Major U.S. Metropolitan Areas

	Men		Women	
	All Persons %	New Immigrants %	All Persons %	New Immigrants %
Chicago	9.0	6.4	3.6	2.4
Los Angeles-Long Beach	12.4	9.1	4.1	3.1
Miami	15.2	13.8	3.9	3.1
New York-New Jersey	10.6	9.3	2.6	2.3
San Francisco-Oakland	12.7	10.6	4.9	3.8

Source: 1980 Census of Population, 5% Public Use Microdata Sample.
Note: "New Immigrants" include all immigrants who arrived in the United States between 1965 and 1980.

Table 15.2. Self-Employment Trends, 1969–1984, in Four European Countries (employed persons in nonincorporated business as percentage of civilian, nonagricultural employment)

	1969 %	1973 %	1979 %	1981 %	1984 %
France	N.A.	9.7	8.7	8.7	9.1
Germany	7.6	7.6	7.7	7.6	8.2
Netherlands	N.A.	3.7	4.1	5.6	4.9
United Kingdom	7.3	7.3	6.6	7.9	9.6

Source: OECD (1986: 45).

airline tickets), even in areas such as Glasgow, where South Asian settlement has been on a relatively small scale (Krcmar 1984).

In France, immigrants still lag far behind the French national population in their rate of self-employment: In 1984, only 6% of the immigrant population was self-employed, in contrast to 17% for the total population. But the overall trend is toward a narrowing of the gap: While small business is losing its attractiveness for the native French population, the proportion of immigrants working on their own account is steadily increasing. As in other countries, the immigrant effect is more visible in those localities with immigrant concentrations than elsewhere. In Paris, for example, one out of every ten store owners is foreign-born (Ma Mung and Guillon 1986).

Elsewhere on the Continent, the expansion of ethnic business has been held back by restrictive "immigrant policies" that constrain movement out of wage and salary employment. In many areas, the terms of entry for migrant workers do not allow self-employment, and the legal/institutional arrangements for small business constitute a further barrier. Despite this, there is evidence of a growing ethnic small business sector, as we discuss elsewhere in the book from which this article comes. In the Netherlands, the overall rate of self-employment is considerably lower than in France, but substantial business activity has sprung up among Chinese immigrants, and Hindustani and Turkish entrepreneurs have reintroduced garment manufacture to Amsterdam. In Germany, where there has been no national census since the 1970s, reliable national estimates of immigrant business rates do not exist. Nonetheless, the case study literature points to a growth of immigrant entrepreneurship, as economic restructuring has spurred immigrants to seek out alternatives to wage and salary work in the traditional immigrant-employing industries (Blaschke and Ersoz 1986; Morokvasic 1986).

Our interactive model of ethnic business development is built on two dimensions: opportunity structures and characteristics of the ethnic groups. As shown in Figure 15.1, opportunity structures consist of market conditions that may favor products or services oriented toward coethnics and situations in which a wider, nonethnic market might be served. Opportunity structures also include the routes through which access to business is obtained. Group characteristics include premigration circumstances, a group's reaction to conditions in the host society, and resource mobilization through various features of the ethnic community. Ethnic strategies emerge from the interaction of all these factors, as ethnic entrepreneurs adapt to the resources made available in opportunity structures and attempt to carve out their own niches.

....

The Opportunity Structure

We begin with the characteristics of opportunity structures to emphasize the role played by historically contingent circumstances in shaping the prospects open to potential ethnic business owners. Groups can work only with the resources made available to them by their environments, and the structure of opportunities is constantly changing in modern industrial societies. Market conditions may favor only businesses serving an ethnic community's needs, in which case entrepreneurial opportunities are limited. Or market conditions may favor smaller enterprises serving nonethnic populations, in which case opportunities are much greater. Even if market conditions are favorable, immigrant minorities must gain access to business, and nonethnic group members often control such access.

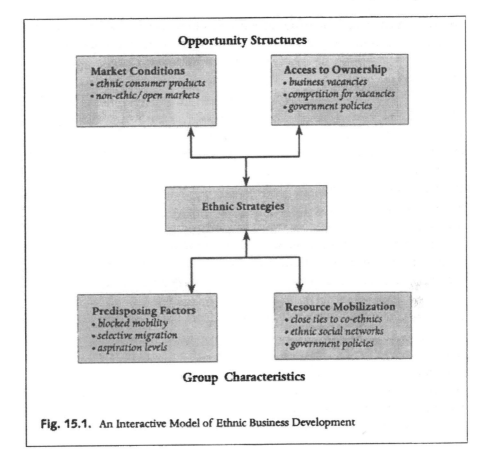

Fig. 15.1. An Interactive Model of Ethnic Business Development

Market Conditions

For a business to arise, there must be some demand for the services it offers. The initial market for immigrant entrepreneurs typically arises within the immigrant community itself—the immigrant community has a special set of needs and preferences that are best served, and sometimes can only be served, by those who share those needs and know them intimately, namely, the members of the immigrant community itself.

Ethnic Consumer Products

Generally, the businesses that develop first are purveyors of culinary products—tropical goods among Hispanics, for example, or Oriental specialties among Asians. Businesses that provide "cultural products"—newspapers, recordings, books, magazines, clothes, jewelry—are also quick to find a niche in the immigrant community. The important point about both types of activity is that they involve a direct connection with the immigrants' homeland and knowledge of tastes and buying preferences—qualities unlikely to be shared by larger, native-owned competitors (Aldrich *et al.* 1985).

Immigrants also have special problems that are caused by the strains of settlement and assimilation, which are aggravated by their distance from the institutionalized mechanisms of service delivery. Consequently, the business of specializing in the problems of immigrant adjustment is another early avenue of economic activity, and immigrant-owned travel agencies and law firms as well as realtors and accountants are common in most immigrant communities. Such businesses frequently perform myriad functions far beyond the simple provision of legal aid or travel information and reservations (Ladbury 1984).

To a large extent, these services to immigrants are unfamiliar and unintelligible to the newcomer unaccustomed to bureaucratic procedures. In some cases, they may impinge on the often dubious legal status of immigrants and their families. Trust is thus an important component of the service, and the need for trust pulls the newcomer toward a business owner of common ethnic background. In addition, in many of the societies from which the immigrants come, people prefer personalistic relationships over reliance on impersonal, formal procedures. Such predispositions further increase the clientele of those businesses that specialize in adjustment problems.

If immigrant business stays limited to the ethnic market, its potential for growth is sharply circumscribed, as shown in studies of white, black, and Puerto Rican businesses in the United States (Aldrich and Reiss 1976) and of Indian and white businesses in the United Kingdom (Aldrich *et al.* 1983). The obstacle to growth is the ethnic market itself, which can support only a restricted number of businesses because it is quantitatively small and because the ethnic population is too impoverished to provide sufficient buying power. Moreover, the environment confronting the ethnic entrepreneur is severe: Because exclusion from job opportunities leads many immigrants to seek out business opportunities, business conditions in the ethnic market tend toward a proliferation of small units, overcompetition, and a high failure rate, with the surviving businesses generating scanty returns for their owners.

These conclusions may be too pessimistic because the immigrant market may also serve as an export platform from which ethnic firms may expand.

One case in point is the experience of Cuban refugees in Miami, Florida, discussed elsewhere in the book from which this article comes. The early refugees converged on a depressed area in the central city, where housing costs were low and low-rent storefront vacant space was available. As the refugee population grew, and the customer base expanded, retail businesses proliferated (Mohl 1983). The availability of a nearby, low-cost labor force linked together through informal networks further enabled Cuban entrepreneurs to branch out in other industries, such as garments or construction, where a nonethnic clientele could be secured. Once in place, these "export industries" then served as a base for additional expansion of the ethnic economy: The export industries generated a surplus that trickled down to merchants serving the local, specialized needs of the Cuban communities. The export industries also enabled ethnic entrepreneurs to diversify, by moving backward or forward into related industries. As the vibrant Cuban ethnic economy has turned Miami into a center for investments from Latin America as well as an entrepôt for trade with that area, Cuban entrepreneurs have been able to move into more sophisticated and higher-profit fields (Levine 1985).

The same pattern of development can be detected among the Chinese refugees who have settled in Paris in growing numbers since 1975. A variety of factors have facilitated the development of a burgeoning Chinese business sector: population concentration, especially in the 13th arrondissement; specialized and distinctive consumption tastes; informal capital-raising networks; and linkages to sources of financing and cheap consumer goods in the Far East. Chinese entrepreneurs have quickly used their access to their ethnic market to develop ties to French customers and suppliers and reduce their dependence on Asian customers:

Already, shops producing beancurd have been started in the Parisian region and in Paris itself. In the 13th arrondissement, the Sojato company, for example, produces several tons of beancurd each day, furnishing it at the same time to local merchants of the neighborhoods and to wholesalers at the Halles de Rungis. Other enterprises making fresh food are in the planning stages. . . . An opening is perceptible toward non-Asian suppliers and at the same time toward a more diversified clientele (the stores make an ever greater effort to translate the prices and labels into French). (Guillon and Taboada-Leonetti 1986: 117)

These examples notwithstanding, we note that the growth potential of immigrant business hinges on its access to customers beyond the ethnic community. The crucial question, then, concerns the types of economic environments that might support neophyte immigrant entrepreneurs.

Roger Waldinger, et al.

Immigrant Business in the Open Market

The structure of industry is a powerful constraint on the creation of new business organizations. New firms are unlikely to arise in industries characterized by extensive scale economies and entry costs. However, most Western economies contain niches where techniques of mass production or mass distribution do not prevail. Under these circumstances, immigrant businesses can grow in the open market.

Underserved or abandoned markets. One such niche consists of markets that are underserved and often abandoned by the large mass marketing organizations. The fact that immigrants are so heavily concentrated in the core of urban centers means that they live in areas that are at once ill-suited to the technological and organizational conditions of large enterprise and favorable to small enterprises. The agglomeration of urban populations allows immigrants to start businesses with virtually no capital at all, as demonstrated by the experience of Senegalese traders in Paris (Salem 1984) and the upsurge of street peddling among a variety of immigrant groups in the United States (Greenberg et al. 1980).

A more important influence is the cost structure of the food retailing industry: Overhead costs in central city locations keep store sizes down, thus diminishing the scale economies that give large chain operations an advantage over small independent grocery stores. In France, where food distribution is increasingly concentrated in large suburban supermarkets, or *hypermarchés*, immigrant retailers have found a niche as small neighborhood retailers (Simon and Ma Mung 1987). Retailing in the United Kingdom is experiencing a similar trend; for example, two firms account for more than half of all package grocery sales in London. But the inner urban areas of largely working-class populations are shunned by the large chains, and Asian shopkeepers now dominate these areas, whatever the ethnic origins of local residents (Ward 1986, 1987). Similarly, in New York City, large national chains play a very limited role in the food retailing industry; consequently, the industry has been entered easily by small immigrant concerns that do well in competing against local, nonimmigrant chains that lack the economies of scale to achieve significant market power (Waldinger 1986).

Within the central cities of the United States, black urban ghettos are particularly underserved by retail chains. For example, North Lawndale, a heavily black community in Chicago of over 60,000 persons, contains only one supermarket (Wacquant and Wilson 1988). In turn, black neighborhoods such as North Lawndale have seen an influx of Korean, Arab, and other immigrant merchants who thrive in the absence of competition from larger, native-owned-and-operated organizations. In general, this pattern of immigrants selling to a

362

nonimmigrant clientele can be characterized as a "middleman minority" situation, which is discussed elsewhere in the book from which this article comes.

Low economies of scale. Markets where economies of scale are so low that immigrant entrepreneurs can achieve the highest levels of efficiency by engaging in self-exploitation are another fertile field for immigrant business. Given the competitive weakness of native-owned food stores, as noted above, self-exploitation is a strategy that small immigrant store owners can successfully pursue. As Ma Mung and Guillon (1986) observed, the immigrant-owned neighborhood shops of Paris offer the same products as their French counterparts, but provide different services: longer hours, year-round operation, easily available credit, and sales of very small quantities. Another case in point is the taxi industry in the United States, where immigrants have been able to move rapidly into ownership positions. What is distinctive about the taxi industry is that virtually no advantages accrue to the large firm. Because the owner-operator of a single cab operates at essentially the same costs as a fleet of 20 to 30 cabs, the key to cost reduction is keeping the vehicle on the road for the longest possible time. Thus if immigrants are amenable to self-exploitation or, better yet, can pool resources to buy a taxi and then split shifts so that the cab is in use 24 hours a day, they can effectively compete with native-owned firms (Russell 1985; Orlick 1987).

Instability and uncertainty. A niche for immigrant firms also arises in markets affected by instability or uncertainty. When demand falls into stable and unstable portions, and the two components can be separated from one another, industries may be segmented into noncompeting branches (Piore 1980): One branch is dominated by larger firms, handling staple products; a second, composed of small-scale firms, caters to the unpredictable and/or fluctuating portion of demand. Hence segmentation processes in industries like clothing or construction give rise to small-scale sectors specializing in products that larger firms cannot effectively supply. As we show elsewhere in the book from which this article comes the small-scale sector, with its low entry barriers and high labor-to-capital ratios, offers immigrant entrepreneurs an accessible route into the general market.

Ethnic goods. A final niche in the general market arises where the demand for exotic goods among the native population allows immigrants to convert both the contents and the symbols of ethnicity into profit-making commodities. Selling exotic goods and services offers a fruitful path of business expansion because immigrants have a special product that only they can supply or, at the very least, present in conditions that are seemingly authentic (Palmer 1984). Immigrants not only lack competitors in "exotic markets," they can also offer their products at relatively low prices and thereby capture a clientele priced out of the businesses run by native entrepreneurs (see Ma Mung and Guillon 1986). Indeed, the demand for exotic products such as Indian cuisine in the United Kingdom and Indonesian cuisine in the Netherlands may become so dominant as to force many native businesses offering traditional alternatives out of business.

In conclusion, what distinguishes the variety of processes giving rise to immigrant business is an environment supportive of neophyte capitalists and the small concerns that they establish. Ethnic consumer tastes provide a protected market position, in part because the members of the community may have a cultural preference for dealing with coethnics, and in part because the costs of learning the specific wants and tastes of the immigrant groups are such as to discourage native firms from doing so, especially at an early stage when the community is small and not readily visible to outsiders (Aldrich *et al.* 1985).

If the ethnic market allows the immigrant to maintain a business at somewhat higher-than-average costs, the other processes outlined above reduce the cost difference between native and immigrant firms. Small capital-to-labor ratios keep entry barriers low, and consequently immigrant businesses should be most common in industries where this condition prevails. Where there are problems in substituting capital for labor because changes in demand might idle expensive machines, immigrant businesses with labor-intensive processes can operate close to the prevailing efficiencies. When small markets inhibit the realization of economies of scale, small firms can achieve efficiencies close to or better than their larger competitors and without the heavy overhead and administrative costs that the latter must shoulder.

A second characteristic of industries supportive of immigrant firms is that the technical barriers to entry are also low. The best example is taxis, in which the essential skill—driving—is one that almost everybody has. More commonly, the required skills do not involve high levels of specialization and can be learned through informal, on-the-job training and developed through work experience.

Consequently, the crucial factor is whether the would-be entrepreneur can pick up the needed business know-how while still an employee. One case in point is the rehabilitation-and-renovations sector in construction: Not only are jobs smaller in size, but fewer master construction skills are needed, making on-the-job training easier to obtain. A similar situation applies in another province of immigrant businesses—restaurants—where the hierarchy of skills ranges from dishwashers at the bottom to cooks at the top. Although one way of going to the top in this industry is going to a culinary school, a newcomer can also move up through observation and learning by doing: today, a dishwasher, tomorrow a sandwich man; eventually, a cook.

Access to Ownership

Given the existence of markets conducive to small business, the would-be immigrant entrepreneur still needs access to ownership opportunities. Immigrants' access to ownership positions largely depends on two factors: (1) the number of vacant business-ownership positions, and the extent to which natives are vying for those slots, and (2) government policies toward immigrants.

Business Vacancies

In the immigrant-receiving countries of the late nineteenth and early twentieth centuries, rapid economic growth created new industries, allowing immigrants to take up business activities without substantial competition from, or displacement of, natives. As we show elsewhere in the book from which this article comes, the clothing industry offers the classic illustration of this process: Because the influx of Jewish immigrants to Paris, London, and New York coincided with a burgeoning demand for factory-made clothes from the 1880s on, immigrants could move into newly emerging small business positions. In the late twentieth century, however, economic growth is proceeding more slowly; there are relatively fewer opportunities for the self-employed, even though the ranks of those working on their own account have generally increased during the past 10 to 15 years. Under these conditions, ownership opportunities for immigrants are principally determined by the supply of native entrepreneurs. Should the supply of native owners for a small business industry dwindle, immigrants may take over as replacement owners.

At the neighborhood level, replacement opportunities for immigrant owners selling to their coethnic neighbors emerge as a result of ecological succession (Aldrich and Reiss 1976). As the native group in a residential area no longer replaces itself, native entrepreneurs seek out business opportunities outside the local area. Given a naturally high rate of failure among all small businesses, the absence of members from the older established group willing to open up new firms in "changed" neighborhoods creates vacancies for potential immigrant business people.

In the general economy, the crucial factor is that the petite bourgeoisie often does not reproduce itself, but survives through the recruitment of owners from lower social classes (Bechhofer and Elliot 1981). To some extent, it is the very marginality of the small business position that discourages heirs from taking up their parents' modest enterprises. As Berteaux and Berteaux-Wiame (1981: 166) write about artisanal bakers in France:

If the baker's trade was still a good trade, as it was for centuries, the sons of bakers would have chosen this profession and one of them would be ready to take over his parent's business. . . . But the baker's trade is not what it used to be. . . . So most bakers orient their sons away from the trade. . . . So when the time for retirement comes, they do not find any baker's child to take over the business; neither their own nor the children of their colleagues.

In the central cities of the United States, where small business has been concentrated among European immigrants and their descendants, the changing social structure of Italian, Jewish, and other European ancestry groups has further diminished the allure of petty enterprise. Assimilation, high levels of educational attainment, and the dwindling of corporate discrimination have lowered the barriers to desirable positions in large organizations. Among groups like Italians or Jews, self-employment tends to be higher among fathers than among sons, and higher among fathers of older cohorts than among their younger counterparts (Goldscheider and Kobrin 1980; Cohen 1983). Similar processes have been observed among the long-established Jewish population in the United Kingdom (Pollins 1984).

A variety of studies note how the growth of replacement demand has altered the ethnic complexion of the small business class. A large proportion of Moroccan storekeepers in Paris have taken over small neighborhood shops from older French owners in areas of relatively low immigrant settlement. Ma Mung and Guillon (1986: 122–123) pointed out that French owners who sold their businesses were "a relatively aged commercial population which had not found a buyer among those French to whom they would have . . . preferred to have sold rather than to 'foreigners.'" Similarly, in New York, Korean grocery store owners have taken over from Jewish or Italian proprietors who were just too old, tired, and scared of crime to keep on minding their stores.

Korean immigrants are able to buy shops from white minority shopkeepers, especially Jews, because the second- or third-generation children of these older immigrants have already entered the mainstream of the American occupational structure, and so they are reluctant to take over their parents' businesses. In fact, experienced Korean shopkeepers have advised less experienced Korean businessmen that "the prospect is very good if you buy a store in a good location from old Jewish people." (Kim, 1981: 111;.

When native groups falter in their recruitment to small business, their share of the small business sector inevitably declines, if for no other reason than the high death rate to which all small businesses are prone. Birch's (1987) studies, for example, have shown that 8% of all firms in U.S. metropolitan areas are lost each year, which means that half of all firms in any area must be replaced every five years for the area simply to break even. For small firms and for new businesses, the failure rates are higher still; indeed, the majority of new businesses do not last longer than four years.

The burgeoning of immigrant business in New York's clothing industry shows how the diverging appeal of small business for immigrants and natives creates a favorable environment for immigrant entrepreneurship by reducing the competition for business positions. Immigrant clothing factories fail at a higher rate than their native-owned counterparts, but the crucial difference is that immigrants set up new businesses at a very high rate. By contrast, there are virtually no natives replacing other natives whose businesses fail. The remaining native proprietors are the aging owners of long-established factories, with little hope for the industry (Waldinger 1986).

Government Policies

Access to ownership is also affected by government policies setting the terms on which immigrants enter and by policies affecting the ease with which businesses can be started. In most societies, new immigrants, because of their terms of entry, are free to settle wherever job opportunities are best. However, governments often attempt to influence where immigrants settle. In the United States, for example, the government tried to spread Cuban and Vietnamese refugees across the country. The policy failed for Cubans, as they recongregated back in the Miami area. In England, the government tried to direct the flow of Asian refugees from Uganda in the early 1970s, again with little long-term success. In Germany, the government initially treated Turkish workers as only temporary residents, making it difficult for them to bring their families with them. Nonetheless, families did reconstitute in German cities, creating markets for ethnic goods and services.

National and local governments vary in the extent to which they set restrictive conditions on which businesses can be started. In the Netherlands, for example, in some trades licenses are required and prospective entrepreneurs must show that there is a "need" for their business. In Germany, the legal right to open a business is contingent upon obtaining a residence permit, which is awarded after many years of labor migrant status. Formal requirements for starting craft and trade firms in various sectors were liberalized in the 1980s, making it easier for immigrants to open businesses.

Group Characteristics

Thus far, we have discussed two opportunity-structure conditions for the development of immigrant business: a niche in which the small business can viably function and access to ownership positions. But if there is a demand for small business activities, why do immigrants tend to emerge as the replacement group? We hypothesize that some immigrants are predisposed toward business and that they can also draw on informal ethnic resources that give them a competitive edge. We emphasize the fit between immigrant firms and the environments in which they function, including not only economic and social conditions but also the unique historical conditions encountered at the time of immigration.

Predisposing Factors

The reasons that immigrants emerge as a replacement group rest on a complex of interacting economic, social, and psychological factors. Blocked mobility is a powerful spur to business activity. Immigrants suffer from a variety of impediments in the labor market: unfamiliarity with the language of the host country, inadequate or inappropriate skills, age, and discrimination. Lacking the same opportunities for stable career employment as natives, immigrants are more likely to strike out on their own and to experience less aversion to the substantial risks that this course entails.

Immigrants' limited range of job- and income-generating activities also spurs them to acquire business skills. Native workers will tend not to acquire particular skills if the returns to the needed investment in education and training are lower than those for comparable jobs. By contrast, the same skills might offer immigrants the best return, precisely because they lack access to better remunerated jobs (Bailey 1987). Immigrants' willingness to put in long hours—needed to generate working capital or to maintain economies of scale—is similarly conditioned. For those without access to jobs with high rates of hourly return, such activities as driving a cab or running a store from early morning to late night offer the best available rewards for their work effort.

There are also psychological components to the entry of immigrants into small business. Much of the sociological literature has characterized the small business owner as an anachronistic type impelled by a need for autonomy and independence (Mills 1958). Auster and Aldrich (1984) noted that this approach assumes that entrepreneurship reflects the decisions of isolated individuals and thus ignores the issue of why certain groups disproportionately channel new recruits into small business.

The traditional perspective also fails to account for the social pressures that conditions groups and individuals for small business activity, including immigration itself. The process of leaving one's home to take up life in a new society is self-selective: The workers who enter the immigration stream tend to be more able, better prepared, and more inclined toward risk than those who stay home. These same characteristics also give immigrants an advantage in competition with native groups in the low-wage labor market, against whom they compare favorably in terms of motivation, risk propensity, and an ability to adjust to change (Chiswick 1978). Immigrants are also more satisfied than native-born workers with low profits from small business because of wage differences between their origin and destination countries (Light 1984).

Immigrants' social origins also alter the way they perceive the chances of getting ahead, because they have a more favorable view of low-level work than do natives. Immigrants perceive their jobs' status, as well as economic rewards, in terms of the much different job hierarchies of their home societies (Piore 1979). Quite the same disparity would give the immigrant a distinctive frame of reference from which to assess the attractiveness of small business opportunities that open up as previously incumbent groups move on to other pursuits. A young native aspiring to work as a manager behind the desk in a clean, air-conditioned bank might well look askance at the idea of taking over the neighborhood grocery store or small local factory that becomes vacant when an aging owner retires. By contrast, in a newcomer's eyes, taking over a petty proprietorship is likely to be a positive alternative to working for someone else, as well as the best chance of getting ahead. Immigrants in general and sojourners in particular are more concerned with economic mobility than with social status.

Resource Mobilization

Resource mobilization is intimately bound up with the dynamics of ethnic identity, and, therefore, we present our conceptualization of ethnicity before turning to the routes through which resources are acquired.

Roger Waldinger, et al.

Conceptualization of Ethnicity

Ethnic is an adjective that refers to differences between categories of people (Peterson 1980). By contrast, when it is linked to the noun *group*, it implies that members have some awareness of group membership. In the book from which this article comes, we begin with the assumption that what is "ethnic" about "ethnic business" may be no more than a set of connections and regular patterns of interaction among people sharing common national background or migration experiences. Consequently, our concern here begins with the subcultural dimension of ethnicity—that is to say, the social structures through which members of an ethnic group are attached to one another and the ways in which those social structures are used. These social structures consist, broadly speaking, of two parts: (1) the networks of kinship and friendship around which ethnic communities are arranged (Zimmer and Aldrich 1987) and (2) the interlacing of these networks with positions in the economy (jobs), in space (housing), and in civil society (institutions).

From our perspective, ethnicity—that is, self-identification with a particular ethnic group—is neither primordial nor imported prior to contact with a host society. Rather, ethnicity is a *possible* outcome of the patterns by which intra- and intergroup interactions are structured. Our central contention is that ethnicity is acquired when the social connections among ethnic group members help establish distinct occupational industrial, or spatial concentrations. Once established, these concentrations promote frequent and intensive face-to-face interactions that breed a sense of commonality and identification with members of the same ethnic group. Ethnic concentrations may also give rise to common ethnic interests, reinforcing a sense of identity. In addition, industrial or business concentrations foster competitive cross-ethnic contact, which in turn promotes ethnic consciousness and solidarity.

Our conceptualization implies that the emergence of ethnic communities and networks may generate the infrastructure and resources for ethnic small businesses *before* a sense of group awareness develops. Once in place, an ethnic business niche may give rise to, or strengthen, group consciousness. Ethnic entrepreneurs, as we note elsewhere in the book from which this article comes, may find themselves in conflict with other ethnic groups or with state officials. As a group's level of self-employment rises, the protection and growth of the ethnic business niche may come to define the group's interests and, therefore, the meaning of ethnicity.

Close Ties Between Coethnics

Information about the host society (accurate or misleading) is transmitted through communication or personal interaction between migrants and their home communities, and the picture portrayed by the migrant prompts other natives to take their chances abroad. A similar chain of events conditions the process of settlement: Once arrived in the new society, who does one turn to but those friends or relatives already situated with a home and a job? To be sure, home and job are not quite as glittering as the newcomers had imagined or the settler had promised. The new arrivals frequently secure jobs where many, or even most, of the workers are immigrants as well.

Because of a preference for familiarity, the efficiency of personal contacts, and social distance from the host society's institutions of assistance, immigrants rely on connections with settlers to find shelter and work and thus find themselves in the ethnic occupation-and-residential ghetto. Should this process repeat itself time and again, two consequences ensue. First, intense interaction within a common milieu intensifies the feeling of commonality and membership with the group. Second, there is the buildup of that critical mass needed for formal ethnic institutions—a church, a mutual aid society, perhaps a trade union, maybe a political club—which in turn serve to reinforce ethnic identity.

Thus far, this is a familiar, though greatly simplified, story; however, we will use it to extract several less familiar lessons. The first is that immigrants may be vulnerable and oppressed, but, because they can draw on connections of mutuality and support, they can also create resources that offset the harshness of the environment they encounter. The second is that the social structures of the immigrant community breed organizations, both informal and formal, in a context that might otherwise tend toward anomie. The third lesson, of particular importance to the discussion that follows, is that such informal organizational resources might give immigrants an advantage against natives should the institutionalized arrangements that normally connect individuals with organizations be undeveloped and/or malfunctioning.

Ethnic Social Networks

Because entrepreneurs need to mobilize scarce and, therefore, valued resources, activating strong ties to kin and coethnics is important in the formation and maintenance of immigrant firms, as we shall discuss at greater length elsewhere in the book from which this article comes. Strong ties are likely to be particularly important to immigrant business owners, who start out with few resources and lack access to mainstream sources of credit or technical assistance. Such ties are embedded in the migration experience: The immigration process selects immigrants who are integrated into kinship networks, and the tendency of immigrants to move under the auspices of settlers and their subsequent interdependence for information and support fosters a reciprocal flow of exchanges. Of course, the characteristics of the migration process are likely to affect the closeness and density of ties within immigrant communities. Migration streams characterized by circular movements, frequent return migrations, or a preponderance of single individuals are less likely to support closely tied networks than those in which households move on a permanent basis. Closely tied networks are likely to unravel over time because settlement makes migrants less dependent on one another and may also give them the skills needed to enter mainstream institutions (Bailey 1987; Portes 1987).

The very process of entry into a new society, in which newcomers both occupy distinct positions and find themselves in conflict with natives, hastens ethnic group formation (Olzak 1983). Conditions that raise the salience of group boundaries and identity, leading persons to form new social ties and action-sets, increase the likelihood of entrepreneurial attempts and raise the probability of success (Aldrich and Zimmer 1986). The more deeply entrepreneurs are embedded within their networks of kin or coethnics, the more salient ethnic group boundaries will be. Therefore, it is more likely that immigrants will engage in the receipt and transmittal of business support and information with other coethnics. Moreover, the circumstances of migration spur the conscious widening of connections within the ethnic community. Even among communities made up of permanent immigrants, home-country familial networks are unlikely to be transplanted fully. Precisely because connections to kin are truncated, nonkin ties must be cultivated for social and economic support (Lessinger 1985).

Such closely tied social networks provide the confidentiality and social control required for the types of informal credit-raising mechanisms that Ivan Light and other subsequent analysts have identified for Japanese, West Indians, Jews, Koreans, Chinese, Tunisians, and others (Boubakri 1985; Guillon and Taboada-Leonetti 1986; Light 1972, 1980; Tenenbaum 1986). Other groups have managed to leap over capital barriers without access to rotating credit associations or their analogues. However, informal ties to other coethnics with capital have a strong impact on the ability to gain start-up capital, as Portes (1987) has shown for the Cubans.

In addition to capital, owners also need to rely on trusted acquaintances to obtain reliable information about permits, laws, available business sites, management practices, and reliable suppliers. Relatives or friends with business experience are likely to be a source of good and low-cost information. Where such ties do not flow from a home-society context, they can be created after migration, as in the case of Koreans in New York who attend churches because "they are looking for jobs or job information, want to obtain business information, make business contacts, conduct business negotiations, or seek private loans" (Kim 1987).

Partners are also to be secured through contacts with coethnics. Partnership is a crucial ingredient, allowing immigrant owners to pool capital, reduce the need for outside labor, and maintain outside wage-earning activities, thereby reducing risk. Informal networks within an ethnic community also enable entrepreneurs to connect with persons in higher positions. Immigrants excluded from the formal credit system may develop close ties to higher-status members of an ethnic community and thereby secure loans or money partners. Professionals within the ethnic community provide a wide variety of valued services (Ladbury 1984).

Labor recruitment. Small business industries such as clothing, restaurants, construction, or retail are the environments in which new immigrant businesses have sprung up. In these industries, size of establishments and competitive conditions constrain the development of internal labor markets. Firms turn to the external market to secure a labor force and, consequently, the factors that influence employment and training characteristics are generated outside the firm (Granovetter and Tilly 1988).

The central issue confronting small firms is how to increase the probability of hiring workers who are capable of learning required skills and who will remain with the firm and apply their skills there. "Hiring," as Spence (1974: 2–3) has put it, "is investing under uncertainty." Employers are uncertain about the productive capabilities of job applicants prior to hiring and even for some time after the hiring decision has been made. In many cases, native workers have dropped out of the labor supply in which immigrants are concentrated (see Waldinger and Lapp 1988 for an example). Native employers, therefore, have little choice but to recruit immigrants, and this dependence causes special problems in stabilizing the employment relationship.

Trust may be low due to stereotyping of immigrant labor; in addition, situational constraints may provide little room for trust to develop. For example, high turnover—which may arise because of seasonality, frequent travel to home societies, or return migration—will hinder the development of stable relationships on which trust might be based. A firm with high turnover is also apt to be caught in a vicious circle, because the costs of constantly hiring make it uneconomical to exercise much discretion over the recruitment process.

Whereas native employers confront a shortage of native workers, immigrant employers usually have no such problem. They recruit an attached labor force by mobilizing direct connections to the ethnic community from which they emigrated. One means of securing a labor force is to recruit family members. Because the characteristics of kin, unlike those of strangers, are known and familiar, their behavior is likely to be predictable, if not reliable. Furthermore, trust may already inhere in the family relationship.

Newcomers turn to settlers for help in job finding and may first seek out employment in an immigrant firm where they can work in a familiar environment with others who know their language. Newcomers' dependence on their bosses/patrons makes them likely to accept conditions that may fall below standard; it is also the case that owners will be more likely to place trust in workers who depend on them.

Native-and immigrant-owned firms further differ in their handling of internal strains. Where management and labor are ethnically distinct, social distance tends to preclude managerial acceptance of informal shop-floor norms. Repeated conflict over production quotas, behavioral rules, absenteeism, and instability tends to take on an explicitly racial character as management interprets workers' behavior in racially stereotyped ways. When immigrant or minority workers are employed by members of the majority group, the economic disparities between the two groups fuel discontent with wages, personnel policies, and general working conditions, making work just another instance of inequitable treatment (Waldinger 1986).

In immigrant firms, however, ethnicity provides a common ground on which the rules of the workplace are negotiated. The social structures around which the immigrant firm is organized help stabilize the employment relationship; they are also relationships of meaning suffused with expectations that actors have of one another. One consequence is that authority can be secured on the basis of personal loyalties and ethnic allegiance rather than on the basis of harsh discipline, driving, and direct-control techniques. Furthermore, ethnic commonality provides a repertoire of symbols and customs that can be invoked to underline cultural interests and similarities in the face of a potentially conflict-laden situation (Wong 1987).

If ethnic commonality is a device for securing the immigrant worker's loyalty, the expectations bound up in the ethnic employment exchange impinge on the owner's latitude as well. Immigrant workers can anticipate that the standards of conduct prevailing in the broader ethnic community will extend to the workplace as well (see, for example, Herman 1979). The immigrant firm is also likely to offer an environment where the worker is sheltered from some of the rules and regulations of the host society: a place where hours are not carefully watched, wages are paid in cash or under the table, and machinery is used for personal needs (Gold 1985). Similarly, the terms under which immigrant owners obtain kin or hometown friends as laborers may include an understanding that the employment relationship is meant to be reciprocal (Ladbury 1984). In return for the immigrant worker's effort and constancy, the immigrant owner may be expected to make a place for newly arrived relatives, to help out with financial problems, or even to provide a loan needed for starting up a new business.

Ascribed ties, such as ethnic commonality, may also make relations between businesses more effective. The cost of transactions between firms is likely to be lower when they have a basis of trusting each other and can thus work more effectively together. Owners in ethnic business communities may be involved in such regular cooperative activities with suppliers, subcontractors and customers, thus justifying the label "custom of cooperation" (Dei Ottati 1986). These may be business/residential communities that are ethnically very distinct, such as, for example, Pakistanis living in a particular urban district in Britain or village/small town communities in which the "industrial district" consists largely of families with recent background in agriculture. In each case, the "custom of cooperation" is underpinned by a range of sanctions, positive and negative, that structure village life, with the prospect that firms that betray trust lose further orders as word of their opportunistic behavior spreads.

Government Policies

Governments vary substantially in the level of economic assistance they provide to immigrants and ethnic minorities. In the United States, minority businesses were ignored by the federal government until the 1960s, when the civil rights movement, civil disorders, and other political conditions coalesced into support for "black capitalism." Minority set-aside provisions were introduced into government contracting procedures, and special minority enterprise investment programs were created. The amount of money allocated was never very large, but the effort was a politically significant symbol of minority business's importance in American society. The long-term economic significance of these programs was small, and little concrete evidence of their consequences could be found in the 1980s.

The British government's interest in minority business was also heightened by widespread civil unrest, which occurred in 1981. Subsequent investigations showed that few government measures had specifically targeted minority businesses, but since 1986, the central government has taken some steps to reach minorities in England's largest cities. Most programs directed to ethnic businesses, however, have been implemented by local authorities.

West Germany, the Netherlands, France, and most other European countries have no funding programs directed primarily at immigrant businesses. If ethnic minorities and immigrants do benefit, they do so as part of the small business constituency, not as members of an ethnic minority.

Differences Among Ethnic and Immigrant Groups

Why do some ethnic and immigrant groups do better in business than others? The historical record shows considerable disparities in self-employment among the various European immigrant and Afro-American populations in the United States and the various immigrant groups in Europe. Jews, for example, were far more successful in business in the United States than were the Irish, and Italians achieved higher rates of self-employment than did the Poles. Similar differences hold for the newcomers who arrived in the United States between 1970 and 1980. According to the *Census of Population*, Koreans ranked first, with 11.5% self-employed; lagging far behind were the Mexicans, among whom less than 2% worked for themselves. In the United Kingdom, South Asians (Indians and Pakistanis) have recently achieved rates of self-employment much higher than the native population, whereas West Indians are underrepresented in self-employment (Ward 1987). In France, Moroccans, Tunisians, and Chinese have high levels of business activity, whereas immigrants from Spain and Portugal are rarely involved in business ventures (Ma Mung and Guillon 1986; Guillon and Taboada-Leonetti 1986).

Various explanations have been proposed for these differences. We believe the most useful approach is multivariate, which implies that the terms of the interaction among the various factors are indeterminate. What we can do at an analytic level is to specify the variables that affect self-employment outcomes; it remains for empirical work to determine their effects on a case-by-case basis, and we will report on some research findings in the following chapters.

We can separate the conditions that influence the self-employment process into three categories: (1) premigration characteristics, (2) the circumstances of migration and their evolution, and (3) postmigration characteristics. First, premigration attributes include skill, language, business experiences, kinship patterns, and exposure to conditions (such as a high level of urbanization and industrialization) that would foster entrepreneurial attitudes. Second, the circumstances of migration are the conditions under which the immigrants move, whether as temporary workers or as permanent settlers, as well as the factors influencing their settlement type. Third, characteristics such as economic and occupational position and discrimination (or the lack thereof) would fall under the postmigration rubric. Our discussion implies that no single characteristic—whether premigration or postmigration experience or circumstance of migration—will in and of itself determine the level of self-employment; rather, the critical factor will be how these various characteristics interact with one another and with the local opportunity structure.

Premigration Characteristics

The likelihood of succeeding in business is enhanced if immigrants come with skills that are useful to business success in both general and specific ways. A good historical illustration is the case of turn-of-the-century Russian Jews who, by virtue of prior experience in tailoring, a high level of literacy, and a historical orientation toward trading, moved rapidly into entrepreneurial positions in the garment industry in the United States. The educational level of recent immigrants to the United States today is much higher than was true for the earlier immigrant waves, and thus a considerable proportion arrive with general skills that are relevant for business success. But among U.S. immigrants there appears to be only a weak correlation between education and self-employment. It is not the immigrants with the highest or most developed general skills that flock to business; rather, it is those whose general skills are not quite appropriate to the new context.

Relatively fewer immigrants arrive with skills that are specific to the business fields they enter. For example, New York's fur industry contains a high proportion of Greeks, both as workers and as owners, almost all of whom have come from the province of Kastoria, where they were apprenticed as furriers at a relatively young age. Yet the bulk of Greeks in business are active in the restaurant industry, and cooking is not a skill that most Greek males appear to have brought with them, especially when one considers that Greek restaurants mainly specialize in "American food." Thus the crucial issue is how skills are acquired upon arrival in the host society. One answer, which follows from our discussion of ethnicity as organizational resource, is that groups with strong informal networks will do better in transmitting skills to newcomers. However, it is also true that these informal networks are important because of the conditions in small business industries; hence, for all groups, positional factors will be an important influence on self-employment rates.

Occupational training is not the only skill affecting immigrants' chances. Social and cultural differences also affect the job opportunities available, especially language skills. College-educated Koreans, for example, often confront a language barrier in the United States that hampers their chances of employment, especially in jobs requiring higher education and contact with the public (Min 1984).

Circumstances of Migration

Whether newcomers arrive as temporary migrants or as permanent settlers, migration scholars increasingly agree, is a crucial condition of mobility and integration into the host society. Piore (1979) argued that most labor migrations to industrial societies begin as movements of temporary workers. Because workers see themselves as temporary migrants, they constitute a satisfactory work force for dead-end jobs that native workers reject: As long as the migrants maintain the expectation of return to the home country, their concern is with the accumulation of capital to be brought home and invested in a business or farm, not with the attainment of social mobility in the societies to which they have migrated. Even though Piore focused mostly on access to structured job ladders of large organizations, rather than the attainment of business ownership, his argument suggests a framework of evaluating how the circumstances of migration will affect entrepreneurial success.

Whether conditions are perceived as opportunities or obstacles to mobility depends upon the eye of the beholder. The same factors that condition temporary migrants for work in low-level, dead-end jobs will also dampen the frustration that spurs other immigrants to start up in business on their own. As long as migrants anticipate returning home, as long as their stint in the host society is punctuated by periodic trips home, as long as they evaluate success in terms of their original standard of living, they will continue to furnish a supply of low-level labor. But those same low-level jobs will be unacceptable to permanent settlers whose ambitions extend to the positions occupied by natives as well as to the rewards generated by those positions. Consequently, blocked mobility will impinge more severely on settlers than on their counterparts among the birds of passage.

Permanence is also likely to add an edge to the settler's quest for opportunity: If one does not succeed, there is no going back. It is for these reasons that permanent immigrants have a reputation for being more self-assertive than temporary migrant groups. Thus the circumstances of migration breed an affinity with the requirements of entrepreneurial success: Only the driven immigrant will be foolish or desperate enough to start up a business when anyone can observe how many new concerns fall victim to a quick but painful death.

In addition to influencing aspirations, the circumstances of migration are also likely to affect immigrants' behavior in a way that will condition the likelihood of setting up on their own. One characteristic of temporary migrants is that their settlement and work patterns are too haphazard and variable to promote the acquisition of needed business skills and are also disruptive of the informal networks that play such an important role in organizing the immigrant firm and its labor force. By contrast, we can expect permanent immigrants to be more deliberate in their quest for economic progress. For example, P. Young (1983) described the foresight and planning with which Korean greengrocers in New York pursue their trade—they may spend months scouring the city for the best possible location, and often deliberately open stores next to supermarkets so as to capture part of the latter's walk-in trade.

The alternative to this argument is the possibility that immigrants who move as sojourners—with a clear intention of returning home—will opt for business over employment as the better way of rapidly accumulating portable investment capital (Bonacich 1973). There are two major problems with this hypothesis. One is that setting up a business is a more risky endeavor than working for someone else. If we assume that even the most entrepreneurial of sojourning immigrants begin as employees, it is likely that they will accumulate a nest egg that can be either safely banked for returning home or invested in a small business whose chance for success is always open to doubt. Faced with these options, the prudent sojourner is likely to keep on working for someone else, as Ward (1984) has shown in a study of East Asian immigrants in Britain.

Though Bonacich (1973) has argued that these East Asian immigrants illustrate the influence of sojourning on ethnic business activity, Ward's study shows that they are in fact more likely to prefer employment over business in areas where high wages are paid to those prepared to undertake hard and unpleasant work, resorting to business only in those cities where the available jobs are relatively poorly paid. Moreover, Aldrich (1977) found that a sojourning orientation made no difference in the business practices of Asians in London, as owners who intended to return to their native lands used the same competitive business practices as those who had no intention of returning. Aldrich et al. (1983) replicated this finding on another sample of Asian business owners in three English cities.

Another condition of immigrant business activity is settlement pattern. Permanent immigrants usually either come with family or import immediate relatives shortly after settling; temporary immigrants leave family members at home. The consequence for temporary immigrants is that they must continue to funnel remittances that are needed to support relatives still living in the home country rather than use those monies to start up a business. Kessner (1977: 167) pointed out in his comparison of Italian and Jewish immigrants at the turn of the century that "the large sums of money sent back over the ocean to Europe drained [the Italians of] risk capital [for] investment and enterprise." Also, if family members do not migrate with the sojourner, then they will not be available as a source of cheap labor for a small business.

Postmigration Characteristics

Another factor that will exercise a strong effect on self-employment outcomes is a group's position in the economy. This factor follows from the argument made about opportunity structures, namely, that certain environments are more supportive of small businesses than others. The likelihood that immigrants will take advantage of supportive conditions is greatest if immigrants are already concentrated in those industries where small business is the prevailing form.

First, the motivation to go into business presupposes other conditions; for example, having some information about business opportunities that in turn can be used to assess the likelihood that one's efforts will be rewarded. Second, neophyte capitalists will do better if they have some knowledge of the activities that the new role of ownership will entail. Such knowledge is usually better if it is obtained firsthand rather than through indirect methods. One characteristic of environments supportive of small business is precisely that the know-how needed to run a business can be acquired through on-the-job training. Thus immigrant groups concentrated in small business industries will have access to more and better information about small business opportunities and will also have more opportunities to acquire the relevant skills than those groups concentrated in industries where small businesses are not prevalent.

Emphasizing position, however, begs the question of why groups occupy one position and not another. To some extent, this is a matter of prior skill; to some extent, purely random factors come into play, such as arriving at a time or place where small business industries generate a demand for immigrant labor. One important influence is the degree of native-language facility, and looking at the effects of language provides a good illustration of how pre-and postmigration experiences interact to affect self-employment outcomes. Immigrants who arrive in the United States with English-language facility have a broader range of employment opportunities than do those newcomers whose English is virtually nonexistent or barely serviceable. Having a broader range of opportunities, immigrants facile in English are more likely to find employment in industries where the organizational form tends to be large.

Even within a small business industry, some occupations are more strategic than others in terms of providing an employee with exposure to the skills and contacts needed to start up a small business. In the garment industry, for example, the typical new manufacturing business is set up when a salesman and a textile cutter get together: The salesman has the necessary knowledge of the market, and the cutter knows the production side. In restaurants, waiting tables is the logical occupational bridge to becoming a restaurateur: The waiter learns how to size up the customer, direct him or her to the appropriate choice, and then hustle the customer off when a new patron is ready to take the table. In retailing, selling is also the point of departure for many employees who decide to start up on their own.

For prospective immigrant capitalists, the question is how to gain access to these strategic occupations. This problem is particularly serious because many of these occupations involve face-to-face interaction, in which case natives' desire to maximize social distance from immigrants will obstruct the latter's recruitment into these key positions. What is at work is an instance of the principle of cumulative social advantage: Immigrants belonging to a group whose characteristics favour business success will also be more likely to be hired by coethnics and thereby gain access to needed business skills. By contrast, those immigrants whose characteristics are less conducive to entrepreneurship will be more likely to work for natives, which in turn will reduce the likelihood of their gaining access to strategic occupations.

Ethnic Strategies

Ethnic strategies emerge from the adaptations ethnic entrepreneurs make to the resources available to them, building on the characteristics of their groups. As we explore at length elsewhere in the book from which this article comes, ethnic business owners commonly confront seven problems in founding and operating their businesses: (1) acquiring the *information* needed for the establishment and survival of their firms; (2) obtaining the *capital* needed to establish or to expand their business; (3) acquiring the *training and skills* needed to run a small business; (4) recruiting and managing efficient, honest, and cheap *workers*; (5) managing relations with *customers* and *suppliers*; (6) surviving strenuous business *competition*; and (7) protecting themselves from *political attacks*.

Information is typically obtained through owners' personal networks and via various indirect ties that are specifically linked to their ethnic communities. The structures of such networks differ, depending upon the characteristics of the group. Some groups have very hierarchically organized families and a clear sense of family loyalty and obligation, whereas others have more diffusely organized families. Ritualized occasions and large-scale ceremonies also provide opportunities for acquiring information, and some groups have specialized associations and media that disseminate information.

Most entrepreneurs, immigrant or not, raise the bulk of their capital from personal savings. After this primary source, some arrange loans within their communities through institutions such as rotating credit associations. Norms about borrowing from family and friends differ widely across groups, as we show elsewhere in the book from which this article comes.

Training and skills are typically acquired on the job, often while the potential owner is an employee in a coethnic or family member's business. Ties within the ethnic economy widen workers' contacts, increasing the probability of their moving up through a variety of jobs and firms in which skills are acquired.

Family and coethnic labor is critical to most ethnic small businesses. Such labor is largely unpaid. And kin and coethnics work long hours in the service of their employers. Ethnic entrepreneurs manipulate family perseverance and loyalty to their own advantage, but they also incur obligations in doing so.

Customers and clients play a central role in owners' strategies, as building a loyal following is a way of offsetting the high level of uncertainty facing ethnic small businesses. Some owners provide special services, extend credit, and go out of their way to deliver individual services to customers. Often, however, providing special services to coethnics causes trouble for owners, who then are faced with special pleading to take lower profits for their efforts.

The intense competition generated in the niches occupied by ethnic businesses is dealt with in at four ways: through (1) self-exploitation, (2) expanding the business by moving forward or backward in the chain of production or by opening other shops, (3) founding and supporting ethnic trading associations, and (4) cementing alliances to other families through marriage. We discuss these more extensively elsewhere in the book from which this article comes.

Finally, ethnic entrepreneurs often need protection from government officials as well as from rival owners outside their ethnic communities. Government is dealt with in much the same way that businesses always have: bribery, paying penalties, searching for loopholes, and organizing protests.

Ethnic strategies, then, reflect both the opportunity structure within which ethnic businesses operate *and* the particular characteristics of the owner's group. Accordingly, we have placed ethnic strategies of the owner's group. According, we have placed ethnic strategies at the center of Figure 15.1, emphasizing their emergent character. As we discuss elsewhere in the book from which this article comes, the strategies adopted by the various groups we have studied are remarkably similar.

....

Conclusions

This chapter has developed an explanation for immigrant enterprise that emphasizes the interaction between the opportunity structure of the host society and the group characteristics and social structure of the immigrant community. The demand for small business activities emanates from markets whose small size, heterogeneity, or susceptibility to flux and instability limit the potential for mass distribution and mass production. Because such conditions favor small-scale enterprise, they lower the entry barriers to immigrants with limited capital and technical resources. Opportunities for ownership result from the process of ethnic succession: Vacancies for new business owners arise as the older groups that have previously dominated small business activities move into higher social positions.

As for group characteristics, two factors promote recruitment into entrepreneurial positions. First, the situational constraints that immigrants confront sometimes breed a predisposition toward small business and further encourage immigrants to engage in activities—such as working long hours—that are needed to gain minimal efficiencies. Some ethnic groups have cultural norms that create a set of understandings about appropriate behavior and expectations within work settings. Second, resource mobilization is facilitated if immigrant firms can resolve problems by drawing on their connections with a supply of family and ethnic labor. While these factors lift the self-employment rate of the overall immigrant population, levels of business activity vary among specific immigrant groups. A group's success in attaining business ownership is determined by three characteristics—its premigration experiences, the circumstances of its migration and settlement, and its postmigration experiences—and how these characteristics interact with one another and with the local opportunity structure.

References

Aldrich, Howard. (1977). "Testing the Middleman Minority Model of Asian Entrepreneurial Behavior: Preliminary Results from Wandsworth, England." Paper presented at the annual meetings of American Sociological Association, Chicago.

Aldrich, Howard, John Cater, Trevor Jones, and David McEvoy. (1983). "From Periphery to Peripheral: The South Asian Petite Bourgeoisie in England." pp. 1–32 in Ida Harper Simpson and Richard Simpson (eds.), *Research in the Sociology of Work*. Vol. 2. Greenwich, CT: JAI.

Aldrich, Howard, John Cater, Trevor Jones, David McEvoy, and Paul Velleman. (1985). "Ethnic Residential Concentration and the Protected Market Hypothesis." *Social Forces* 63 (4, June): 996–1009.

Aldrich, Howard and Abert J. Reiss, Jr. (1976). "Continuities in the Study of Ecological Succession: Changes in the Race Composition of Neighborhoods and Their Businesses." *American Journal of Sociology* 81 (4, January): 846–866.

Aldrich, Howard and Catherine Zimmer. (1986). "Entrepreneurship Through Social Networks." pp. 3–23 in Donald Sexton and Raymond Smilor (eds.), *The Art and Science of Entrepreneurship*. Cambridge, MA: Ballinger.

Auster, Ellen and Howard Aldrich. (1984). "Small Business Vulnerability, Ethnic Enclaves, and Ethnic Enterprises." pp. 39–54 in Robin Ward and R. Jenkins (eds.), *Ethnic Communities in Business: Strategies for Economic Survival*. Cambridge: Cambridge University Press.

Bailey, Thomas R. (1987). *Immigrant and Native Workers: Contrasts and Competition*. Boulder, CO: Westview.

Bechhofer, Frank and Brian Elliot, eds. (1981). *The Petite Bourgeoisie: Comparative Studies of the Uneasy Stratum*. London: Macmillan.

Berteaux, Daniel and Isabelle Berteaux-Wiame. (1981). "Artisanal Bakery in France: How It Lives and Why It Survives." pp. 155–181 in Frank Bechhofer and Brian Elliot (eds.), *The Petite Bourgeoisie: Comparative Studies of an Uneasy Stratum*. London: Macmillan.

Birch, David. (1987). *Job Creation in America: How Our Smallest Companies Put the Most People to Work*. New York: Free Press.

Blaschke, Jochen and Ahmet Ersoz. (1986). "The Turkish Economy in West Berlin." *International Small Business Journal* 4 (3, Spring): 38–45.

Bonacich, Edna. (1973). "A Theory of Middleman Minorities." *American Sociological Review* 38 (5, October): 583–594.

Boubakri, Hassan. (1985). "Mode de gestion et reinvestissements chez les commerçants tunisiens à Paris." *Revue Européene des Migrations Internationales* 1(1): 49–66.

Chiswick, Barry. (1978). *Human Resources and Income Distribution: Issues and Policies*. New York: Norton.

Cohen, Steven. (1983). *American Modernity and Jewish Identity*. New York: Tavistock.

Dei Ottati, Gabi. (1986). "Distretto industriale, problemi delle transazioni e mercato communitario: prime considerazioni." *Economia e Politica Industriale* 51: 93–121.

Department of Employment. (1988). "Ethnic Origins and the Labour Market." *Employment Gazette* (March): 164–177.

Gold, Steven J. (1985). "Refugee Communities: Soviet Jews and Vietnamese in the San Francisco Bay Area." Ph.D. dissertation, University of California, Berkeley.

Goldscheider, Calvin and Frances Kobrin. (1980). "Ethnic Continuity and the Process of Self-Employment." *Ethnicity* 7 (3, September): 256–278.

Granovetter, Mark and Charles Tilly. (1988). "Inequality and Labor Processes." pp. 175–222 in Neil J. Smelser (ed.), *Handbook of Sociology*. Newbury Park, CA: Sage.

Greenberg, Jerome, Martin Topol, Elaine Sherman, and Kenneth Cooperman. (1980). "The Itinerant Street Vendor: A Form of Nonstore Retailing." *Journal of Retailing* 56 (2, Summer): 66–80.

Guillon, M. and I. Taboada-Leonetti. (1986). *Le Triangle de Choisy. Un Quartier Chinois à Paris*. Paris: Ciemi L'Harmatan.

Herman, Harry Vjekoslav. (1979). "Dishwashers and Proprietors: Macedonians in Toronto's Restaurant Trade." pp. 71–92 in Sandra Wallman (ed.), *Ethnicity at Work*. London: Macmillan.

Kessner, Thomas. (1977). *The Golden Door: Italian and Jewish Immigrant Mobility in New York City*. New York: Oxford University Press.

Kim, Illsoo. (1981). *The New Urban Immigrants: The Korean Community in New York*. Princeton, NJ: Princeton University Press.

Kim, Illsoo, (1987). "The Koreans: Small Business in an Urban Frontier." pp. 219–242 in Nancy Foner (ed.), *New Immigrants in New York City*. New York: Columbia University Press.

Krcmar, Karisa. (1984). "Immigrant Retail in Glasgow." M.B.A. thesis, Strathclyde University, Glasgow.

Ladbury, Sarah. (1984). "Choice, Chance, or No Alternative? Turkish Cypriots in Business in London." pp. 105–124 in Robin Ward and Richard Jenkins (eds.), *Ethnic Communities in Business.* Cambridge: Cambridge University Press.

Lessinger, Johanna. (1985). "Painful Intimacy: The Establishment of Trust in Business Partnerships Among New York's Indian Immigrants." Paper presented at the conference, "The Anthropology of Experience, Feeling, and Emotion in South Asia," Houston, December.

Levine, Barry B. (1985). "The Capital of Latin America." *Wilson Quarterly* 9 (5, Winter): 47–69.

Light, Ivan. (1972). *Ethnic Enterprise in America.* Berkeley: University of California Press.

Light, Ivan. (1980). "Asian Enterprise in America." pp. 33–57 in Scott Cummings (ed.), *Self-Help in America.* Pt. Washington, NY: Kennikat.

Light, Ivan. (1984). "Immigrant and Ethnic Enterprise in North America." *Ethnic and Racial Studies* 7 (2, April): 195–216.

Ma Mung, Emmanuel and Michel Guillon. (1986). "Les commerçants étrangers dans l'agglomération Parisienne." *Revue Européene des Migrations Internationales* 2 (3): 105–134.

Mills, C. Wright. (1958). *The Causes of World War Three.* New York: Simon & Schuster.

Min, Pyong Gap. (1984). "A Structural Analysis of Korean Business in the United States." *Ethnic Groups* 6 (1, June): 1–25.

Mohl, Raymond. (1983). "Miami: The Ethnic Cauldron." In Richard M. Bernard and Bradley R. Rice (eds.), *Sunbelt Cities: Politics and Growth Since World War II.* Austin: University of Texas Press.

Morokvasic, Mirjana. (1986). "Recours aux immigrés dans la confection parisienne. Éléments de comparaison avec la ville de Berlin Quest." pp. 199–242 in *La lutte contre les trafics de la main d'oeuvre en 1985–86.* Paris: la Documentation Francaise.

OECD. (1986a). "Employment in Small and Large Firms: Where Have the Jobs Come From?" *Employment Outlook,* pp. 64–83.

OECD. (1986b). "Self Employment in OECD Countries." *Employment Outlook,* pp. 40–66.

Olzak, Susan. (1983). "Contemporary Ethnic Mobilization." *Annual Review of Sociology* 9: 355–374.

Orlick, Anneliese. (1987). "The Soviet Jews: Life in Brighton Beach, Brooklyn." pp. 273–304 in Nancy Foner (ed.), *New Immigrants in New York City.* New York: Columbia University Press.

Palmer, Robin. (1984). "The Rise of the Britalian Culture Entrepreneur." Pp. 89–104 in Robin Ward and Richard Jenkins (eds.), *Ethnic Communities in Business.* Cambridge: Cambridge University Press.

Petersen, William. (1980). "Concepts of Ethnicity." Pp. 234–242 in Stephen Thernstrom (ed.), *Harvard Encyclopedia of American Ethnic Groups.* Cambridge, MA: Harvard University Press.

Piore, Michael J. (1979). *Birds of Passage: Migrant Labour and Industrial Societies.* London: Cambridge University Press.

Piore, Michael J. (1980). "The Technological Foundations of Dualism and Discontinuity." pp. 55–81 in Suzanne Berger and Michael J. Piore (eds.), *Dualism and Discontinuity in Industrial Society.* Cambridge: Cambridge University Press.

Pollins, Harold. (1984). "The Development of Jewish Business in the United Kingdom." Pp. 73–88 in Robin Ward and Richard Jenkins (eds.), *Ethnic Communities in Business.* Cambridge: Cambridge University Press.

Portes, Alejandro. (1987). "The Social Origins of the Cuban Enclave Economy of Miami." *Sociological Perspectives* 30 (4, October): 340–372.

Rieff, David. (1987). *Going to Miami: Exiles, Tourists, and Refugees in the New America.* New York: Penguin.

Russell, Raymond. (1985). *Sharing Ownership in the Workplace.* Albany: State University of New York Press.

Saifullah Khan, Verity, ed. (1979). *Minority Families in Britain: Support and Stress.* London: Macmillan.

Salem, G. (1984). "Les marchands ambulants et le systeme commercial sénégalais en France." In *Marchands ambulants et commerçants étrangers en France et an Allemagne Federale.* Poitiers: University of Poitiers.

Simon, Gildas and Emmanuel Ma Mung. (1987). "La dynamique des commerces maghrebins et asiatiques et les perspectives du marché intérieur européen." Paper presented at the Atelier Cultures Urbaines, Université Lyon 2, December 17–18.

Spence, Michael. (1974). *Market Signalling.* Cambridge, MA: Harvard University Press.

Tenenbaum, Shelley. (1986). "Immigrants and Capital: Jewish Loan Societies in the United States, 1880–1945." *American Jewish History* 76 (1, September): 67–77.

Wacquant, Lois J.D. and William J. Wilson. (1988). "Beyond Welfare Reform: Poverty, Joblessness and the Social Transformation of the Inner City." Paper presented at the Rockefeller Foundation Conference on Welfare Reform.

Waldinger, Roger. (1986). *Through the Eye of the Needle: Immigrants and Enterprise in New York's Garment Trades.* New York: New York University Press.

Waldinger, Roger and Michael Lapp. (1988). "Immigrants and Their Impact on the New York Garment Industry." Washington, DC: U.S. Department of Labor, International Labor Affairs Bureau, Division of Immigration Policy and Research.

Ward, Robin, (1984). "Minority Settlement and the Local Economy." pp. 198–212 in Bryan Roberts, Ruth Finnegan, and Duncan Gallie (eds.), *Approaches to Economic Life: Economic Restructuring, Employment, and the Social Division of Labor.* Manchester: ESRC and Manchester University Press.

Ward, Robin. (1986). "Evaluation of Shopping Centre Improvements Funded Under the Urban Programme in the West Midlands: The Ethnic Dimension." Working Paper no. 8. Birmingham: Aston University, Public Sector Management Research Unit.

Ward, Robin. (1987). "Small Retailers in Inner Urban Areas." pp. 275–287 in Gerry Johnson (ed.), *Business Strategy and Retailing.* New York: John Wiley.

Ward, Robin and Richard Jenkins, eds. (1984). *Ethnic Communities in Business: Strategies for Economic Survival.* Cambridge: Cambridge University Press.

Ward, Robin, Richard Randall, and Karisa Krcmar. (1986). "Small Firms in the Clothing Industry: The Growth of Minority Enterprise." *International Small Business Journal* 4 (3): 46–56.

Wong, Bernard. (1987). "New Immigrants in New York's Chinatown." pp. 243–272 in Nancy Foner (ed.), *New Immigrants in New York.* New York: Columbia University.

Young, Philip K.Y. (1983). "Family Labor, Sacrifice, and Competition: Korean Greengrocers in New York City." *Amerasia* 10: 53–71.

Zimmer, Catherine and Howard Aldrich. (1987). "Resource Mobilization Through Ethnic Networks: Kinship and Friendship Ties of Shopkeepers in England." *Sociological Perspectives* 30 (4, October): 422–455.

Index

Index

Index

23488650R00231

Made in the USA
Middletown, DE
27 August 2015